Find the Law in the Library

A Guide to Legal Research

Find the LAW in the LIBRARY

A Guide to Legal Research

by John Corbin

American Library Association

Chicago and London 1989

Text design by Gordon Stromberg

Cover design by Stephanie Toral

Composed by Impressions, Inc. in Sabon (text and display) on a Penta-driven
Autologic APS-μ5 photo typesetting system in Primer and Univers

Printed on 50-pound Glatfelter B-16, a pH-neutral stock, and bound in Roxite,
c-grade cloth by Braun-Brumfield, Inc.

The paper used in this publication meets the minimum requirements of
American National Standard for Information Sciences — Permanence of Paper for
Printed Library Materials, ANSI Z39.48-1984. ♾

Pages 777 and 778 from 278 *New York Supplement* and page 409 from 28
New York Digest 3d reprinted with permission of West Publishing Co. Copyright ©
1967 by West Publishing Co.

Pages 14 and 999 from *Shepard's New York Supplement 1970 Part Three*
reprinted by permission of Shepard's/McGraw-Hill.

Page 3 from 41 *New York Jurisprudence* and pages 1–4, 186, and 303 from 46
New York Jurisprudence reprinted by permission of The Lawyers Co-Operative
Publishing Co.

Library of Congress Cataloging-in-Publication Data

Corbin, John.
    Find the law in the library : a guide to legal research / by John
Corbin.
      p.   cm.
    Includes bibliographies.
    ISBN 0-8389-0502-1 (alk. paper)
    1. Legal research—United States. I. American Library
Association.   II. Title.
KF240.C63 1989
349.73′072—dc19
[347.372]   88-29981

Printed in the United States of America.
93 92 91 90 89 5 4 3 2 1

Contents

V. Concerns of the Elderly

Appendixes

Foreword

Books on researching the law and on learning the law itself, or topics within it, represent two different approaches to learning research: as a general procedure or as part of a subject matter. This book combines the two approaches, presenting the general procedures of conducting legal research along with descriptions of hypothetical cases of substantive law that are representative of everyday personal problems. The objective is to provide practicing librarians and library school students with a reference tool that introduces them to legal research techniques and materials in the context of real problems that they are likely to face in the library. The intelligent layperson may also benefit from this book, gaining knowledge of how to understand and solve a personal legal problem. Knowing that they too can examine legal matters, laypersons can better express their interests to their lawyers.

Reference librarians must know the process of finding the law if they are to give guidance that is useful. With this book the reference librarian can determine the kind of legal material a patron requires. Knowledge of legal sources is not enough, however. Librarians must also understand how the sources fit into the overall research process. As contrasted with the occasional use by laypersons, knowledge of the legal research process has a continuing use for librarians, especially those using law collections.

The first part of the book presents a basic procedure for legal research. It provides a brief overview of substantive law and the typical publication patterns for the sources of law, both primary and secondary. It also outlines general principles that may be used by anyone interested in researching a legal problem, and includes a step-by-step example of the application of these principles to a particular problem. For those interested in a more in-depth examination, a number of other research texts are listed in the bibliographies for this section. The remaining sections of the book outline the law as it affects the individual from birth and growth in the family, to community and business relationships, retirement, and matters concerning the final distribution of one's assets. For each individual topic a fact pattern presenting a problem for research is given, followed by a demonstration of how the basic research procedure suggested by this book would be utilized to solve the problem. Variations on the procedure and specific tools to be used have been chosen to fit the case at hand. In some situations the most efficient tools have been sacrificed in order to emphasize the use of specific research tools. The cases can be used as starting points to suggest an approach for the reader to take in researching his or her own problem in the areas in question.

Acknowledgments

I wish to express my thanks to Deonna L. Taylor, reference librarian, New York University Graduate School of Business Administration, for suggesting that I combine library science with my legal experience; Victor A. Triolo, associate professor at Southern Connecticut State College, Division of Library Science and Instructional Technology, without whose assistance and encouragement this project would have never been undertaken; the staff of the Charles B. Sears Law Library, State University of New York at Buffalo, who were always helpful and patient during my years of research; Herbert Bloom, senior editor for the American Library Association, who made suggestions and added encouragement during the development of this project; and Frank G. Houdek, director of the School of Law Library, Southern Illinois University, who clarified and enlarged the presentation and updated the references.

Endless hours were contributed by Ellen M. Reen of Alden, New York, for carefully reviewing the book, checking references, and finding and correcting errors, in addition to making valuable suggestions that make the book more complete, accurate, and readable.

I am also deeply indebted to my friend and wife Sue, who put up with the long arduous process, spending untold hours proofreading, editing, and helping make the end result understandable.

I · The Law

Outline of American Law

The definition of law can be as varied as the need for it dictates. In the broadest sense, it can be construed as the rules of conduct established and enforced by the authority, legislation, or custom of a given community, or, more specifically, as that branch of knowledge dealing with the rules of a community.

Whenever there are two or more people, there must be a set of rules governing their behavior in relationship to each other, even though those rules may never be written, spoken, or even acknowledged. There must be some understanding as to how each member will treat the other and of the consequences of misbehavior. As a group enlarges, relationships multiply, and the need for a more specific set of rules arises. When the community reaches a sufficient size, it becomes necessary to codify these rules, or collect them in one location, for all to see and follow. At this point someone must be responsible for assuring that the rules are enforced and that imposed punishments are carried out. Disputes that arise concerning the rules or their application must be settled, and someone must be appointed as an arbitrator to make the decisions regarding disputes. Someone must also be given the chore of establishing new rules, discarding or modifying old rules, and debating their significance.

In most countries, the task of formulating rules, enforcing the rules, and settling arguments arising under the rules is centered in the hands of a small group. This group becomes the government, making all rules, or laws, seeing that they are followed, and deciding what actions are permitted under these rules. This governmental structure embodies what political scientists call the "Organic Theory of State." This theory, briefly stated, places the state and the interests of the state over the interests of the individual citizen. The interests of the state are supreme, and each citizen must subordinate his or her desires to the best interests of the state, as decided by the ruling segment. In such a situation, a person may be overshadowed by the state. An individual is viewed as an object for which things must be done and as an instrument to be used by the state, in the state's best interests. The only function of a good citizen, according to this theory, is to perform for the goodness of the state. Therefore, the citizen has no rights against the state and no safeguards for his or her liberty. In a court of law, trials between individuals may be allowed, but never a suit by a citizen against the government.

3

The United States operates under the "Mechanistic Theory of State," where the interests of the individual citizen are most important and the state is established by the citizens as a mechanism to accomplish the act of governing. The state has no interests apart from those of the individuals who established it; rather, the state serves as the trustee and protector of the interests of the individuals. Unlike the Organic Theory, the Mechanistic Theory allows citizens to oppose the state on the grounds of conscience and to argue against the state upon Constitutional grounds in a court of law. This emphasis upon individualism under the Mechanistic Theory tends to lead to greater material interest—to the greater material benefit of both the state and the individual—and to a much broader base of freedoms and rights for citizens.

Tired of the oppressive tyranny of the English kings, the Founding Fathers of the United States decided that personal liberty, along with the freedom to worship, communicate, and labor was in peril. They believed that the awesome power of the single ruler or of a small tightly knit governing group should be broken up into three branches, each with a specific purview of political power, and each having the power to check the other's actions. They established the Constitution as the supreme law of the land. Under the Constitution, the federal government was given certain enumerated powers needed to bind the country into a single political unit, and all other powers were reserved for the states or for the people. The federal government was divided into three branches—the executive, legislative, and judicial—each of which was delegated powers to check certain actions of the other two. This balance of power was established to prevent any branch from gaining complete control.

The executive branch of government is charged with executing, or carrying out, the laws of the land as set forth in the Constitution and as enacted into law by Congress. It consists of an elected president and vice president, a cabinet appointed by the president, and several administrative agencies. The executive branch is held in check by the legislature, which passes legislation that must be followed and enforced by the executive branch, and by the judicial branch, which, when requested, decides if the executive branch is following the laws under the Constitution and under the statutes.

The legislative branch provides representation to all states in the task of making the laws. This branch, also known as Congress, is made up of the House of Representatives and the Senate. The number of representatives elected to the House by each state is based upon the population of the state. Each state elects two senators. Bills must be passed by both the Senate and the House of Representatives and then signed by the president before they become law. The president may veto any bill for any reason. However, Congress can override a presidential veto with a two-thirds vote. This policy establishes one check and balance between the executive branch and the legislative branch.

At the apex of the judicial branch of government is the Supreme Court. The Court consists of appointees of the president, the executive branch, who are confirmed by the Senate, the legislative branch. It has certain original jurisdiction (cases that may be brought directly to the Supreme Court by the litigants, such as disputes between states), some concurrent jurisdiction (cases that may be brought directly to the Supreme Court, or were originally initiated in a lower court), and ultimate appellate jurisdiction involving federal law (cases appealed from the lower courts to the Supreme Court).

When cases are referred to it from these areas of jurisdiction, the Supreme Court may exercise its check on the other two branches through a power called "judicial review." This means that, upon receiving a case, the Court may determine if the legislature or the executive branch has acted on the basis of an enumerated or an implied power granted to it by the Constitution.

The United States courts of appeals hear appeals from the main federal trial courts. They are thirteen in number, as set forth below:

Circuit Court of Appeals for the District of Columbia

Circuit Court of Appeals for the First Circuit
    Jurisdiction: Maine, Massachusetts, New Hampshire, Puerto Rico, Rhode Island

Circuit Court of Appeals for the Second Circuit
    Jurisdiction: Connecticut, New York, Vermont

Circuit Court of Appeals for the Third Circuit
    Jurisdiction: Delaware, New Jersey, Pennsylvania, Virgin Islands

Circuit Court of Appeals for the Fourth Circuit
    Jurisdiction: Maryland, North Carolina, South Carolina, Virginia, West Virginia

Circuit Court of Appeals for the Fifth Circuit
    Jurisdiction: District of the Canal Zone, Louisiana, Mississippi, Texas

Circuit Court of Appeals for the Sixth Circuit
    Jurisdiction: Kentucky, Michigan, Ohio, Tennessee

Circuit Court of Appeals for the Seventh District
    Jurisdiction: Illinois, Indiana, Wisconsin

Circuit Court of Appeals for the Eighth Circuit
    Jurisdiction: Arkansas, Iowa, Minnesota, Missouri, Nebraska, North Dakota, South Dakota

Circuit Court of Appeals for the Ninth Circuit
    Jurisdiction: Alaska, Arizona, California, Idaho, Montana, Nevada, Oregon, Washington, Guam, Hawaii, Northern Mariana Islands

Circuit Court of Appeals for the Tenth Circuit
    Jurisdiction: Colorado, Kansas, New Mexico, Oklahoma, Utah, Wyoming

Circuit Court of Appeals for the Eleventh Circuit
    Jurisdiction: Alabama, Florida, Georgia

Circuit Court of Appeals for the Federal Circuit
    Jurisdiction: All federal judicial districts for customs problems, patents, copyrights, and trademarks

The federal trial courts consist of the bankruptcy court, which hears matters of bankruptcy and insolvency; the United States Tax Court, which covers cases involving taxes; the United States Claims Court, which hears claims against the United States; and the district courts, which hear all other matters involving federal law. For a diagram of the whole system, see Figure 1.

Decisions handed down by a district court may be appealed to the United States Court of Appeals within whose geographic jurisdiction the case falls. The appeals court does not hear the case over again, but makes a decision based on the record and arguments presented. The higher court may affirm the decision of the lower court, overturn it, approve it in part, send it back for further consideration, or return it with directions concerning additional proceedings. Either party can appeal a court of appeals decision to the Supreme Court of the United States. This is done by "writ of certiorari," which stems from the ancient common law of England and was carried over to the United States. This writ has been abandoned in many states but is still used in federal practice. In federal practice, the writ is issued by the Supreme Court to an inferior court, requesting that the inferior court produce a certified record of a specified case that was heard by the inferior court. An attorney appealing a case to the Supreme Court will petition the Supreme Court to issue a writ of certiorari concerning a specific case so that the case can be decided by the Supreme Court. The Supreme Court is very selective in the cases it will hear.

Decisions of the United States Supreme Court are final. Its decisions become the official interpretations of the law throughout the country on the particular points decided. A case arising later involving the same facts and the same law is bound to follow this decision. This practice, called "stare decisis," brought from England to America, mandates that a decision—once made—will be followed in later cases.

Decisions of a United States Court of Appeals have finality within their own jurisdiction. Courts within the jurisdiction of a particular appellate court will decide like facts and law according to decisions made earlier by that appellate court and according to the decisions of the Supreme Court. Appellate courts need not follow the decisions of other appellate courts and frequently do not. However, decisions from other jurisdictions may be persuasive. If two appellate jurisdictions decide similar cases differently, and those differences turn

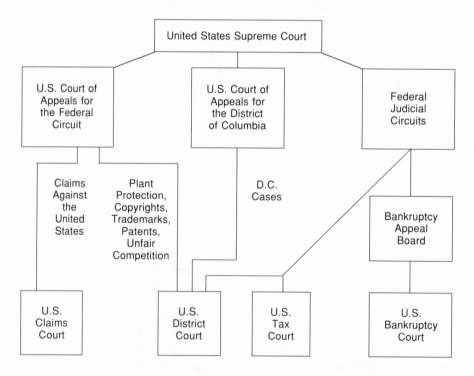

Fig. 1.   Federal Court System Diagram

on matters of interpretation and not on matters of fact, they may be reviewed by the Supreme Court in order to establish one interpretation throughout the country. Decided cases become precedents to be followed and, as such, are an important part of our system of law.

In general, the form of state governments is based on the federal government and consists of an executive department headed by a governor, a legislative branch, and a judicial system. Additional levels of government may underlay this basic structure in the form of county, city, town, and village governments and of special districts such as water districts or lake development districts. These levels may take various forms, and the smaller bodies frequently combine the executive and legislative functions into one body, such as the town selectmen.

Regulatory and administrative agencies, such as the Internal Revenue Service and the Environmental Protection Agency, were established when the size and complexity of our economy necessitated more specific and specialized regulations. Congress delegates to these agencies the power to promulgate rules and regulations that have the force of law, as if Congress itself had passed them. These rules and regulations are published in proposed and final form in the *Federal Register* and are later codified in the *Code of Federal Regulations*. In most cases, appeals from decisions made by the regulatory agencies may be taken to the federal district courts. Agencies and regulatory bodies are grouped under the "administrative law," one of the more complex areas of our legal system because it is the most difficult to locate and identify.

States have also adopted the administrative law approach to solve some of their problems. Some states have fairly well documented rules and regulations, but for most states this material is very difficult to locate. On the local government level, there exist almost no compilations of actions taken by the administrative and regulatory agencies, and therefore each agency must be consulted concerning its regulations.

This, in brief, is the law of the United States—awesome, all encompassing, complex, overlapping, contradictory, and difficult to fathom, but it still works.

Bibliography

(If any of the following works cannot be found in your library or nearest law library, ask your librarian if it can be obtained through interlibrary loan.)

Abshire, David M., and Ralph D. Nurnberger, eds. *The Growing Power of Congress*. Beverly Hills: Sage, 1981. Follows the shift of power between the executive and the legislative branches, including congressional leadership and foreign policymakers. With references and appendixes.

Beitzinger, A. J. *A History of American Political Thought*. New York: Dodd, 1977. A historical review of American politics starting with philosophical and jurisprudential background, covering colonial times, early democratic developments, progress, and challenges.

Christenson, Reo M. *American Politics: Understanding What Counts*. New York: Harper, 1980. This college-level outline of American government, its functions and problems contains a table of presidential elections 1789–1976, the Constitution of the United States and a glossary. Sympathetic toward politicians.

Cueto-Rua, Julio C. *Judicial Methods of Interpretation of the Law*. Baton Rouge: Publications Inst., Paul M. Herbert Law Center, Louisiana State Univ., 1981. A description and analysis of the judicial process. Contains illustrations, bibliography, and index.

Dvorin, Eugene P., and Arthur J. Misner. *Government in American Society: A Reader.* Reading, Mass.: Addison-Wesley, 1968. Conventional text on American government since colonial times. Covers representation, legislation, the executive branch, and the courts. Also includes the Declaration of Independence, Articles of Confederation, and Constitution of the United States; with bibliography.

Fordham, Jefferson B. *Materials on Legislation.* 5th ed. Mineola, N.Y.: Foundation Pr., 1987. Provides historical background on legislative and judicial roles in changing the law, the structure of the legislature, forms of statutes, policy formulation, and legal interpretations. Includes tables of cases and index.

Gibney, Frank, ed. *The U.S. Government: How and Why It Works.* New York: Bantam, 1978. Complied in conjunction with Encyclopedia Britannica, this volume presents a concise overview of the American system of government, including the fourth branch—the American Press.

Grenzke, Janet Miller. *Influence, Change, and the Legislative Process.* Westport, Conn.: Greenwood, 1982. A study of the changes in legislatures and legislators. With tables, figures, appendixes, and index.

Irish, Marian D. et al. *The Politics of American Democracy.* 7th ed. Englewood Cliffs, N.J.: Prentice-Hall, 1981. A basic, simple, easy-to-understand review of American politics describing the function of the parties, legislature, presidency, and judiciary, set in a modern frame of reference.

Keefe, William J., and Morris S. Ogul. *The American Legislative Process, Congress and the States.* Englewood Cliffs, N.J.: Prentice-Hall, 1981. An outline of the legislatures in the political system, their structures, decision-making functions, political parties, and legislative process. Includes notes, tables, and index.

Klein, Fannie J. *Federal and State Court Systems—A Guide.* Cambridge, Mass.: Ballinger, 1977. An overview of court systems, both federal and state, with their structures and jurisdictions, juries, administration, and personnel. With table of contents, figures, tables, and appendixes.

Patrick, John J., and Richard C. Remy. *Civics for Americans.* Glenview, Ill.: Scott, Foresman, 1980. An elementary-level text in civics covering the citizen, national government, economy, and foreign policy. Contains glossary, photos, charts, tables, maps, list of presidents, facts about states, name list of state legislative bodies, flag etiquette, voting population, statistics, and Declaration of Independence.

Wolfinger, Raymond E. et al, *Dynamics of American Politics.* London: Prentice-Hall, 1980. A modern text on American politics, with emphasis on how the political system works rather than on its product. Contains illustrations, charts, tables, photographs, the Constitution of the United States, glossary, and bibliography.

Additional Related Readings

Hahn, Harlan, and William R. Holland. *American Government: Minority Rights Versus Majority Rule.* New York: Wiley, 1976. Explains obstacles confronted by racial and ethnic minority groups, focusing on governmental functions hampering their full participation. Includes a beginning-level discussion of political parties, representation, the Congress, the presidency, the courts, protests, and unrest.

Hetzel, Otto J. *Legislative Law and Process.* Indianapolis: Michi-Bobbs-Merrill, 1980. A coursebook studying legislation and social changes; the relationships among the legislative, executive, and judicial branches of government; and the legislative process. With table of cases, appendix, and index.

Kirk, Russell. *The Roots of American Order.* LaSalle, Ill.: Open Court, 1974. A lucid, informative review of the origins of American law, with background from Hebrew times through Greek, Roman, Anglo-Saxon, French, and American colonial and Revolutionary times, with continuing developments. Contains suggested readings and chronology.

Kolb, Eugene J. *A Framework for Political Analysis.* Englewood Cliffs, N.J.: Prentice-Hall, 1978. A comprehensive primer of political analysis. Provides an introduction to political science, with a basis for understanding the system, government, and political power. Also includes guidelines and tools for a systematic and disciplined political analysis. With bibliography.

Lipset, Seymour M., and Earl Raab. *The Politics of Unreason: Right-Wing Extremism in America, 1790–1977.* 2d ed. New York: Harper, 1978. An analysis of extreme right-wing political groups.

Lockard, Duane. *The Perverted Priorities of American Politics.* New York: Macmillan, 1976. A critical view of politics, questioning priorities in light of hunger, industrial accidents, racial discrimination, pollution, and corruption. Includes suggested readings.

Lockwood, Robert S., and Carol M. Hillier. *Legislative Analysis: With Emphasis on National Security Affairs.* Durham, N.C.: Carolina Academic Pr., 1981. A text on the liaison between the executive and legislative branches of government, with emphasis on its relationship to national security. Appendix included.

Malek, Frederic V. *Washington's Hidden Tragedy: The Failure to Make Government Work.* New York: Free Pr., 1978. Presents the views of a businessman who has worked in the executive branch of government, outlining its deficiencies and inefficiencies, and making recommendations.

Morrow, William L. *Public Administration: Politics, Policy, and the Political System.* 2d ed. New York: Random, 1980. An attempt to study public agencies according to the scientific management approach. Examines the intent of the agencies, their history, theory, organization, and behavior. With diagrams, charts, glossary, and bibliography.

Rehfuss, John. *Public Administration as Political Process.* New York: Scribner, 1973. A bureaucratic approach to government—local, state, federal, and worldwide.

Ripley, Randall B., and Grace A. Franklin. *Congress, the Bureaucracy, and Public Policy.* Homewood, Ill.: Dorsey Pr., 1976. A textbook that relates Congress to the federal bureaucracy. Proposes that the dominant theme of national politics is the desire to minimize conflict, to compromise, and to protect personal careers.

Rose, Richard. *What Is Governing? Purpose and Policy in Washington.* Englewood Cliffs, N.J.: Prentice-Hall, 1978. A study of the purpose of government, relating it to policies of government. Attempts to make politics as important as science in the study of government, using eighteen different models.

Williams, Walter, and Betty Jane Narver. *Government by Agency: Lessons from the Social Program Grants-in-aid Experience.* New York: Academic, 1980. A study of federal grant programs and government operation by agencies.

Worthley, John A. *Public Administration and Legislatures: Examination and Explanation.* Chicago: Nelson-Hall, 1976. An examination of the relationships involving public administration and the legislatures and the treatment of legislatures by public administrators, including a discussion of Watergate. With appendixes, bibliography, name index, and subject index.

Where It Is Recorded

All of these laws, rules, regulations, directives, and guidelines are recorded in a somewhat logical order for everyone to consult. Laws of the United States are proposed in the Congress as either a House of Representatives bill or as a Senate bill. Thousands of bills are introduced each year, and by a process of referring them to the appropriate committees, only a few of them reach the floor of Congress for action. If the committee returns an unfavorable report on a bill, the bill usually does not proceed beyond that point. If a bill is reported on favorably by the committee, it then goes to the floor of the legislative branch that introduced it for debate, amendment, and vote. Surviving this step, the bill goes to the other branch of the legislature, where the process is repeated. If the House and Senate pass different versions of the bill, it is then referred to a conference committee made up of members of both houses who have the responsibility of working out a compromise. In situations where no compromise can be reached, the bill dies. When a compromise is reached, the bill is returned to each branch, where it usually is passed with little difficulty. From Congress the bill goes to the president of the United States for action. The president may sign the bill, making it a law; the president can veto it, returning it to the Congress; or the president can do nothing. Congress by a two-thirds vote may override a veto, and in such cases, the bill becomes law despite the president's action. If the president neither signs the bill nor returns it to Congress with his or her objections within ten days, the bill automatically becomes law. If the president does not act on the bill and Congress adjourns during those ten days, the bill is automatically vetoed (pocket veto). Legislation enacted in all these ways constitutes the statutory law of the United States.

Statutes

Federal

The first written evidence of a law is in the form of a slip law, each printed as a pamphlet or on individual loose sheets. The slip laws are numbered chronologically in the order in which they were passed for each two-year congressional session; so, for example, the first law passed by the Eighty-first Session of Congress would be labeled Public Law 81-1. These laws are later collected and printed into the *Statutes at Large* for that particular session of Congress. The Government Printing Office is usually a couple of years behind in printing the statutes; for example, the 1978 *Statutes* were printed in 1980. The volume contains a listing of the bills enacted into public law by the House of Representatives (HR) number, by House Joint Resolution (HJR) number, by Senate (S) number, and by Senate Joint Resolution (SJR) number. The public laws contained in the volume are listed by session and number, and give the title of the law, a brief description of the law, the date it was passed, and the page on which the complete text is located. In addition to the complete text of public laws, the volume contains the text of reorganization plans of federal agencies, bills enacted into private law, and concurrent resolutions. There is also a subject index and an index of individuals.

Finding the current status of the law using only the *Statutes* is tremendously time-consuming. It involves locating the statute of interest and then examining all the indexes of the *Statutes* from the time the law was enacted up to the present date, looking for amendments to the statute or for its repeal. To overcome this difficulty, Congress in 1925 authorized the publication of the *United States Code (U.S.C.)*, which was first published in 1926.

About a year after the *Statutes at Large* are published, the public laws contained therein are incorporated into the *United States Code* under the proper subject heading and under the section covering that particular law. The 1977 *Supplement* of the *U.S.C.*, for instance, was printed in 1980.

The *U.S.C.* is published and sold by the United States Government Printing Office and consists of all public statutes of general interest that have not been repealed. Every six years, a new edition of the *U.S.C.* is published, incorporating new legislation and eliminating expired and repealed statutes. The *U.S.C.* includes fifty titles, divided into chapters and subdivided into sections. All laws covering the same topic are arranged into one title.

The 1982 edition of the *U.S.C.* is currently being published and incorporates all of the cumulative supplements to the 1976 edition. To find one's way in the *U.S.C.*, there is a comprehensive general subject index.

There is another important difference between the *Statutes at Large* and the *United States Code*. The *Statutes* have all been enacted into law by Congress and signed by the president. Although the *U.S.C.* has been authorized by Congress, only some titles of it have been enacted into positive law. The fifty *U.S.C.* titles each consist of a reorganization of the *Statutes* except for private bills introduced by legislators on behalf of particular constituents. These titles eventually become retroactively enacted as law. Until they are, the relevant *Statutes* are in force and are the positive law.

In addition to statutes, the first volume of the *U.S.C.* contains a list of the members of the House of Representatives Committee on the Judiciary, the titles of the codes by number, a table of contents, titles and chapters, and the organic law of the United States of America, i.e., The Declaration of Independence of 1776, the Articles of Confederation of 1777, the Ordinance of 1787, the Northwest Territory Government, and the Constitution of the United States. The Constitution is followed by an analytical index to the Constitution. Finally come the text of the *U.S.C.* and the index. There, in simplified form, is the statutory law of the United States.

To meet the needs of the researcher, private publishers publish annotated editions of the *U.S.C.* that include many helpful editorial features. In addition to the text of the laws, the annotated editions include references to and brief summaries of court decisions that interpret the law, historical notes indicating the origin of and changes in the law, and cross-references to other useful information. The commercially published annotated editions are printed and updated much faster than the official *U.S.C.* published by the Government Printing Office. Generally, the annotated editions are also easier to use. They include detailed subject indexes and useful tables. Each volume is updated by its own cumulative supplement in the form of a pocket part that fits in the back cover of the volume.

The first of the two major annotated versions of the *U.S.C. The United States Code Service (U.S.C.S.)* published by the Lawyers Cooperative/Bancroft-Whitney was first published as the *Federal Code Annotated*. The wording of the text of the official *U.S.C.* along with its classification by title, chapter, and section are kept, except where the text differs from the wording of the *Statutes*. In those cases, the wording of the *Statutes* is followed. The decisions of courts interpreting sections of the code are annotated for each section. References to other publications, such as the *Code of Federal Regulations, U.S. Supreme Court Reporter,* law review articles, and *American Jurisprudence,* are also included. There is an index to each title as well as a general index to the whole set. The set is kept up to date with annual cumulative pocket part supplements and monthly pamphlets. The monthly pamphlets give the text of new laws, amendments and repeals of the code and of federal court rules, and executive proclamations and orders. The legislative history of each law is given, including citations to the *Congressional Record* to Senate and House reports, and to the *Weekly Compilation of Presidential Documents.*

The other major publisher of an annotated code is West, which publishes the *United States Code Annotated (U.S.C.A.)* This publication follows the *U.S.C.* in titles, chapters, sections, wording, and arrangement. It contains annotations of judicial opinions that have interpreted the provisions of the code and gives historical notes and cross-references to other interpretative aids. There is a multi-volume subject index, editorial notes and discussions, references to the Attorney General's opinions, and cross-reference tables to the *Statutes at Large.* There is also a table that cites the acts by their popular names, allowing the researcher to locate a statute if he or she can remember only its popular name. Like the *U.S.C.S.* the *U.S.C.A.* is updated with annual cumulative pocket parts and monthly pamphlets.

States

States generally follow the same process in developing and in recording their laws as occurs in the federal system. That is, proposed legislation proceeds through an orderly legislative process and is initially published in a slip law form by the state government if the legislation is enacted. At the conclusion of each legislative session, the state usually issues the text of all the laws enacted during that session in a cumulative bound publication. These "session law" volumes contain the laws in the chronological order in which they were enacted, similar to the *Statutes at Large.* As with that set, state session laws are generally not very useful for the typical legal research problem because laws on the same subject are scattered throughout many volumes, making location of relevant materials difficult. To solve this problem, states will occasionally produce codifications of their statutory laws, placing the laws in a logical subject arrangement. These codifications are comparable to the *United States Code*. Once again, however, the delays inherent in government publishing have led commercial publishers to enter the field in the state arena as well, producing annotated editions of state codes. For example, in Massachusetts, West publishes *Massachusetts General Laws Annotated,* while the Lawyers Cooperative publishes the *Annotated Laws of Massachusetts.* Typically, the commercial publishers include an updating service to the codes for subscribers, providing a "legislative service" published in pamphlet form throughout the year that includes the text of new laws passed by the state legislature and also an annual cumulative supplement (often in the form of a pocket part placed into a slot in the back cover of each bound volume in the original set). These supplementary materials should not be overlooked when researching state statutes.

Local

Counties, cities, towns, villages, and districts present a mixed bag. Cities generally operate under a municipal charter that has been adopted by the voters. Under these charters, the legislative bodies pass ordinances, which may be codified in some logical order. These ordinances, along with pertinent state laws, become the statutory law of the cities, towns, and villages. These codes usually include the city charter, text of ordinances currently in force, and some sort of indexing. For example, the General Code Publishing Corporation has published the 1980 looseleaf *Code of the City of Haverhill, Massachusetts,* which includes a list of the city officials; a preface outlining the contents, divisions, and schemes of the code; a table of contents; the city charter; and the code in two parts—administrative and general. It also boasts an appendix within which is included the statutes of Massachusetts, general laws that have been accepted by the city, arranged by year, subject, and statutory reference, and a listing of the special acts affecting the city that have been passed by the Massachusetts legislature. This volume also includes an index and pocket parts containing a zoning map and an organizational chart. Being a looseleaf publication, it is updated annually by replacing the necessary sheets. Not all cities have such a complete coverage of their ordinances.

The General Code Publishing Corporation also works with smaller political units. For instance, it provides the same service for the village of Attica, New York, in the same looseleaf form. The 1980 volume includes a list of the village officials, a preface, a table of contents, the code, and a zoning map.

Few municipalities provide such complete coverage. In many of them it is necessary to search the records of the meetings of the various bodies, such as the city council, covering an indefinite period of time to determine if an action has been taken. Then when the specific section is located, the records must be searched again from the date of the record forward to insure that there have been no amendments or changes. Whatever records are kept, the city, town, or village clerk will be able to provide assistance in locating and obtaining copies of local laws. Clerks seem to have a vast store of knowledge and are almost indispensable when one is working with local governments.

Regulative and Administrative Agencies Regulations

Federal

Today laws are not made by legislatures alone. Administrative bodies are frequently given the authority to make regulations having the force of law. Congress has given such authority to the Securities and Exchange Commission (S.E.C.) and to the Interstate Commerce Commission (I.C.C.), among others. These bodies give notice of proposed regulations in the *Federal Register (Fed. Reg.)*, which also provides a preamble or explanation of the regulations. After the comment period, proposed regulations can be withdrawn, changed and reissued as proposals, or published in final form. Once published in final form, regulations have the force of law as of the effective date indicated.

The *Federal Register* is published daily, Monday through Friday. It provides a uniform system for making available to the public the regulations and legal notices issued by federal agencies. It includes presidential proclamations, executive orders, federal agency documents having general applicability and legal effect, documents required to be published by Congress, and other federal agency documents of public interest. The *Fed. Reg.* also contains many features, such as highlights of the week's activities, a detailed table of contents, rules and regulations going into effect, proposed rules and regulations, notices of hearings, and sunshine act meetings. The readers' aids section includes a list of the parts of the *Code of Federal Regulations (C.F.R.)* affected during the month, a chart indicating which day of the week various agencies are assigned for their publications, and reminders.

The general and the permanent rules of the executive department and of the agencies published in the *Fed. Reg.* are collected and codified annually into the fifty titles of the *C.F.R.* Each title is divided into chapters and further into sections, usually referred to as parts. Titles may be published in more than one volume, each volume having its own detailed table of contents. The annual bound volumes of the *C.F.R.* are kept up to date by the *Register*. The monthly *Lists of Sections Affected (L.S.A.)* is a useful tool for checking if a *C.F.R.* section has been changed by subsequent regulations. The *L.S.A.* is a cumulative table arranged by *C.F.R.* section numbers and refers the researcher to the *Federal Register* page and number where a change appears.

Another useful research tool is the *C.F.R. Index and Finding Aid.* This subject index to the *C.F.R.* also includes various features, such as a table of *C.F.R.* titles and chapters, an alphabetical list of agencies covered by the *C.F.R.*, and a cross-reference table from the *U.S.C.* to the appropriate *C.F.R.* section. Because the subject index is not very detailed, it should be used in conjunction with the table of contents in the appropriate bound volume.

Both the *Code of Federal Regulations* and the *Federal Register* are government publications and are available to the public in all federal depository libraries. Many other libraries make these books available as a service to the public.

State

The federal administrative system is difficult to work with because of its sheer volume, whereas the difficulty in working with state agencies is that each state may differ in how it promulgates and publicizes its regulatory and/or administrative material. Some states have collected this material in one location or publication, while others may have no formal means of publishing this information, forcing the researcher to find and contact the appropriate agency. The Commission on Official Legal Publications for the state of Connecticut, for instance, has published in looseleaf form the *Regulations of Connecticut State Agencies*. Regulations are broken down into headings by title numbers, state agencies, employees, and municipalities. For the state of Delaware, on the other hand, research into state agency rules and regulations is probably best done by the direct approach, i.e., by contacting the individual agencies.

Local

On the local level it is almost always necessary to plow through the contents of the clerk's files and notes. A helpful clerk is the best access and guide.

Court Reporters

Once the laws have been passed and the regulations promulgated, how does one determine what they mean? Reasonable people may differ in their interpretations of the words used, and it is the responsibility of the courts to settle these differences. Judges will look within their jurisdictions or to a superior jurisdiction for cases similar in law and fact to the case before them and will decide the case in a similar manner. This is known as the doctrine of stare decisis. The decisions handed down by the courts make up our common, or case, law, and they are usually recorded in the official reports for a particular jurisdiction. Official reports contain the text of court decisions and are published under the direction of the court, either federal or state. These reporters give the researcher the necessary access to decisions with precedential value. Often in minor or lower courts there are no written reports of judicial decisions. If a written opinion exists, the clerk of the court can usually supply a copy.

A court decision is first issued in a "slip opinion" form by the court itself. These opinions can usually be obtained only from the court clerk, although some courts do make subscriptions to their opinions available. The first regularly published source in which opinions appear are the "advance sheet" pamphlets issued as precursors to the bound reporter volumes. The time lag between the date of decision and the advance sheet varies from jurisdiction to jurisdiction and from publisher to publisher, with a range of anywhere from six weeks to four to six months. Eventually, the publisher cumulates the decisions from several advance sheets and republishes them into a bound reporter volume. These volumes become the permanent record of a court's published decisions. It is important to remember that the cases included in these volumes are generally arranged in chronological order (by date of decision) and are not related to each other by subject in any way. In this sense, the reporters are comparable to session law volumes for legislative enactments.

Federal

Not all of the opinions of the federal district courts are published, but if a federal district court decision is released for publication, it will probably appear in a commercial court reporter. All written opinions of any United States Court of Appeals (formerly the United States Circuit Court of Appeals) that are designated "for publication" are printed in the unofficial reporters of the commercial press. The United States and the unofficial press publish the written decisions of the Supreme Court. The United States Government Printing Office publishes the *United States Reports,* which covers the cases decided by the Supreme Court, and it also publishes the *United States Claims Court Reports,* which covers the cases decided by the Supreme Court involving cases from the United States Claims Court. As with the official *Statutes,* these volumes are not annotated and are a year or two behind in their publication.

Again commercial publishers fill the gap left by slow government publications. West Publishing Company publishes the *Supreme Court Reporter* which covers Supreme Court cases, and the *Federal Reporter* which covers decisions of the United States Courts of Appeals and of the Temporary Emergency Court of Appeals. The *Federal Supplement* reports decisions made by the United States Claims Court since October 1, 1982, by the United States district courts, by the United States Court of International Trade, and by the Judicial Panel on Multi-District Litigation. Other specialty reporters make research in their specialties simpler, such as *West's Bankruptcy Reporter,* which covers selected decisions from the United States district courts involving matters of bankruptcy and decisions of the United States bankruptcy courts, as well as reprints from the *Federal Reporter* and from the *Supreme Court Reporter* of decisions involving bankruptcy.

The Lawyers Cooperative/Bancroft-Whitney publishes the *U.S. Supreme Court Reports, Lawyers' Edition, 2d Series,* which covers the full decisions of the Supreme Court; the *American Law Reports,* which covers selected leading cases from all jurisdictions on all legal subjects, providing extensive discussions of the law involved; and *ALR Federal,* which gives the same service as the preceding volume but is limited to the federal courts.

State

Official state reports are those published under the direction of the state courts. Some states publish their own, but most state reports are published by the commercial press. *New Mexico Reports,* for example, is published by West and consists of reprints from the *Pacific Reporter,* also published by West. The Lawyers Cooperative/Bancroft-Whitney publishes the official reports of both the Michigan Court of Appeals and the Michigan Supreme Court. As with the federal courts, the commercial press publishes cases of the highest court in each state and sometimes of the trial courts on a selective basis. For example, West publishes seven reports that include decisions from states in selected regions of the country. Together these reporters comprise the "National Reporter System" and constitute a source for state cases totally apart from official governmental publication. Because of the delays inherent in governmental publication, researchers often rely on the regional reporters that make up this system for access to cases, rather than on the official state sources. These multi-volume sets are the *Atlantic, Northeastern, Northwestern, Pacific, Southeastern, Southern,* and *Southwestern Reporters.*

The Lawyers Cooperative/Bancroft-Whitney has approached the reporter system with a theory of selectivity. Whereas West gives comprehensive coverage, the Lawyers Cooperative selects only significant decisions, decisions regarding points of law not previously covered, those that change the law, or those pointing toward a new legal trend. In its *American Law Reports (A.L.R.),* leading cases are selected for inclusion. The text of the decision is followed by essays on the legal topics involved; annotations, including reasons for the general rules set forth; discussions of other cases in point, analyzed by jurisdiction; commentaries on the application of the rules to specific facts; and definitions of words and phrases. The series extends back to 1760 and has gone through various changes in name: *American Law Reports, Annotated,* published in seventy-five volumes from 1919 through 1948; *American Law Reports, Annotated, Second Series (A.L.R. 2d),* published in fifty-two volumes from 1948 through 1965; *American Law Reports, Annotated, Third Series (A.L.R. 3d),* published from 1966 to 1980; and *American Law Reports, Annotated, Fourth Series (A.L.R. 4th),* 1980– , bringing the reports up to date. *A.L.R. 4th* will be kept current through the use of pocket part supplements. The Lawyers Cooperative also publishes the *American Law Reports, Federal (A.L.R. Fed.),* which covers from 1969 through the present. Cross-references in all *A.L.R.* sets connect the cases with the other components of the *Total Client-Service Library,* published by the Lawyers Cooperative/Bancroft-Whitney so that the researcher can move easily into other materials on the same subject. A multi-volume *Index to Annotations* provides a convenient, efficient entry into the annotations of each *A.L.R.* set. A combination of the following—descriptive words, facts, legal concepts—is used in the index. Explanatory illustrations show the structure of the index and its proper use.

Local

Most often the only reports of the actions of a local court are found in the records kept by the court clerk or by the local magistrate.

Digests

As noted earlier, court reporters publish cases roughly in the order in which they are decided. This arrangement is not conducive to efficient case law research, since most often one wishes to locate all the cases relating to a specific topic, no matter when the case was decided. Without some kind of subject-oriented tool, the researcher would have to search through the indexes of hundreds of individual reporter volumes in order to accomplish this task. Thus, just as codes are provided to facilitate research into chronologically published legislative enactments, a tool known as a digest has traditionally been used to assist in case law research.

Legal digests consist of brief statements of facts and/or court decisions arranged by subject and subdivided according to the jurisdiction and type of court. A digest serves as an annotated subject index to the reported case law of the particular jurisdiction covered. Each digest contains its own general subject index to lead the researcher to the specific topic of interest and includes cross-references.

There are a variety of digests. The most comprehensive is West's American Digest System, which covers all reported cases in the country, both state and federal. Beyond this there are various special digests, in the federal area the *United States Supreme Court Digest* by West, and the *United States Supreme Court Digest, Annotated,* by the Lawyers Cooperative/Bancroft-Whitney Co.

West has also published a variety of other special digests covering the federal court system, including military justice claims and bankruptcy. West also publishes digests for most states, as well as most of the regional reporters. The digests all follow the same format as indicated below.

The digest system of West collects the headnotes from both federal and state cases, assigning the headnotes a key number from the West Key Number Classification Schedule. Headnotes are usually prepared by the editors of court reporter volumes and appear before the printed opinion, giving a brief summary of the legal rules or facts of the case. The key number is a fixed, permanent number given to a specific point of case law. It consists of a topic and a number uniquely assigned to a specific legal point, e.g., Torts ⚷ 127. The headnotes and case citations are arranged in the digests by key numbers. Thus, once a key number for a specific point of law has been identified, the digest can be used to find all cases covering that point. The American Digest System claims to be a complete digest of all reported cases in the United States. Under each key number (arranged alphabetically by topic and numerically by number within that topic), the summaries of the decisions are set forth alphabetically by states. The components of the American Digest System are the *Century Edition*, which covers cases from 1658 to 1896; the *First Decennial Digest*, which covers cases from 1897 to 1906; the *Second Decennial Digest* through the *Eighth Decennial Digest*, which cover the years 1907 through 1976 in ten-year increments each; and the *Ninth Decennial Digest*, in two parts, which covers the years 1977 through 1986. The *General Digest, Seventh Series* will appear annually to update the *Ninth Decennial Digest* until West is ready to issue a new decennial.

West's digest system also includes special digests. *U. S. Supreme Court Digest* is a complete index to decisions of the United States Supreme Court. The *Federal Digest, West's Modern Federal Practice Digest, West's Federal Practice Digest, 2d Ed.* and *West's Federal Practice Digest, 3d Ed.* cover all of the federal courts, including the U. S. Supreme Court. *West's Bankruptcy Digest* covers all cases reported in the *West's Bankruptcy Reporter,* and the *Court of Claims Digest* indexes the cases of the U.S. Court of Claims.

Also, reporters for the following regions are covered by West Key Number Digests: Atlantic, Northwestern, Pacific, Southeastern, and Southern. Many states have their own digests, as well. West also publishes a number of state digests that follow this same Key Number System. These are set forth below.

WEST'S STATE DIGESTS

Alabama	Hawaii	Minnesota	Oregon
Alaska	Idaho	Mississippi	Pennsylvania
Arizona	Illinois	Missouri	Rhode Island
Arkansas	Indiana	Montana	South Carolina
California	Iowa	Nebraska	Tennessee
Colorado	Kansas	New Hampshire	Texas
Connecticut	Kentucky	New Jersey	Vermont
Dakota	Louisiana	New Mexico	Virginia
District of	Maine	New York	Washington
Columbia	Maryland	North Carolina	West Virginia
Florida	Massachusetts	Ohio	Wisconsin
Georgia	Michigan	Oklahoma	Wyoming

Secondary Authority Sources

Statutes, administrative regulations, and court decisions are considered primary legal authorities. These are sources produced by governmental bodies empowered to create the law. In order to understand what the law is on a particular subject, a researcher must locate all of those primary authorities which relate to that subject. Thus, the ultimate goal of legal research is to identify relevant primary authorities. It has already been noted (and it will be further explained later) that there are a number of tools that provide direct access to primary authorities; nevertheless, one of the most effective legal research techniques is indirect access through secondary authorities. Secondary authorities are those sources produced by individuals outside the government, such as law professors and attorneys, who do not have any responsibility for creating the law. However, the scholarly or professional credentials that many of these individuals possess often give great persuasive value to their comments, even when these remarks contradict previously established legal rules. More importantly for purposes of this discussion, most secondary authorities are filled with citations to primary authorities, and thus they can greatly assist the researcher in locating cases, statutes, or administrative regulations or decisions on the topics addressed. Because they are written in clear prose and already include a synthesis of the law on these topics, secondary authorities are often easier to understand (especially for the novice researcher) than are the indexes, digests, and other research tools that provide direct access to primary authorities. Consequently, it is not unusual to begin researching a problem by consulting one or more secondary authorities before even considering sources of primary authority. The following sections discuss some of the more important forms of secondary authority.

Encyclopedias

A general encyclopedia consists of a book, or set of books, giving information on all branches of knowledge in the form of articles that are alphabetically arranged according to subject. There are also special encyclopedias that provide information about a particular field of knowledge. A legal encyclopedia is a special encyclopedia that offers not only a brief overview and outline of the law but that also gives annotated references to cases for a more in-depth study. The most comprehensive coverage of cases is found in *Corpus Juris*, now *Corpus Juris Secundum (C.J.S.)* published by West. It purports to be a complete statement of the entire American law as developed by all reported cases. This multi-volume set is kept up to date by pocket part supplements. Each volume has its own index, plus there is a multi-volume index for the entire set. *C.J.S.* begins with a general statement of items included and is arranged alphabetically by topic.

The Lawyers Cooperative's *American Jurisprudence*, now in its second edition *(Am. Jur.2d)*, has a slightly different approach. It also is a multi-volume encyclopedia, with volume indexes and a multi-volume general index, which is updated by pocket parts. It claims to provide a comprehensive modern text statement of American law, both state and federal, procedural and substantive. It does not list all published cases as does *C.J.S.* but instead selects the cases it feels will be leading cases representative of the topic involved. It also is arranged alphabetically by topic, and for each topic it gives a scope note, a listing of items that are treated under other topics, and a general legal outline of the topic along with definitions, various elements, procedures, effects, and rights. What *Am. Jur.2d* may lack in repetitive case listings is made up for with this work's critical analysis and discussion of topics.

General legal encyclopedias such as *C.J.S.* and *Am. Jur.2d* are useful for the researcher who is trying to get a broad overview of a topic, without any particular concern about jurisdiction. If jurisdiction is relevant, however, it is preferable to consult a local encyclopedia, if one is available for the jurisdiction in question. Thus, if the researcher wants to know how the state of Illinois treats the issue of common law marriage, it is more effective to use *Illinois Jurisprudence* rather than *C.J.S.* or *Am. Jur.2d.* This publication serves the same purpose and works the same way as the latter two; the only difference is that it is limited to a discussion of relevant Illinois authorities, rather than covering material from all fifty states.

Treatises

Another type of secondary authority that is a fruitful source both for a synthesis of the law and for references to primary authorities is material referred to generically as the "treatise." Basically commentaries on or expositions of the law, treatises may vary in format and include single-volume "hornbooks" (direct statements of legal rules, often used by law students), practitioner-oriented looseleaf publications supplemented with replacement pages, and multi-volume scholarly works. Subjects range from large (e.g., an examination of an entire field, such as property or torts) to small (e.g., a single component of a field, such as residential landlord and tenant problems within the area of property). Treatises generally are supplemented in some fashion, either by pocket parts, looseleaf replacement pages, paperback supplements, or revised volumes. Access is usually by table of contents and subject index. As with legal encyclopedias, the value of treatises lies in their capacity to explain an unfamiliar subject to a researcher while also providing leads to relevant primary authorities.

Legal Periodicals: The Leading Edge

For the most recent thinking on a point of law, an additional type of secondary authority, the legal periodical, should be examined. Legal periodicals are published in a variety of ways, including law reviews published by various law schools, bar association journals such as the *American Bar Association Journal* and *The Record of the Association of the Bar of the City of New York*, specialized bar group journals such as the *Journal of the Patent Office Society*, and legal newspapers. Periodicals cover many legal topics and discuss the newest concepts of law, putting them on the leading edge of the law. From the new thoughts found in these articles and the references provided, new legal trends can be predicted and background material provided that is not easily found elsewhere.

Additional Special Aids

In addition to the primary and secondary sources already discussed, a number of special aids exist that help in updating research work and that are useful in situations where a direct approach may not be possible. Included are such works as *Black's Law Dictionary*, which is used to determine the exact legal meaning of words used by judges and lawyers, and *Shepard's Citations*, which is used to discover later cases referring to the one the researcher is examining. Looseleaf services provide a rapid updating of the law, and *Martindale-Hubbell Law Directory* gives brief outlines of the laws of the various states and of selected foreign countries.

Another approach to legal research is through *Words and Phrases*, by West, updated with pocket parts. Its emphasis is noted in the book's opening quote from Justice Holmes in *Town v. Eisner*, 245 U.S. 418 at 425: "A word is not a crystal, transparent, and unchanged, it is the skin of a living thought and may vary greatly in color and content according to the circumstances and the time in which it is used." *Words and Phrases* is alphabetical by topic and provides a digest of cases that interpret words. Its practical constructions and definitions of words and phrases are set forth by state and federal court decisions going back to the earliest of times. This book is also cross-referenced to the West Key Number System and includes an index. This tool is very useful if the particular research problem involves the definition of a specific word or phrase.

For a quick, brief statement of the general law, researchers can consult Joan Robinson's *American Legal Almanac* (Oceana, 1978). It has forty-five charts and divides its coverage into four parts: (1) Law and Family, (2) Law and Livelihood, (3) Law and Living, and (4) Individuals and Society. Again, pocket parts are used for updating.

Looseleaf services consist of one or more ring binders into which are inserted pages of information. Replacement pages may be issued frequently by the publisher so that these services can provide up-to-date material in their special area of law. Generally, the looseleaf services cover areas of law in which it is necessary for lawyers to have the most current material immediately. Examples of this type include *U.S. Law Week* and the *Supreme Court Bulletin*. These services are also used in areas where publication is irregular, such as the administrative codes of various cities. The most popular looseleaf services cover specific topics of law, along with comments. Examples include the *Labor Relations Reporter* and *U.S. Tax Cases*. These works combine all of the material in one area of law, regardless of jurisdiction; provide the full text of statutes and regulations; and follow up with historical notes, annotations, and commentaries. Each service has its own format and organization; therefore, it is necessary to read each publication's "How to Use" section every time an unfamiliar service is used.

For a brief statement of the laws of each state, the District of Columbia, Puerto Rico, and the Virgin Islands; U.S. patent, copyright, and trademark laws; the laws of Canada and the Canadian provinces; and the laws of selected foreign countries, volume 8 of the *Martindale-Hubbell Law Directory* is an excellent beginning. The first seven volumes compose a directory of lawyers arranged geographically by state and by city.

Volume 8 is divided into eight parts. The first part is a digest of the laws of each state, the District of Columbia, Puerto Rico, and the Virgin Islands. The laws are set forth under about one hundred principal topics, with numerous subheadings, including citations to the National Reporter System.

Part two digests United States copyright, patent, and trademark laws, and part three is a Canadian law digest. A foreign law digest makes up the fourth part, while the fifth part concerns itself with the composition and operations of the federal court system. Part six gives the complete text of many uniform acts passed by many states, and part seven sets forth international conventions to which the United States is a party. The eighth part gives considerable information on the American Bar Association and its activities. This yearly publication is kept current with supplements.

Updating Statutes and Cases

Once a statute or case in point is located, the researcher must make sure that the law stated is still valid and that its interpretations are consistent. If the law has changed, it is vital to discover in what respects it has been altered. Shepard's has devised an efficient system for assuring that research can be brought up to date, popularly called "Shepardizing." Books titled *Shepard's Citations* are published for all state and federal statutes, the major courts, and selected government agencies. Citations of statutes or cases, taken from the codes or from reporters, form the foundation of this system. Under each citation are listed any later cases that refer to a particular citation, using a coding system that allows the researcher to determine the action taken. The preface explains the system's scope, coverage, and analysis, including an illustration of its proper use. Symbols and abbreviations are also explained for use in analyzing the results of decisions. A more complete description of this system and an example of its use are presented later in "How to Find It."

Indexes

For help in locating appropriate articles in this vast array of publications, several indexes have been developed. For current publications, the *Index to Legal Periodicals* covers nearly four hundred publications in three-year cumulations, annual supplements, and monthly advance sheets. It chooses from a fixed list of law or law-related periodicals.

Information Access Company under the auspices of the American Association of Law Libraries produces the *Current Law Index* and the *Legal Resource Index,* which index over seven hundred legal periodicals. Their coverage begins in 1980. The *Current Law Index* is a printed index that includes a subject index, an author index, a table of cases, and a table of statutes. It is published in eight monthly issues, three quarterly cumulations, and a single annual cumulation. The *Legal Resource Index* is produced in both microform and in machine-readable form searchable through DIALOG Information Systems. This index provides access to the same information found in the *Current Law Index* plus legal-related material from the *Magazine Index* and from the *National Newspaper Index*.

The *Index to Periodical Articles Related to Law* (*I.P.A.R.L.*) is designed specifically to provide access to articles pertaining to legal matters published in journals not included in the *Index to Legal Periodicals*. It is published quarterly with annual and ten-year cumulations. It focuses on non-legal periodicals such as *Playboy*, *Fortune*, the *New Yorker*, *Esquire*, *American Behavioral Scientist*, *Journal of the American Medical Association*, *Political Science Quarterly*, *Scientific American*, and *Foreign Affairs* for the occasional law-related articles that appear in such publications.

How to Find It

There are innumerable methods for conducting any type of research, and legal research is no exception. Before one can develop an individualized procedure for legal research however, a logical, systematic method must be established. This method will form a solid scientific base from which the art of legal research may blossom. As a research style develops, some of the scientific steps may be eliminated, the approach refined, and some of the time required reduced. Care should be taken to see that accuracy is not sacrificed for the sake of saving time. A clear understanding of the material in the preceding section, "Where It Is Recorded," is essential before proceeding.

Legal research can be very complicated; therefore, one must plan an approach before beginning in order to ensure that nothing is overlooked. The aim is to reach the primary sources of law (statutes and cases) so that one can gain an understanding from them of how the law will be applied to solve one's particular problem. There are so many statutes and cases that research is essentially a process of elimination. To aid in this process, there are descriptive materials (e.g., encyclopedias, treatises, journal articles) that give a general background and lead to other sources. If the researcher has some idea of where he or she is going, the finding aids (e.g., digests, indexes, and codes) will lead him or her to specific cases and statutes covering the points of law of interest.

Many researchers find checklists to be valuable tools to ensuring that all necessary bases are covered and for indicating the present status of the project. The first checklist to be considered will be the "Search Process Flow Chart" (Fig. 2 below), which presents an outline of strategy to be used during the search. Without a strategy, the examination of information tends to be hit or miss, with the researcher trying first one method then switching to another when an enticing bit of information is uncovered. This process leads to confusion regarding the status of the project at any one time. A checklist is just a guide, however, and need not be followed religiously. It will always be a good point of reference when one finds oneself going off in the wrong direction or when the research is resumed after an interruption. As one becomes more adept, individual variations will appear and shortcuts can be used as long as there is no sacrifice of accuracy.

The search is undertaken to find the correct rules of law to be applied to a given situation. In the beginning, probably all that the researcher knows is a

24

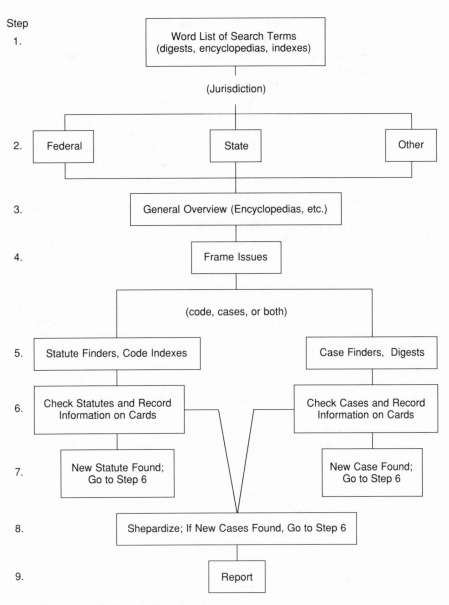

Fig. 2. Search Process Flow Chart

few facts. It is essential that the facts be carefully determined, both in the interest of accuracy and because facts alter cases. Once the facts have been determined, the fun begins.

The Search Process Flow Chart lists nine steps in the process. This chart assumes that the facts have been investigated and studied and that they are entered on a card and firmly set in mind. Step 1, "Word List of Search Terms," is the generation of a list of key words from the factual situation that will be used in one's search of sources of law, statutes, and cases. Key words obtained from a factual situation consist of those words that one would expect to find in decisions of cases involving like circumstances. For instance, in the case of a person slipping on a banana peel in a grocery store, key words from the factual situation might be *banana peel, grocery store, floor,* etc. Key words in a legal reference from these facts might be *liability* or *damages.*

Systems for generating a search term list may vary, but the objective is the same—to assist researchers in finding the words or phrases from the factual situation that will enable them to access the legal literature through existing indexes and digests. The process of extracting words from facts that are pertinent to and useful in research is difficult. Publishers of legal materials attempt to make this process easier by using common descriptive words in their headnotes, indexes, and digests. Experience with legal literature is the best way to familiarize oneself with the terminology used and needed to become a proficient researcher.

The Lawyers Cooperative/Bancroft-Whitney—the publishers of a variety of statute books, reporters, digests, and encyclopedias—has suggested the use of their simple "TAPP" system when looking for search terms. The TAPP system, along with all of the other systems used for finding search terms, is intended to be easily remembered and suggest the main areas in which to look to find key words. The TAPP system works as follows: *T* means to look for *things* in the facts that are important to your situation, such as a floor or a store; *A* means an *act* of some person or a failure to act when required to do so, such as when shopping, minding a store, or eating a banana; *P* refers to a *person,* such as a customer or a shopkeeper; and the second *P* signifies a *place,* such as a store or a sidewalk. One or more of these points (*T, A, P,* or *P*) can be used in legal research; but, naturally, the more access points one uses, the greater chance one has of finding a key word that clicks. The TAPP system is especially useful with Lawyers Cooperative/Bancroft-Whitney publications because it is interwoven into their Total Client Service Library. This means that topics are consistent throughout Lawyers Cooperative/Bancroft-Whitney publications so that once one finds a pertinent topic, one can use it to find appropriate material throughout the search.

West has devised a different method of identifying their material from the one mentioned above. Their digest topics form the basis of identifying specific points of law found in a particular case. The digest of topics is further broken down into key numbers that identify more specific treatments of the topic. Digest topics and key numbers are permanent, fixed, and consistent in all current West digests and reporters. For example, under the digest topic "negligence," key number 32 covers the "Care as to licensees or persons invited"; and as a more specific subsection key number, 32(2.8) covers "Business visitors, and store and restaurant patrons." Therefore, if a key number is located in one volume, it can be used to find the same topic and same breakdown into key numbers in the other volumes. Each case in West's reporters include headnotes, a short paragraph consisting of a brief statement of the facts, a brief statement of the rules of law applied by the court in a particular situation, and an accompanying key number.

Again, the researcher must find the right term that is needed to lead to the topic in question. *West's Law Finder,* a research manual for lawyers, sets forth a slightly different method of finding the right descriptive terms, legal topics, or cases, that will lead into the key number system. West's descriptive word process involves finding words that describe the facts or the legal situation to be searched in the indexes of the company's digests and encyclopedias. West's descriptive words consist of five elements: (1) parties, (2) places and things, (3) basis of action, (4) defense, and (5) relief. There are so many legal topics and key numbers that West suggests not relying on memory but instead suggests checking the publisher's outline of law, which divides the law into seven main divisions; many subdivisions can also be found in the front of digest volumes. Words can also be gathered from the descriptive word indexes, which provide search words and references to the proper topics and key numbers in each digest.

J. Myron Jacobstein and Roy M. Mersky's *Fundamentals of Legal Research* outlines a slightly different system from this one for analyzing the facts that are needed to find search words. These authors use what they call the "TARP" rule. Using this rule, *T* stands for *thing*, *A* stands for the *action* to be taken, *R* stands for *relief*, and *P* stands for *persons*.

The rule followed in this book will be called the "CORP" rule. *CORP* is easy to remember. Each letter identifies a concept for which key words can be found and used as access points for unlocking information about legal concepts and issues contained in various research sources. The actual words to be used as access points will be taken from the facts of each individual situation, so CORP is not a magical tool but rather a device to jog one's imagination and to ensure that one is thorough and systematic in gathering search terms to be used with indexes and similar research sources. The CORP rule establishes the general outline of any legal research project, starting with the estalishment of terms to be searched for.

C stands for the *cause* of action, or on the other side, the defense. In the case of a person slipping on a banana peel in a grocery store, the cause of action might be a claim for negligence against the grocery store operator, and an index search under *negligence* might be required.

O stands for the *object* or thing involved. In the case above, the banana peel might be an important object, so *banana peel* might be used in searching indexes.

R stands for *restitution*. What sort of assistance is the person seeking from the court? Does he or she want an amount of money to which he or she feels entitled as the result of the action or inaction of the other party? Does the individual want the court to force the other party to take a particular action or to cease some activity in which that party is already engaged? In the banana peel case, for instance, the individual who slipped on the peel may want the grocery store operator to compensate him or her for doctor bills incurred because of the fall. The restitution sought in this case then might be listed in an index under *compensation, damages,* or *doctor bills.*

P stands for the *parties* involved. In this same case, we would have a person who has been invited onto the premises for the purpose of purchasing goods. The other party is the shopkeeper. It is important that the parties be identified according to their interests in each situation. That is, they should not be called just Mr. Brown or Ms. Smith but also identified as a customer and a shopkeeper, respectively.

Once the researcher has settled on the search terms, the next factor to consider is jurisdiction, or Step 2 in the Search Process Flow Chart. Jurisdiction, for the purpose of this discussion, is the power given to the courts by a constitution or legislature to make decisions involving persons or property within set bounds. It may come about because of the geographic location of the person or object involved, or it may be granted over certain things, parties, or actions. For example, the Constitution of the United States gives the federal government jurisdiction over certain functions, such as interstate commerce; but until the federal government acts, the states may exercise their own jurisdiction. Once the federal government has acted in this area, its actions supersede the functions of the states. It is important to decide jurisdiction initially, because laws vary from one jurisdiction to another and one must examine the law books of the jurisdiction within which the action took place.

Step 3, "General Overview," should be used if one knows little or nothing about the subject or needs a refresher in that area. This step is extremely important because it provides the researcher with a concise discussion of the law, which is already synthesized by the author from the primary sources, e.g., cases, statutes, and administrative regulations and decisions. Without such commentary, the newcomer to a particular field is likely to become lost in the maze of digest paragraphs and legalistic language used in statutes, finding it very difficult to make sense out of the materials. The best sources for such an overview are often legal encyclopedias, either those that are national in scope (i.e., C.J.S. and Am. Jur.2d) or the local ones published for specific states. The latter narrow the information down to a manageable size. In addition to encyclopedias, the treatises or textbooks that exist for many subjects of law may be consulted for valuable background information. Any information, cases, or statutes that one finds concerning the problem under investigation should be written on cards as outlined below. Remember, this step may be skipped if one does not need background on a certain subject.

Step 4 concerns the legal issues presented by the factual situation. "Framing a Legal Issue" means formulating a legal question (or questions) to be answered by one's research. Attorneys spend their law school years learning how to frame legal issues and continue to learn how to do so throughout their careers, so this is by no means a simple task. Still, this process is essential to the ultimate success of one's research because it is impossible to judge the relevancy of materials and authorities one has found unless one knows exactly what question one is trying to answer. Many novice researchers waste precious time meandering through law books because they have not taken the time beforehand to analyze their problem and to decide what it is they wish to find.

Defining the framing of legal issues is easy, but describing the process is difficult, if not impossible. The process requires an extensive use of the imagination and the help of the above-mentioned outline of the law which is provided in the front of the West's digests. Framing the legal issues begins with a careful analysis of the facts in order to discover the problem or problems. Once the problems are discovered, the right questions must be asked. These questions will help direct the researcher to answers. Imagination comes into play in making up the questions. Here is where new case law is made—lawyers with imagination come up with questions no one else has considered. Since this book is a guide to beginning legal research, it will not include such a soaring of the imagination but instead will concentrate on the basic research process that creates the foundation for understanding the law.

In Step 5, one searches for answers either in statutes or cases, or both. This step refers one to the materials in which one may find leads to the cases or statutes that make up the primary sources of the law for which one is searching. If statutes are involved, the general indexes of codes should be searched for the words in the key word list. Digests and indexes serve this same purpose when one is seeking the law as set forth in legal cases.

Step 6 is the examination of the cases and statutes located, and the recording of that information for use in solving the issues. Naturally, only the information concerning the particular issue in question should be considered at this point. If other points come to mind, they should be noted separately and considered later because there should be a single-mindedness about following one point at a time. If in the examination of a statute or case, new cases or statutes appear concerning the immediate legal issue, Step 7 indicates that they should be given the same examination as the originally located material received in Step 6 (examination and recording).

The cases found may be several years old. What if a statute changed the law, or another judge decided the same facts and law differently? Step 8, "Shepardizing," refers to a process that is designed to follow the history of a case or statute from the time of its decision or enactment to date. This process will be explained in greater detail below.

Step 9 of the Search Process Flow Chart suggests that once one has all the facts and has ascertained the law, this information should be condensed and consolidated into a report. Not only is this step essential to carry out when one is working for others; it is also useful when one is doing work for oneself. Following this step makes one rethink the problem and reduce it to its essentials. (An example of a report can be found at the end of next section.)

During the process of gathering and reporting on statutes and cases, the researcher should refer to these items in a uniform manner. To aid lawyers, researchers, and authors, the Harvard Law Review Association has published *A Uniform System of Citation*, now in its 14th edition (1986). This concise work begins with the general rules of citation and style, and covers cases, constitutions, statutes, legislative material, administrative and executive material, international material, books, pamphlets, unpublished material, periodicals, newspapers, and services. Specific citation forms and abbreviations are listed for the United States, the fifty states, other common law jurisdictions, and other jurisdictions. In the back there is a comprehensive index.

Cases for instance, are generally found in volumes, and each case begins on a separate page in the volume. In state and federal reports, the cases tend to be more or less chronological. In the reporters that cover a variety of states, on the other hand, will not be so arranged. Cases are identified by the last names of the parties—first the plaintiff's name, followed by the abbreviation for *versus* (v.), and then by the defendant's name. The case name is followed by the number of the volume within which the case is recorded, the abbreviation of the reporter or reports containing the case, the page where the case begins, and the date, as noted below:

Plaintiff	versus	Defendant	Vol.	Rept.	Pg.	Date
Jones	v.	Smith,	321	Mass.	286	(1967)

or

Jones v. Smith, 321 Mass. 286 (1967)

With the Search Process Flow Chart and CORP in mind as aids, the researcher must develop a logical approach to the research. Any systematic method can be used. The use of 4″ x 6″ index cards, for example, allows considerable room for notes; cards also are convenient to carry and can be rearranged in any desirable order to make a file.

The first card should outline the facts of the case as they appear at the time. If the alleged facts change because of the discovery of new evidence as the case develops, it is a simple matter to substitute a new card so that the facts are correct in light of the latest evidence. After the fact card, the next card develops an issue involved in the case, one legal issue per card. In addition to stating the specific issue, the issue card also lists the research materials considered useful in solving this particular issue. Following each issue card come cards for each of the useful references found, indicating the information that was found and any related references to be investigated. After all these references have been examined, the next issue is considered, and the process is repeated. When the project is finished, the cards are assembled in a logical order, as indicated in the card display in Figure 3.

Each card must be dated and identified by the name of the person for whom the project is undertaken, by the name of the party of interest, and by the problem. In the case of Joe Bleau, shown below in Figure 4, he is doing the project for himself.

In the hope that a step-by-step walk through the research process will help fix the suggested steps in the mind of the reader and illuminate the complications and confusions that can arise during that process, the remainder of this section is devoted to a specific example of its use. If possible, it would be advisable to take an afternoon off, go to the nearest law library, and follow the solution of the example in the available New York State reference materials.

For background material on the tools to be used in legal research, review the section of this book titled "Where It Is Recorded." See the Glossary for the meanings of unfamiliar terms that appear in the following example; and see Appendix A for abbreviations.

Solving the Problem of Joe Bleau and the Banana Peel

The first card also should contain a concise statement of the operative facts involved. The facts should be specific and concise, covering O for the object involved and P for the parties involved, and giving the parties' legal status in the particular case. The statement of fact card or cards set forth the facts as the researcher has discovered them, and these cards must be revised if new relevant facts are later discovered. A summary of the researcher's factual examination of the accident in the sample case shown here should also appear on the fact card (Fig. 5).

Before using a legal encyclopedia or an outline of the law to form our word list (Step 1 in the Research Process Flow Chart), it is a good idea to review the facts, define the parties, and review CORP. Mr. Bleau is a "person," but that category is much too broad. Does he fit into a class having something to do with the accident? Yes, he was a purchaser in the store, i.e., a consumer, or a "party" under CORP. Stores are maintained to invite people to enter and to

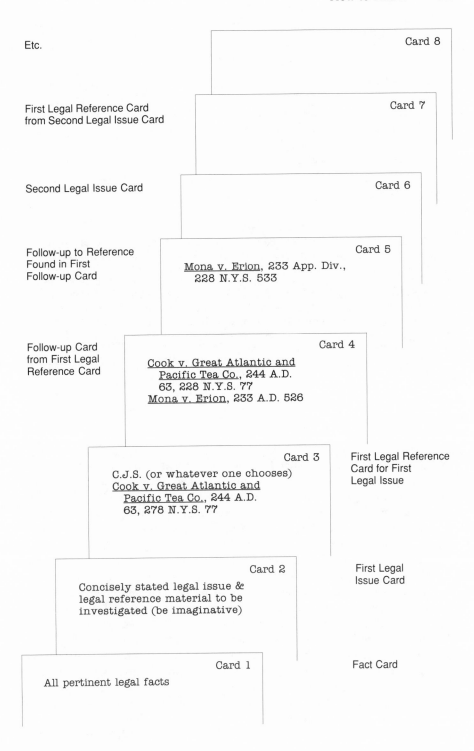

Etc.   Card 8

First Legal Reference Card   Card 7
from Second Legal Issue Card

Second Legal Issue Card   Card 6

Follow-up to Reference   Card 5
Found in First   Mona v. Erion, 233 App. Div.,
Follow-up Card   228 N.Y.S. 533

Follow-up Card   Card 4
from First Legal   Cook v. Great Atlantic and
Reference Card   Pacific Tea Co., 244 A.D.
                               63, 228 N.Y.S. 77
                            Mona v. Erion, 233 A.D. 526

                                                           Card 3   First Legal Reference
                      C.J.S. (or whatever one chooses)   Card for First
                      Cook v. Great Atlantic and   Legal Issue
                         Pacific Tea Co., 244 A.D.
                         63, 278 N.Y.S. 77

                                                  Card 2   First Legal
                  Concisely stated legal issue &   Issue Card
                  legal reference material to be
                  investigated (be imaginative)

                                          Card 1   Fact Card
         All pertinent legal facts

Fig. 3.   Card Display (Card Headings Omitted)

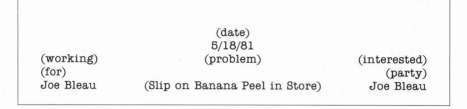

(date)
5/18/81
(working)   (problem)   (interested)
(for)   (party)
Joe Bleau   (Slip on Banana Peel in Store)   Joe Bleau

Fig. 4. Card Heading

5/18/81
Joe Bleau   (Slip on Banana Peel on Floor)   Joe Bleau
Statement of facts: Joe Bleau of Apt. 4E, 1862 Beach St., Tuxedoville, N.Y., on Feb. 5, 1981, at about 2:30 PM entered the A&P store
at 2619 Main St. in said town to purchase groceries. While shopping in the aisle containing fruits and vegetables, he slipped on
a banana peel, which he had not seen, on the floor. He fell,
injuring his hip. The store operator, Mr. I. M. Quick, came immediately, ascertained that Mr. Bleau was injured, and called an
ambulance, which arrived about 3:00 PM, taking Mr. Bleau to
Memorial Hospital, where it was discovered that he had a broken
hip.

Fig. 5. Fact Card

shop, i.e., to do business. Therefore, Mr. Bleau was more than a visitor or a guest; his presence was for a business purpose. The A&P—also a "party" under CORP—obviously is operating a store, and without customers it will fail. The store thus goes to elaborate means to lure shoppers inside to purchase wares. It does not invite customers to "hang out"; in fact, the store probably has a No Loitering sign or two on the premises.

Now that the parties are identified and recognizable as classes—a customer in a store and a shopkeeper—and the location of the accident is established— in the store—what relationships come into play? Accidents do happen; some cannot be avoided. Others occur because someone did, or did not do, some- thing. Unavoidable accidents are called "acts of God" and cannot be prevented. Accidents caused by someone doing something that he or she should not have done, or not doing something that should have been done, arise from negligence. Do the facts in our case give us enough information to discover if negligence (cause of action under CORP) was involved, and if so, was the negligence on the part of the store? Suppose a young lad—another *P* for *party*—a neighbor of Mr. Bleau, saw him coming down the aisle and decided to have some fun. He threw the banana peel on the floor to see what would happen. This act is not negligence but a deliberate act. Is the store responsible? Or, perhaps someone unknowingly knocked the banana peel onto the floor just before Mr. Bleau rounded the corner. Is the store responsible for this act that it certainly did not even know about? If the peel had been on the floor for a couple of hours, long enough for store employees to have seen it and picked it up, does this have any effect upon the negligence of the store? What degree of care does the store owe its customers? And what about Mr. Bleau himself? How much responsibility should he take for his own safety? Finally, what does Mr. Bleau claim as his damages—medical and hospital expenses, perhaps loss of wages, or even conscious pain and suffering—*R* for *restitution* under CORP? As these questions arise, the simple case of slipping on a banana peel demonstrates the complexities of the law. All of the above information is important and can alter the legal results. As each point is raised, further investigation will be needed, and the range of the concise statement of facts is increased.

It turns out that another customer, Ms. James, had walked down the aisle a half hour before Mr. Bleau and had seen the banana peel on the floor. She did not report it, and no one connected with the store admitted being aware that the banana peel had fallen onto the floor. Nor could anyone be found who knew how it got there. Mr. Bleau, in walking down the produce lane, was intently interested in apples and oranges, and did not see the cause of his downfall resting on the floor. This information should be added to the fact card (Fig. 6).

Referring to our Search Process Flow Chart, Step 1, we make up a word list. We have already thought of some terms in going through CORP—*storekeeper, customer, negligence, injury*. Opening a digest to Digest Topics, we come across *damages* and *negligence*. No tremendous list, but enough to start.

Step 2 concerns jurisdiction. The accident happened in New York State, and that appears to be the most likely jurisdiction. Therefore, our search will be confined to New York material as far as possible.

Step 3 takes us to an investigation of encyclopedias and textbooks because we are really not confident enough that our word list will help us find our topic, and we need a review of the subject. We select *New York Jurisprudence,* an

---

3/29/82

Joe Bleau   (Slip on Banana Peel in Store)   Joe Bleau

Statement of facts: Joe Bleau of Apt. 4E, 1862 Beach St., Tuxedoville, N.Y., on Feb. 12, 1981, about 2:30 PM entered the A&P store at 2619 Main St. in said town to purchase groceries. While shopping in the fruit and vegetable aisle, concentrating on apples and oranges, he slipped on a banana peel, which he had not seen, and fell, injuring his hip. The store operator, Mr. I. M. Quick, came immediately, ascertained that Mr. Bleau was injured, and called an ambulance, which arrived about 3:00 PM, taking Mr. Bleau to Memorial Hospital, where it was discovered that he had a broken hip. Ms. James, another customer, had seen the banana peel on the floor about 2:00 PM on the day of the accident but reported it to no one. No employee of the store admitted being aware of the banana peel on the floor. Mr. Bleau suffered a loss of wages amounting to $8,500, was out of work for six months, had hospital and doctor bills amounting to $15,350, and now walks painfully with the aid of a cane.

Fig. 6. Corrected Fact Card

encyclopedia published by the Lawyers Cooperative/Bancroft-Whitney. This title was chosen over other encyclopedias because it involves only New York State law and will be much quicker than searching through a general encyclopedia covering all state and federal material. The encyclopedia will include references to federal law or cases that in any way alter New York law. In looking through the index, we discover "Shopkeepers," and under this heading we come across "Premises Liability, Sec. 146" (Fig. 7), a likely start. This information is entered on a separate card as shown in Figure 8.

This information gives us some idea of the law involving our situation and some cases, one of them concerning a store and a customer. The case of *Cook v. Great Atlantic & Pacific Tea Co.* we mark with an "x" for further study.

Now that we have a general idea of what we are looking for, Step 4 of our Search Process Flow Chart suggests that we frame some legal issues from the facts. Several legal issues can be framed from what we now know. The issues should be consolidated whenever possible; however, it may be that some issues will become subdivisions of others.

A legal issue is a question posed by the facts of a situation that may be answered by the application of certain legal concepts. Several legal issues may be involved in any one situation, and they should be answered separately. The framing, or construction, of legal issues includes all elements of the CORP rule (Cause of action, Object involved, Restitution sought, and Parties involved), combined within the framework of the law. The above-mentioned Outline of the Law and the Digest Topics found in West's digests can be useful in framing issues. In Mr. Bleau's case, only three issues have been formed, and only issue one will be pursued as an example. Applying CORP and our imagination, combined with logic and West's Outline of the Law and Digest Topics, we come up with the following issues (Figs. 9–11).

We arrange the cards in logical order while considering the issues and exhaust the research for one issue completely before moving on to the other issues. One issue will suffice for this discussion to demonstrate the method to be used. Each issue card contains one legal question that must be answered and applied to the case at hand. The issue cards are used to recite the issue and also to list the logical sources of research information on the specific issue. As each source is exhausted, it is checked off on the card. We arrange the sources in a logical order of search to give ourselves the quickest path to a solution. For example, if a statute is involved, the statute itself may be the first source to examine, since it is likely to be controlling over any case law and since an annotated code will easily lead us to any cases pertaining to the statute anyway.

Using our Search Process Flow Chart, Step 5 leads us to case or statute finders—in this situation, case finders. These are usually written on the issue cards so that as each issue comes up, the references are available. In our example, we have already discovered a case that we will investigate; however, we will still enter the information on the issue card (Fig. 12).

As each source is investigated, we check it off on the card to indicate that it has been examined. Some sources will be useful, while others will not. The ones found useful deserve a card of their own, as indicated below. Perhaps, however, sufficient information is located in *New York Jurisprudence (N.Y. Jur.)* so that it becomes unnecessary to check *Am. Jur.2d* and the rest of the

PREMISES LIABILITY

would naturally produce a crowd, fails to provide supervisors whose presence could reasonably be expected to prevent such a violation of the rules.[8] However, even if under the circumstances an owner of premises on which a playground is furnished for the use of resident children should have a duty to provide adequate supervision over the activities conducted thereon, liability cannot be predicated upon a failure to provide supervision if there is no causal relation between the alleged breach of duty and the injury for which recovery is sought.[9]

B. Liability for Injuries Caused by Defects in Premises Intended for a Particular Use or Purpose

→   ### 1. Stores and Shops

a. In General

§ 146. Duty of care and liability generally.

The proprietor of a store or shop, whether he is the owner of the premises or not, owes to his customers and other invitees a duty to exercise prudence and care in keeping his premises in a condition which will not expose them unreasonably or unnecessarily to danger, and the measure of this duty is the standard of reasonable prudence and care.[10] This duty extends to

8. Where those in control of a large public housing project provided a water spray on a hot day for the benefit of children, at a place where bicycle riding should have been anticipated in the light of past failures to suppress the practice by effective enforcement of rules forbidding it, the owner of the premises was held liable where a child playing in the water was run down by a bicycle, in the absence of a guard to police the area. Da Rocha v New York City Housing Authority (Sup) 109 NYS2d 263, affd 282 AD 728, 122 NYS2d 397.

9. Hansen v New York City Housing Authority, 271 AD 986, 68 NYS2d 71, assuming, but not deciding, that a public housing authority might have such a duty.

10. Miller v Gimbel Bros., Inc. 262 NY 107, 186 NE 410.
Greene v Sibley, Lindsay & Curr Co. 257 NY 190, 177 NE 416.
Hart v Grennell, 122 NY 371, 25 NE 354.
Cejka v Macy & Co. 3 AD2d 535, 162 NYS2d 207, affd 4 NY2d 785, 173 NYS2d 24, 149 NE2d 525.
Powers v Montgomery Ward & Co. 251 AD 120, 295 NYS 712, affd 276 NY 600, 12 NE2d 595.
→ Cook v Great Atlantic & Pacific Tea Co. 244 AD 63, 278 NYS 777, affd 268 NY 599, 198 NE 423.
Stark v Franklin Simon & Co. 237 AD 42, 260 NYS 691.
Mona v Erion, 223 AD 526, 228 NYS 533.
Higgins v Ruppert, 124 AD 530, 108 NYS 919.

303

Fig. 7. 46 N.Y. Jur., Sec. 146, "Premises Liability"

4/12/82

Joe Bleau   (Slip on Banana Peel in Store)   Joe Bleau
46 N.Y. Jur., "Premises Liability," Sec. 146, Duty of care and
liability, generally.

"The proprietor of a store or shop, whether he is the owner of
the premises or not, owes his customers and other invitees a duty
to exercise prudence and care in keeping his premises in a condition which will not expose them unreasonably or unnecessarily
to danger, and the measure of this duty is the standard of reasonable prudence and care."[10]

10. Miller v. Gimbal Bros., Inc., 262 N.Y. 107, 186 N.E. 410.
     Greene v. Sibley, Lindsay & Curr Co., 257 N.Y. 190, 177 N.E.
       416.
     Hart v. Grennell, 122 N.Y. 371, 25 N.E. 354.
     Cejka v. Macy & Co., 3 A.D.2d 535, 162 N.Y.S.2d 207, aff'd, 4
       N.Y.2d 785, 173 N.Y.S.2d 24, 149 N.E.2d 525.
     Powers v. Montgomery Ward & Co., 251 A.D. 120, 295 N.Y.S.
       712, aff'd, 276 N.Y. 600, 12 N.E. 423.
   x Cook v. Great Atlantic & Pacific Tea Co., 244 A.D. 63, 278 N.Y.S.
       777, aff'd, 268 N.Y. 599, 198 N.E. 423.
     Stark v. Franklin Simon & Co., 237 A.D. 42, 260 N.Y.S. 691.
     Mona v. Erion, 223 A.D. 526, 228 N.Y.S. 533.
     Higgins v. Ruppert, 124 A.D. 530, 108 N.Y.S. 919.

Fig. 8.   46 N.Y. Jur., Sec. 146, "Premises Liability" Card

4/12/82

Joe Bleau   (Slip on Banana Peel in Store)   Joe Bleau
Issue 1. What duty does a store owe its customers to keep the
floor clear of potentially dangerous debris?

Fig. 9.   Issue 1 Card

4/12/82

Joe Bleau   (Slip on Banana Peel in Store)   Joe Bleau
Issue 2. Must the storekeeper have prior knowledge of the dangerous condition causing the accident?

Fig. 10.   Issue 2 Card

references. In this case, it would probably be advisable to check the *New York
Digest* to find a case as close in facts to the present case as possible. In this
exercise, however, this additional step will not be taken.

```
                              4/12/82
Joe Bleau           (Slip on Banana Peel in Store)        Joe Bleau
Issue 3. What is the extent of the liability of a storekeeper to a
customer injured on the premises by the negligence of the store?
```

Fig. 11.   Issue 3 Card

```
                              4/12/82
Joe Bleau           (Slip on Banana Peel in Store)        Joe Bleau
Issue 1. What duty does a store owner owe its customers to keep
the floor clean of potentially dangerous debris?
x  N.Y. Jur. (a New York law encyclopedia by Lawyers Coopera-
       tive/Bancroft-Whitney)
   Am. Jur.2d (a general law encyclopedia by Lawyers Coopera-
       tive/Bancroft-Whitney)
   C.J.S. (a general law encyclopedia by West)
   Library subject cards under "negligence" (for textbooks)
   A.L.R.4th (a general selective reporter with treatise by Lawyers
       Cooperative/Bancroft-Whitney)
   New York Digest (by West, for cases involving our list of terms
       and CORP)
```

Fig. 12.   Expanded Issue 1 Card

As each reference is checked, any pertinent information found is entered on the card made up for that particular reference. If in pursuing the reference, one finds additional references, these references should be noted on the card and followed up later.

Going back to *N.Y. Jur.*, where we had nine cases cited in note 10, only one of them is selected to follow as an example, the one involving a grocery store, *Cook v. Great Atlantic & Pacific Tea Co.*, 244 A.D. 63, 278 N.Y.S. 777, aff'd, 268 N.Y. 599, 198 N.E. 423 (1935).

A variety of abbreviations and citations used above need explaining. The reference 244 A.D. 63 indicates where the original case is reported—in volume 244 of the Appellate Division Reports on page 63. This volume contains the official report of the case. The same case appears in the commercially printed *New York Supplement (N.Y.S.)* reports in volume 278 on page 777. The "aff'd" indicates that the case was affirmed by a higher court, and the reference following it indicates where the affirmation is recorded. 268 N.Y. 599 shows us that the affirmation is recorded in volume 268 of the *New York Reports* on page 599. Again, this volume contains the official report. The same affirmation is also reported in the commercial publication the *Northeastern Reporter* in volume 198 on page 423. In practice, both the original case and the affirmation should be examined, probably in the commercial edition because of its better head-noting. If further interesting references are found (e.g., additional headings, key references, or cases)—in this case, *Cook v. Great Atlantic & Pacific Tea Co.*— they should be followed up on a separate card for each. In this case, the card made for the Cook case gives us the general rule governing a shopkeeper in relation to his customers, and a case reference that was also found under Premises Liability, Sec. 146 of *N.Y. Jur.* (see Fig. 8).

Step 6, Part Two informs us that the cases and statutes found should be entered on our cards. So the case of *Cook v. Great Atlantic and Pacific Tea Co.* has been discovered and examined (Fig. 13), and placed on a card (Fig. 14).

Step 7 informs us that any new cases and statutes we discovered should be investigated as in Step 6. This is what should be done with the case of *Mona v. Eiron* found in the Cook case above, especially since the same case was also referred to in *N.Y. Jur.* under Premises Liability. However, this being an example, we will not take up extra space to demonstrate this additional step.

Note that we are now dealing with a West publication, the *New York Supplement*, and the West Key Number System (Negligence ⚿ 44). In checking the body of the case against headnote 1, we find that the headnote seems to restate the words of Justice Crosby. The case of *Mona v. Erion* was also listed on the card for further checking, especially since it also appeared in the list of cases recited in note 10 of Sec. 146, Premises Liability, in *N.Y. Jur.* Although the official versions of the cases are the last word in the event of an error in the commercially reported versions, for most practical purposes we can rely on the more informative headnoted commercial reports. They are occasionally in error, however; and in these rare cases, it is necessary to check the official version. Each case must be consulted, as one cannot rely entirely on statements in the encyclopedias, footnotes, or headnotes.

In the Cook case above, headnote "1, Negligence ⚿ 44," and the statement following it are both taken from the headnote and placed on the card. As mentioned earlier, the West key number allows one to enter West publications using the key numbers and to use the same reference indicator to find other material involving the issue being researched. Cross-referencing from the digest key number system to *C.J.S.* topics and from *C.J.S.* topics to the key number system is not quite so easy. What cross-referencing is found is usually under the heading of "Library References" both in the digests and in *C.J.S.*, but not always. Library references are found under the topic headings and at the front of the text. Older *C.J.S.* volumes, however, frequently do not give this information under Library References, and in such cases it is advisable to check the pocket parts to see if they contain a reference to the key number system. This circumstance is one of the weaker links in the system.

We began our examination by first looking at *N.Y. Jur.* under Premises Liability and found a pertinent section (146) covering the duty of care and liability in general. This led us through note 10 to the case of *Cook v. Great Atlantic & Pacific Tea Co.*, which we investigated in *N.Y.S.* In checking the case in this commercial publication, we found a headnote stating what appears to be an answer to our issue (headnote 1, Negligence ⚿ 44). We entered this information on our card for the Cook case.

We note that we first entered the Lawyers Cooperative/Bancroft-Whitney's *N.Y. Jur.* under Premises Liability, and we now have a reference to "Negligence" in the West system. It is important to keep the references of these

COOK v. GREAT ATLANTIC & PACIFIC TEA CO.   → 777
278 N.Y.S. ←   Sup. Ct.

Argued before HILL, P. J., and RHODES, McNAMEE, CRAPSER, and HEFFERNAN, JJ.

Sidney B. Pfeifer, of Buffalo, for appellants.

John J. Bennett, Jr., Atty. Gen., for respondent.

PER CURIAM.

Employee was injured while painting premises owned by the employer. The employer was engaged in the furniture business. The employee was not employed in the conduct of the furniture business nor in the operation of its stores nor at their location. The policy of insurance issued by the carrier covered operations of the furniture business solely.

Decision unanimously affirmed, with costs to the State Industrial Board. Matter of Anderson v. Abbott-Cheney Paper Corp'n, 259 N. Y. 26, 180 N. E. 883.

→ 244 App. Div. 63

COOK v. GREAT ATLANTIC & PACIFIC TEA CO. (two cases).

Supreme Court, Appellate Division, Fourth Department.
March 13, 1935.

→ 1. Negligence ☞44

Duty of storekeeper, as regards customers, was to keep premises in reasonably safe condition.

2. Negligence ☞48

Storekeeper is not liable to customer injured on premises unless dangerous condition was known to him or could have been known by exercise of due care.

3. Evidence ☞123(11), 317(9)
Negligence ☞126(2)

Evidence in injured customer's case in chief that storekeeper's employee said, after customer had slipped on cream cheese on floor and fallen, that employee had ordered that floor be cleaned *held* not part of res gestæ nor admissible to prove storekeeper's knowledge of dangerous condition of floor, but inadmissible as hearsay.

───────────────

☞For other cases see same topic & KEY NUMBER in all Key Number Digests & Indexes
278 N.Y.S.—49½

Fig. 13.   Cook v. Great Atlantic and Pacific Tea Co.

Appeal from Monroe County Court.

Actions by Bertine Cook and by Arbor Cook against the Great Atlantic & Pacific Tea Company. From judgments for plaintiffs, for $285 and $500, respectively, entered in county clerk's office on November 14, 1934, and from orders denying new trials, the defendant appeals.

Reversed and new trial ordered.

Argued before TAYLOR, EDGCOMB, THOMPSON, CROSBY, and LEWIS, JJ.

Stephen K. Pollard, of Rochester (Carlyle B. Newcomb, of Rochester, of counsel), for appellant.

Walter S. Forsyth, of Rochester, for respondents.

CROSBY, Justice.

Plaintiff Mrs. Cook has recovered a verdict against defendant for $285, and her husband has a verdict for $500. The verdicts grow out of an injury which Mrs. Cook received by slipping and falling on the floor of defendant's store. Taken at its best, and disregarding the evidence produced by defendant, Mrs. Cook's testimony supports a finding that she slipped on some cottage cheese that had dripped onto the floor from an overfilled pan of cottage cheese that was standing on a counter near an aisle along which she walked in a careful manner.

→[1] The duty of defendant was to keep the premises, to which it invited customers, in a reasonably safe condition. Mona v. Erion, 223 App. Div. 526, 228 N. Y. S. 533.

[2] It has been said by our Court of Appeals that: "Liability does not arise unless the dangerous condition is known, or with the exercise of due care ought to have been known." Junkermann v. Tilyou Realty Co., 213 N. Y. 404, 408, 108 N. E. 190, 191, L. R. A. 1915F, 700.

The only evidence in the record offered to show that defendant knew that the slippery substance was on the floor, or that it had been there for a sufficient length of time so that defendant, in the exercise of diligence, ought to have known it, is found in the testimony of Mrs. Cook. She testified that after slipping and falling she had a conversation with a man behind the counter. She testified that this man "had a white coat on," and "was arranging the food there." We will assume that the man was sufficiently identified as

Fig. 13.   Cook v. Great Atlantic and Pacific Tea Co. (Cont.)

```
                              4/20/82
Joe Bleau          (Slip on Banana Peel in Store)        Joe Bleau
Cook v. Great Atlantic and Pacific Tea Co., 244 A.D. 63, 278 N.Y.S.
    777, aff'd, 268 N.Y. 599, 198 N.E. 423 (1935).
1. Negligence ⬦⚿══ 44 Duty of storekeeper as regards customers
was to keep premises in reasonably safe condition
Mona v. Erion, 223 App. Div. 526, 228 N.Y.S. 533.
```

Fig. 14.   Cook v. Great Atlantic and Pacific Tea Co. Card

two publishers in mind, *and separate,* because they are not interchangeable. We now have two legal concepts to investigate—premises liability and negligence. In *N.Y. Jur.* we have examined premises liability. We will not, however, pursue the concept of negligence in *N.Y. Jur.* at this point because we have cases that seem to answer our question. But if further information is desired, 41 *N.Y. Jur.,* "Negligence" covers negligence in some detail (Fig. 15).

Having discovered the West key number (Negligence ⬦⚿══ 44), we can now enter the West sources. We have the background material we need, and we are now ready to turn to *New York Digest 3d* under "Negligence ⬦⚿══ 44" to find additional cases (Fig. 16).

We complete the research on one issue before proceeding to the next issue. Attempting to research two or three issues at the same time can be quite confusing and can turn a project into complete chaos. The end is near when most references on each point are familiar and have already been consulted. In the beginning, it is better to err on the side of collecting too much material, for any superfluous data can always be discarded later. It is better to follow many legal issues, one at a time, adding new ones as they arise during the project. These, too, can be discarded later if they are found to be irrelevant.

Step 8 has us check to see if the law has changed since the Cook case was first reported. This is done with the aid of *Shepard's Citations.* The case under investigation (i.e., Cook) should be checked in the appropriate Shepard's volume, under its Appellate Court reporting in 278 N.Y.S. 777, and its affirmation in 268 N.Y. 599 should be checked in the appropriate Shepard's New York citator. In *Shepard's New York Supplement Citations,* the citation "278 N.Y.S. 777" first appears in Part Three of the 1970 publication covering *N.Y.S.* reporters, Volumes 150 through 300 (Fig. 17).

Reading the preface tells us that *Shepard's Citations* claims to be a complete citation system showing all citations by the state and federal courts to all cases reported in the *New York Supplement.* This system is continued in the *1970–1980 Supplement,* and in annual and monthly cumulations thereafter, all of which must be checked. Coverage also includes references to encyclopedias and to various legal journals that discuss a particular case. Each case reference is analyzed to determine the effect of the latest decisions upon the original case, i.e., whether it is overruled, distinguished, followed, etc.

Such effects are indicated by a special set of abbreviations, unique to the various units of *Shepard's Citations,* that are explained under "Abbreviations—

NEGLIGENCE

II. FOUNDATION OF LEGAL LIABILITY

§ 3. Generally; "damnum absque injuria" and "unavoidable accident"
§ 4. Intent
§ 5. Contract exempting or limiting liability
§ 6. — Effect of relative bargaining powers of parties

III. ELEMENTS OF ACTIONABLE NEGLIGENCE

A. IN GENERAL

§ 7. Generally
§ 8. Acts of omission and commission
§ 9. Knowledge; foreseeability

B. DUTY TO PERSON INJURED

§ 10. Generally
§ 11. Basis of duty generally
§ 12. Use of own property; sic utere tuo ut alienum non laedas
§ 13. Contract
§ 14. Voluntary assumption of duty

IV. DEGREE AND STANDARD OF CARE

§ 15. Generally; ordinary or reasonable care
§ 16. Standard in measuring conduct
§ 17. Effect of circumstances generally
§ 18. Care commensurate with danger
§ 19. Effect of emergency or sudden danger
§ 20. Exercise of individual's own best judgment
§ 21. Effect of custom and usage
§ 22. Performance of duty voluntarily assumed
§ 23. — Taking care of sick, injured, or an infant
§ 24. Status, capacity, or condition of person injured
§ 25. — Children

V. DEGREES OF NEGLIGENCE; WILFUL, WANTON, AND RECKLESS ACTS

§ 26. Generally
§ 27. Slight, ordinary, gross, and culpable negligence defined
§ 28. Wilful, wanton, and reckless acts

VI. PROXIMATE CAUSE

A. IN GENERAL

§ 29. Generally
§ 30. Definitions

B. TESTS OF PROXIMATE CAUSE

§ 31. Generally; natural and probable consequences
§ 32. Foreseen and foreseeable consequences
§ 33. — Anticipation of particular injury

C. CONCURRENT CAUSES

§ 34. Generally
§ 35. Joint and several liability

3

Fig. 15.   41 N.Y. Jur. "Negligence"

NEGLIGENCE   ⊝⇒44

For references to other topics, see Descriptive-Word Index

Assuming that building owner had failed to make inspections required by industrial code during hand demolition operations, building owner could not be held liable for injuries suffered by demolition contractor's employee when fire escape on which he was working fell, where the danger was not caused by the demolition work, but was present before such work began. Labor Law §§ 241, 241, subd. 6.

Monroe v. City of New York, 414 N.Y.S.2d 718, 67 A.D.2d 89.

Section of Labor Law requiring all areas in which construction, excavation or demolition work is being performed be so constructed, shored, equipped, guarded, arranged, operated and conducted so as to provide reasonable and adequate protection and safety to persons employed therein or lawfully frequenting such places was intended to compel owners and general contractors to become more concerned with safety practices of subcontractors, because they would be exposed to liability without regard to control over the work. Labor Law § 241, subd. 6.

Monroe v. City of New York, 414 N.Y.S.2d 718, 67 A.D.2d 89.

Labor Law provision requiring demolition work to be conducted so as to provide adequate protection to employees imposes a nondelegable duty upon owners and contractors to vicariously respond in damages for injuries sustained due to negligent failure of general contractor or subcontractors to so conduct demolition operation. Labor Law § 241, subd. 6.

Monroe v. City of New York, 414 N.Y.S.2d 718, 67 A.D.2d 89.

N.Y.A.D. 1976. Where a defendant causes or permits slippery condition to exist, there may be liability, and question of liability is for jury.

Kelsey v. Port Authority of New York and New Jersey, 383 N.Y.S.2d 347, 52 A.D.2d 801.

N.Y.A.D. 1975. Person who was on premises for purposes of taking promotional photographs for his employer, and not for the owner of the premises, and who, while searching for a ladder, fell through chute used to feed hay to stock in basement of barn was properly permitted to recover in negligence action brought against owner of the premises.

Parish v. Henneberry Road Farms, Inc., 370 N.Y.S.2d 728, 49 A.D.2d 675, affirmed 386 N.Y.S.2d 580, 39 N.Y.2d 932, 352 N.E.2d 884.

N.Y.A.D. 1970. Even though supervisor was absent, employer which provided skating rink for its employees was not liable for injuries sustained by guest who fell when skater passed her and suddenly turned and began skating against flow of skaters and caught guest's skate.

Baker v. Eastman Kodak Co., 312 N.Y.S.2d 449, 34 A.D.2d 886, affirmed 320 N.Y.S.2d 247, 28 N.Y.2d 636, 269 N.E.2d 36.

N.Y.A.D. 1970. If plaintiff were not an invitee but only a licensee, no duty to her was violated in connection with her fall on defendants' premises, where at most under proof the defendants could properly be charged with only ordinary negligence.

Andlauer v. Caldarell, 311 N.Y.S.2d 593, 34 A.D.2d 725.

N.Y.A.D. 1969. Presence of a one and one-half to two-inch piece of paper, similar to a candy wrapper, on bank's doorstep was not of such a character as to impose liability on bank or of such a nature that probability of injury could have been foreseen in exercise of care and prudence.

Kritz v. Manufacturers Hanover Trust Co., 305 N.Y.S.2d 887, 33 A.D.2d 753.

N.Y.A.D. 1969. A condition which imports even unusual slipperiness of floor does not impose liability on homeowner to licensee even if social visitor would hardly realize danger.

Golding v. Mauss, 305 N.Y.S.2d 1, 33 A.D.2d 64, reversed 313 N.Y.S.2d 399, 27 N.Y.2d 580, 261 N.E.2d 399.

N.Y.A.D. 1968. Highly polished floors in defendant's house, with scatter rug thereon, did not charge defendant, as reasonably, prudent person, with duty of foreseeing that invitee, in exercise of ordinary care, would be exposed to danger through slip and fall.

Mannix v. Matthews, 292 N.Y.S.2d 33, 30 A.D.2d 895.

Mere polishing of floors, creating slippery condition, is not negligence even as to an invitee.

Mannix v. Matthews, 292 N.Y.S.2d 33, 30 A.D.2d 895.

N.Y.A.D. 1968. Fraternal organization which maintained lodge building had duty to take such measures as jury might find reasonable under prevailing weather conditions to reduce danger of a fall by lodge member on snowy steps leading to lodge building.

Mason v. Eagles Lodge, 290 N.Y.S.2d 56, 30 A.D.2d 605.

N.Y.A.D. 1967. Defendant was not negligent in placing ordinary perforated mat, which caused plaintiff's injuries when plaintiff tripped on mat and fell, in front of revolving door of hotel.

Hill v. Hotel Pierre Corp., 284 N.Y.S.2d 403, 28 A.D.2d 1104.

N.Y.A.D. 1967. Plaintiffs could not recover from landowners for injuries sustained in fall by plaintiff-wife who was a social guest-licensee where fall was not caused by trap or an affirmative act of negligence or by hidden, dangerous defect not likely to be discovered by wife.

Levine v. Barfus, 282 N.Y.S.2d 23, 28 A.D.2d 896.

N.Y.A.D. 1967. While conditions of self-service market and probability of spillage from han-

see McKinney's Consolidated Laws of New York

Fig. 16.   28 N.Y. Digest 3d 409

NEW YORK SUPPLEMENT

—721— Case 3 (243AD793) —722— Case 1 (243AD793) —722— Case 2 (243AD800) —722— Case 3 (243AD800) —723— Case 1 (243AD798) —723— Case 2 (243AD796) s268NY726 —723— Case 3 (243AD800) —724— Case 1 (243AD799) a269NY617 —724— Case 2 (243AD795) —725— Case 1 s276S479 (243AD798) —725— Case 2 (243AD790) s270S688 —726— Case 1 (243AD790) s270S688 —726— Case 2 (243AD794) —727— Case 1 (243AD801) —727— Case 2 (243AD818) s270S532 s277S616 s266NY1 —727— Case 3 (243AD812) —728— Case 1 (243AD815) s268NY723 —728— Case 2 (243AD817) —729— Case 1 (243AD820) —729— Case 2 (243AD806) —729— Case 3 (243AD804) —729— Case 4 (243AD803)	—729— Case 5 (243AD803) —730— Case 1 (243AD802) —730— Case 2 (243AD804) —730— Case 3 (243AD804) —731— Case 1 (243AD804) —731— Case 2 (243AD804) —731— Case 3 (243AD804) —731— Case 4 (243AD808) —731— Case 5 (243AD595) —732— Case 1 (243AD555) s266NY155 —732— (243AD816) s283S485 s268NY727 —732— Case 3 (243AD819) —733— Case 1 (243AD815) s267NY [xxxix —733— Case 2 (243AD806) —733— Case 3 (243AD806) —733— Case 4 (243AD818) —734— Case 1 (243AD806) —734— Case 2 (243AD814) —734— Case 3 (243AD853) —735— Case 1 (243AD805) —735— Case 2 (243AD803) —735— Case 3 (243AD818)	—736— Case 1 (243AD819) —736— Case 2 (243AD820) —736— Case 3 (243AD815) —737— (244AD106) 297S2715 192S2d 3625 101AR [1355n —743— (244AD726) s278S745 s278S746 289S1192 295S2d157 —745— Case 1 (243AD803) s278S743 s278S746 —745— Case 2 (243AD812) —746— Case 1 (243AD803) s278S743 s278S745 —746— Case 2 (154M576) 19S2d 1868 j167S2d 477 —752— (154M869) —754— (154M663) —759— (154M667) a282S235 a282S245 —764— (154M569) —766— (154M565) cc253S303 cc255S1012 cc274NY388 —771— (244AD230) a271NY589 46S2d 2440 277S2d3706 —775— (243AD853) 18S2d 1918 71S2d 1615 160S2d 1364 48CaL665 —776— Case 2 (243AD803) m280S1022 108AR813n —777— (244AD63)	a268NY599 p278S385 289S922 36S2d 3267 36S2d 8281 93S2d 2541 j181S2d 298 d253S2d [31014 j261S2d [31006 100AR712n 100AR744n 163AR 80n N M 161P2d 635 404P2d291 —780— (243AD856) 284S151 297S2274 j 35S2d 1911 35S2d 1964 157S2d 2322 13A3292n —781— (244AD195) 224S2d 1207 50FS11019 175AR 620n 26A31244n —785— (244AD238) m269NY517 s272S624 292S370 22S2d 551 29S2d 8884 35S2d 8838 43S2d 8598 47S2d 8148 58S2d 2619 58S2d 8817 73S2d 8535 88S2d 890 d 91S2d 2183 101S2d 8697 174S2d 4641 199S2d 5683 j303NY 1296 337F2d8219 343F2d3462 350F2d31016 241FS 8492 276FS3332 51MnL446 70YLJ182 168AR1468n 21A31429n 74A3 787n Tex 198SW 733 —791— (243AD853) 288S2d1299 —792— (155M91) 271NY1387 Calif 61P2d752 —796— (244AD735) s279S548 s268NY727	—797— (155M168) a284S364 43S2d1442 102AR [1296n —798— (244AD234) —802— (244AD52) s274S183 85S2d 2245 96S2d 352 148AR1327n 148AR1329n —804— (244AD55) 1S2d1195 9S2d2919 44S2d 1296 66S2d 1592 69S2d 1574 93S2d 1622 112S2d 1213 146S2d 1103 54A31436n 62A3 943n Calif 69CaR581 442P2d661 —805— (244AD209) —809— (244AD200) a270N.Y550 s268NY723 25S2d 2225 158AR 277n 158AR 283n 78A3 37n 78A3 48n 78A3 55n —815— (244AD188) r268NY183 s287S690 —823— (244AD252) 12S2d 2974 d 61S2d 2840 e115S2d 2271 159S2d 1563 177S2d 152 288S2d2755 1A3 852n —826— (244AD244) f291S3S3 293S375 20S2d 8738 88F2d3403 110F2d8876 25FS3399 194At203 —832— (244AD54) —833— (243AD855) 210S2d 166 74A3 117n 74A3 186n —834— (244AD702) r270NY184	280S1159 3S2d145 18FS1600 54FS 815 —837— (155M573) a283S996 —838— (243AD855) s289S74 s297S307 s278NY613 38S2d 1960 —839— (155M98) s8S2d196 14S2d 893 49S2d 8890 49S2d 8891 88S2d 3639 34BR398 131AR 478n Okla 85P2d285 —844— Case 1 (243AD851) —844— Case 2 (244AD51) f278S1846 103AR494n —846— Case 1 (243AD852) —846— Case 2 (243AD850) s267NY [xxxviii cc293S283 cc294S538 cc6S2d498 —847— (155M106) 288S269 288S269 290S2427 299S4424 2S2d20339 2S2d7344 6S2d7807 j 21S2d 4522 48S2d 4924 114S2d10293 141S2d 8798 219S2d 1318 262S2d [15229 262S2d8569 j302NY 8160 148F2d4979 148F2d11979 46FS 8467 195FS 1628 109AR [1107n 140AR1391n 140AR1392n 140AR1395n 37A31385n 37A31388n Miss 33So2d 800	Tex 98SW1008 —860— (243AD822) m280S1023 a268NY658 s281S188 s268NY544 285S16 292S1577 4S2d1821 285NY 146 Minn 273NW680 —863— (155M574) 110S2d 1224 —867— (155M577) —870— (154M723) —880— (155M103) 259S2d 1597 —884— (155M581) 46S2d 729 220S2d 1266 —887— (155M49) s265S55 s266S952 s264NY401 287S1823 299S11000 109S2d 2319 196S2d 4828 —891— (155M152) 15S2d 8698 j 15S2d 8733 e57S2d3446 f108S2d 5495 126AR 163n 144AR1160n —895— (154M843) d279NY1262 17S2d 1952 27S2d 1293 82S2d 1475 101AR [1282n 121AR144n —898— (155M35) 292S1307 2S2d1517 2S2d4519 23S2d 144 52S2d 4380 d 52S2d 438 201S2d 1303 134AR 936n S D 107NW 297 —904— (154M779) 282S6287 283S4548 6S2d4604 12S2d 2804 12S2d 6808 81S2d 6840 100S2d 6293	122S2d 4712 130S2d 6486 229S2d 6647 247S2d 6159 109AR13n 109AR42n 144AR1158n 144AR1160n —910— Case 1 (243AD801) —910— Case 2 (243AD802) —910— Case 3 (243AD802) —910— Case 4 (243AD801) —911— Case 1 (243AD814) —911— Case 2 (243AD805) r269NY110 —911— Case 3 (243AD805) s268NY722 —912— Case 1 (243AD805) —912— Case 2 (243AD801) —912— Case 3 (243AD801) a269NY663 —912— Case 4 (243AD802) —913— Case 1 (243AD801) s277S517 s269NY7 —913— Case 2 (243AD801) —913— Case 3 (243AD802) —913— Case 4 (243AD802) —913— Case 5 (243AD801) —914— Case 1 (243AD804) s276S878 —914— Case 2 (243AD811) s281S882 s282NY 732 —914— Case 3 (243AD802)

Fig. 17.   Shepard's N.Y.S. 1970, Part 3

ABBREVIATIONS—ANALYSIS

History of Case

a	(affirmed)	Same case affirmed on appeal.
cc	(connected case)	Different case from case cited but arising out of same subject matter or intimately connected therewith.
D	(dismissed)	Appeal from same case dismissed.
m	(modified)	Same case modified on appeal.
r	(reversed)	Same case reversed on appeal.
s	(same case)	Same case as case cited.
S	(superseded)	Substitution for former opinion.
v	(vacated)	Same case vacated.
US cert den		Certiorari denied by U. S. Supreme Court.
US cert dis		Certiorari dismissed by U. S. Supreme Court.
US reh den		Rehearing denied by U. S. Supreme Court.
US reh dis		Rehearing dismissed by U. S. Supreme Court.

Treatment of Case

c	(criticised)	Soundness of decision or reasoning in cited case criticised for reasons given.
d	(distinguished)	Case at bar different either in law or fact from case cited for reasons given.
e	(explained)	Statement of import of decision in cited case. Not merely a restatement of the facts.
f	(followed)	Cited as controlling.
h	(harmonized)	Apparent inconsistency explained and shown not to exist.
j	(dissenting opinion)	Citation in dissenting opinion.
L	(limited)	Refusal to extend decision of cited case beyond precise issues involved.
o	(overruled)	Ruling in cited case expressly overruled.
p	(parallel)	Citing case substantially alike or on all fours with cited case in its law or facts.
q	(questioned)	Soundness of decision or reasoning in cited case questioned.

NOTES

A superior figure appearing immediately to the left of the page number of any New York or federal court citing reference indicates the particular paragraph of the syllabus or particular headnote of the cited case which states the point of law dealt with in the citing case.

Where the reports of more than one case start on the same page of any volume of reports, Shepard's New York Supplement Citations refers to the cases as "Case 1", "Case 2", etc. and shows the citations to each case accordingly.

Absence from any bound volume or cumulative supplement of a page number for any New York case indicates that the case has not been cited within the scope of that volume or cumulative supplement.

A letter "n" to the right of the citing page number indicates a citation in an annotation. Only the first citation of a case in an annotation or subdivision thereof is shown. A letter "s" to the right of a page number indicates a citation in a supplement to an annotation commencing on that page.

Fig. 18.   Shepard's N.Y.S. 1970, Part 3, "Abbreviations"

Analysis" in the prefatory material that appears in each volume (Fig. 18). Under history of the case, the symbols indicate all of the things that could happen to the case, ranging from being affirmed by a higher court to being modified in some aspect or reversed. Under treatment of the case, other abbreviations may be used to indicate what subsequent court decisions—many having nothing directly to do with the original case—might have said about that case, including criticism of the case, limiting it to its peculiar facts, overruling it, or questioning its soundness. Using these abbreviations and explanations, we can learn much about how subsequent cases have viewed the case in question. It is important for us to discover if the point that interests us has later been overruled by another case. Also of potential interest to us is whether another court has discussed our point of law in a later case or decided such a case in a similar fashion. Some cases may have been distinguished from ours, either in fact or law. All of these things are indicated in *Shepard's Citations* for all jurisdictions that mention our case, and the decision can be discovered through the use of the abbreviations and notes provided.

As shown in Figure 17, the case reported in 278 N.Y.S. 777 is analyzed on page 999, and the volume reported is identified, in this instance, in the upper right-hand corner of the page. The page in question in Volume 278 starts at the bottom of column three and continues to the top of column four. The first citation is "(244 A.D. 63)"; the parentheses indicate that this is a parallel citation, i.e., the same case is also reported in Volume 244 of the *New York Appellate Division Reports* on page 63. This citation is followed by "a268 N.Y. 599," indicating that the case was affirmed by the New York Court of Appeals and that the affirmation is reported in Volume 268 of that reporter on page 599. The next citation is "p278 S 385," and indicates that a case reported in Volume 278 of the *New York Supplement* reporter on page 385 is a parallel case or one substantially like the original case. The citation "36 S2d ³267" indicates that in Volume 36 of the *New York Supplement Second Series* reporter, on page 267, a case discusses the point of law set forth in the third headnote of *Cook v. Great Atlantic & Pacific Tea Co.* (originally reported in 278 N.Y.S. 777), and the case is mentioned by name and reference. Thus, the history of a case can be followed from the time of its original reporting to within a month of the current investigation in order to determine its effect as law. Each reference found that in any way alters the law must be read in its original reporter. All volumes of Shepard's for all cases found must be checked in order to Shepardize the case to date.

Having followed up all the references we found under Premises Liability, Section 146 in *N.Y. Jur.* and any references we found in the follow-up, we now should check our work. The index to *N.Y. Jur.* brought us to Premises Liability, Section 146. After examining this section to be sure we have not missed anything important, we now turn to the beginning of the section on premises liability (Fig. 19). As with all topics discussed in *N.Y. Jur.*, this section starts with a statement of the scope of the topic, followed by cross-references to topics that are treated in other sections. Following the cross-references is a brief outline of the general headings examined in this section, along with a detailed break-down. Looking for help with our one issue—"What duty does a store owe its customers to keep the floor clear of potentially dangerous debris?"—we note

New York Jurisprudence

Volume 46

PREMISES LIABILITY

Gerard B. Crook, Editor

Scope of Topic: This article discusses the duty and liability of owners and occupants of real property as respects injury to persons on or near the premises caused by defects therein or hazards created by the activities of such owners and occupants, their servants and and employees.

Treated elsewhere are the mutual obligations and liabilities of adjoining landowners with respect to injuries arising from negligence or nuisance (see 1 NY Jur, ADJOINING LANDOWNERS §§ 5–12); the duties and liabilities of the occupiers of premises used for various particular types of businesses or activities (see, for example, 2 NY Jur, AIRCRAFT AND AIRPORTS § 20; 3 NY Jur, AMUSEMENTS §§ 25–43; 7 NY Jur, CEMETERIES AND CEMETERY COMPANIES § 26; 22 NY Jur, FAIRS AND EXPOSITIONS §§ 9, 10; 25 NY Jur, GARAGES, FILLING AND PARKING STATIONS §§ 34–36; 26 NY Jur HIGHWAYS, STREETS, AND BRIDGES §§ 365–419; 27 NY Jur §§ 420–LIBRARIES §§ 29, 30; 42 NY Jur, PARKS AND RECREATION CENTERS; 487, 501–530; 27 NY Jur, HOSPITALS AND ASYLUMS § 77; 27 NY Jur, HOTELS, RESTAURANTS, AND MOTELS §§ 43–61; 35 NY Jur, SCHOOLS, UNIVERSITIES, AND COLLEGES); the duties and liabilities of the owners or occupants of premises used as terminals by public carriers (see 7 NY Jur, CARRIERS §§ 2, 26, 330–342), and for railroad rights of way (see RAILROADS). Also treated elsewhere are duty and liability with respect to injury caused by domestic animals (see 3 NY Jur, ANIMALS §§ 25–30, 35–38, 41–51); electricity or gas (see 19 NY Jur, ELECTRICITY, GAS, AND STEAM §§ 67–108); elevators and escalators (see 19 NY Jur, ELEVATORS AND ESCALATORS §§ 9–54); explosives (see 22 NY Jur, EXPLOSIONS AND EX-

Fig. 19. 46 N.Y. Jur., pp. 1–4

PREMISES LIABILITY

PLOSIVES §§ 29–70) ; and fires (see 22 NY Jur, FIRES §§ 10–20). As to the respective rights and liabilities of landlord and tenant where a third party is injured on leased premises, see 34 NY Jur, LAND-LORD AND TENANT §§ 437, 443, 455–477, 487–492.

I. INTRODUCTION (§§ 1–31)

→ II. STATUS OF PERSON INJURED
    A. EFFECT OF STATUS ON DUTIES AND LIABILITY (§§ 32–51)
    → B. CLASSIFICATION OF PERSON INJURED ACCORDING TO STATUS (§§ 52–75)

III. LIABILITY FOR OFF-PREMISES INJURIES (§§ 76–96)

IV. LIABILITY FOR INJURIES ON PARTICULAR PREMISES AND PARTS OF PREMISES
    A. LIABILITY FOR DANGEROUS CONDITIONS OR DEFECTS IN GROUNDS, APPROACHES, AND EXTERIOR PARTS OF STRUCTURES (§§ 97–145)
    B. LIABILITY FOR INJURIES CAUSED BY DEFECTS IN PREMISES INTENDED FOR A PARTICULAR USE OR PURPOSE (§§ 146–264)

I. INTRODUCTION

§ 1. Grounds for liability, generally; persons liable
§ 2. Negligence as a basis for liability
§ 3. — Acts of third persons; employees
§ 4. — Foreseeability of risk
§ 5. — Effect of character of instrumentality and prior occurrences on liability
§ 6. — Proximate cause
§ 7. — Notice and opportunity to repair or warn of a defect as prerequisite to liability
§ 8. Nuisance as a basis for liability
§ 9. — Statutory nuisances
§ 10. — Characteristics of a nuisance
§ 11. Distinction between negligence and nuisance
§ 12. Statutes, ordinances, and regulations as a basis for liability, generally
§ 13. — New York City Administrative Code
§ 14. Violations of statutes as imposing absolute liability
§ 15. Effect of violations of other statutes; violations as evidence of negligence
§ 16. Effect of violations of ordinances and administrative regulations
§ 17. Effect of occupation and control on liability, generally
§ 18. When liability first attaches
§ 19. — Transferee's responsibility for pre-existing nuisance
§ 20. Delegation of duty; independent contractors
§ 21. Dual or divided control of premises or instrumentality
§ 22. — Effect of divided control on applicability of res ipsa loquitur doctrine
§ 23. Termination of control, generally

Fig. 19.   46 N.Y. Jur., pp. 1–4 (Cont.)

　　　　　PREMISES LIABILITY

→ **II. STATUS OF PERSON INJURED**

A. Effect of Status on Duties and Liability

1. Trespassers

2. Licensees

3. Public Officers and Employees

4. Invitees and Persons Rightfully on the Premises

→ B. Classification of Person Injured According to Status

1. In General

3

Fig. 19.   46 N.Y. Jur., pp. 1–4 (Cont.)

PREMISES LIABILITY

4

Fig. 19.   46 N.Y. Jur., pp. 1–4 (Cont.)

that Section II B covers "Classification of Person Injured According to Status" (Secs. 52–75).

Continuing in the detailed list of contents under Section II B, we find that Section 70 specifically covers "Customers of stores and other commercial institutions." Turning to Section 70 (Fig. 20), we find a further discussion of our issue; and in footnote 15, a cross-reference to the previously examined Section 146 will give us a new section of *N.Y. Jur.* to investigate under this one issue.

When one issue has been completely researched, we then take up the next issue and repeat the process. We hold off numbering the cards until the project is completed, for then they can be organized logically, numbered, and used to make a report of the entire project.

Even if the project is one's own, it is useful to prepare a report (Step 9) because it forces one to rethink, recheck, and organize the material gathered. A report should identify itself, giving the identity of the person requesting it and of the person performing the work, and specifying the subject and the date. A brief statement of the facts as finally determined is necessary to outline the limits of the investigation. The report cannot be considered a memorandum of law, for only an attorney can prepare these. It should, however, follow the form of an objective memorandum in that it emphasizes both the strengths and weaknesses of the position to be taken on both sides of the issue, and in this sense it can be considered a law library research report. After the facts are stated, the issue or issues should be set forth, followed by a discussion of the relevant authorities discovered. The discussion should be detailed enough so that a conclusion can be drawn. For an example of a report, consult the end of the following section, titled "Marriage."

Checklist

Step 1—Word List of Search Terms   For word lists, cull evidence as set forth in the facts using CORP: *C* course of action, *O* object involved, *R* restitution sought, and *P* parties involved. Compare facts with the Digest Topics and Outline of Law found in West's current digests. Investigate indexes of encyclopedias and statutes.

Step 2—Jurisdiction   The two main jurisdictions to consider are state and federal. There may be a choice of jurisdictions, in which case it is necessary to compare the law as it applies to the researcher's case in both jurisdictions.

Step 3—General Overview of Law   For a general background of law, investigate encyclopedias *(Corpus Juris Secundum (C.J.S.)* and *American Jurisprudence (Am. Jur.))* and texts on the subject. Special encyclopedias for states and subjects also exist. Check library card catalogs for any textbook on the subject. Also check the *Index to Legal Periodicals* or the *Current Law Index* and the *Index to Periodical Articles Related to Law.*

Step 4—Frame Issue   Examine the facts as discovered, use the CORP checklist, and compare terms with the Digest Topics and Outline of Law found in current West's digests. Ask questions that will specifically lead to the solution of the problem.

fers no direct or indirect economic benefit on the occupant acquires invitee status,[10] and such an entrant may be found to be a
licensee or trespasser if the implied invitation extends only to
those possessing certain qualifications,[11] or is an invitation to enter
for a limited purpose.[12] Also one who goes beyond the geographi-
cal scope of an implied invitation loses invitee status[13] if the
premises, or the part used by the visitor, have not been made
available for public use as a passageway.[14]

→ ## § 70. Customers of stores and other commercial institutions.

The cases involving injuries to customers on the premises of
shops and stores, and to the patrons of other commercial institutions, which are discussed elsewhere in this article in connection
with defects in particular types of premises,[15] all treat an injured
customer as an invitee while he is on a portion of the premises
on which customers have an express or implied invitation to go,
from the time he first enters such premises until he leaves them,
provided the customer does not exceed the scope of the implied
invitation extended to him by entering portions of the premises
into which customers are not invited or expected to go. Thus,
a merchant engaged in wholesale operations, who without making any special effort to attract retail trade makes occasional
small retail sales on the premises as an incident of his general
business, does not extend to customers seeking to make a retail

10. One who enters another's place
of business solely to seek rest or
shelter is a licensee and not an
invitee. Converse v Walker, 30
Hun 596.

11. Feuerstein v Mariani (City Ct
NY) 133 NYS2d 774, holding that
a child who could not read and
who was incompetent to transact
business could not have been re-
sponding to a sign inviting inspection of premises for sale.

12. Fischer v Amity Harbor Corp.
237 AD 196, 261 NYS 41, wherein
a plaintiff who, in order to go
swimming in adjacent waters,
entered a real-estate development
offering lots for sale, but not

bathing facilities to the public for
compensation, was held to be a
licensee.

13. § 56, supra.

14. Rosenthal v United Dressed
Beef Co. 52 Misc 166, 101 NYS
532, holding that one who passed
through business premises to
reach adjoining premises to which
access could have been had directly from the street was a licensee.

→ 15. §§ 146–182, infra (shops and
stores); §§ 183–189, infra (offices, office buildings, and
lofts); § 193, infra (laundries
and drycleaning establish-
ments).

186

Fig. 20. 46 N.Y. Jur., Sec. 70

Step 5—Statute and Case Finders   To find statutes, check the indexes to codes. Jurisdictions may have their codes published by several publishers; for example, the federal code can be examined in *U.S.C., U.S.C.A.,* and *U.S.C.S.* For cases, investigate the digests under the relevant topic of law. Cases and codes are frequently referred to in other cases, encyclopedias, and texts. For local situations, confer with the city or town clerk, and check the records of the local governmental body.

Step 6—Checking and Recording Statutes and Cases   Statutes will be found in the statute books of a particular jurisdiction. Cases will be found in the reporters. Both statutes and reporters may be published by more than one company. It is suggested that they be recorded on 4″ x 6″ cards. For federal administrative law, examine the *Code of Federal Regulations (C.F.R.)* and the *Federal Register (Fed. Reg.).* For state administrative material, check the state administrative codes, if published. For local governmental bodies, check with the clerk, and examine the records.

Step 7—New Statutes or Cases Found   New cases are discovered in the cases one is reading, in the annotations to statutes, and in Shepardizing.

Step 8—Shepardize   The history of cases and statutes can be traced by using *Shepard's Citations* for a particular jurisdiction.

Step 9—Report   The researcher must make up the report; however, a suggested outline can be found in the next section and in all subsequent sections of this book.

Bibliography

(Note: If a book cannot be found in your library or in the nearest law library, ask your librarian if it can be obtained through interlibrary loan.)

Aldrich, Patricia et al. *A Law Librarian's Introduction to Missouri State Publications.* Chicago: Amer. Assn. of Law Libraries, 1980.

Allen, Cameron. *A Guide to New Jersey Legal Bibliography and Legal History.* Littleton, Colo.: Fred B. Rothman, 1984.

Axel-Lute, Paul. *New Jersey Legal Research Handbook.* Newark, N.J.: New Jersey Inst. for Continuing Legal Ed., 1985. Includes bibliography.

Aycock, Margaret et al. *A Law Librarian's Introduction to Virginia State Publications.* Chicago: Amer. Assn. of Law Libraries, 1981.

Bander, Edward J. et al., eds. *Searching the Law.* Dobbs Ferry, N.Y.: Transnational Pubs., 1987.

Beer, Richard L. *An Annotated Guide to Legal Literature of Michigan.* Rochester, Minn.: Fitzsimmons Sales, 1973.

Boner, Marian. *A Reference Guide to Texas Law and Legal History: Sources and Documentation.* Austin, Tex.: Univ. of Texas Pr., 1976.

Botsford, Margot, and Ruth G. Maatz, eds. *Handbook of Legal Research in Massachusetts.* Boston: Massachusetts Continuing Legal Education, Inc., 1982. A looseleaf guide covering general law, administrative law, teaching, and practice in Massachusetts.

Brunner, Thomas W. et al. *The Legal Assistant's Handbook.* Washington, D.C.: Bureau of Nat. Affairs, 1982. A working tool for paralegals, with detailed reference source. Includes index and glossary.

Bysiewicz, Shirley R. *Monarch's Dictionary of Legal Terms.* New York: Monarch Pr., 1983.

Chanin, Leah F. *Reference Guide to Georgia Legal History and Legal Research.* Charlottesville, Va.: Michie Co., 1980.

————, gen. ed. *Specialized Legal Research.* Boston: Little, 1986. Looseleaf.

Chiang, Win-Shin S. *Louisiana Legal Research.* Austin, Tex.: Butterworth Legal Pub., 1985.

Coco, Al. *Finding the Law: A Workbook on Legal Research for Laypersons.* Washington, D.C.: Bureau of Land Management, Department of Interior, 1984. Written for survey personnel and others in government service who do not have a law background but are frequently exposed to the law. Has been selected as a GPO depository item and should be available in the government documents section of any library acting as a depository. Also available at GPO bookstores.

Cohen, Morris L. *Legal Research in a Nutshell.* St. Paul Minn.: West, 1985. Pocket size paperback covering all necessary subjects. Includes index, appendix, and lists.

———— and Robert C. Berrins. *How to Find the Law.* 8th ed. St. Paul, Minn.: West, 1983. American Casebook Series.

Congressional Index (CCH). Looseleaf service covering legislative work of each session of Congress, weekly while in session.

Danner, Richard A. *Legal Research in Wisconsin.* Madison, Wis.: Univ. of Wisconsin Extension Law Dept., 1980.

David, Shirley H. *Research Administrative Law.* St. Paul, Minn.: Advanced Legal Education, Hamline Univ. School of Law, [1979].

Davies, Bernita J. et al. *Research in Illinois Law.* Dobbs Ferry, N.Y.: Oceana, 1954.

Davis, Lyda C. *An Introduction to Maryland State Publications for the Law Librarian.* Chicago: Amer. Assn. of Law Libraries, 1981.

Elias, Stephen. *Legal Research: How to find and understand the law.* 1st ed. Berkeley, Calif.: Nolo Pr., 1982. Complete coverage of research, starting with an overview of the process, and followed by an examination of the necessary tools, examples, and computers. With appendixes and index.

Fariss, Linda K., and Keith A. Buckley. *An Introduction to Indiana State Publications for Law Librarians.* Chicago: Amer. Assn. of Law Libraries, 1982.

Fink, Myron. *Research in California Law.* 2d ed. Buffalo, N.Y.: Dennis, 1964.

Fox, Elyse H., comp. *The Legal Research Dictionary: From Advance Sheets to Pocket Parts.* Newton Highlands, Mass.: Legal Info. Serv., 1987.

French, Harriet I. *Research in Florida Law.* Rev. 2d ed. Dobbs Ferry, N.Y.: Oceana, 1965.

Granberg, Ron. *Introduction to California Law Finding.* Montgomery, Calif.: Why Not Creations, 1977.

Henke, Dan F. *California Law Guide.* 2d ed. Los Angeles: Parker & Son, 1976.

Hill, Paul F. *Nebraska Legal Research and Reference Manual.* St. Paul, Minn.: Mason, 1983. Looseleaf for updating, with bibliography and index.

Honigsberg, Peter Jan. *Clueing into Legal Research: A Simple Guide to Finding the Law.* Berkeley, Calif.: Golden Rain Pr., 1979. Step-by-step legal research process described. Covers definitions, legal systems, cases, statutes, etc.

Jacobs, Roger. *Illinois Legal Research Sourcebook.* Springfield, Ill.: Illinois Inst. for Continuing Legal Ed., 1977.

Jacobstein, J. Myron, and Roy M. Mersky. *Fundamentals of Legal Research.* Mineola, N.Y.: Foundation Pr., 1987. Successor volume to Pollack's *Fundamentals of Legal Research.* 2d ed. by Jacobstein and Mersky. Provides comprehensive coverage for law students, lawyers, and librarians interested in legal research. Textbook accompanied by workbook.

Kauass, Igor I., and Bruce A. Christensen. *Guide to North Carolina Legal Research.* Buffalo, N.Y.: William S. Hein & Co., 1973.

Knudson, William. *Wisconsin Legal Research Guide.* 2d ed. Madison, Wis.: Univ. of Wisconsin, Extension Dept. of Law, 1972.

Kunz, Christina et al. *The Process of Legal Research.* Austin, Tex.: Butterworth, 1985.

Laska, Lewis L. *Tennessee Legal Research Handbook.* Buffalo, N.Y.: William S. Hein & Co., 1977.

Legal Research Beyond Tradition. St. Paul, Minn.: Advanced Legal Education, Hamline Univ. School of Law, 1981.

Legal Research for the Practicing Attorney. St. Paul, Minn.: Advanced Legal Education, Hamline Univ. School of Law, 1979.

Legal Research Guide. Seattle, Wash.: Univ. of Washington School of Law, 1980.

Legal Research Guide for Michigan Libraries. Detroit, Mich.: Public Access to Law Committee, Michigan Ass. of Law Libraries, [1982–1983]. Contains illustrations.

Legal Research Guide for the New Jersey State Library. Trenton, N.J.: New Jersey State Law and Legislative Reference Bureau, 1957.

Lewis, Alfred J. *Using American Law Books*. 2d ed. Dubuque, Iowa: Kendall/Hunt Pub., 1985. An introductory classroom textbook on legal bibliography and research techniques. Contains notes, index, appendixes, and table of citation forms.

Lloyd, David. *Finding the Law: A Guide to Legal Research*. Dobbs Ferry, N.Y.: Oceana, 1974. A guide for first-year law students, covering common and statutory law, periodicals, treatises, and government documents.

Merzon, Melvin S. *Legal Research and Writing: A Guide for Illinois and Federal Law*. Rev. ed. Springfield, Ill.: Illinois Inst. for Continuing Legal Ed., 1985.

Mills, Robin K., and Jan S. Schultz. *South Carolina Legal Research Handbook*. Buffalo, N.Y.: William. S. Hein & Co., 1976. The first work related to legal research in South Carolina. Includes historical information, government operations, and checklists.

Poldervaart, Arie W. *Manual for Effective New Mexico Legal Research*. Albuquerque: Univ. of New Mexico Pr., 1955.

Price, Miles O. et al. *Effective Legal Research*. 4th ed. Boston: Little, 1979. Gives comprehensive coverage for lawyers and law students. Includes the United States, United Kingdom, Canada, Australia, New Zealand, South Africa, and International Law.

Reinertsen, Gail G. and Richard L. Brown. *Guide to Florida Legal Research*. 2d ed. Tallahassee, Fla.: Florida Bar Assn., Continuing Legal Education, 1986.

The Research Group, Inc. *Basic Legal Research Techniques*. Rev. 4th ed. San Mateo, Calif.: Amer. Law Pub. Serv., 1979. Covers court rules, statutes, and administrative law, secondary authority, Shepardizing, and the West Key Number System.

Roberts, Bonita K., and Linda L. Schlueter. *Legal Research Guide: Patterns and Practice*. Charlottesville, Va.: Michie Co., 1986.

Schneider, John J. *Researching Taxation*. St. Paul, Minn.: Advanced Legal Education, Hamline Univ. School of Law, 1970.

Snyder, Fritz. *A Guide to Kansas Legal Research*. Topeka, Kans.: Kansas Bar Assn., 1986.

Soderberg, Arlette. *Researching Labor Law*. St. Paul, Minn.: Advanced Legal Education, Hamline Univ. School of Law, 1979.

———, and Barbara L. Golden. *Minnesota Legal Research Guide*. Buffalo, N.Y.: William S. Hein & Co., 1985.

A Sourcebook for Research in Law and Medicine. Owings Mills, Md.: National Health Pub., 1985.

Statsky, William P. *Legal Research and Writing: Some Starting Points*. 3d ed. St. Paul, Minn.: West, 1984.

———. *Legal Research, Writing, and Analysis*. 2d ed. St. Paul, Minn.: West, 1982. With illustrations, bibliography, and index.

———, and R. John Wernet, Jr. *Case Analysis and Fundamentals of Legal Writing*. St. Paul, Minn.: West, 1984. With bibliography.

Surrency, Erwin C. *Research in Pennsylvania Law*. 2d ed. Dobbs Ferry, N.Y.: Oceana, 1965. Law students and beginning lawyers may find this work useful, if out of date.

Wallach, Kate. *Louisiana Legal Research Manual*. Baton Rouge, La.: Louisiana State Univ. Law School, Inst. of Continuing Legal Ed., 1972.

Wren, Christopher G., and Jill Robinson Wren. *The Legal Research Manual: A Game Plan for Legal Research and Analysis*. Madison, Wis.: A-R Editions, 1986. Contains bibliography and references.

Yoak, Stuary D., and Margaret A. Heinen. *Michigan Legal Documents: An Annotated Bibliography*. Chicago: Amer. Assn. of Law Libraries, 1982.

Young, Nancy J., ed. *Locating the Law: A Handbook for Non-Law Librarians*. Los Angeles: Committee on Public Access to Legal Infor., Southern Calif. Assn. of Law Libraries, 1984. With index and bibliography.

II · The Family

Marriage

According to *Black's Law Dictionary, family* is a word used to designate many relationships. *Webster's Third New International Dictionary* includes under this term the servants of a household, the head of the household, and all persons related to the head by blood or marriage. The original meaning of *family* was "servant or slave." The most common meaning now implies a father, mother, children, and immediate blood relatives living together under a single roof. This meaning implies that the head of the family has the right to direct and control the family's actions and has an obligation to support the other family members. This interpretation, in turn, implies obedience and partial dependence on the part of the other members. A family is more than a mere contract; it is a relationship entered into in good faith based upon mutual gratuitous services, and it is also a social status. Changing life-styles and substructural variations have given rise to looser definitions of a family (e.g., the "Charles Manson Family"), but the legal family still consists of a man and a woman joined in marriage with their children and blood relatives.

Marriage is the civil status of one man and one woman united by contract and mutual consent. It implies mutual duties and obligations to each other and to the community. These duties are imposed by the association of two people in marriage founded on the distinction of sex. Marriage is a civil contract established by law and having certain duties and rights, irrespective of the wishes of the parties. Marriage is the foundation of the family and of society, is basic to morality and civilization, and is of vital interest to the state. The growing trend toward cohabitation without marriage may be a revolt against the state-imposed duties and obligations that are placed upon married couples. In any event, the state is a party to the marriage contract, and each state has its own regulations for marriage as well as for its dissolution. The state statutes concerning marriage and divorce must be investigated for the appropriate jurisdiction.

Marriage by definition being based on a difference in sex is limited to relationships between a man and a woman, and as yet no state allows legal marriages between members of the same sex, although there appears to be some pressure to change this situation. This pressure may be in line with the modern trend to consider marriage a business transaction, with all rights determined by the law of contracts.

Marriages between certain blood relatives are generally prohibited, e.g., between brother and sister, parent and child, grandparent and grandchild. In some jurisdictions, first cousins are also prohibited from marrying. Beyond first cousins, individuals are usually free to marry as they desire. Some states also prohibit marriages when the parties are related by affinity, or by marriage.

Introduction to Research Problem

A few states still recognize common-law marriages—those marriages not solemnized by a ceremony and not having the benefit of a license, but consisting of a man and a woman holding themselves out to the public as husband and wife. A valid marriage in one state will generally be recognized and considered valid in any state to which the parties move after marriage. So a common-law marriage that is legal in the jurisdiction where it was contracted will be recognized in the other states, even though the marriage would not be valid if originally performed in the second state. Exceptions arise where the marriage is deemed repugnant to public policy or goes against the laws of nature as generally recognized in Christian countries. As determined by individual state statutes, each state has a minimum age for marriage, generally lower for women than for men, and usually ranging from the age of sixteen through twenty-one. Marrying under the minimum age, however, does not necessarily mean that the marriage is void; the marriage may be only voidable. Courts have been known to give permission for minors to marry in certain circumstances. A voidable marriage can be voided by the court only upon the request of the minor's parents or guardian. Once the participants reach the statutory age, the marriage will be affirmed if they continue to live together.

The seriousness of marriage to society, is demonstrated by the part the state plays in each marriage. Marriage affects the distribution of property upon a spouse's death, for a man, for instance, cannot cut his wife completely out of his will. The state by statute says that she is entitled to a one-third interest in what he possessed, which is sometimes called the "dower rights." Social security and veterans benefits flow to wives but not to those who have been merely cohabitating. Children born out of wedlock generally inherit only through their mother, although there are hints of changes in this area. Even the tax situation, especially estate and inheritance taxes, favors marriage. Thus it becomes important in many cases to determine whether or not a couple fall within this preferred status of marriage. A recent federal statute requires the signature of a spouse if pension benefits are left by a worker to anyone other than the spouse (26 U.S.C. 417).

In the following example, for background material on the tools used in legal research, review the section titled "Where It Is Recorded"; and for an example of a legal research problem, see "How to Find It." For unfamiliar terms, see the Glossary. See Appendix A for abbreviations. The legal explanations and the issues selected here are not comprehensive due to space limitations. Should the researcher become interested in a legal problem not covered in the background material, in the introduction, or in the research problem, he or she should note the question, and, using the procedures suggested in this book, perform his or her own legal research to discover the answer.

Research Problem

The research tools to be used in this section consist of the Search Process Flow Chart, the CORP rule, statutes, reporters, citators, and digests.

Let us now examine a situation that by today's "soap opera" standards is simplistic. In 1950 Billie Jo, age eighteen, left the farm in rural Alabama and migrated to Mobile, where she met a city slicker named Charlie Red, age twenty-five. Charlie Red convinced Billie Jo that he was madly in love with her, and they agreed to set up housekeeping, rented an apartment, signed the lease as husband and wife, and generally were considered as such by their neighbors. After the birth of their second child in 1954, they moved to Weeki Wachee, Florida. By 1960 Charlie Red was tired of Billie Jo and took off for New York City, where he met and married, with full ceremony, Florence. This union also produced two children before Charlie Red died in 1975. Imagine the surprise Florence received when Billie Jo showed up in surrogate court claiming to be the wife of Charlie Red. Let us consider that the facts as stated have been established, and we now must discover the law.

The first step is to put the pertinent facts on a fact card (Fig. 21).

One of the first steps to take in a search is to organize one's approach. A flow chart of the search process may be found in Figure 2, page 25. A checklist to accompany the flow chart begins on page 51. We learn in Step 1 that we must make up a list of search terms. From the facts, we pick out the obvious terms—*marriage, husband and wife,* and *widow.* To aid in this search for proper terms, we can also use the CORP rule (see page 27), thinking of Cause of action, Object involved, Restitution sought, and Parties involved. Here we might pick up an additional term, *divorce.* Also of help in the selection of terms is the "Outline of the Law" in the front of West's digests, from which we might select the search terms *domicile, absentees,* and *illegitimate children.* Turning to the Digest of Topics, also found in West's digests, *fraud* and *wills* might be selected from this alphabetical list of topics for consideration. Out of our list of terms—*absentees, divorce, domicile, fraud, husband and wife, illegitimate children,*

11/12/75

Mr. Lawyer   (Marriage Validity)   Florence Red

Facts: Sometime in 1950, Billie Jo and Charlie Red lived together in Mobile, Alabama, both being of age to marry. They signed leases as husband and wife, told the neighbors they were married, produced two children, and were considered by their neighbors to be married. They moved to Florida in 1954, where Charlie Red deserted Billie Jo and moved to New York City in 1960. While in New York, Charlie Red married Florence, with a license and full ceremony. They also had two children. Charlie Red died in 1975 in New York. Florence discovered, while probating Charlie Red's estate, that Billie Jo claimed to be his wife.

Fig. 21. Marriage Fact Card

marriage, widow, and *wills*—we pick the one most likely to lead us to the law books that will in turn lead us to the proper law to be applied. Probably *marriage* has the best prospect, so we will concentrate on this word initially.

Step 2 of the chart asks about jurisdiction. In this case, there is a strong possibility that we will have two states—New York, where Charlie Red married Florence and died, and Alabama, where it is possible that he married Billie Jo. Thus, we limit our search to the necessary volumes, i.e., those covering New York and Alabama statutes and cases.

Step 3 is intended to give us a general overview of the law and possibly cases covering our subject. This area is covered by encyclopedias and textbooks. In this case, we remember that marriage is governed by the state legislatures, and therefore it might be advisable to first check the statutes of the states involved.

Step 4 calls for the framing of issues. What issues are involved? The first one would be whether New York State recognizes a common-law marriage if the marriage was performed in another state. If it does, the second issue would be the validity of the common-law marriage. And a third issue might be the status of the marriage between Charlie Red and Florence. Since this section deals specifically with marriage, we will not now dwell on some of the other important problems marriage presents, such as the legitimacy of the children of Florence and various property rights; these issues will be taken up in a later section.

The problem might be approached by first looking at the validity of the Alabama marriage or by first finding out if New York State would recognize the Alabama common-law marriage if such a marriage existed. We will take the latter approach simply because Mr. Lawyer is currently operating in New York State and on behalf of Florence, who lives there. This choice also gives us an opportunity to use another approach. In the preceding section, we started our examination with an encyclopedia; here we will start with a statute. The basic question seems to be the validity of marriages, so that issue is selected for the initial approach.

A sound approach to the research of this issue would be to first consult a statute book, a case digest book covering New York law, and an encyclopedia covering New York cases, as shown on the following card (Fig. 22).

We have listed the research tools in the order in which we feel they will be most useful. We continue with Step 5 and examine first the nearby New

---

```
                          11/15/75
Mr. Lawyer              (Marriage Validity)              Florence Red
Issue 1. Is an Alabama common-law marriage recognized as valid in
New York State?
x  N.Y. Statutes (for statutes concerning marriage)
   New York Digest (for cases involving marriage)
   N.Y. Jur. (for encyclopedic coverage of marriage)
```

Fig. 22. Marriage Issue 1 Card

York State statutes, entering by way of the general index under "Marriage." There may be several statute books published by different companies. In this case, we are looking at the New York statutes as found in the *New York Consolidated Law Service* published by the Lawyers Cooperative/Bancroft-Whitney. Here we find that most of the entries that are listed involving marriage in the general index fall under the heading of "Domestic Relations." So we now go to the volumes containing statutes concerning domestic relations. Looking on the spines of the volumes, we find that Volume 8 and Volume 8A cover domestic relations.

Step 6 calls for an investigation of the records we found listed in the index. Looking in N.Y. Domestic Relations Law, Sec. 11 (Consol.), we find that "no marriage shall be valid unless solemnized. . . ." At the end of the section, we check the case notes and find that note 16 concerns common-law marriages. In most commercial publications covering state and federal statutes, notes on various aspects of the law's application are set forth.

In the case notes, we find the case of *Re Bloch's Estate,* 79 N.Y.S.2d 6 (Surr. Ct. 1948), which states, "Common law marriage has been abolished in this state since April 29, 1933." Further down the section under case notes we come across Section 19, titled "Sister State or Foreign Country." Under this section, there is a case stating that the "State of New York will recognize common-law marriages if validly contracted under the law of another state." *Merritt v. Chevrolet Tonawanda Div., General Motors Corp.,* 50 A.D.2d 1018, 377 N.Y.S.2d 663 (1975). A card made up for New York statutes would look something like the following (Fig. 23).

This brings us to Step 7, which says that if we find a new case or statute, we should return to Step 6 and investigate what we have found. Remembering that these notations are taken from headnotes, we take a look at the actual cases to make sure that the case actually says what the headnote reports, and then we make a card for the case (Fig. 24).

Having answered the question by checking the statutes and cases, we check the statutes on the issue card and the Merritt case on the *New York Consol-*

```
                               11/15/75
Mr. Lawyer              (Marriage Validity)            Florence Red
N.Y. Domestic Relations Law, Sec. 11 (Consol.)
Sec. 11. No marriage shall be valid unless solemnized
                              . . .
Case Note 16. Common-law marriage abolished in this state since
     April 29, 1933.
Re Bloch's Estate, 79 N.Y.S.2d 6 (Surr. Ct. 1948).
Case Note 19. Sister State or foreign county.
     "State of New York will recognize common-law marriage if
     validly contracted under the laws of another state."
x  Merritt v. Chevrolet Tonawanda Div., General Motors Corp., 50
       A.D.2d 1018, 377 N.Y.S.2d 663 (1975).
```

Fig. 23.   N.Y. Domestic Relations Law, Sec. 11 (Consol.) Card

```
                        11/20/75
Mr. Lawyer            (Marriage Validity)           Florence Red
Merritt v. Chevrolet Tonawanda Div., General Motors Corp., 377
N.Y.S.2d 633, 50 A.D.2d 1018 (1975).
    "Although the state of New York no longer recognizes common-
law marriages, it will recognize such marriages if validly contracted
under the laws of another state."
```

Fig. 24.   Merritt v. Chevrolet Tonawanda Div., General Motors Corp. Card

```
                        11/20/75
Mr. Lawyer            (Marriage Validity)           Florence Red
Issue 2. Was a common-law marriage in 1950 valid if performed in
Alabama, and what were its requirements?
x  Alabama Code
x  6th Decennial Digest (1946–1956)
```

Fig. 25.   Marriage Issue 2 Card

idated Law Service card; there is no need to investigate *N.Y. Jur.* or the *New York Digest.* Had the question not been adequately answered by an examination of the information found in the statute books, we would have continued by examining the digests or *N.Y. Jur.*

Although common-law marriages are no longer permitted within New York State, we have a case in 1975—the date of death of Charlie Red—stating that if the common-law marriage was considered valid in the state where it was performed, it will be recognized as valid in New York State. Because the case was decided the same year that Charlie Red died, we do not have to continue with Step 8, Shepardizing; we already know what law was in existence at our critical date. This brings up the second issue, the validity of the Alabama common-law marriage between Billie Jo and Charlie Red.

The first issue having been decided, we now move on to the second issue and repeat the process. The facts remain the same, and Steps 1 through 3 remain the same. Step 4 calls for the framing of the second issue, which we put on a card (Fig. 25). We have discovered that a common-law marriage will be recognized in New York State if the marriage was valid in the state where it was performed. This issue calls for a search of Alabama law.

The New York State library we are currently working in is not strong on Alabama law and has no encyclopedia or digest for Alabama, so we have chosen to start with the Alabama Code. Not having an Alabama digest available, we decide to list the general digest system covering the years in question (i.e., the *Sixth Decennial Digest* covering the years 1946–1956), which includes Alabama cases on our subject.

Step 5 suggests checking statute finders. Looking in the general index of the Alabama Code for Marriage, we are referred to Title 34 of the *Code of Alabama, Recompiled 1958*, which covers marital relations; Chapter 1 is entitled "Marriage." Section 9 of this chapter states that a marriage is not to be solemnized without a license. In the notes under this point, we find that a common-law marriage made by consent of the parties, without ceremony or solemnization, and followed by cohabitation is recognized in Alabama. *Herd v. Herd*, 194 Ala. 613, 69 So. 885 (1915): *Rogers v. McLeskey* 225 Ala. 148, 142 So. 526 (1932). Therefore, we check off the Alabama Code on the issue card and make a card for the Alabama Code.

Step 6 calls for checking the statutes we have found. This we do, and we put our findings on a card (Fig. 26).

Step 7 informs us that if we find new statutes or cases, they should be checked and recorded as in Step 6. We will now work with West's *Southern Reporter* because, handily, it is located on the same floor we are now on (we could have gone to the floor where the Alabama reports are shelved). We look at *Herd v. Herd*, 69 So. 885 (1915). Headnote 3, "Marriage 🔑 20—Common-law marriage—recognition" seems appropriate. It is interesting to note that the editors have added a note: "—for other cases, see Marriage, Cent. Dig., Sections 12-14: Dec. Dig. 🔑 20." Naturally, we can use "Marriage 🔑 20" in the digests from the *Decennial Digest* to date because it is a West publication and therefore uses the key number system. Now we can make a card for the Herd case (Fig. 27), checking it off on the Alabama Code card.

We will not follow up on the Rogers case at this point, although it is an interesting one. We know that common-law marriages were acceptable in Alabama in 1915, but how about in 1950? We find this information by checking the digest in an attempt to locate cases covering the validity of common-law marriages in Alabama decided during the years involved. We can shorten the search process by using West's Key Number System, searching under "Marriage 🔑 20." Here we will find all recorded cases in the country covering this specific topic and listed alphabetically by state. Therefore, we turn to "Marriage 🔑 20," search for Alabama, and then examine the cases found thereunder for one similar to our case.

	11/20/75	
Mr. Lawyer	(Marriage Validity)	Florence Red

Ala. Code (1958)

Title 34, Marital Relations, Ch. 1 Marriage, Sec. 9. A marriage is not to be solemnized without a license.

Notes: x <u>Herd v. Herd</u>, 194 Ala. 613, 69 So. 885 (1915). The common-law mode of marriage by consent of the parties, without ceremony or solemnization, followed by cohabitation is recognized in Alabama. <u>Rogers v. McLeskey</u>, (1932) 225 Ala. 148, 142 So. 526 (1932).

Fig. 26. Ala. Code 1958, Title 34, Marital Relations, Ch. 1 Marriage, Sec. 9 Card

11/20/75

Mr. Lawyer   (Marriage Validity)   Florence Red

Herd v. Herd, 194 Ala. 613, 69 So. 885 (1915).

"The common-law mode of marriage is recognized as valid in this state, and to constitute such a marriage it is only necessary that there shall exist a mutual consent between the parties to be husband and wife, followed by cohabitation and living together as husband and wife."

Fig. 27.   Herd v. Herd Card

11/20/75

Mr. Lawyer   (Marriage Validity)   Florence Red

Beck v. Beck, 268 Ala. 692, 246 So.2d 420, Supreme Court of Alabama (1971).

1. Cases are replete with statements to the effect that the common-law mode of marriage is recognized as valid in this state.

2. No ceremony and no particular words are necessary to constitute a valid common-law marriage.

3. But to constitute such a marriage, there must first be a present agreement, a mutual understanding to presently enter into the marriage relationship, permanently and exclusively of all others.

Fig. 28.   Beck v. Beck Card

In the *Sixth Decennial Digest* covering 1946 through 1956, and in the *Seventh Decennial Digest* covering 1956 through 1966, no Alabama cases are shown under "Marriage 🔑 20." However, the *Eighth Decennial Digest* gives us two cases: *Beck v. Beck*, 286 Ala. 692, 246 So.2d 420, (1971) and *O'Dell v. O'Dell*, 57 Ala. App. 185, 362 So.2d 747. *Beck v. Beck* gives us the information we need, so we make another card (Fig. 28).

There is no need to follow Step 8, Shepardizing, here because we are working within a limited time frame (1915–1971), which already brackets our target year of 1950. The second issue is now answered—a common-law marriage in Alabama was valid in 1950, and it involves the consent and agreement of the parties, followed by cohabitation. It appears that Billie Jo and Charlie Red were legally married in Alabama, he deserted her in Florida, and he became a bigamist in New York.

Having completed Steps 1 through 3, we are again at Step 4, framing an issue. The final issue is the status of the marriage between Charlie Red and Florence in New York. We now make up a card for issue three (Fig. 29).

Step 5 brings us to West's *New York Digest 3d*. Looking under Marriage, we come across "Marriage 🔑 11—Prior Existing Marriage." We find headnotes for two cases, almost on point, that are worth investigating, as well as

```
                              11/20/75
Mr. Lawyer              (Marriage Validity)          Florence Red
Issue 3. What is the status of a marriage in New York between two
people, one of whom was previously married to a wife still living
and never divorced?
x  N.Y. Digest
x  N.Y. Statutes
   N.Y. Jur.
```

Fig. 29. Marriage Issue 3 Card

```
                              11/27/75
Mr. Lawyer              (Marriage Validity)          Florence Red
West's N.Y. Digest 3d, Marriage ⟨key⟩ 11—Prior Existing Marriage.
Gonzalez v. Gonzalez, 34 Misc.2d 193, 228 N.Y.S.2d 4. Ref. to Do-
   mestic Relations Law, Sec. 6
Brown v. Brown, 51 Misc.2d 839, 274 N.Y.S.2d 484
x  Ref. to Domestic Relations Law, Secs. 220, 221
```

Fig. 30. West's N.Y. Digest 3d, "Marriage ⟨key⟩ 11—Prior Existing Marriage" Card

```
                              11/27/75
Mr. Lawyer              (Marriage Validity)          Florence Red
N.Y. Domestic Relations Law, Sec. 6 (McKinney).
   "A marriage is absolutely void if contracted by a person whose
husband or wife by a former marriage is living, unless . . ." (excep-
tions not here relevant).
```

Fig. 31. N.Y. Domestic Relations Law, Sec. 6 (McKinney) Card

references to some statutory authorities. The card for *N.Y. Digest 3d* would include the references to the cases and statutes as follows (Fig. 30).

Before looking into these cases, we continue with Step 6 by checking the New York state statutes, remembering that marriage is controlled by the legislature. Here we find a statement that ends our examination of this issue, and we make a card for it (Fig. 31).

This time we are in the library on the floor containing *McKinney's Consolidated Laws of New York Annotated,* so these are the statute books we will now use. We find under "Domestic Relations Law: Marriage, Section 6" the following information, which we put on a card.

The cases could have been put on cards as confirmation, but the statute seems to answer our question. Step 8, Shepardizing, we will again omit because we are leaving our situation back in 1975. Now that we know the bad news for Florence, we should put it into some sort of logical order and make a report to her lawyer. This step (Step 9) we will do in the form of a "Law Library Research Report." Once the legal issues have been resolved, the problems not covered by law must be addressed. These include the practicality of pursuing and the financial ability to pursue the issue to the desired conclusion. Having the law on one's side does not necessarily mean that one has the power to enforce it.

Law Library Research Report

Title: Marriage Validity

Requested by: Mr. Lawyer

Client: Florence Red

Submitted by: J. Corbin

Date Submitted: January 2, 1976

Statement of Facts   Billie Jo lived with Charlie Red in Mobile, Alabama, signed leases as husband and wife, and produced two children between 1950 and 1954. In 1954 the family moved to Florida, where Charlie Red deserted Billie Jo and the children in 1960. He moved to New York City, and in a formal wedding ceremony, he married Florence. Charlie Red and Florence had two children before his death in 1975. Florence proceeded to probate his estate in surrogate court in New York as his surviving widow. Billie Jo filed an objection.

First Question Presented   Is an Alabama common-law marriage recognized as valid in New York State?

Brief Answer   A marriage valid in the state where it was performed will be recognized as valid in New York State.

Discussion   While New York State has not allowed common-law marriages to take place within its bounds since April 29, 1933 (*N.Y. Domestic Relations, Sec. 11 (Consol.)*) (*Re Bloch's Estate*, 79 N.Y.S.2d 6 (Surr. Ct. 1948)), it will recognize common-law marriages that are valid under the law of the state where they were contracted (*Merritt v. Chevrolet Tonawanda Div., General Motors Corp.* 50 A.D.2d 1018, 377 N.Y.S.2d 663 (1975)).

Second Question Presented   Was a common-law marriage allowed in Alabama in 1950, and if so, what were its requirements?

Brief Answer   Common-law marriages were recognized in Alabama in 1950 if there was a mutual consent of the parties to be husband and wife, followed by cohabitation.

Discussion   Two types of marriages exist in Alabama from before 1950 to date: (1) a solemnized marriage with a properly issued license, and (2) a common-law marriage consisting of mutual consent to be husband and wife, followed by cohabitation. *Ala. Code,* "Marital Relations—Marriage," Sec. 9 (1958), *Herd v. Herd,* 194 Ala. 613, 69 So. 885 (1915); *Rogers v. McLeskey,* 225 Ala. 148, 142 So. 526 (1932); *Beck v. Beck,* 286 Ala. 692, 246 So.2d 420 (1971).

Third Question Presented   What is the status of two people married in a formal ceremony in New York if one of the parties was previously married to a person still living and not divorced?

Brief Answer   The second purported marriage is void, and the innocent party to it is not married. The other party remains married to the first wife or husband.

Discussion   N.Y. Domestic Relations Law, "Marriage," Sec. 6 states that a marriage is absolutely void if contracted by a person whose husband or wife by a former marriage is living.

Bibliography

(Note: If a book cannot be found in your library or in the nearest law library, ask your librarian if it can be obtained through interlibrary loan.)

Barton, Chris. *Cohabitation Contracts: Extra-Marital Partnerships and Law Reform.* Brookfield, Vt.: Gower Pub., 1985.

Bureau of National Affairs. *The Family Law Reporter.* Washington, D.C.: BNA Bks., 1984. Weekly reports of court actions, and federal and state legislatures relative to family law. Looseleaf.

Canudo, Eugene R. *Marriage, Divorce, and Adoption (N.Y.).* Binghamton, N.Y.: Gould, 1979.

Desk Guide to the Uniform Marriage and Divorce Act. Rev. ed. Washington, D.C.: BNA Bks., 1982.

Eddy, R. Lee. *What You Should Know About Marriage, Divorce, Annulment, Separation, and Community Property in Louisiana.* Smithtown, N.Y.: Exposition Pr., 1975.

Green, Samuel, and John V. Long. *Marriage and Family Law Agreements.* Colorado Springs, Colo.: Shepard's/McGraw-Hill, 1984.

Kline, Adam. *Marriage and Family Law for Washington.* Vancouver, B.C.: Internatl. Self-Counsel Pr., 1979.

Kuchler, Frances W. H., gen. ed. *Law of Engagement and Marriage.* Dobbs Ferry N.Y.: Oceana, 1978. Legal Almanac Series No. 59. Excellent for easy understanding of background and general principles. Contains glossary, references, and index. Appendix gives forms of ceremonies for Protestant, Roman Catholic, and Jewish certificates of marriage.

Krause, Harry D. *Family Law in a Nutshell.* 2d ed. St. Paul, Minn.: West, 1986.

Redden, Kenneth R. *Federal Regulation of Family Law.* Charlottesville, Va.: Michie Co., 1982. Annual supplements.

Rutkin, Arnold H. *Family Law and Practice.* 4 vols. Albany, N.Y.: Matthew Bender & Co., 1985. In looseleaf for updating.

Weyrauch, Walter O., and Sanford N. Katz. *American Family Law in Transition.* Washington, D.C.: Bureau of Natl. Affairs, 1983. A casebook that develops the theory of family.

Children

The legal definition of an infant differs from the popular conception of an infant as helpless, unable to care for itself, and dependent upon the full support of others. The legal definition of an infant is anyone who has not reached the age of majority. Therefore, when one is searching for any legal information involving children, the term *infant* must be considered. Generally, until a child reaches the age of majority, it has no legal right to leave the home of its parents and to choose one of its own. The common law vests parental rights in the father, and only reverence and respect in the mother. The modern tendency is to equalize the rights and obligations of both the mother and the father. The age of majority, i.e., when an individual may manage his or her own affairs, is established by the various state legislatures and differs in relation to the purpose involved. States set the age at which males and females can marry—frequently establishing different ages for each—taking into account differences in the two sexes' physical and emotional development. The legal ages for drinking, driving an automobile, and obtaining hunting and fishing licenses may all be different from one another, thus allowing an infant to gradually participate in various activities before reaching the generally accepted age of majority—twenty-one. For example, courts have permitted marriage by minors before reaching the statutory age allowing them to marry. The limitations placed on infants in the various states may be removed in certain specific situations if sanctioned by the legislature.

Infants are entitled to certain things from parents. Parents are obligated to provide control, custody, and support for their infants, and to give them protection, medical care, religious education, discipline, education, and advice. A South Dakota case (*Monen v. Monen*, 645 S.D. 581, 269 N.W. 85) states that "the parent has the liberty of extreme solicitude for the welfare of the child even after marriage, and may advise freely and frequently and even foolishly."

The relationship between parents and children has historically been considered as a status and not as a contract or property right. As a status, it is a reciprocal relationship, and the parents have the right to have the services and earnings of the infant, and the rights of control, custody, and obedience. The support an infant is entitled to is judged by the infant's needs, the parents' station in life, and the parents' financial ability. Support is not limited to necessities. At the other end of the spectrum, the common law does not require children to support parents in any way; however, some states by statute now do require children to support parents in certain situations.

The authority of parents—except as altered by statutes—is considered almost absolute, unless the situation endangers the safety or morals of an infant. Parents have wide discretion, extending even to choosing with whom the infant may associate. They can employ corporal punishment as long as it is not excessive, immoderate, or unreasonable. The abuse of this right has brought about a proliferation of "child abuse" statutes. Children who are abused, or who are deprived of parental control and care, can become wards of the state. This authority is often delegated to the children's court or to state welfare agencies. Generally, this area involves infants who are abused, delinquent, needing supervision, deprived, abandoned, neglected, or incorrigible. In these situations, the court can terminate parental rights and place the infant in a foster home or in an institution.

The common law places no liability on parents for any tort, or damage, caused by a minor child just because he or she happens to be the parent of the child, even if the parent was present when the act occurred. Statutes in a majority of the states have changed this aspect of the law, making parents responsible in a limited way for damages caused by the willful, malicious, intentional, or unlawful acts of their minor children.

To protect minors, most states have regulated the commercial obligations in which minors may engage. Minors may be liable to pay for the necessities of life. Many states have passed legislation binding minors to repay loans taken out for educational purposes. However, generally, the signature of a minor is not binding. A minor can rescind a contract, return property obtained under the contract, take back property transferred under a contract, and obtain the return of any money paid. This right makes it difficult for a minor to purchase, mortgage, or lease real estate, including an apartment. This right to rescind contracts does not extend to the marriage contract, however. The state has an interest in marriage and in the family, so a marriage contracted by a minor cannot be rescinded or voided without the permission of the state.

A husband has the legal obligation to support his wife and child regardless of his age. A minor father is liable for the support of his child from the moment the child is conceived, including providing payment for doctors' bills, nurses, prenatal care, expenses of birth, hospital bills, support, and education, whether or not the father is married to the mother.

One of the great American traditions has been that everyone has an opportunity to obtain an education. We have built up an elaborate free educational system and have established age brackets within which everyone must attend school. The father, as the head of the family, has historically been the one charged with determining the educational needs of his children. Poverty or unwillingness to work did not relieve him of this responsibility. This historic power has been altered in most states. State laws now require children to attend school between certain ages, the state now sets minimum required subjects, and many other standards have been introduced, thereby reducing the historic complete control of the father over the education of his children.

Generally, teachers have been given the same rights and controls over students as the parents have for enforcing reasonable regulations, caring for the health and physical condition of students, handling emergencies, etc. Teachers are not entitled to exercise any cruel or abusive treatment, or to give out excessive punishment. This area of the law has seen much activity recently as students seek greater freedom.

Introduction to Research Problem

The welfare of children has been a function of the states, with each state taking care of its own orphans and deserted children. This care originally amounted to no more than housing children in an institution until they were old enough to fend for themselves. As the inhumanity of this situation became more publicized, children came under the control of state agencies that supervised the process of placing them in foster homes and finding parents worthy of adopting them. Each state, being independent in this area, developed its own procedures, resulting in a bureaucratic hierarchy. This bureaucratic structure in theory led to more perfect adoptions, but it also slowed the entire process of adoption. The process required much investigation of the adopting parents by state social workers, as well as a considerable amount of paperwork. When the adopting parents lived in one state and the child in another, things tended to become confused. This confusion led to the promulgation of an interstate adoption code that attempted to unify the proceedings of each state and to simplify the entire adoption process. Adopting the code was the prerogative of each state, with some States adopting it in toto, some in part, and some not at all. This situation had the effect of adding another layer of paperwork and investigation to the bureaucratic structure, tending to dampen interest in interstate adoptions.

In the following example, for background material on the tools used in legal research, review the section titled "Where It Is Recorded"; and for an example of a legal research problem, see "How to Find It." For unfamiliar terms, see the Glossary. See Appendix A for abbreviations. The legal explanations and issues selected here are not comprehensive due to space limitations. Should the researcher become interested in a legal problem not covered by the background material, by the introduction, or by the research problem, he or she should note the question and, using the procedures suggested in this book, perform his or her own legal research to discover the answer.

Research Problem

The research tools used in this problem consist of the Search Process Flow Chart, the CORP rule, and various statutes.

At this point, let us consider a simple case—the adoption by a couple residing in New York of a child who is about to be born in Connecticut. Jane Doe, an unmarried teenager, is in panic upon discovering that she is pregnant. John Row, the expectant father, is also upset. They both had planned on obtaining further education, and the pregnancy has upset their plans to have bright careers. Neither of them wishes to marry at this point in life, as marriage will close off too many options. Jane's mother, Joy, is also upset, and no one wants

John's parents to be told about the pregnancy. Jane had expressed a wish to have the child but now has decided to give it up for adoption.

Joy thinks that adoption might not be too bad an idea, especially since it is a bit late to consider not having the child. Under the circumstances, everyone believes that adoption might be the best thing for all, including the baby. So Joy investigates the adoption proceedings in her state—Connecticut. Beyond the blinding emotional upset stands the legal entanglements about which she knows very little. However, she picks up her cards, her pen, and her copy of the Search Process Flow Chart, and heads for her local law library. The first thing to be done is to outline the facts of the situation. So she sits down at a desk in the library and enters the facts as they appear to her on a card (Fig. 32).

The chart indicates in Step 1 that Joy should first make a list of terms to be examined. She naturally thinks of *adoption, minors, youths,* and *juveniles,* but what other words might be useful? The librarian directs Joy to West's digests, suggesting that there she can find an outline of the law, plus an alphabetical list of topics that might be helpful. The Outline of the Law consists of seven categories—Persons, Property, Contracts, Torts, Crimes, Remedies, and Government—the most promising of which is "Persons" Under Persons, Joy picks up the words *illegimate children, infants, adoption, husband and wife, marriage,* and *parent and child.* The Digest Topics contribute *abortion,* which has been ruled out, and *guardian and ward.*

This process has given her a list of search terms to work with—*abortion, adoption, guardian and ward, husband and wife, illegitimate children, infant, marriage, minors, parent and child,* and *youths.* Out of this list of terms, there appears to be only one term that covers her daughter's specific situation without going into all of the other ramifications that are not pertinent at this point. That term is *adoption,* and this is the term that Joy will investigate.

At this point, she also checks the CORP rule to see if she has forgotten a Cause of action, an Object involved, Restitution sought, or Parties involved. "Parties" still appears to be the best bet for starters. Remembering that her jurisdiction is Connecticut (Step 2 on her chart) and that this question will be controlled by statutes, Joy decides to work directly with the statutes instead of starting with a legal encyclopedia or a textbook, deliberately bypassing Step 3. Her next step, Step 4, is to determine the legal issues with which she is concerned. Considering this to be only a cursory search, conducted mainly to gain some

---

7/5/69

Joy Doe   (Adoptions)   Jane Doe

Statement of facts: Jane Doe and John Row are about to have a child out of wedlock. Abortion is out of the question, John's parents do not know of the situation, and no one wishes to inform them. Jane and John do not wish to marry at this point in their lives, and neither of them wants to keep the child. Jane's mother does not want to keep the child either. The consensus is that the child should be given up for adoption as soon as it is born.

Fig. 32.   Adoption Fact Card

understanding of the situation, Joy confines herself to the question of what steps are involved in an adoption in Connecticut, and she makes a card for this issue only (Fig. 33).

Since she is determined to start her search with the statutes, Joy examines a copy of the *Connecticut General Statutes Annotated*. Looking in the general index under "Adoption of Children" (using her primary word from the word list and applying Step 5—code indexes as a statute finder), she finds the title "Adoptions, Definitions," which refers her to Title 45, Section 61b. Selecting the statute book, Joy finds that Section 61b is part of Chapter 778 entitled "Adoptions." Running down the sections, Joy finds that Section 61(j) catches her eye. It states "When child free for adoption."

Step 6 calls for investigating this statute, which Joy does, and she makes a note of its contents on another card (Fig. 34).

It appears that to have a child born in Connecticut be free for adoption, parental rights must be terminated. Running down the listings under Section 61, Joy notes that Subsection (c) continues with further information. This information requires a card of its own (Fig. 35).

Still further down in Section 61 is Subsection(i) concerning what persons may give a child for adoption, which calls for another card (Fig. 36).

The issue is getting complicated. First, parental rights must be terminated; second, a statutory parent must be appointed; and then the statutory parent may apply to have the child placed for adoption. And there is more. As she looks through the index at the head of Title 45, Joy notices Section 63. It

---

7/5/69

Joy Doe   (Adoptions)   Jane Doe

Issue: What are the laws and procedures in Connecticut concerning the adoption of children born out of wedlock?

x Connecticut General Statutes

Fig. 33.   Adoption Issue Card

7/5/69

Joy Doe   (Adoptions)   Jane Doe

Conn. Gen. Stat. Ann., Title 45, Sec. 61(j). When child free for adoption.

"A minor child shall be considered free for adoption and the court of probate may grant an application for appointment of a statutory parent if any of the following have occurred, (a) The child has no living parents; (b) The parents were removed as guardians . . . ; (c) All parental rights have been terminated under Connecticut law; (d) Any child from outside the United States. . . ."

Fig. 34.   Conn. Gen. Stat. Ann., Title 45, Sec. 61(j) Card

```
                              7/5/69
Joy Doe                     (Adoptions)                    Jane Doe
Conn. Gen. Stat. Ann., Title 45, Sec. 61(c).
     "(a) Any of the following persons may petition the court of
probate to terminate parental rights of all persons who may have
parental rights regarding any minor child. If adoption is contem-
plated, petition the court for the appointment of a statutory parent
or for the termination of parental rights of any one parent provided
the application so states: [(1)(a) and (1)(b) not applicable]
     "(1)(c) appointment of guardian ad litem, who must approve the
application in writing if any petitioner is a minor."
```

Fig. 35.   Conn. Gen. Stat. Ann., Title 45, Sec. 61(c) Card

```
                              7/5/69
Joy Doe                     (Adoptions)                    Jane Doe
Conn. Gen. Stat. Ann., Title 45, Sec. 61(i). Who may give child in
adoption.
     (a) The following persons may give a child in adoption. (i) Statu-
tory parent . . . (other sections apply only to members of the child's
family wishing to adopt).
```

Fig. 36.   Conn. Gen. Stat. Ann., Title 45, Sec. 61(i) Card

concerns applications for and agreements of adoption. She makes another card for Title 45, Section 63, "Application for and Agreement of Adoption" (Fig. 37).

Joy has found nothing in the statutes indicating that there will be additional problems if the adopting parents are from out of state. She had seen something about the Uniform Interstate Adoption Laws, but she did not look into them. She recalls that uniform laws are promulgated by the National Conference of Commissioners on Uniform State Laws as a way of promoting consistent treatment under the law of an area of activity that often touches more than one state jurisdiction. States are encouraged, though not required, to adopt the acts as promulgated, thereby establishing uniformity of regulation and reciprocity of enforcement across state borders. The drive toward uniformity has been especially significant in family law-related areas. The text of such laws can be found in a publication called *Uniform Laws Annotated*. The version of the law that is passed by a particular state, including whatever amendments the state made to the original act, is published in the regular source for that state's legislative enactments.

Before pursuing this lead, however, Joy remembers that information concerning the functions of state agencies is best discovered through direct contact with the agency. Therefore, she calls the Office of the Commissioner of Children

---

7/5/69
Joy Doe   (Adoptions)   Jane Doe
Conn. Gen. Stat. Ann., Title 45, Sec. 63(a)(1).

"(1) Each adoption matter shall be instituted by filing an application in a court of probate, together with the written agreement of adoption in duplicate. One of the duplicates shall be forwarded to the Commissioner of Children and Youth Services.

"(2) The application shall incorporate . . .

"(3) An application for the adoption of a minor child not related to the adopting parties shall not be accepted by the court of probate unless the child sought to be adopted has been placed for adoption by the Commissioner of Children and Youth Services or a child-placing agency . . . and the placement for adoption has been approved by the Commissioner or a child-placing agency.

"(5)(b)(1) The court of probate shall request said Commissioner or a child-placing agency to make an investigation and written report to it in duplicate, within the ninety-day period. . . ."

Fig. 37.   Conn. Gen. Stat. Ann., Title 45, Sec. 63(a)(1) Card

and Youth Services, and her concern grows. She is told that her daughter's child will have to be taken from the hospital either by its mother, by the Commissioner's office, or by an approved agency. Until the necessary paperwork is completed, the child will be either with its mother, in a foster home, or in an institution. None of these alternatives appeals either to Jane or to Joy. Joy is told that private adoptions are not looked upon favorably and that all adoptions must be sponsored by the Commissioner of Children and Youth Services or an agency approved by that office. The agency worker also tells Joy that the person having the most say in the placement of the child is the caseworker assigned to the case. She also says that it appears most unlikely that these individuals would favor the adoption of the child by parties outside the state when there are so many requests within the state for children.

Joy's telephone conversations with the Office of the Commissioner of Children and Youth Services confirm that indeed the child must be taken from the hospital either by its mother, by a representative of the Commissioner of Children and Youth Services, or by a child placement agency approved by said Commissioner. The child would then remain in the custody of either its mother, a foster home, or an institution. Out-of-state adoptions are frowned upon because there are too many people in the state of Connecticut looking for children to adopt.

Joy has a sleepless night, but the next morning she has a solution. Not all problems are best solved by consulting with law books and lawyers. Frequently, a practical solution saves time, money, and heartaches. Joy decides to move to New York with Jane and to have the baby be born in New York, where half of the problems will be eliminated.

In spite of the fact that she never completed Step 7 or Step 8 on her chart, Joy does feel the need to make a law library research report of her work (Step 9) so that she can review the facts quickly when she talks with her lawyer. Once the legal issues have been resolved, there are always problems not covered by law that must be addressed. These problems involve the practicality of pursuing and the financial ability to pursue the issue to the desired conclusion. Joy knows that having the law on one's side does not necessarily mean that one has the power to enforce it.

Law Library Research Report

Title: Adoption

Requested by: Jane and Joy Doe

Submitted by: Joy Doe

Date Submitted: July 7, 1979

Statement of Facts   Jane Doe and John Row are about to have a child out of wedlock. Abortion is out of the question, John's parents do not know of the situation, and no one wishes to inform them. Jane and John do not want to marry at this point in their lives, and neither of them wants to keep the child. Jane's mother does not want to keep the child either. The consensus is that the child should be given up for adoption as soon as it is born.

Question Presented   What are the laws and procedures in Connecticut concerning the adoption of children out of wedlock?

Brief Answer and Discussion   Before a child can be adopted out of its natural family in Connecticut, the rights of its natural parents must be terminated (Conn. Gen. Stat., Title 45, Sec. 61(j)) and a statutory parent must be appointed by the court (Conn. Gen. Stat., Title 45, Sec. 61(c)), who then has the authority to give the child up for adoption (Conn. Gen. Stat., Title 45, Sec. 61(i)). A petition must be filed along with a written agreement for adoption in duplicate—one copy of which goes to the Commissioner of Children and Youth Services—and the child must be placed for adoption by the Commissioner of Children and Youth Services or by a child placement agency approved by said Commissioner (Conn. Gen. Stat., Title 45, Sec. 63(a)(1)).

Bibliography

(Note: If a book cannot be found in your library or in the nearest law library, ask your librarian if it can be obtained through interlibrary loan.)

ABA *Juvenile & Child Welfare Law Reporter*. Washington, D.C.: Amer. Bar Assn., Natl. Legal Resource Ctr. for Child Advocacy and Protection, 1986– . A monthly journal that includes abstracts of recent court decisions, reports on legislative activity, substantive articles, and bibliographies of recent literature in the field.

Cohen, Howard. *Equal Rights for Children*. Totowa, N.J.: Rowman & Littlefield, 1980. Investigates the rights of children in the light of human justice, social justice, and political justice. Contains notes, bibliography, and index.

Davis, Samuel M. *Rights of Juveniles: The Juvenile Justice System*. 2d ed. New York: Clark Boardman, 1980. A review of juvenile proceedings, as influenced by constitutional requirements mandated by United States Supreme Court decisions. Written for a general audience with the intention of benefiting lawyers, judges, law and undergraduate students, and interested nonlawyers. In looseleaf for updating.

———, and Mortimer D. Schwartz. *Children's Rights and the Law.* Lexington, Mass.: Lexington Bks., 1987.

DeFrancis, Vincent, and Carol L. Lucht. *Child Abuse Legislation in the '70's.* Denver, Colo.: Amer. Humane Assn., 1974. A report of the study of child abuse-reporting legislation. Records the state of the law in each state, with analysis and comments. Includes references.

Goldstein, Joseph et al. *Before the Best Interest of the Child.* New York: Free Pr., 1979. A study of when the state should be involved in relationships between parents and children. With notes and index.

———. *Beyond the Best Interests of the Child.* New York: Free Pr., 1973, 1979. A study of child placement, giving guidelines. With notes and index.

Gottesman, Roberta. *The Child and the Law.* St. Paul, Minn.: West, 1981.

Guggenheim, Martin, and Alan Sussman. *The Rights of Young People.* New York: Bantam, 1985. ACLU Handbook

Horowitz, Robert M., and Howard A. Davidson, eds. *Legal Rights of Children.* Colorado Springs, Colo.: Shepard's/McGraw-Hill, 1984.

Houlgate, Laurence D. *The Child and the State: A Normative Theory of Juvenile Rights.* Baltimore, Mo.: The Johns Hopkins Univ. Pr., 1980. Theory of juvenile rights and its application. Contains notes and index.

Juvenile and Family Law Digest. Reno, Nev.: Natl. Council of Juvenile and Family Court Judges, 1981– . A monthly publication containing digests of relevant state court opinions. Cumulative index published annually.

Kfoury, Paul R. *Children Before the Court: Reflections on Legal Issues Affecting Minors.* Stoneham, Mass.: Butterworth, 1987.

Loeb, Robert H., Jr. *Your Legal Rights as a Minor.* Rev. 2d ed. New York: Watts, 1978. Excellent coverage for minors, including contracts, marriage, labor, schools, police, parents, and child abuse.

Protecting Children through the Legal System. Washington, D.C.: Amer. Bar Assoc., 1981.

Sloan, Irving J. *Youth and the Law.* 4th ed. Dobbs Ferry, N.Y.: Oceana, 1981. Legal Almanac Series No. 46. Written for youth to guide them in their legal rights and responsibilities. Contains glossary, excerpts from acts, and forms.

Weinstein, Noah. *Legal Rights of Children.* Reno, Nev.: Natl. Council of Juvenile Court Judges, 1974. Published for use in training juvenile court judges. Largely concerned with criminal law. Includes table of cases.

Divorce

At one time, carrying over from our background of English law, divorce was the sole concern of the Ecclesiastic Court, as it still is within the Catholic religion. Divorces were granted infrequently and only for the most compelling reasons, leaving many unhappily married couples leading a life of so-called quiet desperation. In the United States, these duties of the Ecclesiastic Court fell to the courts in equity, and by statutes, gradually into the probate, surrogate, or divorce courts. Some states still vest jurisdiction over divorces in their general trial courts having equity jurisdiction; but with the appearance of the specialized probate courts, this jurisdiction is seldom, if ever, used.

Except where governed by a state constitution, divorce, along with marriage, depends entirely on state statutes. The state is a party to every divorce, and even though a divorce may be requested by only one of the spouses, the spouses agreement in seeking a divorce does not guarantee that the court will grant it. The difference between a marriage contract and other contracts was stated by the United States Supreme Court in *Maynard v. Hill*, 125 U.S. 190:

> Other contracts may be modified, restricted, enlarged, or entirely released upon consent of the parties. Not so with marriage. The relationship once formed, the law steps in and holds the parties to various obligations and liabilities. It [marriage] is an institution, in the maintenance of which in its purity the public is deeply interested. For it is the foundation of the family, and of society, without which there would be neither civilization nor progress.

Divorce is governed by the domicile of the parties and of the marriage. A divorce granted to spouse "A" domiciled in state "X" may have no effect on spouse "B" domiciled in state "Y," unless state "X" at the same time had jurisdiction over both spouses and over the marriage.

An event happening before the marriage cannot be grounds for divorce. However, an act committed or a promise made before the marriage may be grounds for an annulment of the marriage under certain circumstances. A divorce states that two people, although once having been married to each other, are legally separated and are free to remarry. An annulment of a marriage states that legally the two people were never married and that the marriage proceedings were null and void.

A legal separation, i.e., the act of living apart for justifiable cause, is granted by the courts in situations where the parties do not want a divorce but no longer want to live together as husband and wife; the couple instead want to continue their own separate lives, free of the entanglements of marriage. Generally, the grounds required for a legal separation are similar to those required for a divorce.

For many years, the only ground for divorce in New York State was adultery. New York and other states with excessively limited grounds for divorce, which did not take into consideration the actual facts of life, contributed to frauds being perpetrated upon the court through faked evidence of marital wrongdoing and through the popularity of the so-called Reno or Mexican divorce.

Introduction to Research Problem

No problem exists concerning the validity of a divorce if the divorce is granted in a state where the parties resided as husband and wife and if both are domiciled in that state. There are three domiciles to be considered—that of the husband, that of the wife, and that of the marriage. When a husband and wife cohabitate in a state, that is the state with jurisdiction over the marriage. If one of the spouses moves to another state, the domicile of the marriage remains where the parties last lived together as husband and wife. A wife can leave her husband in one state and move to another state, and by meeting the requirements of the second state, she can obtain a divorce from her husband that will be valid in the state where she resides. However, the divorce will have no effect on property rights involving property in the state she left. If her minor children did not accompany her, she also may not be able to obtain custody of them. This area of divorce law becomes very complex, but it is always important to remember the domicile of the husband, the domicile of the wife, the domicile of the marriage, and the state statutes when one is trying to figure out interstate divorces.

The concept of divorce is grounded in the belief that one party has injured the other and the marriage by his or her behavior. In other words, one party is at fault, and the other party is innocent of any wrongdoing concerning the marriage. This concept of fault allows the party without fault to obtain a divorce, and it frequently penalizes the other party with excessive support claims. If it should happen that both parties are at fault, the law exercises the old rule of equity—the "clean hands" doctrine—which states that "the party requesting relief must approach the court with clean hands" (being without fault him- or herself). If the court finds both parties to be at fault, there will be no divorce, and they will be stuck with each other. The clean hands doctrine may not be the only reason for refusing a divorce. The court may find it has no jurisdiction over the parties. But the doctrine makes the most dramatic example for court refusal, although it is slowly becoming moot as no-fault divorce becomes the standard in more and more states.

The modernization of statutes has broadened the grounds for divorce in many states. In addition to adultery, some states, but not all, include such grounds as cruelty, bigamy, conviction of a felony, conduct causing fear of physical harm, conduct causing mental suffering, neglect of duty, desertion for a period of time established by statute, voluntary separation for a statutory period of time, incompatibility, non-support of the wife, drug habits, or personal indignities. Other states have turned to "no fault" divorce laws, allowing people to divorce without requiring that one person be at fault, and granting a divorce on the grounds of simple "irreconcilable differences."

In the following example, remember that the Search Process Flow Chart is found in Figure 2 on page 25; the checklist to accompany it begins on page 51. For background material on the tools used in legal research, review the section titled "Where It Is Recorded"; and for an example of these tools' use in a legal research problem, see "How to Find It." For unfamiliar terms, see the Glossary. See Appendix A for abbreviations. The legal explanations and the issues selected here are not comprehensive due to space limitations. Should the researcher become interested in a legal problem not covered by the background material, by the introduction, or by the research problem, he or she should note the question; and using the procedures suggested in this book, the researcher should perform his or her own legal research to discover the answer.

Research Problem

The research tools used in this problem consist of the Search Process Flow Chart, the CORP rule, encyclopedias, and statutes.

Jane Doe eventually did marry John Row, in Connecticut. The Rows raised three additional children, and the computer industry put John in the chips. Their move to Silicon Valley was exciting but palled in a couple of years. The life-style was too fast for Jane, and Jane was becoming too dull for John. John accepted another position in New York City, but Jane was reluctant to move. John left anyway, taking only one of their automobiles, stocks and bonds in his name, and the money in the couple's joint bank account. He left Jane their house, a modest savings account in her name, and their membership in the golf club. Jane was a bit shaken; but taking hold of the situation, she managed to keep the rest of the family together, all the time hoping that John would return. John did not return, and in a few months he wrote her a "Dear Jane" letter telling her that he was divorcing her in New York on the grounds of desertion. In a state of shock, Jane asked herself, "Can he do this to me? Can I do something about this situation here, such as divorcing John? We need money, but how can I keep the assets I have?"

Not all of these questions are answered in law books, but after the emotional storm had blown itself out, Jane decided to look into her rights. She picked up her note cards, and, like her mother before her, headed for the law library. Having learned a bit about legal research from her mother, Jane first made out a card describing the facts of the situation as she saw them (Fig. 38).

Jane also had remembered to bring along her copy of the Search Process Flow Chart, which was given to her by her mother. After sitting for awhile, composing herself, she looked at the Search Process Flow Chart and saw that Step 1 called for a list of terms to be searched to help her enter the legal material. Using the CORP rule, she thought immediately of C for cause of action, and came up with the terms *divorce* and *desertion*. Her mother had told her not to rely upon her memory but to check in West's digests for that publisher's Outline of the Law and Digest Topics to help her find more and ap-

```
                            11/4/76
Jane Row                   (Divorce)                    Jane Row
Facts: Parties married in Connecticut in 1969, having three chil-
dren, ages 6, 4, and 2. They moved to California in 1972. In June
1976 husband left his wife and family, saying that he was going
to New York to work. He took an automobile, stocks and bonds in
his name, and the money out of their joint account. In October
1976 wife received a letter telling her that her husband was di-
vorcing her in New York on grounds of desertion.
```

Fig. 38.   Divorce Fact Card

propriate terms to be used in her search. The seven sections of the Outline of the Law—(1) Persons, (2) Property, (3) Contracts, (4) Torts, (5) Crimes, (6) Remedies, and (7) Government—led her to "Persons" as the best place to start. Because Jane lived in California, and John lived in New York, *domicile* was included in her list. Because John had moved, *absentee* seemed useful also. Jane also noted the categories of *husband and wife* and *marriage*, which she wrote down. Her list thus consisted of *absentee, divorce, domicile, husband and wife,* and *marriage.*

Jane's primary concern involved the problem of whether or not John, who had left her in California, could obtain a divorce in New York. Therefore, *divorce* was chosen as the search term to be used initially.

Step 2 of Jane's chart asked her to consider what jurisdiction or jurisdictions concerned her case. John had stated that he was divorcing her in New York, so the state of New York was one jurisdiction. Jane lived in California and therefore might have had some rights that protected her in California, so she considered this jurisdiction too. She selected New York to research first.

Step 3 indicated that an encyclopedia or a textbook might be a good starting place for her because she knew almost nothing about the subject. Jane told the librarian the problem she was researching, which allowed the librarian to bring her own knowledge and experience into play. The helpful librarian guided Jane to the encyclopedia *New York Jurisprudence 2d,* which was shelved following the *New York Reports,* and picked 45 N.Y. *Jur.2d,* "Domestic Relations" for Jane to investigate. She did know what her problem would be, so she made up an issue card (Step 4) before opening the book (Fig. 39).

Looking at the book in her hand, she began Step 3 and checked the index to obtain a general overview of the subject. Two sections stood out: 47 N.Y. *Jur.2d,* Domestic Relations, Sec. 1106, covering "Abandonment," and Sec. 961, covering "Residency Requirements for a Divorce." She studied these sections and entered the information on a card (Fig. 40).

"He hasn't lived in New York long enough to divorce me there!" thought Jane. Returning the *N.Y. Jur.2d* to the shelf, she proceeded to Step 5 (locating statutes and cases) and looked in the index of *McKinney's Consolidated Laws of New York Annotated.* She discovered that her subject came under the domestic relations laws, and Article 10, "Action for Divorce," caught her eye.

11/4/76

Jane Row   (Divorce)   Jane Row
Issue 1. Can a husband living in California with his wife and
children in 1976, leave for New York to work, and divorce his
California wife in New York on the grounds of desertion?
x N.Y. Jur.2d
x New York Statutes

Fig. 39.   Divorce Issue 1 Card

11/4/76

Jane Row   (Divorce)   Jane Row
47 N.Y.Jur.2d. Domestic Relations.
   Sec. 1106. Abandonment for one year is grounds for divorce.
   Sec. 961. Residence requirements allow a divorce of parties married in the state of New York, or both currently residing in New
York, to obtain a divorce after one year's residency. Other cases
(including the present situation) require a two-year residency.

Fig. 40.   47 N.Y. Jur.2d, "Domestic Relations" Card

11/4/76

Jane Row   (Divorce)   Jane Row
McKinney's Consolidated Laws of New York Ann. Domestic Relations Laws (Book 14).
   Sec. 170, Action for Divorce.
   "An action for divorce may be maintained by a husband or wife
to procure a judgment divorcing the parties and dissolving the
marriage on any of the following grounds: . . .
   "(2) The abandonment of the plaintiff by the defendant for a
period of one or more years. . . ."

Fig. 41.   McKinney's Consolidated Laws of New York Ann. "Domestic Relations
           Laws" (Book 14) Card

Retrieving this volume, she discovered that Section 170 outlined the action for
divorce, and here she made another card (Fig. 41).
   "He hasn't been in New York long enough to divorce me," she thought
again. "What can I do here in California to protect the assets he left and save
them for myself and the children to live on?" She found no interesting cases
in the annotations, and the statute was up to date, thus taking care of Step 6
and making Steps 7 and 8 unnecessary. She then turned her attention to Cali-

fornia law. She reconsidered the question, "What can I do here in California to protect the assets he left and save them for myself and the children to live on?"

There was no need to repeat Steps 1 and 2 at this point. Step 3 told Jane that she should examine a California encyclopedia for a lead into the California part of her problem. This brought her to Step 4 (framing the second issue), which she put down on the next card (Fig. 42).

Returning to Step 3, Jane reshelved *N.Y. Jur.2d* and *McKinney's Consolidated Laws of New York Annotated,* and quickly found *California Jurisprudence 3d.* Examining the index for "Divorce," Jane found that the information she needed was recorded under "Family Law." Going down the sections in the table of contents for Family Law, she found several sections that interested her, and she put them on another card (Fig. 43).

Jane was beginning to feel a bit better, or at least slightly more secure financially. She realized that she had to continue the research project beyond the secondary material—the encyclopedias—and turned to *Deering's California Code Annotated.* In the index (Step 5), she located under Family Law a section entitled "Dissolution of Marriage." Turning to this area of the statute, she

---

11/4/76

Jane Row   (Divorce)   Jane Row

Issue 2. Can a wife deserted less than a year ago in California obtain a divorce from her husband living in New York and retain the assets he left in California?

x California Jur.

x California Statutes

Fig. 42.   Divorce Issue 2 Card

11/4/76

Jane Row   (Divorce)   Jane Row

33 Calif. Jur.3d, Family Law.

Sec. 584. There are now only two grounds for divorce in California— irreconcilable differences that have caused irremediable break-down of the marriage, and insanity.

Sec. 612. Service by publication on a non-resident will be sufficient for a divorce, but any action requiring something from the other party will require obtaining jurisdiction over that person.

Sec. 774. The court can exercise the same jurisdiction over the community property of a spouse served by publication as it has over a spouse served within the state.

Sec. 782. The court can make additional awards when it determines that property has been deliberately misappropriated.

Fig. 43.   33 Calif. Jur.3d "Family Law" Card

discovered that grounds for dissolution were covered in Section 4506, which she entered on a card (Fig. 44).

Jane's next concern was to make sure that the divorce would be binding on both parties ("How can I be sure that he will be subject to a California judgment?"). Checking the index again, she found under "Civil Actions" the term *jurisdiction*, and under this term, *process* Section 415.40 covered "Service Outside State: When Complete," and Section 415.50 covered "Service by Publication." She made one card to cover both of these sections (Fig. 45).

Browsing through the Family Law headings, Jane found two more interesting sections, Section 4813, covering "Jurisdiction Over Property When Service is by Publication," and Section 4800, covering the "Court's Division of Community Property." She made cards for each of these areas (Figs. 46 and 47).

In making the card for Section 4800, Jane decided to paraphrase the contents instead of copying the entire section (Fig. 47).

For her present psychological needs, Jane was satisfied. The way she saw the situation, John eventually could divorce her in New York once he had lived there for one year. But he would not be able to do anything with the assets he left in California without returning in person. On the other hand, it appeared that Jane might be able to obtain a divorce in California, have the community property separated from her personal property, ask the judge to divide the community property, and then if she could show that John left with substantial other community property, she could request the judge to make an additional award to her out of John's share of the community property. She then proceeded to Step 9 and put together the results of her examination. By putting this information in the form of a law library research report, it was easier to understand when she discussed her problem with an attorney. She knew that once the legal issues were resolved, there would always be problems not covered by law that needed to be addressed. These included the practicality of pursuing, and the financial ability to pursue, the issues to the desired conclusion. Jane also knew that having the law on one's side did not necessarily mean that one had the power to enforce it.

11/4/76

Jane Row   (Divorce)   Jane Row
Deering's California Code, Annotated. Family Law—Dissolution of Marriage.

"Sec. 4506. [Grounds for Dissolution or Separation]

"A court may decree a dissolution of the marriage or legal separation on either of the following grounds, which shall be pleaded generally:

"(1) Irreconcilable differences, which have caused the irredeemable breakdown of the marriage.

"(2) Incurable Insanity."

Fig. 44.   Deering's California Code, Annotated, "Family Law—Dissolution of Marriage," Sec. 4506 Card

11/4/76

Jane Row   (Divorce)   Jane Row

Deering's California Code, Annotated. Civil Actions.

"Sec. 415.40. [Service outside state: When complete]

"A summons may be served on a person outside this state in any manner provided by this article or by sending a copy of the summons and of the complaint to the person to be served by any form of airmail requiring a return receipt. Service of a summons by this form of mail is deemed complete on the 10th day after such mailing.

"Sec. 414:50.' [Service by publication: Prerequisite findings on affidavit: Order for publication in named newspaper: When service complete: Service other than by publication ordered]

"(a) A summons may be served by publication if upon affidavit it appears to the satisfaction of the court in which the action is pending that the party to be served cannot with reasonable diligence be served in another manner specified in this article and that:

"(1) A cause of action exists against the party upon whom service is to be made or he is a necessary or proper party to the action; or

"(2) The party to be served has or claims an interest in real or personal property in this state that is subject to the jurisdiction of the court or the relief demanded in the action consists wholly or in part in excluding such party from any interest in such property.

"(b) The court shall order the summons to be published in a named newspaper, published in this state, that is most likely to give actual notice to the party to be served and direct that a copy of the summons and of the complaint be forthwith mailed to such party if his address is ascertained before expiration of the time prescribed for publication. Except as otherwise provided by statute, the publication shall be made as provided by Section 6064 of the Government Code unless the court in its discretion orders publication for a longer period.

"(c) Service of a summons in this manner is deemed complete on the last day of publication.

"(d) Notwithstanding an order for publication of the summons, a summons may be served in another manner authorized by this chapter, in which event such service shall supersede any published summons."

Fig. 45.   Deering's California Code, Annotated, "Civil Actions," Sec. 415.40 Card

Law Library Research Report

Title: Divorce

Requested by: Jane Row

Submitted by: Jane Row

Date Submitted: November 6, 1976

11/4/76

Jane Row   (Divorce)   Jane Row

Deering's California Code, Annotated. Family Law—Dissolution of Marriage.

"Sec. 4813. [Jurisdiction over property of spouse when service by publication]

"When service of summons is made pursuant to Section 415.50 of the Code of Civil Procedure upon a spouse in a proceeding under the provisions of this part, the court, without the aid of attachment thereof or the appointment of a receiver, shall have and may exercise the same jurisdiction over all of the following:

"(a) The community real property of the spouse so served situated in this state as it has or may exercise over the community real property of a spouse in a proceeding under this part who is personally served with process within this state.

"(b) The quasi-community real property of the spouse so served situated in this state as it has or may exercise over the quasi-community real property of a spouse in a proceeding under this part who is personally served with process within this state."

Fig. 46.   Deering's California Code, Annotated, "Family Law—Dissolution of Marriage," Sec. 4813 Card

11/4/76

Jane Row   (Divorce)   Jane Row

Deering's California Code, Annotated. Family Law—Dissolution of Marriage.

Sec. 4800. Court's equal division of community and quasi-community property

(a) The court may divide community property and quasi-community property equally, or (b) as follows:

(1) In a manner to effect a substantially equal division of the property,

(2) Awarding additional property to one party if the other has deliberately misappropriated property.

(3) Provisions for property under $5,000 in value.

(4) Educational loans.

(c) Community property personal injury damages.

(d) The court may make such orders as it deems necessary to carry out the purpose of this section.

Fig. 47.   Deering's California Code, Annotated, "Family Law—Dissolution of Marriage," Sec. 4800 Card

Statement of Facts   Parties married in Connecticut in 1969, and having three children, ages 6, 4, and 2, moved to California in 1972. In June 1976 husband left his wife and family, saying that he was going to New York to work. He took an automobile, stocks and bonds in his name, and the money out of the couple's joint account. In October 1976 the wife received a letter telling her that her husband was divorcing her in New York on the grounds of desertion.

First Question Presented   Can a person moving from California to New York divorce the spouse remaining in California on the grounds of desertion?

Brief Answer   A person moving to New York State and leaving a spouse in California may not bring proceedings for divorce on the grounds of desertion for less than one year.

Discussion   A one-year period of desertion is required in New York State for filing for a divorce on the grounds of desertion. *McKinney's Consolidated Laws of New York Annotated,* "Domestic Relations," Sec. 170(2).

John, who moved to New York State from California less than a year ago, cannot at this time divorce his wife, Jane, who is still living in California.

Second Question Presented   What actions can the spouse remaining in California take for her protection after her husband has moved to New York and expressed his intention to obtain a divorce?

Brief Answer And Discussion   In California there are only two grounds for divorce: (1) irreconcilable differences causing an irremediable breakdown of the marriage, and (2) incurable insanity *(Deering's California Code, Ann.,* "Family Law," Sec. 4506). Service by publication is sufficient to obtain a divorce from a spouse who resides outside the jurisdiction *(Deering's California Code, Ann.,* "Civil Actions," Secs. 415.40 and 415.50). Jurisdiction over property in California can be obtained through service by publication *(Deering's California Code, Ann.,* "Family Law," Sec. 4813). The court can make a division of the property in the state, including additional awards when it is determined that property has been deliberately misappropriated *(Deering's California Code, Ann.,* "Family Law," Sec. 4800).

Bibliography

(*Note:* If a book cannot be found in your library or in the nearest law library, ask your librarian if it can be obtained through interlibrary loan.)

Arendell, Terry. *Mothers and Divorce: Legal, Economic, and Social Dilemmas.* Berkeley, Calif.: Univ. of Calif. Pr., 1986.

Atkinson, Jeff. *Modern Child Custody Practice.* 2 vols. New York: Kluwer Law Bk. Pubs., 1986.

Douthwait, Graham. *Unmarried Couples and the Law.* Indianapolis, Ind.: Allen Smith, 1979. A comprehensive study of marriage and life-styles, giving ramifications of the many variations. Covers children, property rights, and taxation. Also gives commentary on the whole scene, state by state.

Englebardt, Leland S., II. *Living Together, What's the Law?* New York: Crown, 1981. A review of marriage, cohabitation, and parenting in light of the Marvin case, listing all states and outlining the current law in each state. Includes sample contracts to help one avoid problems.

Goldberg, Barth H. *Valuation of Divorce Assets.* St. Paul, Minn.: West, 1984.

Harwood, Norma. *A Woman's Legal Guide to Separation and Divorce in All 50 States.* New York: Scribner, 1985.

Krauskopf, Joan M., ed. *Marital and Non-Marital Contracts: Preventive Law for the Family.* Chicago: Amer. Bar Assn., 1979. An investigation into marriage contracts. With forms and exhibits.

Kressel, Kenneth. *The Process of Divorce: How Professionals and Couples Negotiate Settlements.* New York: Basic Books, 1985.

The Practical Lawyer's Manual on Divorce and Separation. Philadelphia: Amer. Law Inst.-Amer. Bar Assn., 1985.

Rothenberg, Waldo G. *Tax and Estate Planning for Divorce and Separation.* Rochester, N.Y.: Lawyers Cooperative, 1985.

Taft, Robert S. *Tax Aspects of Divorce and Separation.* New York: Law Journal Seminars Pr., 1984. Provides easy-to-read coverage of topics, with sample agreements, forms, and documents. In looseleaf.

Valuation and Distribution of Marital Property. 2 vols. Albany, N.Y.: Matthew Bender & Co., 1984–. In looseleaf for updating.

Wheeler, Michael A. *Divided Children: A Legal Guide for Divorcing Parents.* New York: Norton, 1980.

Wishard, William R., and Laurie Wishard. *Men's Rights: A Handbook for the '80's.* San Francisco: Cragmont, 1980. Examines the problems of men in their relationships with women and children. Covers marriage, agreements, credit, living together (under *Marvin v. Marvin),* divorce and separation, property settlements, children, and custody. Contains appendix, bibliography, and index.

Personal Property

Property generally includes everything that can be possessed. Originally, personal property included only household furnishings and ornaments. Now the term *personal property* is generally recognized as including all moveables. Even a building can be considered personal property if it is placed upon rented land with the provision included in the lease that the building may be removed at the termination of the lease. Personal property can be the object itself, such as an automobile, or the right to use the object, such as a lease of the automobile, or the evidence of the right to use the object, such as the paper upon which the lease is written. Personal property includes the right to keep, use, enjoy, and dispose of the property within the bounds of any restrictions placed upon this right.

Personal property is something we are all involved with every day but to which we seldom give any consideration. Personal property is generally defined by defining what it is *not*. The usual explanation is that personal property is all property that is not real estate. Definitions of quasi-personal property, called mixed property, include items that may be either real or personal property, having qualities of both. In any given jurisdiction, it is best to check the statutes because, frequently, personal property is defined by the legislature. Generally, personal property includes both tangible property and intangible property. Tangible property is that which can be touched, such as money, shoes, or furniture. Intangible property is represented by some other means; for example, the evidence of a debt is the note from the debtor. The note itself is tangible, but it only represents the actual debt. The debt itself is intangible, yet it is an item of personal property.

Ownership of property includes certain rights, such as the right to use the property, to posses it, to move it about as one desires, to loan it, to rent it to others, to borrow money using it as security, or to dispose of it in any manner. There are also obligations attached to property ownership. One obligation is not to use personal property in such a manner as to injure others. Also, taxes frequently must be paid on the ownership or possession of personal property; and under certain circumstances, the state can confiscate personal property. At times, restraints are placed by statutes upon the use of personal property, and one may not use personal property in a manner that is considered contrary to public policy. Public policy encompasses the general principles by which a government is guided in the management of public affairs. For example, a contract not to compete is personal property; however, the contract may or may not be valid according to the interpretation of its terms. This type of contract may sometimes be considered as going against public policy because it tends to restrain trade. However, valid reasons for such contracts are recognized, and if the contracts are reasonable in scope and time, and serve a useful business purpose, they are permitted.

The stealing of personal property does not change the property's ownership, or the right of possession. Therefore, the original owner of stolen property may repossess it wherever it can be found.

Some objects are excluded from any definition of personal property. These things are free in nature, and until taken possession of in some manner, they are not the personal property of anyone. The air moving freely overhead, for instance, belongs to no one, unless a windmill is erected to harness the power of the wind. Running water is not personal property as it courses down the stream; but should someone legally dam the stream, the water collected in the dam may become personal property that is used to create power, cool equipment, bathe in, or drink. Wild animals and birds fall into this category also; they are owned by no individual in their wild state. However, should a hunter take possession of one of them, that animal then becomes his or her personal property simply by the act of taking. Likewise, goods that have been abandoned by a former owner may become the personal property of the person who picks them up and possesses them. The new owner's claim is then good against all the world.

There is a lot of case law involving personal property, and there will be much more in the future. However, some of the confusion has been removed by the adoption of the Uniform Commercial Code by almost all jurisdictions. Even here variations exist, but the general principles are maintained so that more or less uniform interpretations exist from jurisdiction to jurisdiction. The fact that the code has wide acceptance makes it vital to investigate the commercial code of the jurisdiction within which the researcher is operating when dealing with matters concerning personal property.

A good share of the code addresses commercial operations, which have little effect upon individual citizens who are going about their daily lives. The areas involving the individual the most are the purchase, sale, delivery, and financing of household goods and automobiles. One entire section of the code is set aside to deal with household purchases.

Introduction to Research Problem

Rights and obligations arise upon the mere taking of property, such as occurs when one person leaves his or her tiger lily plant with a neighbor while on vacation. The situation of one person's having possession of property belonging to another is covered by the law of bailment and is also consolidated into the Uniform Commercial Code. Individuals are involved with bailment more often than they might expect: It is a bailment when one leaves one's car in a garage or parking lot while one shops, when one leaves one's coat with the hat-check person or one's dog in a kennel for a week, and when one borrows one's neighbor's lawnmower. For a bailment to arise, there must be possession, control, and the intent to control the chattel, all vested in the bailee. A bailee is not an insurer, but he or she may be liable for damages or loss if he or she lacked care in keeping the goods.

According to common law, innkeepers are liable for the goods of their guests during their stay at the inn. This liability may be reduced if the innkeeper has a contract with visitors limiting liability. The liability may also be shifted if the innkeeper has a safe deposit box available for the use of guests, advertises it, draws guests' attention to it, and guests decline to accept the offer. The common-law liability of the innkeeper is also substantially reduced by statute, and again, the Uniform Commercial Code in effect in the jurisdiction of interest should be examined.

Common carriers—those in business to transport people or goods and who offer their services to the general public—are also considered bailees. They are generally considered as insurers of their cargo; however, again this liability can be, and frequently is, limited by contract.

In the following example, remember that the Search Process Flow Chart is found in Figure 2, page 25; a checklist to accompany it appears on page 51. For information on the tools used in legal research, review the section titled "Where It Is Recorded"; and for an example of the use of these tools in a legal research problem, see "How to Find It." For unfamiliar terms, see the Glossary. See Appendix A for abbreviations.

The legal explanations and the issues selected here are not comprehensive due to space limitations. Should the researcher become interested in a legal problem not covered by the background material, by the introduction, or by the research problem, he or she should note the question, and using the procedures suggested in this book, perform his on her own legal research to discover the answer.

The facts supplied in this example are used to develop a list of terms from the case, to examine the legal indexes of statutes and cases, and to frame the issues. Index cards are used because of their versatility, transportability, and flexibility in substitution and arrangement.

Research Problem

The research tools used in this problem consist of the Search Process Flow Chart, the CORP rule, a legal dictionary, an encyclopedia, statutes, and reporters.

On his way to New York, John stopped in Atlanta, Georgia, to visit his best friend and college roommate, Joe. The discussion turned to hobbies, and John said he was now into building model airplanes. He happened to bring his favorite one with him, a free-flying computerized biplane that could perform amazing stunts. The two friends took it to a nearby field and spent an afternoon in frivolous fun, flying the biplane. Joe was delighted, and John finally said, "I'm headed for New York City and can't use it there. Why don't you keep it for me until I find a place where I can fly it? You have the basic skills, so you might as well enjoy it." Joe was overjoyed and thanked John, saying, "I'll take good care of it for you, and I'll certainly have fun flying it. Thanks a million!"

Joe did just that; he even joined a model airplane club and made some of his own planes, but the one John had let him use was by far his favorite and the favorite of the club as well. With this biplane the club won all of the stunting contests they entered. Nothing was heard from John for six months, a year, two years, until finally one day a letter arrived telling Joe that John now had a place on Long Island, that there was a lot of room to fly model airplanes, and that John was joining one of the three clubs in the area. John's job situation had settled down, and he wanted Joe to ship his airplane back to him.

Joe and his club had become very attached to the airplane; and coming up in six months, they had a very important contest in which they had entered John's biplane. After all this time, they had assumed that John had given up all thoughts of flying, and that they, for all practical purposes, owned the plane. They told Joe that he just couldn't send the plane off to John, at least not right now. So Joe wrote to John, telling him that Joe had not heard from him for two years, that he assumed John no longer wanted the airplane, that he and his club had become very attached to it, and that he just couldn't bring himself to send the model plane to New York.

This news naturally upset John. He went to the Columbia University Law School library to solve his problem. There he made up a fact card and reviewed it to be sure that it was accurate (Fig. 48).

John took out his Search Process Flow Chart, which he found to be very useful in keeping the project progressing step by step to a solution. He also reviewed the CORP rule: C for cause of action (John loaned his airplane to Joe, who refused to return it upon demand), O for object involved (the airplane or some other object of personal property), R for restitution sought (John wishes to have Joe return the airplane, probably calling for an injunction ordering its return), and P for parties involved (John, who lent the airplane, and Joe, who accepted it).

Proceeding with Step 1 on the Search Process Flow Chart, John looked for terms to include on his word list of search terms. He remembered that it was a good idea not to rely on his own memory and imagination when searching for terms. A more exact approach was to use the facts of each situation and then to go through the Outline of the Law and the Digest Topics found in West's digests. Running through the Digest Topics, John saw *bailment* and *conversion*. *Black's Law Dictionary* informed him that *conversion* means "the unlawful appropriation and use of the property of another." *Damages* was also included on his list because it was uncertain at this point what options were open to John. The Outline of the Law in the digest led from the heading

---

6/18/78

John   (Refusal to Return Airplane)   John

Facts: While John was moving from California to New York City, he passed through Atlanta, Georgia, stopping to visit his old friend, Joe. John left his special model airplane with Joe, telling him that he would call for it later. Two years later, John wrote to Joe requesting that the airplane be shipped to him in New York. Joe refused.

Fig. 48.   Bailment Fact Card

"Property" to the word *conversion*, and under "Contracts" to *bailment*. Turning again to *Black's Law Dictionary*, John discovered that a bailment exists when one person, the bailor, lends property to another, the bailee, the property to be held by the bailee in trust for a specific purpose and then returned to the bailor when the purpose has been completed. This information gave him a search term list consisting of *bailment, conversion*, and *damages*. The most promising word for a start appeared to be *bailment*, so this term was chosen as the first search word.

Jurisdiction is the concern of Step 2. John would have a difficult time getting jurisdiction over Joe in New York State as long as Joe stayed in Georgia. So if John were to do anything, he would have to do it in Georgia; and in his investigation, John had to use Georgia law.

Step 3 suggests the use of a general encyclopedia or a textbook as a source for general background information when one does not know much about a subject, so John picked up the encyclopedia Corpus Juris Secundum. He could just as well have relied on the other major general legal encyclopedia, *American Jurisprudence 2d*, for it too provides a basic commentary on most legal subjects, synthesizing case decisions from all the states and from the federal courts into a cohesive statement about the current state of the law. Another advantage of this latter work is the extensive footnotes that are given to substantiate the statement, often providing a direct lead to relevant case law.

John first checked the encyclopedia *C.J.S.* for a lead to the general principles. Under "Personal Property," he found "Bailments," Sections 1 and 12 to be interesting. The "Analysis" under Bailments added another interesting section, Section 8, "Bailments for Mutual Benefit." John started writing the card for *C.J.S.* (Fig. 49).

The next step, Step 4, was to establish the issues and make up the issue cards (Fig. 50).

Now that John had a general idea of the subject, it was time to get more specific, and Step 5 told him that he should look for statute finders, which would include the index to the Georgia statutes. Using the search word *bailment*, he examined the index of the *Code of Georgia Annotated*, put a check mark on the issue card, and entered his findings on new cards, Step 6 (Fig. 51).

John applied the above information to his own situation, and it appeared that when he loaned Joe his airplane to use while he was unable to fly it in New York, a bailment situation arose in Georgia. Under that bailment situation,

---

6/18/78

John   (Refusal to Return Airplane)   John

C.J.S., Bailments: Section 1 defines <u>bailment</u> as one person holding the property of another for some purpose, the property to be returned or delivered upon instructions from the bailor.

   Section 8, Bailments for Mutual Benefit, states that a bailment for mutual benefit arises when both parties derive a benefit from the bailment.

Fig. 49. C.J.S., "Bailments," Sec. 1 and Sec. 8 Card

6/18/78

John   (Refusal to Return Airplane)   John

Issue 1. What legal relationships result in John's leaving his airplane with Joe, and what obligations have been assumed as a result thereof?

x Georgia Statutes, Bailments
   Georgia Digest, Bailments

Fig. 50.   Bailment Issue 1 Card

6/18/78

John   (Refusal to Return Airplane)   John

Code of Georgia Ann., Bailments.

Sec. 12-101, Definition. This section states that "a bailment is a delivery of goods or property for the execution of a special object, beneficial to either the bailor, bailee, or both, and upon a contract, express or implied, to carry out this object and dispose of the property in conformity with the purpose of the trust."

Sec. 12-501, Kinds of Loans. Loan for consumption. "Loans are of two kinds, for consumption or for use. A loan for consumption is where the article is not to be returned in specie, but in kind; this is a sale, and not a bailment."

Definition. "A loan is a bailment of an article for a certain time to be used by borrower without paying for its use. 52 App. 58, 59 (182 SE 205), 71 App. 298, 299 (30 SE2d 792)."

Sec. 12-502. "Loan for Use defined. A Loan for use is the gratuitous grant of an article to another for use, to be returned in specie [the exact thing], and may be either for a certain time or indefinitely, and at the will of the grantor."

Fig. 51.   Code of Georgia Ann., "Bailments" Card

Joe was obligated to return the airplane upon John's request. This information seemed to answer the question posed by issue one.

Leaving issue one with Step 6, John then turned to the question of what could be done about the situation. He was in New York, his airplane was in Georgia, and he wanted it back, or at least to be paid for it.

Steps 1 and 2 in the Search Process Flow Chart remained the same for the second issue, so John went back to Step 3, searching the encyclopedia, *C.J.S.* Step 4 brought him to framing the second issue, which was entered on a card (Fig. 52).

Next John went back to *C.J.S.* under Bailments. Following through with Step 5, John checked the subtitles for the search term and found Sections 31 and 37 to be potentially useful here. A card was made for *C.J.S.*, Bailments, Sections 31 and 37 (Fig. 53).

6/18/78

John   (Refusal to Return Airplane)   John

Issue 2. What remedy does John, in New York, have against Joe, in Georgia, either to force the return of the loaned airplane or to be paid for it?

x C.J.S., Bailments

x Georgia Statutes

x Georgia Digest

Fig. 52.   Bailment Issue 2 Card

6/18/78

John   (Refusal to Return Airplane)   John

C.J.S., Bailments.

   Section 31. Lists several ways that conversion of the property by the bailee can be accomplished, including converting it to one's own use.

   Section 37. This section covers the refusal of the bailee to redeliver the property to the bailor at the completion of the bailment. It states that upon the termination of the bailment, the bailee must redeliver the property to the bailor. Non-delivery of the goods is considered evidence of conversion.

Fig. 53.   C.J.S., "Bailments" Card

For a more specific examination of the problem in light of Georgia law, John looked at the *Georgia Digest* under Bailment to see what the cases said about his possible remedies, returning to Step 5. The digest listed many of the items examined above and also something interesting under "Bailment ☞ 16, Conversion by Bailee." Here John found the case of *Traylor v. Hyatt Corp.,* 178 S.E.2d 289, 122 Ga.App. 633 (1970), indicating that John might sue in trover, which is an ancient action to recover damages for goods withheld or used illegally by another, if Joe has wrongfully withheld the airplane. Moving on to Step 6, John investigated this case and entered it on a card (Fig. 54).

Returning to Step 5 again, John continued the digest search and discovered another case that gave a little broader scope concerning the remedies available to him. John investigated this case and entered it on a separate card (Fig. 55).

John found nothing new in these cases to follow up (Step 7). After Shepardizing both of the above cases and the Georgia code concerning bailment (Step 8), and finding no changes to be concerned with, John drew some conclusions concerning his problem. It appeared that John bailed his airplane to Joe when he lent it to him and that Joe had an obligation to return the plane to John under the terms of the oral bailment. John had the option either of suing Joe for damages in converting his property or of asking the court to issue

```
                              6/18/78
John                  (Refusal to Return Airplane)              John
Traylor v. Hyatt Corp., 122 Ga.App. 633 (1970).
     An action for the recovery of damages for the loss of a son's
clothing from an automobile left in a garage of the Hyatt Corpora-
tion. On page 634, Judge Eberhardt states, "A bailment relationship
is, as between the bailor and bailee, sufficient to support an action
in trover when the chattel bailed is converted or wrongfully with-
held from the bailor."
```

Fig. 54.   Traylor v. Hyatt Corp. Card

```
                              6/18/78
John                  (Refusal to Return Airplane)              John
AAA Parking, Inc. v. Black, 139 S.E.2d 437, 439, 110 Ga.App. 554
(1964).
     On page 555, Judge Hall quoted from Parker Motor Company v.
Spiegal, 33 Ga.App. 795, 796, 127 S.E. 797, 798: "[By] setting up a
breach of the duty [plaintiff] may elect as to his remedy, and may
rely upon either his right under the contract or proceed for damages
as in a case of tort."
```

Fig. 55.   AAA Parking, Inc. v. Black Card

an injunction ordering Joe to return the airplane. However, whatever he decided to do, John had to hire a lawyer in Georgia.

Once the legal issues were resolved the problems not covered by law had to be addressed. These involved the practicality of pursuing and the financial ability to pursue the issue to the desired conclusion. Having the law on John's side did not necessarily mean that he had the power to enforce it.

Now John had to make a decision. He was already at odds with his best friend, and his airplane was gone. Did he want to spend the money and effort required to get the plane back, and risk further damage to their relationship? To make the decision easier, John put together a law library research report covering the problem (Step 9).

Law Library Research Report

Title: Bailment of Airplane

Requested by: John Row

Submitted by: John Row

Date Submitted: June 20, 1978

Statement of Facts   While John was moving from California to New York City, he passed through Atlanta, Georgia, stopping to visit his old friend

Joe. John left his special model airplane with Joe, telling him that he would call for it later. Two years later, John wrote to Joe requesting that the airplane be shipped to him in New York. Joe refused.

First Question Presented   What legal relationships result from John's leaving his airplane with Joe, and what obligations have been assumed as a result thereof?

Brief Answer   By leaving his airplane with Joe in Georgia, John created a bailment for use.

Discussion   A bailment is the delivery of goods or property for the execution of a special object, beneficial to either the bailor, the bailee, or both, and upon a contract, express or implied, to carry out this object and dispose of the property in conformity with the purpose of the trust (Code of Georgia Ann., Bailments, Sec. 12–101, Definition).

A loan for use is a gratuitous grant of an article to another for use, to be returned in specie (the exact thing) and at the will of the grantor. The loan may be either for a certain time or indefinite (Code of Georgia Ann., Bailments, Sec. 12–502).

Second Question Presented   What remedy does John, in New York, have against Joe, in Georgia, either to force the return of the loaned airplane or to be paid for it?

Brief Answer   John, the bailor, has the option either of suing Joe, the bailee, in Georgia for damages in converting John's property or of asking the court for an injunction ordering Joe to return the airplane.

Discussion   A bailment relationship is sufficient to support an action in trover when the chattel bailed is converted or wrongfully withheld from the bailor *(Traylor v. Hyatt Corp.,* 122 Ga.App. 633 (1970)). The bailor may elect to his or her rights under the contract and retrieve the bailed property, or proceed for damages in tort *(AAA Parking, Inc. v. Black,* 139 S.E.2d 437, 110 Ga.App. 554 (1964)).

Bibliography

(Note: The looseleaf materials listed below may present the best overview and provide the most up-to-date information. These materials are not completely described here because the services are tremendously expensive for individuals to purchase, the titles identify the topics, their formats are relatively similar, and most of them can be found in law libraries.

If a book cannot be found in your library or in the nearest law library, ask your librarian if it can be obtained through interlibrary loan.)

Alderman, Richard M. *A Transactional Guide to the Uniform Commercial Code.* 2d ed. 2 vols. Philadelphia: Amer. Law Inst. Amer. Bar Assn., 1983.

Anderson, Ronald A. *Anderson on the Uniform Commercial Code.* 3d ed. Rochester, N.Y.: Lawyers Cooperative/Bancroft-Whitney, 1981– . Kept up to date with pocket supplements.

Brown, Ray Andrews. *The Law of Personal Property.* 3d ed. Chicago: Callaghan & Co., 1975. A conventional text covering ownership and classes of property, acquisition, loss, gifts, sales, bailments, liens, and pledges.

Burke, D. Barlow. *Personal Property in a Nutshell.* St. Paul, Minn.: West, 1983.

Consumer & Commercial—Credit Union Guide. (P-H) Looseleaf.

Consumer Credit Guide. (CCH) Looseleaf.

Felsenfield, Carl, and Alan Siegel. *Writing Contracts in Plain English.* St. Paul, Minn.: West, 1981. Presents a step-by-step method for writing understandable legal documents. Calls for an analysis of the substance of the contract and an understanding of its uses; describes how to organize its sections and choose the proper language. With appendix, index, and forms.

Hemphill, Charles F., Jr. *The Consumer Protection Handbook: A Legal Guide.* Englewood Cliffs, N.J.: Prentice-Hall, 1981. Describes how to avoid swindles, traps, and other deceptive practices. A clear, concise sourcebook covering what to do if one suffers injury from a product or a service. Covers consumer fraud, advertising, mail order, door-to-door sales, guarantees and warranties, sales contracts, product safety, debt delinquency, loan defaults, consumer credit, housing, attorneys, and small claims.

Reiley, Eldon H. *Guidebook to Security Interests in Personal Property.* 2d ed. New York: Clark Boardman, 1986– .

Stone, Bradford. *Uniform Commercial Code in a Nutshell.* 2d ed. St. Paul, Minn.: West, 1984.

White, James J., and Robert S. Summers. *Handbook of the Law Under the Uniform Commercial Code.* 2d ed. St. Paul, Minn.: West, 1980.

Landlord and Tenant

The relationship between a landlord and a tenant is a contractual one. The landlord is the person owning, or having possession of and the right to occupy, certain real estate; and the tenant is the person leasing that real estate, giving him or her the right of occupancy for a specific period of time and for a specified rent. At the termination of the contract, the rights of occupancy revert to the landlord. The lessee may sublet the property to another, unless the original lease prohibits it. This is one of the reasonable restrictions a landlord may place upon the property being leased. Other reasonable restrictions include prohibiting animals and prohibiting the use of the property for other than a specified purpose, such as preventing a business use in residential property. The lease gives the tenant the exclusive right of occupancy of the property; however, he or she may not make any material alterations on the property without the landlord's consent.

Uninhabitability of the premises, according to common law, is not considered an eviction by the landlord. However, in many jurisdictions, if the premises are not habitable due to the landlord's neglect, uninhabitability may be considered a constructive eviction of the tenant. If the property is not heated, for example, and the lease requires the landlord to furnish heat; or if the water does not reach the leased premises; or if the electric system is out of order, and no electricity is available, there may be a claim of constructive eviction. The tenant must move out within a reasonable period of time to treat any of these conditions as an eviction and as a breach of the lease contract.

If a landlord agrees to make repairs to the property and fails to do so, he or she may then become liable for injury to the tenant if the injury is caused by the lack of repairs. The common areas in the building and the grounds that are under the landlord's control must be kept in repair and free from defects that may injure tenants or their visitors. On the other hand, the tenant has the responsibility of keeping the leased premises in good repair and of returning this property to the landlord at the termination of the lease in the same condition it was in at the beginning of the tenancy, subject to reasonable wear and tear.

Introduction to Research Problem

If the tenant remains on the premises after the termination of the lease without the permission of the landlord, the tenant may be treated as a trespasser

100

and be evicted by the landlord. The landlord may at his or her option treat the tenant as a tenant at will, which means that the tenant may stay on the property as long as the landlord allows, but the tenant can be evicted at any time.

Statutes have changed many of the common-law concepts of landlord and tenant relationships. Abuses by so-called slum landlords have caused states and cities to enact laws governing residences; these laws frequently are enforced through the fire code or sanitation code. Housing shortages and high rents have brought about rent controls in many jurisdictions, sometimes leading to undesired results when landlords no longer receive sufficient rent to make repairs and improvements. Large areas of some cities are now abandoned as a result of the unworkability of the local housing ordinances. In many jurisdictions, laws also have been passed making it unlawful for a landlord to evict a tenant in retaliation for any legal act done by the tenant.

For background material on the tools used in legal research, review the section titled "Where It Is Recorded"; and for an example of the use of these tools in a legal research problem, see "How to Find It." See the Glossary for unfamiliar terms and Appendix A for abbreviations.

The legal explanations and the issues selected here are not comprehensive due to space limitations. Should the researcher become interested in a legal problem not covered by the background material, by the introduction, or by the research problem, he or she should note the question and, using the procedures suggested in this book, perform his or her own legal research to discover the answer.

Research Problem

The research tools used in this problem consist of the Search Process Flow Chart, the CORP rule, legal treatises, a legal dictionary, statutes, and reporters.

John's eldest daughter, Alice, studied real estate in school and decided that Hawaii held the best prospects for her talents. In her haste, Alice purchased a string of garden apartments, almost all of which were leased, and proceeded to get acquainted with her property and tenants. She reviewed the current leases, checked on the condition of the property, and began talking with everyone concerned. One of her most frequent conversationalists was Zora, an interesting, intense, intelligent, single-minded person, who was outspoken in her views of the existing political and economic system. Zora insisted on her rights, including those as a tenant, and became somewhat of a pest, later a nuisance, and finally a problem. Alice was very patient with her but grew to intensely dislike Zora and her forcefully stated views.

Zora's lease expired in April, but Alice did nothing about the expired lease except to keep collecting rent. Zora had made public statements that drew unfavorable newspaper reviews and occasionally caused congestion around the apartment complex. She headed a sort of tenants committee that was organized to improve the conditions of their tenancy, including repairing some sewer pipes, placing railings on dangerous stairs, planting decorative trees and flowers on the premises, and installing a swimming pool.

Such activity upset Alice, and eventually, in September, she found another tenant who was willing to rent Zora's apartment at an increased rent. So on

September 25, Alice sent a notice to Zora explaining that her tenancy would expire on November 1 and that she was to be out of the building by that time. Zora increased her incendiary activities, and by November 2, she still had not moved out. Alice started summary proceedings for eviction and was surprised to find that Zora resisted. Zora replied in her answer to the complaint that she was being harassed because of her political views, that Alice's actions were in retaliation for Zora's activities, and that retaliatory eviction was illegal. This charge was something that Alice had not learned in school, so she called her father in New York, told him the story, and asked, "What is this all about? What can I do?"

After calming his daughter down and telling her he would look into the matter, John trudged off to the Columbia University Law School library to research the problem. He figured he would be able to research the problem himself if he were willing to invest the time; after all, he had already been through the process because of the airplane problem.

Since John was generally unfamiliar with the law regarding relations between landlords and tenants, he decided that he should begin his research by getting a general overview of the subject. He recalled that examining a treatise is often a good way to get such an overview because the author tries to distill the principles derived from cases, statutes, and regulations into a straightforward explanation of the law. For a novice in the field, John recalled, it is often easier to gain an understanding of the law by following this approach initially rather than by starting with the primary authorities themselves. Investigating the subject catalog in the library under the heading "Landlord and Tenant," he discovered a treatise titled *American Law of Landlord and Tenant* by Robert J. Schoschinski (1980). The catalog card also told John that the treatise was kept up to date with pocket supplements, so he was reasonably sure that he would get current information from the book. Taking out his 4" x 6" cards, a copy of the Search Process Flow Chart, and the requested book by Schoschinski, John reviewed the CORP rule: *C* for cause of action, *O* for object, *R* for restitution and *P* for parties. He also remembered that the rule was to be used in conjunction with the facts of the case in order to insure coverage of all aspects of the case, and in order to create a word list for searching indexes for statutes and cases. So before undertaking anything else, John made up a fact card (Fig. 56).

Turning to the Search Process Flow Chart, John saw that Step 1 suggests compiling a list of search words to be used in conjunction with the facts he had just entered on a card. He thought of *landlord and tenant* and was also given *retaliatory eviction* by Alice. John remembered that he should not rely on his own memory but should use the Outline of the Law and the Digest Topics found in West's digests. In the Outline of the Law under "Property," he located no new terms. From the Digest Topics he added *civil rights, condominium,* and *ejectment.* This gave him the following list of words to be used in searching: *civil rights, condominium, ejectment, landlord and tenant,* and *retaliatory eviction.* He decided to begin with the most specific topic in the list, which was *retaliatory eviction.* John knew that it is generally a good idea to begin with the most specific term when searching in an index, since relevant material will be found immediately if the index uses that term; if it does not,

12/27/81

Alice   (Landlord's Retaliatory Eviction)   Alice

Facts: Alice purchased real estate in Hawaii consisting of garden apartments. Becoming a landlord, she inherited some tenants with leases and some without. Zora, a tenant, had a lease that expired in April and was not renewed. The landlord kept collecting rent, and the tenant kept paying the same rent as was stated in the lease. The tenant had been active politically, causing some discomfort to the landlord because the tenant's activities had attracted adverse attention to the garden apartments. Zora, the tenant, headed a tenants association, which forced improvements consisting of repairing sewer pipes and replacing railings, and which was requesting decorative plantings and a swimming pool. Alice, the landlady, found another tenant who was willing to pay more for the apartment, so she sent a notice to Zora on September 25 informing Zora that she was to vacate the apartment by November 1. Zora did not vacate the premises, and the landlady started the summary process for eviction. The tenant replied, claiming "retaliatory eviction."

Fig. 56. Eviction Fact Card

John knew that he could always expand his search by going to more general terms, such as *civil rights* or *landlord and tenant* in this instance.

The chart indicates that the next step (Step 2) is to consider jurisdiction. In Alice's case, it appeared that Hawaii was the only jurisdiction to be considered.

Step 3 suggests conducting a general overview. In this case, instead of using an encyclopedia, John decided to use a text—the Schoschinski book. In the index he found his subject: Retaliatory Eviction, Generally, Sec. 12:1 to 13; Activities of Tenant, Sections 12:3, 9; Conduct of Landlord, Sections 12:4, 10; Decisions of Law, Sections 12:1 to 7; Eviction, Landlord's Retaliatory motivation for, Section 6:17; Legislation as preempting common-law developments, Section 12:13; Pleading Retaliation, time limitations in, Section 12:6; Presumptions and burden of proof, Sections 12:5, 11; Remedies, Sections 12:7, 12; and Tenancy at will, termination by retaliatory action, Section 12:18. Seeing "tenancy at will" made John wonder what other types of tenancies there are. In the index he saw that there are estates for years, holdover tenancies, periodic tenancies, tenancies at sufferance, and tenancies at will. Remembering that a law dictionary can be used to define terms, John located one in the library. A quick check of *Black's Law Dictionary* revealed information that he put on a card for further reference (Fig. 57).

Periodic tenancy, tenancy at sufferance, and tenancy at will all sounded as if they might apply, so John went back to the index of the Schoschinski book to pick out some general information on the subject (Fig. 58).

John made a note to check the case noted on the Schoschinski card. Schoschinski (in Sec. 12:2 under "Landlord Retaliatory Action," note 19) lists another Hawaii case to be checked later, *Windward Partners v. Delos Santos*, 59 Hawaii 104, 577 P.2d 326 (1978). In Section 12:1 the landmark case in the

12/27/81

Alice   (Landlord's Retaliatory Eviction)   Alice

Black's Law Dictionary:

Estate for Years—Estate less than a freehold where a person has an interest in land for some fixed period of time.

Holdover Tenant—A tenant who retains possession after the expiration of a lease or after a tenancy at will has been terminated.

Periodic Tenancy—Tenancy from week to week, month to month, or year to year.

Tenant at Sufferance—One who after rightfully being in possession of rented premises remains on the premises after his or her right is terminated.

Tenancy at Will—One who holds possession of premises by permission of the owner but without a fixed term.

Fig. 57.   Black's Law Dictionary Card

12/27/81

Alice   (Landlord's Retaliatory Eviction)   Alice

Schoschinski, Robert S., American Law of Landlord and Tenant (1980).

Sec. 2:10. Periodic tenancies continue for a certain period of time and for successive equal periods of time unless terminated at the end of any period by notice from either party.

Sec. 2:16. Tenancy at will endures only so long as both parties agree.

Sec. 2:23. Holdover tenancy states that when a tenant remains on the premises after his or her tenancy is terminated, he or she is classed as a tenant at sufferance. The landlord may either evict or hold the tenant to a new tenancy. The new tenancy will depend upon the old one. If the original lease was for a year, some states hold that a tenancy for a year results, while others hold that a holdover tenancy is from month to month. Some states have statutes dealing with holdovers. In the pocket part of the book under this section, there is a reference to a case from Hawaii, Hawaiian Electric Co. v. DeSantos, 621 P.2d 971 (1980).

Fig. 58.   Schoschinski Card 1

nation is listed as *Edwards v. Habib,* 130 App. D.C. 126, 397 F.2d 687 (1968), cert. denied, 393 U.S. 1016. Under Section 12:13, note 34, another Hawaiian case is listed, *Aluli v. Trusdell,* 54 Hawaii 417, 508 P.2d 1217 (1973), cert. denied, 414 U.S. 1040. John added these cases to a continuing list on the original Schoschinski card (Fig. 59). John realized, however, that to be sure of finding all relevant Hawaiian cases, he would eventually need to use the *Hawaii Digest,* or, at a minimum, a treatise dealing specifically with landlord and tenant law in Hawaii. He knew that a general work such as Schoschinski's book cannot

```
                          12/27/81
Alice              (Landlord's Retaliatory Eviction)            Alice
Robert S. Schoschinski, American Law of Landlord and Tenant (1980).
    Sec. 12:2, Landlord Retaliatory Action. note 19, Windward Part-
ners v. Delos Santos, 59 Hawaii 104, 577 P.2d 326 (1978).
    Sec. 12:1, note Edwards v. Habib, 130 App. D.C. 126, 397 F.2d 687
(1968), cert. denied, 393 U.S. 1016. (landmark case)
    Sec. 12:13, note 34, Aluli v. Trusdell, 54 Hawaii 417, 508 P.2d 1217
(1973), cert. denied, 414 U.S. 1040.
```

Fig. 59. Schoschinski Card 2

```
                          12/27/81
Alice              (Landlord's Retaliatory Eviction)            Alice
Issue: What conditions must exist to support a claim of "landlord's
retaliatory eviction" as a valid defense in the eviction suit brought
in Hawaii?
x  Hawaii Revised Statutes
x  Windward Partners v. Delos Santos, 59 Hawaii 104, 577 P.2d 326
       (1978).
   Edwards v. Habib, 130 App. D.C. 126, 397 F.2d 687 (1968), cert.
       denied, 393 U.S. 1016. (landmark case)
x  Aluli v. Trusdell, 54 Hawaii 417, 508 P.2d 1217 (1973), cert. denied,
       414 U.S. 1040.
   Hawaiian Electric Co. v. DeSantos, 621 P.2d 971 (1980).
```

Fig. 60. Eviction Issue Card

possibly list all cases from every jurisdiction. Still, at least he knew that there
are some cases in Hawaii involving the problem of landlord retaliation.

Step 4 calls for the framing of issues, now that John had a general idea
of what was involved in the problem. This task gave him some trouble, but he
finally came up with the following information and entered it on a card (Fig.
60), along with the primary sources of law he discovered in the Schoschinski
work (Step 5).

Step 5 was also included in the listing of cases and statutes on the issue
card because the Schoschinski work was used as a case finder as well as for a
general overview of the subject.

Continuing with Step 6 of the Search Process Flow Chart, John investigated
these items and entered them on cards. He found hints that some states have
statutes covering the exact subject of Alice's problem. John also remembered
that landlord and tenant rights are often covered by state legislation, so he knew
that as a general rule a researcher should always review the state code when
faced with any question dealing with landlord and tenant relations. John therefore took a quick look at the statutes of Hawaii, using the general index to

find any provisions relating to the status of holdover tenants, as tenant status might make a difference. He listed his findings on the cards (Fig. 61).

That information solved the problem of the type of tenancy. It appeared that Alice and Zora had, by statute, created a tenancy from month to month when Zora let her lease expire and when Alice continued to collect rent monthly with no other changes. Continuing with the Hawaii Revised Statutes card, John listed the following information:

> Sec. 521-71(a). When a tenancy is month to month, the landlord or the tenant may terminate the rental agreement upon his notifying the other party at least twenty-eight days in advance of the anticipated termination. . . . (Pocket part supplement indicates no change through 1981.)

It seemed that Alice had done the right thing—she gave notice to Zora on September 25 to vacate the apartment on November 1, which was beyond the required twenty-eight days.

John then checked the Aluli and Windward cases and put them on cards, as they were pertinent to his needs (Figs. 62 and 63).

The code involved in the Windward case above was the Residential Landlord-Tenant Code, Hawaii Rev. Stat., Sec. 521-74. Step 7 of the Search Process

---

12/27/81

Alice   (Landlord's Retaliatory Eviction)   Alice
Hawaii Rev. Stat.
　　Sec. 521-71. Covers the termination of tenancy, landlord's remedies for holdover tenants. "(c) . . . The landlord may bring a summary proceeding for recovery of possession of the dwelling unit at any time during the first sixty days of holdover, except that the landlord's acceptance of rent in advance after the first month of holdover shall create a month-to-month tenancy in the absence of an agreement between the parties to the contrary at the time of such acceptance." (Pocket part checked; no change through end of 1981.)

Fig. 61.　Hawaii Revised Statutes, Sec. 521-71 Card

12/27/81

Alice   (Landlord's Retaliatory Eviction)   Alice
Aluli v. Trusdell, 54 Hawaii 417, 508 P.2d 1217 (1973), cert. denied, 414 U.S. 1040.
　　Landlord properly evicted a month-to-month tenant, and the tenant claimed in defense that the landlord had evicted him because he had been active in a tenants organization, and his first amendment rights were thereby violated. The court said that the landlord's action did not take away any rights and that the tenant could still attend meetings and speak out about the conditions of the premises.

Fig. 62.　Aluli v. Trusdell Card

12/27/81

Alice   (Landlord's Retaliatory Eviction)   Alice
Windward Partners v. Delos Santos, 59 Hawaii 104, 577 P.2d 326
(1978).

    Landlord attempted to evict tenants because they opposed land-
lord's attempt to redesignate the land use from agricultural to urban.
The court said that although the conduct of the tenants was not
included in the protected activities listed in the Hawaii Rev. Stat.,
Sec. 521-74(a) (Retaliatory Eviction and Rent Increases Prohibited),
the defense could be raised because the ". . . code does not purport
to be the sole exclusive expression of the rights and remedies available to landlords and tenants." Allowing landlords to retaliate in
such cases as this would frustrate the provisions of the act covering
land use, which requires public hearings before allowing land use
changes.

Fig. 63.   Windward Partners v. Delos Santos Card

12/27/81

Alice   (Landlord's Retaliatory Eviction)   Alice
Hawaii Rev. Stat., Sec. 521-74(a)

    "Notwithstanding that the tenant has no written rental agree-
ment or that it has expired, so long as the tenant continues to
tender the usual rent to the landlord or proceeds to tender receipts
for rent lawfully withheld, no action or proceeding to recover possession of the dwelling unit may be maintained against the tenant,
nor shall the landlord otherwise cause the tenant to quit the dwelling unit involuntarily, nor demand an increase in rent from the
tenant, nor decrease the service to which the tenant has been entitled, after:

"(1) The tenant has complained in good faith to the department of
    health, landlord, building department, office of consumer pro-
    tection, or any other governmental agency concerned with land-
    lord-tenant disputes, of conditions in or affecting his dwelling
    unit which constitutes a violation of a health law or regulation
    or of any provision of this chapter; or

"(2) The department of health or other government agency has filed
    a notice or complaint of a violation of a health law or regulation
    or any provision of this chapter; or

"(3) The tenant has in good faith requested repairs under section
    521-63 or 521-64."

Fig. 64.   Hawaii Revised Statutes, Sec. 521-74(a) Card

Flow Chart says that if the researcher discovers new material, he or she should
go back to Step 6 and check that material. Doing this, John decided that he
had to make a card for the first part of Section 521-74 of the code, involving
evictions (Fig. 64).

The courts seem to have extended the protection given to tenants beyond what is listed in the statute by stating that the statute is not exclusive and that tenants have a common-law remedy in equity. Following Step 8 (Shepardizing the cases to date for any changes) revealed nothing new. John felt that Alice's case might end up in an interesting court fight and that he really did not have enough legal expertise to advise his daughter. So he wrote her a letter, including a law library research report of his findings (Step 9), suggesting that she take the report to her lawyer, who might find that the research already done by John would save time. John also suggested that once the legal issues were resolved there always are problems not covered by law that must be addressed. These include the practicality of pursuing and the financial ability to pursue the issue to the desired conclusion. Having the law on one's side, John reminded his daughter, does not necessarily mean that one has the power to enforce it.

Law Library Research Report

Title: Landlord Retaliatory Eviction
Requested by: Alice Row
Submitted by: John Row
Date Submitted: January 2, 1982

Statement of Facts   Alice purchased real estate in Hawaii consisting of garden apartments. Becoming a landlord, she inherited some tenants with leases and some without. Zora, a tenant, had a lease that expired in April and was not renewed. The landlord kept collecting rent, and the tenant kept paying the same rent as was stated in the lease. The tenant had been active politically, causing some problems for the landlord because the tenant's activities attracted adverse attention to the garden apartments. Zora, the tenant, headed a tenants association, which forced improvements consisting of repairing sewer pipes and replacing railings, and which now was requesting decorative plantings and a swimming pool. Alice, the landlady, found another tenant who was willing to pay more for the apartment. She sent a notice on September 25 to Zora, notifying her that Zora was to vacate the premises on November 1. Zora did not vacate the apartment, and the landlady started summary proceedings for eviction. The tenant replied, claiming "retaliatory eviction."

Question Presented   What conditions must exist to support a claim of "landlord's retaliatory eviction" as a valid defense in the eviction suit brought by Zora in Hawaii?

Brief Answer   The response of "landlord retaliation" does not appear to have merit in this case. The landlady followed the required steps for eviction and appeared to have a valid reason for the eviction. However, the situation is clouded by two recent cases.

Discussion   The landlord complied with all of the steps needed to terminate the tenancy under Hawaii Rev. Stat., Sec. 521-71 and 521-71 (a), which set forth proceedings required before bringing summary proceedings to recover possession of property.

Two more or less contradictory cases have clouded the answer by reading into the statute extensions of its coverage. *Aluli v. Trusdell,* 54 Hawaii 417, 508 P.2d 1217 (1973), cert. denied, 414 U.S. 1040, states that the first amendment rights of a complaining tenant were not violated by the evicting landlord because the tenant could still attend meetings of the tenants association and speak out against conditions on the premises.

The second case, *Windward Partners v. Delos Santos,* 59 Hawaii 104, 577 P.2d 326 (1978), concerned the eviction of tenants who opposed their landlord's attempt to convert his land from agricultural to urban. Here the court brought in Hawaii Rev. Stat., 521-74(a) (Retaliatory Eviction and Rent Increases Prohibited), stating that the statute does not purport to be the exclusive remedy available and that to allow landlords to retaliate in such cases would frustrate the intent of the act. Hawaii Rev. Stat., Sec. 521-74(a) does not appear to apply to Alice's situation.

Bibliography

(Note: The looseleaf materials listed below may set forth the best overview and provide the most up-to-date information. They are not completely described here because the services are tremendously expensive for individuals to purchase, the titles identify the topics, their formats are relatively similar, and most of these materials can be found in law libraries.

Because landlord-tenant relationships are generally governed by state law, there are many treatises that focus on such provisions in a particular state. Examples include *California Landlord and Tenant Law and Procedure* (Goddard) and *New York City Tenant Handbook: Your Legal Rights and How to Use Them* (Striker and Shapiro). These state-specific items are too numerous to include in this bibliography. Consequently, you should always check in a local law library for such materials when dealing with problems in the area of landlord and tenant law.

If a book cannot be found in your library or in the nearest law library, ask your librarian if it can be obtained through interlibrary loan.)

Blumberg, Richard E., and James R. Grow. *The Rights of Tenants.* New York: Avon, 1978. A guide for tenants covering leases, housing codes, remedies, deposits, utility shutoffs, discrimination, and organizations. Appendixes cover standard forms, leases, legal procedures, inspection and inventory, basic legal research, and ACLU policy. Includes chapter notes.

Equal Opportunity in Housing. (P-H) Looseleaf.

Hill, David S. *Landlord and Tenant Law in a Nutshell.* St. Paul, Minn.: West, 1986. Contains most of the rules of landlord and tenant law, with some background. Also includes tables and index.

Housing and Development Reporter. (BNA) Looseleaf.

Jessup, Libby F. *Landlord and Tenant.* Dobbs Ferry, N.Y.: Oceana, 1974. Provides historical background, chart of states giving tenancies and their terminations, hints to tenants as to what is desirable in a lease, and a special section on urban tenancies, evictions, and tenants' rights. Uniform Residential Landlord and Tenants Act, glossary, and index included.

Rose, Jerome G. *Landlords and Tenants.* New Brunswick, N.J.: Transaction Bks., 1973. Comprehensive coverage of residential rental relationships and guide for both landlord and tenant. Covers government housing; recommends legal reforms. With appendixes, chapter notes, and index.

Schoschinski, Robert S. *American Law of Landlord and Tenant.* Rochester, N.Y.: The Lawyers Cooperative/Bancroft-Whitney, 1980. An excellent, complete, and comprehensive textbook on all aspects of the subject. Contains footnotes, index, and table of cases; updated with pocket parts.

Real Property

Real property includes all rights and interests in things that are real, i.e., land, and in things that are permanently attached to the land. It may also include the right to use, or to the profits from the use of, someone else's land. The most important right in land is ownership, which, within certain increasing limits, gives a person the right to use the land as he or she wishes without having to account to anyone.

In most states, the law concerning real estate came to us from England, where it evolved from the feudal system. Under the feudal system from the time of the Norman Conquest, all lands were held by the king. The king granted the use of the land to his subjects, conditioned upon the performance of certain duties or services. The occupant of the land was said to have tenure and in turn could create a subtenure, as could his subtenant, ad infinitum. In the chain of tenure holders (called "mesne lords") various types of holdings could exist. For instance, Lord "A" might own the right of military service from the occupant of the land, while Lord "B" might hold the right to collect rents. Upon the death of the tenant, the law stated that the estate descended to the tenant's firstborn son, subject to the claims of the mesne lords above the deceased. Upon death, a pecuniary payment was due, most likely the forerunner of today's estate and inheritance taxes. A tenant could probably dispose of his holdings to another as long as such action did not injure in any way the interests of the lord.

The principles of real estate law developed under the feudal system were carried over from England to the United States and are still embodied in our common law. One of the most important of these principles, or theories, is that of "estates." This theory allowed the rights of possession and enjoyment to be divided according to time, as measured in days, weeks, months, years, or lifetimes. This division gave us the classification of estates. For example, the "freehold estate," which is held for an unspecified period of time, includes estates that can be inherited and life estates which are not inherited. Estates for less than a freehold include estates for years, tenancies at will, tenancies from year to year, and tenancies at sufferance.

In the United States, a person who is the sole owner of property may leave real estate under a will to anyone he or she wishes. In the absence of a will, the property will upon death descend to the heirs as defined by the statutes of the state within which the land is situated. Most real estate is transferred by a deed. A deed is a legal document that is signed, sealed, and acknowledged by the owner, and delivered to the new owner. Frequently, statutes outline the form that a deed must take. In addition to its execution by the seller, the deed must contain the name and address of the purchaser, an adequate description of the property to be conveyed, and the consideration given for the sale. The consideration need not be monetary; love and affection are sufficient. So that the public may become aware of land transfers, deeds and mortgages are recorded in the office called for in the state statutes, e.g., in New York State, the Office of the County Clerks; in Massachusetts, the Registry of Deeds; and in Connecticut, the town or city clerk. Recording the deed also protects the purchaser because it puts the world on notice that he or she is the new owner.

Real estate may also be pledged to secure a debt, which is usually a note for a certain amount of money. The security interest is called a mortgage, which is recorded in the same manner as the deed and is notice to all that the mortgagee has an interest in the specified real estate. If the mortgagee's interest is not satisfied, he or she may foreclose the mortgage and take possession of the property even though it may have been conveyed to someone else.

Before an individual purchases property, or loans money with real estate as security, prudence dictates that he or she examine the record title to the property. This examination consists of checking all the records that might in any way affect the real estate, and may extend from searching the registry records, where deeds and mortgages are recorded, to consulting the registry of probate or surrogate, where wills and probate matters are decided, and finally, to checking the records on liens against personal property such as furnaces, which may be installed in real estate and thereby become a part of the real estate. This report of the condition of the title is either prepared by an attorney or examined by an attorney before the actual transfer, and if defects are discovered, they are altered, removed, corrected, adjusted, compromised, or accepted.

Titles have historically been examined from a recognized root, such as a government grant or a railroad grant, or for a fixed, arbitrary period of time, i.e., twenty years, forty years, sixty years, or one hundred years. It is becoming increasingly difficult and unnecessary to trace the ownership of real estate back to its original grant from a government. The current process of examining titles is cumbersome, time consuming, expensive, and, in view of modern business methods, inefficient. Businesspeople are increasingly demanding faster service and results instead of conferences and arguments. The introduction of computers and microfiche has improved the speed and accuracy of the process, a long-needed step that it is hoped will continue. Microfiche has made it possible to store on film copies of records consisting of deeds, mortgages, attachments, indexes, and other helpful title-searching aids, thereby allowing tremendous space saving. The computer, in addition to space saving, allows rapid access to the databases that store the records.

Introduction to Research Problem

Each state has sovereignty over its own land; therefore, the statutes of each state must be examined to discover the peculiar quirks of that state's real estate law. However, in spite of the purely local nature of real estate, the federal government has found ways to impose federal regulations upon local real estate transactions. This government regulation falls into the area of interstate commerce and came about because some real estate developers and condominium builders used questionable methods in their advertising and sales.

For background material on the tools used in legal research, review the section titled "Where It Is Recorded"; and for an example of the use of these tools in a legal research problem, see "How to Find It." See the Glossary for unfamiliar terms and Appendix A for abbreviations.

The legal explanations and the issues selected here are not comprehensive due to space limitations. Should the researcher become interested in a legal problem not covered by the background material, by the introduction, or by the research problem, he or she should note the question, and, using the procedures suggested in this book, perform his or her own legal research to discover the answer.

Research Problem

The research tools used in this problem consist of the Search Process Flow Chart, the CORP rule, statutes, and administrative agency regulations found in the *Code of Federal Regulations (C.F.R.)* and in the *Federal Register (Fed. Reg.)*.

One of John's brothers, JJ, developed sales ability as he went through high school. Loving the outdoors, JJ purchased 813 acres of land in rural Pennsylvania. It consisted of about forty acres of flatland fronting on a hardtop road, with the balance made up of rolling, forested hills with several brooks running through it and a dirt road meandering from the hardtop road to the back, splitting the total acreage into two sections—one section of about 313 acres, and the other of about 500 acres. JJ, being ambitious, built himself a cabin on the property, scooped out a wide spot in one of the brooks, and placed a small dam across it, forming a nice pond of about four acres. The setting looked so nice that JJ decided to develop the land and share its beauty with others. He figured that if he put in roads, reserving about thirteen acres for himself, he would have 800 acres to develop, from which he could make a very nice profit, in spite of the fairly high development costs. Not counting the roads and the recreational areas, he should have about 150 four-acre lots for sale.

His attorney worked out a satisfactory plan in accordance with the Pennsylvania Environmental Master Plan (Pennsylvania Code, Title 25). JJ had the survey and testing work done, and complied with the few local regulations. A plan of the development—including the roads, recreation areas, ponds, and lots—was properly recorded. JJ then collected a staff of hotshot real estate people to sell the lots, and advertised the development in newspapers, magazines, and by direct mail. His ads stated that the lots were for sale, financing was available, and the installation of roads, water, sewers, and electricity were to be completed within two years.

JJ set up an open house offering gifts to those attending, and he generally carried on a high-pressure sales campaign. At this point, he had only bulldozed out the roads and staked the lots, waiting to collect money from the sales before putting in the water, electricity, recreational areas, and blacktopped roads. Within a month, he had sold twenty-seven lots to people from the local area, New York, Pennsylvania, and Ohio. Most of them were on a contract to sell the land, and most of the sales were owner-financed. Some buyers had gone to a local bank recommended by JJ to obtain their money. None of the contracts mentioned a time limit for installing roads, water, sewers, and electricity; indeed, the contracts did not even indicate that this work would be done. A few of the purchasers asked for a return of their money after they had recovered from the high-pressure sales pitch, but JJ was relying on his silver tongue to talk them into staying.

Finally, JJ was visited by a representative of the Office of the Director of Land Sales of the Enforcement Division Office of Interstate Land Sales, H.U.D., informing him that he was in violation of the Interstate Land Sales Full Disclosure Act of 1970, 15 U.S.C., Sec. 1700 et seq. The violation existed because no statement of record had been filed by JJ, and he did not include in his sales contracts any reference to the completion of his roads, electric, water, and sewage systems as required. JJ fumed, said that he was doing business only in Pennsylvania, that he had no loans from H.U.D. and didn't anticipate any, and that therefore it was none of H.U.D.'s business how he sold his land. After calming down a bit, JJ did tell the agent that he would check with his attorney and get back to him. This he did. JJ's lawyer gave you the job of doing some quick preliminary research into the problem. A conference with the volatile JJ produced the following facts, which you put on the first card (Fig. 65).

10/18/79

Mr. Lawyer   (Violation of 15 U.S.C., Sec. 1700)   JJ

Facts: JJ purchased 813 acres of land in Pa., built himself a pond, and proceeded to develop the remaining land for camping homesites. He complied with all the Pa. and local regulations, and had a survey of the development recorded showing roads, ponds, recreation areas, and 153 lots. He bulldozed roads and staked out the lots, ponds, and recreation areas, but he held up on putting in water, electricity, sewage, and finished roads until he obtained enough money from the sales of lots to complete them. He hired salespeople and carried on an aggressive sales campaign in newspapers, magazines, and by direct mail, promising roads, water, sewers, and electricity within two years, and offering gifts to those attending the open house. His promises of utilities and roads, however, never found their way into any of the land sales contracts. He had seven requests for the return of deposits, but he was trying to talk these purchasers into staying. He was later visited by a representative of H.U.D., Office of Land Sales Enforcement Division, Office of Interstate Land Sales Registration, who informed him that he was selling in violation of the Federal Interstate Land Sales Act, 15 U.S.C., Sec. 1700 et seq. because he had not registered with H.U.D. and his contracts did not include references to roads, a water system, electrical installations, or sewer connections, in spite of the fact that he had advertised them. JJ had never heard of the act.

Fig. 65.   Interstate Real Estate Sales Fact Card

You thank JJ for his time, escape from his tobacco-chewing presence, and head for the law library with your 4″ x 6″ cards, your Search Process Flow Chart, and your CORP rule.

Step 1 on the chart leads you to a search for words, which, used in conjunction with the facts of the case, will lead you to statute and case finders to solve the problem. The problem has been considerably shortened here because you already have a lead, the federal Interstate Land Sales Full Disclosure Act of 1970 (15 U.S.C., Sec. 1700 et seq.). Step 2 is also easily taken care of because you know that the federal jurisdiction is causing the problem. There is no need for Step 3 (consult a text or encyclopedia for a general overview) at this point because you can assume that the statute will provide sufficient background. However, it might be useful at a later point in the research process to locate and review a secondary authority (such as a treatise, encyclopedia, or legal periodical article) that contains a discussion of this statute, since it is often difficult to understand the requirements of a complex act without some assistance from such a commentary.

Step 4 calls for the framing of the issue involved in the case, which is entered on a card (Fig. 66).

There is no need for Step 5 because the relevant statute has been identified. You can now proceed directly to the primary source of the law. You go to the U.S.C.A., pick out Title 15, and turn to Section 1700, which brings you to Step 6—checking the statute and recording it on a card.

In checking Section 1700 et seq., you find your attention drawn to Section 1703, "Requirements respecting sale or lease of lots." You make a card for this information (Fig. 67).

That section covers more federal regulating than one would ever have imagined concerning local real estate. The portions that concern JJ are Section 1703 (1)(A), which makes it unlawful for him to use the mails to sell unless a statement of record with respect to such lots is in effect, and Section 1703 (2)(D), which makes it unlawful for him to sell if representing that roads, sewers, water, gas or electric services, or recreational amenities will be provided or completed by the developer without stipulating in the contract of sale that such services will be provided or completed.

The situation seems negative for JJ at this point. He appears to have violated federal regulations about which he knew nothing. Grasping at straws, he wonders what is the authority of H.U.D. and the agent that approached him?

10/20/79

Mr. Lawyer   (Violation of 15 U.S.C., Sec. 1700)   JJ

Issue: Has JJ violated 15 U.S.C., Sec. 1700 et seq. by not filing a statement of record with H.U.D. and by not including in each sales contract a statement concerning the completion of the installation of roads, sewers, water, and electricity?

x 15 U.S.C.A. 1700 et seq.

Fig. 66.   Interstate Real Estate Sales Issue Card

10/18/79
Mr. Lawyer   (Violation of 15 U.S.C., Sec. 1700)   JJ
15 U.S.C.A., Sec. 1700 et seq.
"Sec. 1703. Requirements Respecting Sale or lease of lots.
"(a) Prohibited activities. It shall be unlawful for any developer or agent, directly or indirectly, to make use of any means or instruments of transportation or communication in interstate commerce, or the mails:

"(1) with respect to the sale or lease of any lot not exempt under section 1403 (15 U.S.C. 1702)

"(A) to sell or lease any lot unless a statement of record with respect to such lot is in effect in accordance with section 1407 (15 U.S.C. 1706);

"(B) to sell or lease any lot unless a printed property report meeting the requirements of section 1408 (15 U.S.C. 1707) has been furnished to the purchaser or lessee in advance of the signing of any contract or agreement by such purchaser or lessee;

"(C) to sell or lease any lot where any part of the statement of record or the property report contained an untrue statement of a material fact or omitted to state a material fact required to be stated therein pursuant to sections 1405 through 1408 of this title (15 U.S.C. 1704 through 1707) or any regulations thereunder; or

"(D) to display or deliver to prospective purchasers or lessees advertising and promotional material which is inconsistent with information required to be disclosed in the property report; or

"(2) with respect to the sale or lease, or offer to sell or lease, any lot not exempt under section 1403(a) (15 U.S.C. 1702(a))

"(A) to employ any device, scheme, or artifice to defraud;

"(B) to obtain money or property by means of any untrue statement of material fact, or any omission to state a material fact necessary in order to make the statement made (in light of the circumstances in which they were made and within the context of the overall offer and sale or lease) not misleading, with respect to any information pertinent to the lot or subdivision;

"(C) to engage in any transaction, practice, or course of business which operates or would operate as a fraud or deceit upon a purchaser; or

"(D) to represent that roads, sewers, water, gas, or electric service, or recreational amenities will be provided or completed by the developer without stipulating in the contract of sale or lease that such services or amenities will be provided or completed."

Fig. 67. 15 U.S.C.A., Sec. 1700 et seq. Card

You know that inasmuch as the secretary of H.U.D. is responsible for carrying out the act, it becomes important to determine what rules and regulations have been promulgated by that individual. This brings you to Step 7—H.U.D. regulations—and you return to Step 6 to investigate them.

H.U.D. is a federal government agency and as such makes rules and regulations covering the areas assigned. The rules and regulations of administrative agencies have the effect of law once they are published in the *Federal Register (Fed. Reg.)*. The regulations are collected annually and codified by subject matter in the *Code of Federal Regulations (C.F.R.)*. Each revision of the C.F.R. contains the text of regulations still in force, including the new ones and deleting those that have been repealed or replaced. Between the annual revisions of the individual titles of the C.F.R., the *Fed. Reg.* is used to keep the regulations current. To use the *Fed. Reg.* as an updating tool, you need to consult two tables—the *Cumulative List of C.F.R. Sections Affected* (published separately on a monthly basis) and the *Cumulative List of C.F.R. Parts Affected* (contained in each issue of the *Fed. Reg.*). The C.F.R. can be entered through the yearly index, which alphabetically lists both subjects and agencies. If a statute is known, there is also a "Parallel Table of Authorities and Rules" contained in the C.F.R. *Index and Finding Aids* volume, which indicates the location of any rules in the C.F.R. that have been promulgated under the authority of federal statutes. Remember, for the most up-to-date information on regulations not yet included in the C.F.R., the *Fed. Reg.* must be consulted.

The rules and regulations of H.U.D. (or any other federal administrative agency) are found in the C.F.R. Since in JJ's case you know the statutory authority under which any relevant regulations would have been enacted (i.e., 15 U.S.C., Sec. 1700 et seq.), you can use the Parallel Table of Authorities and Rules in the C.F.R. *Index* to locate those regulations. Reading across from 15 U.S.C., Sec. 1701 et seq. in the Parallel Table provides you with a reference to 24 C.F.R., Sec. 1710. When you refer to that section, you quickly determine that the entire Section 1700 includes regulations relating to the applicable act. Because regulations are often crucial to the implementation of the statutory provisions, you immediately investigate these sections (Fig. 68).

It appears that the Office of Director of Land Sales Enforcement Division has been established in 24 C.F.R., Sec. 1700.85 and that the land sales involving interstate advertising must be registered with the secretary of H.U.D. under 24 C.F.R., Sec. 1700.1. The latest supplemental materials for the federal statutes and the *Fed. Reg.* for the H.U.D. regulations are checked to date (Step 8). Finding no changes, you proceed to Step 9 and put together a report.

You know that once the legal issues have been resolved, the problems not covered by law must be addressed. These include the practicality of pursuing and the financial ability to pursue the issue to the desired conclusion. As you know, having the law on your side does not necessarily mean that you have the power to enforce it.

```
                                    10/18/79
Mr. Lawyer        (Violation of 15 U.S.C., Sec. 1700)               JJ
24 C.F.R., Sec. 1700 et seq.
     Part 1700.1 states, "A land developer is required by the Interstate
Land Sales Full Disclosure Act . . . enacted on August 1, 1968 . . . to
make full disclosure in the sale or lease of certain undeveloped,
subdivided land. The act makes it unlawful . . . for any developer to
sell or lease, by use of mail or by any means in interstate commerce,
any such land offered as part of a common promotional plan unless
the land is registered with the Secretary of Housing and Urban
Development and a printed property report is furnished to the pur-
chaser or lessee in advance of the signing of an agreement for sale
or lease."
     Part 1700.85 establishes the Office of Director of Land Sales En-
forcement Division and sets forth his or her duties and powers.
     Part 1710 covers land registration and gives the requirements in
great detail.
     Part 1715 covers the purchaser's rights of revocation, illegal sales
practices, and standards.
     Part 1715.25 details misleading sales practices.
     Part 1720 sets forth the details of formal procedures and rules of
practice, covering rules and rule making, filing assistance, formal
investigations, and adjudicatory proceedings.
     Part 1730 covers the application of the regulations for filing.
```

Fig. 68.   24 C.F.R., Sec. 1700 et seq. Card

Law Library Research Report

Title: Violation of 15 U.S.C., Sec. 1700, Interstate Land Sales

Requested by: Mr. Lawyer

Submitted by: (Your Name)

Date Submitted: October 22, 1979

Statement of Facts   JJ purchased 813 acres of land in Pennsylvania, kept part, and developed the remaining land for camping homesites. He complied with all state and local regulations and recorded a survey of the development showing roads, ponds, recreation areas, and 153 lots. He bulldozed roads and staked out the lots, ponds, and recreation areas, but he held up on putting in water, electricity, sewage, and finished roads until he could obtain enough money from the sales of lots to complete them. He hired salespeople and carried on an aggressive sales campaign in newspapers, magazines, and by direct mail, promising roads, water, sewers, and electricity within two years and offering gifts to those attending the open house. His promise to install utilities and roads, however, was not written into any of the land sales contracts. Seven people requested the return of deposits, unsuccessfully. JJ was later visited by a representative of the H.U.D. Office of Land Sales Enforcement Division, Office of Interstate Land Sales Registration, who informed him that he was selling in violation of the Federal Interstate Land Sales Act, 15 U.S.C., Sec. 1700 et seq. because he had not registered his land for sale with H.U.D. and he had never included in his contracts references to when he would complete his roads, water system, electric installations, or sewer connections. He had never even heard of the act.

Question Presented   Has JJ violated 15 U.S.C., Sec. 1700 et seq. by not filing a statement of record with H.U.D. and by not including in each sales contract a statement concerning the completion of the installation of roads, sewers, water, and electricity?

Brief Answer   It appears that JJ has violated the statute recorded in 15 U.S.C., Sec. 1700 et seq. and also the regulations of H.U.D. found in 24 C.F.R., Sec. 1700 et seq.

Discussion   15 U.S.C., Sec. 1703 (1)(A) and H.U.D. regulations found in 24 C.F.R., Sec. 1700.0 require that a person selling real estate using the mails or interstate commerce must record a statement with H.U.D. 15 U.S.C., Sec. 1703 (2)(D) requires that the seller of a lot covered by this statute include in any contract of sale a stipulation concerning such services as roads, electricity, water, sewage, and other amenities that the seller advertises he or she will provide.

JJ never filed as required, and he did not know about the statutory condition. He advertised that he would provide roads, water, electricity, and sewers within two years, but he neglected to put this information in any of his contracts of sale, contrary to the statute.

Bibliography

(Note: The looseleaf materials listed below may set forth the best overview and provide the most up-to-date information. They are not completely described here because the services are tremendously expensive for individuals to purchase, the titles identify the topics, their formats are relatively similar, and most of these materials can be found in law libraries.

If a book cannot be found in your library or in the nearest law library, ask your librarian if it can be obtained through interlibrary loan.)

Arnold, Alvin L. et al. *Modern Real Estate and Mortgage Forms: Basic Forms and Agreements.* 3d ed. Boston: Warren, Gorham, & Lamont, 1986– . In looseleaf for updating.

Barnett, Peter M., and Joseph A. McKenzie. *Alternative Mortgage Instruments.* Boston: Warren, Gorham, & Lamont, 1984– . In looseleaf for updating.

Bernhardt, Roger. *Real Property in a Nutshell.* 2d ed. St. Paul, Minn.: West, 1981.

Bruce, Jon W. *Real Estate Finance in a Nutshell.* 2d ed. St. Paul, Minn.: West, 1985.

Casner, James A., ed. *American Law of Property.* 7 vols. Boston: Little, 1954– . Kept up to date by pocket supplements.

Colt, Charles S. *Introduction to Real Estate Law.* 2d ed. Chicago: Real Estate Educ., 1985.

Cribbet, John E. *Principles of the Law of Property.* 2d ed. Mineola, N.Y.: Foundation Pr., 1975. A basic textbook mostly concerning real estate. Designed to cover the "big picture" and also to indicate the changing nature of real property law.

Housing & Development Reporter. (BNA) Looseleaf.

Kehoe, Patrick E. *Cooperatives and Condominiums.* Dobbs Ferry, N.Y.: Oceana, 1974. Provides brief outline of historic ownership, background on condominiums and cooperatives, organizational setup of each, hints, and guides for purchasers. With appendixes and index.

Land Use Law & Zoning Law Digest. (Amer. Soc. of Planning Officials) Looseleaf.

National Property Law Digest. (NPLD) Looseleaf.

Powell, Richard R. *The Law of Real Property.* Albany, N.Y.: Matthew Bender & Co., 1949– . In looseleaf for updating.

Rohan, Patrick J. *Home Owners Association and Planned Unit Developments—Law and Practice*. New York: Matthew Bender & Co., 1981. Covers legal, economic, and other aspects of homeowners association and planned unit developments, ranging from historical developments and basic concepts through enabling legislation, regulations, creation of associations, financing and marketing, operations and management, liabilities, insurance, taxes, and termination. Supplemented by replacing ring binder units.

————, Bernard H. Goldstein, and Charles S. Bobis. *Real Estate Brokerage Law and Practice*. New York: Matthew Bender & Co., 1985– . In looseleaf for updating.

Tifany, Herbert Thorndike. *The Law of Real Property*. 3d ed. 6 vols. Edited by Basil Jones. Chicago: Callaghan and Co., 1939. Provides complete and comprehensive coverage of real estate law from the feudal system to date, covering estates, tenancies, trusts, future interest, ownerships, public rights, wills, tax sales, titles, mortgages, and much more. Contains table of cases and index. Kept up to date with cumulative pocket parts.

Zoning and Planning Report. (Clark Boardman) Looseleaf.

III · The Community

Tort

Tort is a term used in civil law, in contrast to criminal law, to denote an injury done to one person by another. The definitions of this term are at times inconsistent and confusing. It is said that if a person commits an act that he or she should not have committed, or does not act when he or she should have, and another person is injured by the act or its omission, a tort has been committed. Therefore, an act can be both a crime against the state and a tort against a person at the same time. For example, if John strikes Jane for no reason at all, he commits the crime of assault and battery, which is punishable by the state, and he also commits a tort against Jane. The injury need not be physical in nature against a person; the property of an individual can also be injured, as in the case of a person setting fire to someone's house or running an automobile across the lawn of a neighbor. A person's reputation or standing in a community can also be damaged, although here the rules are changed slightly.

Ancient rules of legal procedure were very rigid, and at times it was difficult to fit injuries into specific causes of action. Tort appears to have arisen out of the need to address these injuries and has resulted in a mixed bag of cases all being subsumed under one name. Pleadings in general are more relaxed now, and it is no longer very important to pick the exact cause of action in order to start a lawsuit. In many jurisdictions, a person can start an action under contract law, tort law, or both, without being more specific in his or her pleadings.

Whether or not a person meant to injure another is generally immaterial. Legal intent is declared if the actor knew that his or her action invaded the rights of another, even if he or she did not necessarily mean to injure the other person. It is said that malice may make a bad act worse but in itself does not constitute a tort. So if John harbored ill will against Jane but did nothing more, he has committed no tort. But in striking her, regardless of his feelings, he has injured her and committed a tort against her. Malice *is* necessary in some torts—for example, slander. Generally, however, it is the act itself that breaches duty and causes injury. Thus, moral turpitude is not actionable as a tort, for it can only make a bad act worse.

For a tort to exist, the duty required must be a legal duty and not merely a moral obligation. If there is no legal duty to act or to refrain from acting, then no grounds for tort exist. For instance, a person may be reprehensible for not coming to the aid of a neighbor in time of distress, but if there is only a moral obligation, he or she will not be held liable at law for his or her dereliction of this moral duty.

Interference with intangible relationships is also protected under the broad term *tort*. If "A" has a contract to perform services for "B," for example, and "C" approaches "B" in a malicious manner and with such false information as to induce "B" to refuse to perform the contract, "A" can sue "C" under tort law for interfering with the contract. In addition to personal property and contract rights, the rights of reputation in the community, privacy, marriage, social relationships, and free worship are also protected.

Introduction to Research Problem

A stricter liability is placed on people who are engaged in inherently dangerous activities. For example, a person who stores gasoline in huge storage tanks on his or her property is held responsible for seeing that the material does not injure a neighbor. This duty is based on the theory that everyone knows that the gasoline is dangerous, and therefore a person who takes upon him- or herself the task of storing the gasoline—knowing its dangers—must be held strictly responsible for its proper use and safety.

This theory of "strict liability" is frequently extended into the field of product liability. A manufacturer who produces a product, advertises its use, and sells it for that particular use, knowing that the product has certain latent dangers, can be held accountable under tort law for injuries suffered as a result of those inherent dangers. Strict liability is also extended into the area of instrumentalities dangerous to children; children, attracted by the play possibilities involved with the product and oblivious to any dangers, are protected under tort law from product injury.

Remember, for background material on the tools used in legal research, review the section titled "Where It Is Recorded," and for an example of the use of these tools in a legal research problem, see "How to Find It." See the Glossary for unfamiliar terms, and see Appendix A for abbreviations.

The legal explanations and the issues selected here are not comprehensive due to space limitations. Should the researcher become interested in a legal problem not covered by the background material, by the introduction, or by the research problem, he or she should note the question, and, using the procedures suggested in this book, perform his or her own legal research to discover the answer.

Research Problem

The research tools used in this problem consist of the Search Process Flow Chart, the CORP rule, an encyclopedia, and the digest system.

Alice, in Hawaii, discovers that one of her tenement houses is infested with roaches and other vermin. At the request of the two remaining tenants, she moves the tenants into other units until the house is fumigated. She hires RoachFree exterminators, who do a competent and careful job, placing heavy canvas over the house and sealing the house so that the fumes cannot escape. The exterminators fill the enclosure for forty-eight hours with very toxic poison to kill the pests, place signs on all sides warning of the danger, and add their name and telephone number to the signs.

The next day, four children—ages eight to thirteen—from the removed families remember the toys they left behind and return to the house. After consulting among themselves, two of the children decide that they will go inside if the other two will stand guard to see that no one interferes. Ten minutes after entering, one of the children staggers out, choking, and says that the other boy has collapsed inside and that he cannot be pulled out. The children race home and tell one of their mothers what has happened; she immediately calls the paramedics. As soon as they see the sign, the paramedics call RoachFree to find out what poison was used in the building. RoachFree dispatches a truck immediately, along with gas masks, and starts a search of the building.

While RoachFree is searching the building, the paramedics call their hospital to alert the hospital to the fact that the paramedics have two children who entered a building that was being fumigated. The paramedics give the hospital the name of the poison that was used and start treating the boy who escaped. As soon as the other boy is out of the building, both boys are rushed to the hospital. The boy who collapsed in the building dies, and the other one recovers but has considerable damage to his nervous system, requiring years of treatment.

The parents of the children go to their attorney to see if they have a case against the building owner or RoachFree for the death and injury their children suffered. The attorney asks, did either of the parties do something they should not have done, or did they neglect to do something they should have done? Obviously, the parties were dealing with dangerous materials, but does that make them absolute insurers against any possible harm to the general public? The lawyer also mentions something about an "attractive nuisance."

After the parents have gone home and the lawyer has made her notes, she calls you, gives you her notes, and requests that you investigate the laws of Hawaii concerning "attractive nuisances."

With the Search Process Flow Chart, the lawyer's notes, the CORP rule (C for cause of action, O for object, R for restitution, and P for parties), and your ubiquitous 4″ x 6″ cards packed in your briefcase, you head for the law library.

Finding a free desk in a quiet section of the library close to the materials you need, you open the briefcase, remove your working tools, look at the Search Process Flow Chart for a quick review of the research process, and then make out the fact card (Fig. 69).

The Search Process Flow Chart indicates that first you need to form a list of words to use in searching indexes to help you locate the primary law, i.e., statutes and cases. The first thing that comes to mind relating to Step 1 is the phrase given to you by Mr. Lawyer, *attractive nuisance*. You review the CORP rule. C stands for a cause of action, and this brings to mind *negligence*. O for object brings up the word *poison*. R for restitution suggests the word *damages*. And P for *parties* brings up *children*. However, remembering not to rely entirely on memory, you examine the Outline of the Law in a digest volume. You find the words *poison, nuisance,* and *damages* there, but they are already on your

2/12/84

Ms Lawyer   (Attractive Nuisance)   Parents

Facts: Alice, in Hawaii, discovers that one of her tenement houses is infested with roaches and other vermin. At the request of the two remaining tenants, she moves the tenants into other units until the house is fumigated. She hires RoachFree exterminators, who place heavy canvas over the house, thereby sealing it so that the fumes cannot escape. The exterminators fill the enclosure for forty-eight hours with very toxic poison to kill the pests, place signs on all sides warning of the danger, and add their name and telephone number to the signs.

The next day, two children from the removed families enter the house, leaving two others outside. The children range in age from eight to thirteen. Ten minutes after entering, one of the boys staggers out, choking, and says that the other boy has collapsed inside and cannot be pulled out. Paramedics are summoned, and as soon as they see the sign, they call RoachFree to find out what poison was used in the building. RoachFree dispatches a truck and begins a search of the building, while the paramedics alert the hospital to the incident and start treating the boy who escaped. Both boys are rushed to the hospital, where the boy who collapsed in the building dies. The other boy recovers, but he has considerable damage to his nervous system, which will require years of treatment.

Fig. 69.   Attractive Nuisance Fact Card

list. Next, in the same volume, you review the Digest Topics and discover the words *consumer protection, custom and usage, death,* and *health and environment.* From this list of nine words, it appears that *attractive nuisance, negligence,* and *poison* are the most likely to lead you to the law of interest.

The jurisdiction to be examined (Step 2) is Hawaii; and to help yourself feel secure in this area of the law, Step 3 suggests that you consult a legal encyclopedia or a textbook to get a general overview of the subject. Looking in the general index of *American Jurisprudence 2d (Am. Jur.2d)*, a legal encyclopedia, under "attractive nuisance," you find a reference to "Premises Liability." Turning to Premises Liability, Section 137 et seq., you put the general information on a card (Fig. 70).

From the looks of the Index information, most of the things involved in your problem are listed under Premises Liability in *Am. Jur.2d.* Checking the spines of the *Am. Jur.2d* volumes, you find that Premises Liability is in Volume 62. *Am. Jur.2d* is an annotated encyclopedia; therefore, the information set forth in this volume includes footnotes to cases from various jurisdictions. You begin making more cards for *Am. Jur.2d* (Fig. 71).

Now that you have some background on the subject, you are ready to follow Step 4, which is to frame and record an issue (Fig. 72).

Step 5 instructs you that the next investigation should be into statute and case finders. Checking the general index to the *Hawaiian Statutes* reveals that there is no listing for attractive nuisance and that nothing of interest is listed under "Nuisance, Dwellings" or under any other likely subject heading. For a

2/12/84
Ms Lawyer   (Attractive Nuisance)   Parents
Am. Jur.2d, Index under Premises Liability
Generally—Premises Liability, Sec. 137 et seq.
Barricades, Owner's duty to erect—Premises Liability, Sec. 167
Building & Construction—Building & Construction, Sec. 133; Premises Liability, Sec. 173
Contributory Negligence of Children—Premises Liability, Sec. 289
Precautions to be taken—Premises Liability, Sec. 167
Third Persons, conditions on property—Premises Liability, Sec. 185
Vacant House—Premises Liability, Sec. 173
Warnings—Premises Liability, Sec. 163 & 179

Fig. 70.   Am. Jur.2d, Premises Liability Card

2/12/84
Ms Lawyer   (Attractive Nuisance)   Parents
62 Am. Jur.2d, Premises Liability
Although some states have legislation covering the subject, not all jurisdictions find the "attractive nuisance" doctrine acceptable. In looking over the notes in Am. Jur.2d, you find no Hawaii cases. (Possibly the question has not been presented to a Hawaiian court.)
"Sec. 137. If certain conditions are met, an owner or occupant of land may be held responsible for injuries to trespassing or intruding children caused by dangerous conditions upon the premises, although there would be no liability if the trespasser had been an adult.
"This doctrine is also known as the 'Turntable Doctrine,' 'Infant Trespasser,' 'Dangerous Instrumentality,' 'Dangerous Agency,' 'Playground Rule,' 'Trap,' 'Implied Invitation,' or 'Special Rule.'
"One who maintains on his premises a condition dangerous to children of tender age by reason of their inability to appreciate the danger, is charged with using reasonable care to protect them against the dangers."
"Sec. 167. Special precautions are required in proportion to the foreseeable risk, such as making repairs, hiring guards, installing safety devices, erecting fences."
"Sec. 173. A vacant house is not an attractive nuisance per se."
"Sec. 185. A person responsible for creating or maintaining a dangerous condition on the premises of another may be held liable for injury to a child."
"Sec. 289. In some jurisdictions children below a certain age are deemed incapable of contributory negligence."

Fig. 71.   62 Am. Jur.2d, Premises Liability Card

2/12/84

Ms Lawyer   (Attractive Nuisance)   Parents

Issue: Is a house that is being fumigated, well covered, and posted
with warning signs considered an "attractive nuisance" to children
between the ages of eight and thirteen in Hawaii?

Fig. 72. Attractive Nuisance Issue Card

2/12/84

Ms Lawyer   (Attractive Nuisance)   Parents

Digests: Beginning with 8th Decennial, 1966–1976; 9th Decennial,
Part 1, 1976–1981; and General Digest, 6th Series, to date.

Negligence (1) Acts or omissions constituting negligence: (c) Condition and use of land, buildings, etc.

    🔑 32(4) Children and others under disability.

    🔑 33 Care to Trespassers:

        (1) In general.

        (3) Children.

    🔑 39 Places attractive to children.

Fig. 73. Attractive Nuisance, Digest System Card

case finder, you decide to choose West's *Eighth Decennial Digest* covering the years 1966–1976 as your starting point. If you had access to a *Hawaii Digest,* it might make more sense to use it instead, since the digest would cover only Hawaii decisions; but you realize that any Hawaii decisions will also be included in the units of West's American Digest System, since those units provide nationwide coverage. Also, by using the various decennial digests, you will be able to locate cases from other jurisdictions that might prove persuasive to the Hawaii courts if there are no Hawaii decisions on your particular legal point. You enter the headings you want to examine on another card (Fig. 73).

Checking these leads in all of the volumes listed above is a time-consuming task, but it is necessary if you are to have a complete search made of Hawaii case law. Bringing a search in the decennial digests up to date by using the *General Digest* is essential for thorough research.

In all, only two Hawaiian cases are found, both irrelevant. The first, under negligence 🔑 32(1) *Poston v. U.S.,* 396 F.2d 103 (1968), involves a backhoe operator cutting an electric line; and the second, under negligence 🔑 33(1) *Farrion v. Payaton,* 57 Hawaii 620, 562 P.2d 799 (1977), involves a dog bite. No Hawaii cases appear under the other key numbers noted. At this point in the search, you might consider pursuing whether there are relevant decisions from other states, especially if you decide that this is a case of first impression in Hawaii. In such instances, the court will often look to other jurisdictions for guidance; however, the court is in no way bound by decisions from other states.

Since you are doing only preliminary research at this time, you decide to stop your search for case law with what you have discovered in Hawaii.

There being no statutes to investigate and no cases to examine, Step 6 (check statutes and cases), Step 7 (check newly found statutes and cases), and Step 8 (Shepardizing) are all eliminated for this exercise, leaving you with Step 9—preparing a report of your research for Ms Lawyer. Once Ms Lawyer has studied the case, she will be able to appraise the legal situation. Once the legal issues have been resolved, however, the problems not covered by law must be addressed. These include the practicality of pursuing and the financial ability to pursue the issue to the desired conclusion. Having the law on your side does not necessarily mean that you have the power to enforce it.

Law Library Research Report

Title: Attractive Nuisance

Requested by: Ms Lawyer

Submitted by: (Your Name)

Date Submitted: February 14, 1984

Statement of Facts   Alice, in Hawaii, discovers that one of her tenement houses is infested with vermin; she therefore hires RoachFree exterminators. They place heavy canvas over the house to seal it, and they fill the enclosure for forty-eight hours with toxic poison, place signs on all sides warning of the danger, and add their name and telephone number to the signs.

The next day, two children, ages eight and thirteen, enter the house. Ten minutes after entering, one of the boys staggers out, choking, and says that the other boy has collapsed inside and cannot be pulled out. Paramedics are summoned. They immediately call RoachFree to find out what poison was used in the building. RoachFree searches the building while the paramedics alert the hospital. The boys are rushed to the hospital, where the boy who collapsed in the building dies. The other boy recovers but he has considerable damage to his nervous system, which will require years of treatment.

Question Presented   Is a house that is being fumigated, well covered, and posted with warning signs considered an "attractive nuisance" to children between the ages of eight and thirteen in Hawaii?

Brief Answer   There is no statute covering this subject in Hawaii, and there have been no cases involving attractive nuisance since 1966. It thus may be necessary to use statutes and cases from other jurisdictions, although some jurisdictions have rejected the doctrine of attractive nuisance.

Discussion   The Index of the *Hawaii Rev. Stat.* has been examined and makes no reference to the subject. The Digest System also has been examined from the *Eighth Decennial Digest* (1966–1976) through the *General Digest*, 6th Series, Volume 22, and no cases in Hawaii have been found covering the subject. Topics covered in the Digest System include the following:

Negligence (1) Acts or omissions constituting negligence:
(c) Condition and use of land, buildings, etc.
🔑 32(4) Children and others under disability.
🔑 33 Care to Trespassers:
(1) In general.
(3) Children.
🔑 39 Places attractive to children.

Bibliography

(Note: The looseleaf materials listed below may set forth the best overview and provide the most up-to-date information. They are not completely described here because the services are tremendously expensive for individuals to purchase, the titles identify the topics, their formats are relatively similar, and most of these materials can be found in law libraries.

If a book cannot be found in your library or in the nearest law library, ask your librarian if it can be obtained through interlibrary loan.)

Consumer Product Safety Guide. (CCH) Looseleaf.

Dooley, James A. *Modern Tort Law, Liabilities & Litigation.* 4 vols. Chicago: Callaghan & Co., 1977. Kept up to date with annual pocket supplements.

Harper, Fowler, Fleming James, and Oscar S. Gray. *The Law of Torts.* 6 vols. 2d ed. Boston: Little, 1986. The standard treatise in the field; widely accepted. Covers all aspects of tort law, including analysis of both cases and statutes. Heavily footnoted. Kept up to date with annual pocket supplements.

Malone, Wex S. *Torts in a Nutshell.* St. Paul, Minn.: West, 1979. A brief outline of the law, including family relationships, social relationships, and trade relationships. Includes table of cases and notes.

Minzer, Marilyn, ed. dir. *Damages in Tort Actions.* 9 vols. New York: Matthew Bender & Co., 1982– . Discusses damages in the context of many different types of actions and the types of damages that may be awarded (e.g., pain and suffering, loss of earnings). Includes practice commentaries and a separate practice guide volume (e.g., preparing for trial, trial techniques, and forms). Separate volumes examine the evaluation and proof of economic loss. In looseleaf for updating.

Page, Joseph A. *The Law of Premises Liability.* Cincinnati, Ohio: Anderson, 1976. Provides comprehensive coverage of the law involving real estate and torts, including trespassers, tenants, etc. With footnotes, bibliography, table of cases, and index.

Pegalis, Steven E., and Harvey F. Wachsman. *American Law of Medical Malpractice.* Rochester, N.Y.: Lawyers Cooperative/Bancroft-Whitney, 1980. A general overview focusing on physicians' liabilities and duties, and finishing specifically with obstetrics. Contains a mock trial; kept up to date with pocket parts. Future volumes highlighting other subjects expected.

Product Liability Reports. (CCH) Looseleaf.

Product Safety & Liability Reporter. (BNA) Looseleaf.

Prosser, William L. *Prosser and Keeton on Torts.* 5th ed. Edited by Page Keeton. St. Paul, Minn.: West, 1984. The standard one-volume work in the field.

Rosenthal, Douglas E. *Lawyer and Client: Who's in Charge?* New Brunswick, N.J.: Transaction Bks., 1977; Rutgers Univ., 1974. An examination of the problem of how much a client should participate in the decision making encountered in legal actions, especially in cases of personal injury. In contrast with the usual passive role played by the client, the author suggests that most clients can understand what is going on and should acquaint themselves with the problems in order to participate actively in the decisions, to produce a more effective outcome. Contains tables, figures, appendixes, and index.

Schwartz, Victor. *Comparative Negligence.* 2d ed. Charlottesville, Va.: Michie Co., 1986.

Speiser, Stuart M., Charles F. Krause, and Alfred W. Gans. *The American Law of Torts.* Rochester, N.Y.: Lawyers Cooperative/Bancroft-Whitney, 1983– . Gives comprehensive coverage of all substantive aspects of tort law, with discussion of all leading cases and references to all decisions from all jurisdictions decided from 1975 to date. Includes bibliographies of books and articles after every chapter. Kept up to date with annual pocket part supplements.

Criminal Law

In a broad sense, criminal law includes the activities of legislatures, which pass criminal statutes; of executive departments, which enforce them; and of the court systems, which interpret statutes and apply them to individual cases. The department most consistently involved in criminal law is the Criminal Justice Department of the executive branch. The Criminal Justice Department has the responsibility of enforcing the laws passed by the legislature and of presenting cases to the courts for decisions and sentencing.

Philosophically, society has the right to protect itself and its members from antisocial acts. Legally, the power to so act comes from the constitutions of the federal and state governments, which assign to the legislatures the power to define crimes and to establish punishments for them. Cities, counties, towns, villages, and districts in turn derive their powers to define and punish crimes from the state legislatures.

The three basic aims of criminal law are to suppress crime, protect the public, and punish criminals. It is sometimes argued that another aim of the criminal justice system is to rehabilitate the criminal. Most people would agree that no effective method for rehabilitating criminals has yet been instituted, although the criminal justice establishment gives lip service to this theory.

A criminal is a person who commits an offense, or violates a public law. A single act may be both a crime, which is punishable by the state, and a tort, for which the injured individual can sue to collect damages in a civil action against the perpetrator. A single act may also result in the commission of more than one crime, and the person committing the single act can be tried and punished for each of the crimes committed by this single act.

It is the offense against the public that is punished by the state in its own name. The crime need not be an immoral act; frequently, in fact, morality has nothing to do with the crime. Some crimes may be common-law crimes, although most have now been codified into statutes. For a person to be guilty of a statutory crime, the statute must have been in effect before the so-called criminal act was committed. In general, the states administer criminal justice, although the Congress has preempted the states in certain areas and defined a considerable number of acts as federal crimes.

Statutes set various degrees of crimes, depending on the circumstances and conditions surrounding a particular act. According to common law, a person committing the act becomes a principal in the first degree. One who aids the person in committing a crime, such as a lookout or a driver, is a principal in the second degree. This model has been altered in most states, so that all persons involved in the crime are now treated as principals. One who is involved in any portion of the criminal activity before its actual commission (e.g., aiding in the planning, providing equipment) is considered an accessory before the fact, and a person involved in any portion of the criminal activity after the crime has been committed (e.g., concealing either the loot or the criminal) becomes an accessory after the fact.

There are two basic types of crimes: felony and misdemeanor. Originally, a felon forfeited all lands and goods, but this stipulation has been abolished in all jurisdictions. Felonies are identified by the type of punishment that can be imposed for the commission of a certain act. Basically, a felony is an act that can be punished by death or by imprisonment in a penitentiary. However, the fact that a judge gives a lesser punishment for a crime does not necessarily identify the crime as a misdemeanor; that crime still may be a felony, depending upon the punishment that *can* be imposed. A misdemeanor is any crime that is not considered a felony. Most of the common-law felonies are carried over into the statutes, and the statutes have added many other felonies as well.

The age of the person committing a crime is taken into consideration in common law. Children under seven years of age are conclusively presumed incapable of committing a crime; and although children between the ages of seven and fourteen also are presumed incapable, the presumption can be rebutted. From the age of fourteen on, children are presumed capable of committing crimes. However, states have made numerous revisions in the common law concerning age.

Today states stipulate that a person must have the mental capacity to commit a crime, i.e., the perpetrator must be a free agent, have the choice between right and wrong, and choose to act wrongly. In Old English law, insanity was not a defense against committing a crime but instead was ground for a pardon. In modern law, the insane cannot commit crimes because they know not what they are doing, and intent is missing. For some crimes intent is disregarded, however, and legal intent is found by presuming that a person intended the foreseeable results of his or her actions, regardless of his or her personal thoughts. A simple example of legal intent is the violation of a speed limit law.

Several states have now passed laws compensating the victims of crimes. Where these acts have been adopted, it is customary to stipulate that such reimbursement provides the entire remedy available and that the victim then cannot sue for damages in a civil action.

Introduction to Research Problem

For anyone to set fire to buildings and property is illegal. Such an act is called "arson," and anyone convicted of the act can be imprisoned or fined. Arson is involved in the burning of buildings either by or on behalf of the owners in order to collect insurance money, or by individuals who get a perverse thrill out of seeing things burn. At times arson is used to cover up other crimes, such as murder or robbery. The fact that a person owns the burned-down property does not eliminate the possibility that he or she committed the arson, especially if the property is covered by insurance. An arsonist who has burned his or her own property and who uses the mails to send in claims to receive a check from the insurance company is performing an act of interstate commerce, which comes under the control of the United States government. The specific act in this instance is called mail fraud.

For background material on the tools used in legal research, review the section titled "Where It Is Recorded," and for an example of the use of these tools in a legal research problem, see "How to Find It." See the Glossary for unfamiliar terms and Appendix A for abbreviations.

The legal explanations and the issues selected here are not comprehensive due to space limitations. Should the researcher become interested in a legal problem not covered by the background material, by the introduction, or by the research problem, he or she should note the question, and, using the procedures suggested in this book, perform his or her own legal research to discover the answer.

Research Problem

The research tools used in this problem consist of the Search Process Flow Chart, the CORP rule, statutes, citators, and reporters.

Flash has been marginally criminal all of his life. He is intelligent, streetwise, and educated, and he pushes the laws to their limit whenever possible. This behavior sometimes seems like a game he plays to see how far he can go without getting caught. His activities span the spectrum, ranging from car sales and oil speculations, to investing in grain elevators, silver mines, the bonds of various foreign countries, and, most recently, real estate.

Using a portion of his profits from these various ventures, Flash has decided to present a facade of respectability by becoming a "land baron." He therefore purchases several multiple dwellings in Pennsylvania, some industrial buildings, a loft, and a garage, all of which he insures to the limit or above with an insurance company in Maine. The first problem arises when an oil truck, left in the garage overnight for repairs, explodes, burning the garage and its contents to the ground. After collecting from his insurance company, Flash purchases a tavern–rooming house.

The next dramatic event occurs when some oily waste rags spontaneously burst into flames in Flash's loft, resulting in another complete loss and another good settlement from the Maine insurance company. The fires are investigated by the insurance company and by the fire marshall; and in spite of some suspicious information, there is insufficient evidence for refusing to pay the claims.

Flash puts the money from the loft into the tavern–rooming house and inflates the insurance to $475,000. The rooming house is usually about 75 percent occupied, and the tavern produces extraordinary income—at first. As time goes on, the novelty of the tavern dissipates, and patronage falls off, partly due to the bartender's personality. In an attempt to build back the bar business,

Flash takes over the bartender's position. This new responsibility requires late hours, and usually Flash is the last person to leave in the early morning hours.

About a month later, Flash is awakened at five o'clock in the morning by the police and is informed that his tavern–rooming house is burning. Fortunately, the tenants have escaped, but again, the building is a complete loss. The insurance company, suspicious, quizzes him about his loss, especially about several valuable paintings listed as contents of the tavern, which Flash claims went up in smoke with the building. Nothing can be proven, and arson cannot definitely be established, so Flash finally receives a check for a compromised figure of $425,000 mailed from insurance company headquarters in Maine to Flash in Pennsylvania.

While visiting an auction gallery, one of the agents of the insurance company stumbles across one of the pictures Flash claimed had been burned. Again questions are raised, but Flash denies having any knowledge of how the picture survived and ended up in the gallery. Still there is insufficient evidence to establish arson, but the insurance company becomes very upset and asks its attorneys if they can find some way to take care of Flash.

Mr. Attorney, a sharp country lawyer from Maine, considers a charge of mail fraud. To do research into the question, he calls his research assistant, Ms Dash.

Ms Dash, an efficient character, picks up her Search Process Flow Chart, her 4″ x 6″ cards, and her CORP rule, and promptly places the known facts on her cards for easy reference (Fig. 74).

Ms Dash glances quickly at her Search Process Flow Chart, reviews the CORP rule *(C* for cause of action, *O* for object, *R* for restitution, and *P* for

---

10/20/80

Mr. Attorney   (Mail Fraud)   Insurance Co.

Facts: Flash, a resident of Pennsylvania, purchased several parcels of real estate in Pennsylvania, insuring them all with Insurance Co. headquartered in Maine. One purchase, a garage, was destroyed by fire, resulting in a settlement from the insurance company. Shortly after the settlement, Flash purchased a tavern–rooming house. A loft owned by Flash, also heavily insured with our client, was destroyed in a second fire of suspicious origin, although arson could not be established. Flash insured his tavern–rooming house for $475,000 to cover the cost and renovations, and specifically to include several valuable paintings. The tavern–rooming house burned under suspicious circumstances, but again arson could not be established. The insurance company settled the claim and sent a check from their headquarters in Maine to Flash, the owner, in Pennsylvania in the amount of $425,000 on November 7, 1977.

At a later date, an alert agent for Insurance Co. located one of the pictures Flash had claimed was destroyed in the fire. The painting was on sale for $87,500 in an art gallery. Flash denied having any knowledge of how the painting survived and ended up in the gallery.

Fig. 74.   Mail Fraud Fact Card

parties), and decides that the only word she needs (Step 1) is *mail fraud*, a term provided by her boss. The jurisdiction (Step 2) would be federal because the federal government controls the mails and makes the laws concerning mail. Step 3 (conducting a general overview using a text or encyclopedia) can be bypassed at this point in the research because Ms Dash's boss has told her that all the background information she needs is contained in the *United States Code Annotated (U.S.C.A.)*. She also realizes that if she becomes confused by what she finds in the *U.S.C.A.*, she can always return to Step 3 and refer to an encyclopedia or treatise for background information. Framing the issue (Step 4) is next, and this information she enters on one of her 4" x 6" cards (Fig. 75).

Step 5 (searching statute finders) in this case involves looking through indexes of the federal statutes concerning mail fraud. Ms Dash proceeds to the excellent law library provided by the insurance company and settles down with her cards at a desk near the *U.S.C.A.*. In the general index under "Mail or Mailing," she runs across "Fraud," and under this heading she finds "Schemes, etc., to defraud or for obtaining money or property by means of fraudulent pretenses, etc., penalties, 18 U.S.C.A., Sec. 1341, 1342." Also, under "Sentences and Punishment" is "Swindles, etc., 18 U.S.C.A., Sec. 1341". She adds this information to a card for quick reference (Fig. 76).

Returning the index to the shelf, Ms Dash brings back 18 U.S.C.A., Sec. 1081-1690, Crimes and Criminal Procedures, and checks the original volume. Volume 18 is dated 1966, but there is a supplementary pamphlet for 1966 through 1980 that she also takes. Following Step 6, she turns to Section 1341 to make her card (Fig. 77). (*Note:* A new volume was issued in late 1984, and

---

10/20/80
Mr. Attorney   (Mail Fraud)   Insurance Co.
Issue: Does the receipt of a settlement check by mail from an out-of-state insurance company for a fraudulent insurance claim constitute mail fraud?

Fig. 75.   Mail Fraud Issue Card

10/20/80
Mr. Attorney   (Mail Fraud)   Insurance Co.
U.S.C.A. (1971) General Index, Mail or Mailing.
    Schemes, etc., to defraud or for obtaining money or property by means of fraudulent pretenses, etc.
Penalties, 18 U.S.C.A., Sec. 1341, 1342.
Sentences and Punishment.
Swindles, etc., 18 U.S.C.A., Sec. 1341.

Fig. 76.   Mail Fraud, 18 U.S.C.A. Index Card

10/20/80

Mr. Attorney   (Mail Fraud)   Insurance Co.

18 U.S.C.A., Sec. 1341, Frauds and Swindles

"Whoever having devised or intending to devise any scheme or artifice to defraud, or for obtaining money or property by means of false or fraudulent pretense, representations, or promises ... for the purpose of executing such scheme or artifice or attempting to do so, places in any post office or authorized depository for mail matter, any matter or thing whatever to be sent or delivered by the Postal Service, or takes or receives therefrom, any such matter or thing, or knowingly causes to be delivered by mail according to the direction thereon, ... any such matter or thing, shall be fined not more than $1,000 or imprisoned not more than five years, or both."

Notes of Decisions from the Supp. Pamphlet.

Insurance Fraud 53b.

Notes of Decisions from Title 18.

Note 44, Intent, Generally.

"Fraudulent Intent, as a mental element of crime, may be inferred from a series of seemingly isolated acts if they are sufficiently numerous, even though each act standing by itself may seem unimportant." Nassan v. U.S., 126 F.2d 613 (C.C.A., Md., 1942).

Note 63: "Reasonable Probability of Use. Under this section prohibiting the use of the mails to defraud, it is immaterial whether the probably likely use of the mails was contemplated either at the onset or during performance of the scheme." Abbott v. U.S., 239 F.2d 310 (C.C.A., Tex., 1956).

Note 64: "Gist of Offense. If a person devises a scheme to defraud in the execution of which a letter is mailed, the crime of 'Using the Mails in Executing a Scheme to Defraud' is committed, and it is immaterial whether the person or persons devising the scheme had intended to use the mails or whether anybody was actually defrauded." Stapp v. U.S., 120 F.2d 898 (C.C.A., Tex., 1941).

Note 71: "Person to Whom Mail Sent. The letter need not be to or from intended victim." Stewart v. U.S., 300 F. 769 (C.C.A., Mo., 1924).

Fig. 77.   Mail Fraud, 18 U.S.C.A., Sec. 1341 Card

by the time this reference was checked in 1985, the supplementary pamphlet no longer existed. The references to cases found in the pamphlet (including the ones used in this example) apparently were not all copied into the new volume.)

With these notes, Ms Dash proceeds to investigate the cases she has found in order to build a case against Flash, and these cases are entered on her cards (Figs. 78–81).

Nothing Ms Dash has found in the cases indicates that she should examine further cases (Step 7), so she proceeds to Step 8 and Shepardizes the cases she entered on the cards. *Shepard's Citations* gives her a history of each case from the time of its decision to date by listing all cases that have referred to the prime case, identifying them by numbered paragraph in the case, and indicating dispositions with specific letters. This step returns her to Step 6, and she examines each of the cases that she found in *Shepard's Citations*.

10/20/80

Mr. Attorney   (Mail Fraud)   Insurance Co.
Stapp v. U.S., 120 F.2d 898 (5th Cir., 1941)
    Foster, C.J., at 899(1) states, "The law is well settled that if a person devises a scheme to defraud, in the execution of which a letter is mailed, the crime denounced by the statute is committed. It is immaterial whether the person or persons had intended to use the mails or whether anybody was actually defrauded."
    Shepardize: x 152 F.2d 59
                x 51 F.Supp. 15

Fig. 78. Stapp v. U.S. Card

10/20/80

Mr. Attorney   (Mail Fraud)   Insurance Co.
Abbott v. U.S., 239 F.2d 310 (C.A., Tex., 1956)
    John R. Brown, J., stated at 314(6-7), ". . . immaterial whether the probable, likely use of the mails was contemplated either at the outset or during the performance of the scheme."
    Shepardize: x 253 F.2d 109
                x 265 F.2d 705
                x 282 F.2d 204
                x 307 F.2d 557
                x 259 F.S. 570

Fig. 79. Abbott v. U.S. Card

For *Stapp v. U.S.*, 120 F.2d 898 (1941), Ms Dash makes two cards, one for each of the two cases she found through Shepardizing (Figs. 82 and 83).

For *Abbott v. U.S.*, 239 F.2d 310 (1956), Ms Dash makes five cards, one for each of the five cases she found in *Shepard's Citations* under the Abbott case (Figs. 84–88).

For *Nassan v. U.S.*, 126 F.2d 613 (4th Cir., 1942), Ms Dash makes two cards, one for each of the cases she discovered while Shepardizing the Nassan case (Figs. 89 and 90).

For *Stewart v. U.S.*, 300 F. 769 (8th Cir., 1924), Ms Dash finds one case by Shepardizing and makes a card for it (Fig. 91), even though this case probably will not be used in her report. The case does not seem to be quite on the point she wishes to make, but that fact can be decided later.

Ms Dash repeats this process, Shepardizing the cases she has found and recorded. Because she finds nothing new, we will not repeat the process of placing all of the newly decided cases on cards; the process is already sufficiently outlined here.

Ms Dash's next act, according to Step 9, is to make a report of her discoveries to her employer, Mr. Attorney, which she does in the form of a

10/20/80

Mr. Attorney   (Mail Fraud)   Insurance Co.

Nassan v. U.S., 126 F.2d 613 (4th Cir., Md., 1942)

At 615(1), "This court has had recent occasion to consider the element of fraudulent intent as used in the Mail Fraud Statute. In Aiken v. U.S. (4th Cir.), 108 F.2d 182, 183, Judge Dobie said: 'Fraudulent intent, as a mental element of crime (it has been observed), is too often difficult to prove by direct and convincing evidence. In many cases it must be inferred from a series of seemingly isolated acts and instances which have been . . . aptly described as badges of fraud. When these are sufficiently numerous, they may in their totality properly justify an inference of a fraudulent intent; and this is true even though each act or instance, standing by itself, may seem rather unimportant. . . .' "

Shepardize: x 155 F.2d 744
        x 279 F.2d 179

Fig. 80.   Nassan v. U.S. Card

10/20/80

Mr. Attorney   (Mail Fraud)   Insurance Co.

Stewart v. U.S., 300 F. 769 (8th Cir., Mo., 1924)

Sanborn, J., at 775, stated, ". . . it is not indispensable that the letter mailed in executing such a scheme . . . should be directed or sent to or received from one of the intended victims of fraud. Preeman v. U.S., 244 F. 1, 156 C.C.A. 429."

Shepardize: x 34 F.S. 987D

Fig. 81.   Stewart v. U.S. Card

10/20/80

Mr. Attorney   (Mail Fraud)   Insurance Co.

Sheridan v. U.S., 152 F.2d 57 (6th Cir., 1945)

Martin, J., at 59(2) cited the Stapp case in confirmation of a point of law he made in the case he was then deciding.

Fig. 82.   Sheridan v. U.S. Card

law library research report. Mr. Attorney will be able to size up the legal aspects of the case and report to his client. Once the legal issues have been resolved, the problems not covered by law must be addressed. These involve the practicality of pursuing and the financial ability to pursue the issue to the desired

---

10/20/80

Mr. Attorney   (Mail Fraud)   Insurance Co.
U.S. v. Decker et al., 51 F.Supp. 15 (D.Md., 1943)
    Chestnut, J., at 19 distinguished the facts in the Stapp case from the facts in the case he was then deciding.

Fig. 83. U.S. v. Decker et al. Card

10/20/80

Mr. Attorney   (Mail Fraud)   Insurance Co.
Gregory v. U.S., 253 F.2d 104 (5th Cir., 1958)
    John R. Brown, J., at 109 used the Abbott case as a precedent for his decision in Paragraph 3 of the case he was deciding.

Fig. 84. Gregory v. U.S. Card

10/20/80

Mr. Attorney   (Mail Fraud)   Insurance Co.
U.S. v. Froman, 265 F.2d 702 (2d Cir., 1959)
    Hincks, J., at 705 used both the Gregory case and the Abbott case as precedents for Paragraphs 3 and 4 of his decision.

Fig. 85. U.S. v. Froman Card

conclusion. Having the law on one's side does not necessarily mean that one has the power to enforce it.

Law Library Research Report

Title: Mail Fraud

Requested by: Mr. Attorney

Submitted by: Ms Dash

Date Submitted: October 20, 1980

Statement of Facts   Flash, a resident of Pennsylvania, purchased several parcels of real estate in Pennsylvania, insuring them all with Insurance Co. headquartered in Maine. One purchase, a garage, was destroyed by fire, resulting in a settlement from the insurance company. Shortly after the settlement, Flash purchased a tavern–rooming house. A loft owned by Flash, also heavily insured with our client, was destroyed in a second fire of suspicious origin, although

---

10/20/80
Mr. Attorney   (Mail Fraud)   Insurance Co.
Hooper v. Mountain States Securities Corp., 282 F.2d 195 (5th Cir., 1960)
    John R. Brown, J., at 204 used both the Gregory case and the Abbott case in support of Paragraph 10 of his decision.

Fig. 86.   Hooper v. Mountain States Securities Corp. Card

10/20/80
Mr. Attorney   (Mail Fraud)   Insurance Co.
Dranow v. U.S., 307 F.2d 545 (8th Cir., 1962)
    Ridge, J., at 557 quoted from the Abbott case to support his decision in Paragraphs 7 and 8.

Fig. 87.   Dranow v. U.S. Card

10/20/80
Mr. Attorney   (Mail Fraud)   Insurance Co.
U.S. v. Beckley, 259 F.Supp. 567 (D.C., Ga., 1965)
    Sloan, J., at 570 cited the Abbott case in support of his decision in Paragraph 1 of the case he was deciding.

Fig. 88.   U.S. v. Beckley Card

arson could not be established. Flash insured his tavern–rooming house for $475,000 to cover renovations and, specifically, several valuable paintings. The tavern–rooming house burned under suspicious circumstances, but again arson could not be established. The insurance company settled the claim and sent a check from its headquarters in Maine to Flash, the owner, in Pennsylvania in the amount of $425,000 on November 7, 1977.

At a later date, an alert agent for Insurance Co. located one of the pictures Flash had claimed was destroyed in the fire. Flash denied having any knowledge of how the painting survived and ended up in the gallery.

Question Presented   Assuming that Flash knew that a picture found in the gallery had not burned, does his making out an insurance claim for its destruction and receiving a check covering its loss mailed by the insurance company in Maine to him in Pennsylvania constitute mail fraud?

```
                              10/20/80
Mr. Attorney              (Mail Fraud)              Insurance Co.
Deaver v. U.S., 155 F.2d 740 (D.D.C., 1946)
    Clark, J., at 744 used the Nassan case as precedent for the state-
ment, "The fraudulent nature of the plan may be inferred from a
series of isolated acts."
```

Fig. 89.   Deaver v. U.S. Card

```
                              10/20/80
Mr. Attorney              (Mail Fraud)              Insurance Co.
U.S. v. Vandersee, 279 F.2d 176 (3d Cir., 1960)
    McLaughlin, J., at 179 used the Nassan case as a precedent for
the proposition that a fraudulent intent may be inferred from a
series of seemingly isolated acts.
```

Fig. 90.   U.S. v. Vandersee Card

```
                              10/20/80
Mr. Attorney              (Mail Fraud)              Insurance Co.
U.S. v. Leche, 34 F.Supp. 982 (Dist. Ct., W.D., La., 1940)
    Dawkins, J., at 987 distinguished Paragraph 2 of the Stewart case
from the one he was then deciding.
```

Fig. 91.   U.S. v. Leche Card

Brief Answer   There is a strong possibility that Flash can be indicted for mail fraud on the facts as presented. A sufficiently strong case of mail fraud can be built on circumstantial evidence consisting of a series of seemingly unrelated acts to show fraudulent intent, and it is immaterial whether the use of the mails was contemplated as long as the mails were actually used.

Discussion   18 U.S.C.A., Sec. 1341, Frauds and Swindles states that,

> Whoever having devised or intending to devise any scheme or artifice to defraud, or for obtaining money or property by means of false or fraudulent pretenses, representations, or promises . . . for the purpose of executing such scheme or artifice, or attempting to do so, places in any post office or authorized depository for mail matter, any matter or thing whatever to be sent or delivered by the Postal Service, or takes or receives therefrom, any such matter or thing, or knowingly causes to be delivered by mail according

to the directions thereon, . . . any such matter or thing, shall be fined not more than $1,000 or imprisoned not more than five years, or both.

A "fraudulent intent," as a mental element of crime, may be inferred from a series of seemingly isolated acts if they are sufficiently numerous, even though each act standing by itself may seem unimportant. *Nassan v. U.S.*, 126 F.2d 613 (C.C.A., Md., 1942)

Under this section prohibiting the use of the mails to defraud, it is immaterial whether the probable, likely use of the mails was contemplated either at the onset or during the performance of the scheme. *Abbott v. U.S.*, 239 F.2d 310 (C.A., Tex., 1956)

If a person devises a scheme to defraud in the execution of which a letter is mailed, the crime of "Using the Mails in Executing a Scheme to Defraud" is committed, and it is immaterial whether the person or persons devising the scheme had intended to use the mails or whether anybody was actually defrauded. *Stapp v. U.S.*, 120 F.2d 898 (C.C.A., Tex., 1941)

Bibliography

(Note: The looseleaf materials listed below may set forth the best overview and provide the most up-to-date information. They are not completely described here because the services are tremendously expensive for individuals to purchase, the titles identify the topics, their formats are relatively similar, and most of these materials can be found in law libraries.

If a book cannot be found in your library or in the nearest law library, ask your librarian if it can be obtained through interlibrary loan.)

Amsterdam, Anthony G. *Trial Manual for the Defense of Criminal Cases—4.* 4th ed. 2 vols. Philadelphia: Amer. Law Inst.-Amer. Bar Assn., 1984- . Includes bibliographies and index. In looseleaf for updating.

Brent, Stephen, and Sharon P. Stiller. *Handling Drunk Driving Cases.* Rochester, N.Y.: Lawyers Cooperative/Bancroft-Whitney, 1985.

Cook, Joseph G. *Constitutional Rights of the Accused.* 2d ed. 4 vols. Rochester, N.Y.: Lawyers Cooperative/Bancroft-Whitney, 1985–1986. Kept up to date by pocket parts.

Criminal Law Reporter. (BNA) Looseleaf.

Erickson, William H., William D. Neighbors, and B. J. George, Jr. *United States Supreme Court Cases and Comments: Criminal Law and Procedure.* New York: Matthew Bender & Co., 1985- . Includes index. In looseleaf for updating.

Israel, Jerold H. *Criminal Procedure: Constitutional Limitations in a Nutshell.* St. Paul, Minn.: West, 1988.

La Fave, Wayne R., and Austin W. Scott, Jr. *Criminal Law.* 2d ed. 3 vols. St. Paul, Minn.: West, 1984. Kept up to date with pocket supplements.

Loewy, Arnold H. *Criminal Law in a Nutshell.* 2d ed. St. Paul, Minn.: West, 1987.

McNeely, R. L., and Carl E. Pope, eds. *Race, Crime, and Criminal Justice.* Beverly Hills, Calif.: Sage, 1981. Covers race-related problems and criminal justice, with proposals for change. Contains author biographies, chapter references, and tables.

Naftalis, Gary P., ed. *White Collar Crimes.* Philadelphia: Amer. Law Inst.-Amer. Bar Assn. Committee on Continuing Professional Ed., 1980. Covers antitrust violations as crimes, conspiracies, federal securities laws, prosecutions, tax evasion, extortion, corporate criminal liability, legal representation, testimony, and sentencing. Includes subject index, tables, and notes.

The Practical Lawyer's Manual on Criminal Law and Procedure. Philadelphia: Amer. Law Inst.-Amer. Bar Assn., 1985.

Ringel, William E. *Searches and Seizures, Arrests and Confessions.* 2d ed. 2 vols. Prepared by Justin D. Franklin and Steven C. Bell. New York: Clark Boardman, 1980, 1981, 1982. Written for lawyers, judges, and law enforcement officials to present current law as interpreted by the various courts. Includes table of cases, general index, and footnotes. Ring binder; updated annually.

Search & Seizure Law Report. (Clark Boardman) Looseleaf.

Singer, Shelvin, and Marshall J. Hartman. *Constitutional Criminal Procedure Handbook.* New York: Wiley, 1986. Kept up to date with pocket supplements.

Torcia, Charles E. *Wharton's Criminal Law.* 14th ed. 3 vols. Rochester, N.Y.: Lawyers Cooperative, 1978. Provides complete textbook coverage of criminal law, covering mostly case law. With footnotes and general index. Updated with cumulative pocket parts.

Way, H. Frank. *Criminal Justice and the American Constitution.* North Scituate, Mass.: Duxbury, 1980. Covers constitutional law, arrest, search, seizure, self-incrimination, grand jury, bail, pleas and bargaining, double jeopardy, sentencing and punishment, and the legal rights of prisoners in a textbook/casebook format. Contains notes, Constitution of the United States, table of cases, and index.

Environment

At the time of the signing of the Constitution, our country consisted of vast reserves of natural resources and few people. The natural resources were so abundant, and seemingly inexhaustible, that there was a tendency to waste them. Forests were burned, topsoil stripped, land worn out by failure to rotate crops, open sores created by pit and strip mining, and wastes deposited on the land and in the rivers and lakes. As the population increased, so did the devastation, and warnings appeared indicating that we really did not have endless reserves of forests, minerals, wildlife, rivers, and lakes. Outcroppings of underground fires from mining operations burned out of control. Rivers and lakes, including the Great Lakes, became polluted by the dumping of wastes from cities and factories, which endangered the supply of drinking water. Fish and the thriving fishing industry on the lakes were destroyed. In the expansive farmlands of the midwestern United States, destructive farming practices made the land unproductive, resulting in the Great Dust Bowl that drove thousands of farmers into unemployment.

This devastation has not been limited to the United States. Observe how the heavy logging operations in Haiti have removed almost all forms of flora and fauna from various areas of that country. Some scientists for years have condemned our lack of interest in preserving our planet for future generations, exclaiming that the world will soon be unable to feed its inhabitants, that our air will be unfit to breathe, that our water supply will be polluted and diminished, and that our birds and animal life will be depleted due to the heavy and indiscriminate use of insecticides, but these scientists are largely voices crying in the wilderness.

Attempts have been made to clean up the environment. Some have been successful, such as the cleanup of the Great Lakes, and some, not so successful, such as the water use situation in Florida, where vast amounts of water are used in the phosphate industry. A variety of relatively small organizations, including the Audubon Society and the Sierra Club, have started campaigns to save the wilderness, the birds, and the alligator, and they have been successful up to a point.

The jolt that finally made Americans realize the gravity of the situation and understand that our resources really are limited was the gas crunch. When people witnessed the price of gasoline going from thirty-nine cents a gallon to a dollar and a half or more, when they parked in line for hours to get gasoline for their automobiles, and when they couldn't get it, a new level of awareness was realized.

The exhaustion of regional, national, and worldwide resources is too important to be left in the hands of corporations and individuals whose declared objective is to make money. Some means of control must be established; and in this country, such control must stem from the Constitution and the statutes.

Governments have always claimed the power to perform all acts that are necessary to protect and to promote the health and safety of the public. This claim is expressed in legal language in the case of *U.S. v. Sutter*, D.C. (Cal.), 127 F. Supp. 109 on page 118, where it is written that the state is organized for the purpose of government, that it must be able to defend itself from destruction, and for that purpose its citizens must be well and able bodied. From this case it is easy to see how the state has expanded its control over public health and safety, decreeing that regulations should be liberally construed. And this aim has been fulfilled. In keeping its citizens "well and able bodied" in order to defend the state, vast networks of administrative bodies have been established, creating millions of jobs and adding millions of dollars from tax assessments. Sanitary and health districts have been established by states as mechanisms to carry out this public purpose, and these districts have such duties and powers as the legislature gives them. Boards of health, health departments, health officers, and the like have come into existence to handle the health problems created by an increased population. The spread of communicable diseases has called for the eradication and control of those diseases in order to prevent their spread. This goal has led to the establishment of new methods to discover sources of disease, the closing of public buildings, the requiring of vaccinations and quarantines, and the use of other health measures that are deemed reasonable.

This program of protecting public health has been expanded to cover building safety codes, fire regulations, the condemnation of buildings as unsafe or unhealthful, the institution of housing regulations, and the growth of redevelopment authorities to clear slum areas. The program also extends into government control over occupations such as those practiced by barbers, beauty operators, animal care workers, and undertakers. Other health measures involve birth and death reports, burial permits and permits to transport dead bodies, control of the sale of contraceptive devices, garbage collection, water fluoridation, bathing and swimming codes, tobacco and its advertising, places of mass gatherings, and the list goes on.

Frequently, the agency developing, supervising, and running a public health program is also the agency charged with enforcing regulations. So, for example, the board of health that is acting under a city ordinance giving it the power to establish rules for healthful housing is also charged with seeing that those rules are followed, usually by making inspections and reports. If the board's recommendations are not followed, the board can assess penalties, which are enforced by the courts. These penalties may consist of fines, injunctions ordering that certain acts be performed, or criminal prosecution.

For years, the federal government has been involved in a minor way with environmental control through its conservation acts. Title 16 of the *United States Code (U.S.C.)* covers the conservation of such things as national parks and forests, historic sites, soil, water, timber, wildlife, and power, and coastal zone management. But the first big step into complete control of the environment was taken with the establishment of the National Environmental Policy, 42 U.S.C., Chapter 55, Sections 4321–4370. This policy is popularly known by its short title, "National Environmental Policy Act of 1969." The stated purpose of this act is to "encourage productive and enjoyable harmony between man and his environment; to promote efforts which will prevent or eliminate damage to the environment and biosphere and stimulate the health and welfare of man; to enrich the understanding of the ecological systems and natural resources important to the Nation; and to establish a Council on Environmental Quality." In conformity with this act, the president sent Reorganization Plan No. 3 of 1970 to Congress, establishing the Environmental Protection Agency and transferring conservation functions to this agency. Later executive orders have covered such areas as "Environmental Safeguards on Activities for Animal Damage Control on Federal Lands" and "Use of Off-Road Vehicles on Public Lands."

Subchapter 1—Policies and Goals, Section 4331 sets forth Congress' declarations of national environmental policy. This policy recognizes that the results of humanity's impact on the environment in which it lives must be controlled, or the nation will soon find itself with no environment. Congress has declared that it is the policy of the federal government, in cooperation with the states, local governments, and individuals, to create and maintain conditions under which people and nature can exist productively and harmoniously. To this end, the federal government is assigned to coordinate plans and functions, and the states are assigned to carry out those plans.

Congress followed this ambitious statement by enacting Title 42, U.S.C., Sections 4371–4374, Environmental Quality Improvement, popularly known as the "Environmental Quality Improvement Act of 1970." This act reported congressional findings and established an Office of Environmental Quality, staffing it with compensated employees and stating their duties, authority, and appropriations. The congressional findings, declaration, and purpose are found in Section 4371.

Another vast program established in 1972 was the Noise Control Act of 1972, 42 U.S.C., Sections 4901–4918, which set standards for noise levels for a variety of things, ranging from aircraft and manufacturing plants to railroads and automobiles. Enforcement procedures were also established, calling for the issuing of orders and criminal citations. In addition, provisions were made for citizens to sue for violations of the noise standards.

The atmosphere was included in this conservation program by the passage of the Air Quality and Emissions Limitations Pollution Prevention and Control Act, 42 U.S.C., Sections 7401–7642 in 1977, which again placed the burden upon the states to carry out the mandates and standards set forth by the federal government, with the assistance of federal knowledge and funding.

Space does not permit a detailed investigation of these preservation statutes, for they are much too complex in their writing and even more complex in their interpretation into action, resulting in considerable confusion when cases reach the judicial branch of the government. However, the Air Quality act does include measures for the prevention of significant deterioration of air quality, Sections 7407–7491; Plan requirements for non-attainment areas, Sections 7501–7508; Emission standards for moving sources, Sections 7521–7551;

Aircraft emission standards, Sections 7571–7574; and Noise pollution, Sections 7641–7642.

Naturally, huge bureaucracies have been formed to support these lofty preservation schemes. This cost, added to the economic cost of complying with the established standards, has given some people second thoughts, as indicated by current literature. In any event, it has been discovered that in some areas a moderation of these goals or a relaxation of time schedules is required to make these laudable policies economically practical.

An indication of the bureaucratic red tape that is involved in setting various environmental issues appeared in the August 8, 1982, issue of the *New York Times* on page 41. The article described the killing of coyotes in the western states because they were gobbling up sheep herds. Ranchers wanted to use a poison called sodium monoflouroacetate to eradicate the coyotes, but environmentalists claimed that the poison caused inhumane deaths and could injure other wildlife. In July 1981, the Environmental Protection Agency held hearings that the agency said were intended to find out whether or not hearings should be held. The real hearings on the coyote issue opened in April 1982, with promises by both sides to appeal any decision to the courts. These promises could delay any final decision for years.

Introduction to Research Problem

Another interesting area of conservation law was covered by the passage of Chapter 59, Urban National Growth Policy and New Community Development Act, 42 U.S.C., Sections 4501–4532, popularly known as the "Urban Growth and New Community Development Act of 1970." The congressional statement of purpose is set forth in Section 4501 as follows:

> It is the policy of the Congress and the purpose of this chapter to provide for the development of a national urban growth policy and to encourage the rational, orderly, efficient, and economic growth, development, and redevelopment of our States, metropolitan areas, cities, counties, towns, and communities in predominantly rural areas which demonstrate a special potential for accelerated growth; to encourage the prudent use and conservation of our natural resources; and to encourage and support development which will assure our communities of adequate tax bases, community services, job opportunities, and well-balanced neighborhoods in socially, economically, and physically attractive living environments.

In 1972 the Water Pollution Prevention and Control Act was passed (33 U.S.C., Sections 1251–1376) and was known by its short title as the "Federal Water Pollution Control Act Amendments of 1972," which in turn was extensively expanded by the 1977 amendment, the Federal Water Pollution Act, known by its short title as the "Clean Water Act of 1977." By definition, this act includes within its compass almost all of the lakes, ponds, rivers, streams, and brooks in the United States. Like the other acts, it provides that the states perform the work by following national guidelines and with the aid of federal funds. The act's declaration of goals and policy is in the same tone as that of the other acts.

Remember, for background material on the tools used in legal research, review the section titled "Where It Is Recorded"; and for an example of the use of these tools in a legal research problem, see "How to Find It." See the Glossary for unfamiliar terms and Appendix A for abbreviations. The legal explanations and the issues selected here are not comprehensive due to space limitations. Should the researcher become interested in a legal problem not covered by the background material, by the introduction, or by the research problem, he or she should note the question, and, using the procedures suggested in this book, perform his or her own legal research to discover the answer.

Research Problem

The research tools used in this problem consist of the Search Process Flow Chart, the CORP rule, and statutes.

Richard's family had been farmers in Minnesota for generations. Gradually, they concentrated on hog farming, and through this activity they branched out into collecting garbage. Originally, they collected the garbage, trucked it to their farm, and separated out what the hogs could not eat and threw it into a depression on their 325-acre farm. The farm was far enough removed from civilization at that time that no one was bothered by the hog operation or by the farmers' disposal methods. As time went by, the government's food inspection process became stricter, and for Richard's family to produce saleable hogs, it became necessary for the hogs to be fed on grain, or if garbage was used, the garbage had to be steam cooked before being thrown to the hogs. The family used these methods for awhile, but the methods eventually became expensive and time consuming, as well as smelly and bothersome. Richard, a bright, forward-looking lad, believed that people would always have trash that needed to be disposed of and that the disposal part of the family's operation could be continued—indeed expanded—while they gave up the hogs.

In 1961 Richard convinced the family to deed him 250 acres of the homestead—including the trash dump—to be used as an experiment. Richard talked with his friendly banker, told him he was becoming a "garbologist," and arranged a loan to purchase three garbage trucks, a bulldozer, and a dump truck. He then aggressively went after trash bids from towns, cities, and industries in the area. The operation was so successful that Richard purchased two large roll-off trucks and six roll-off containers for use with stores and industries. This setup meant that the containers were rolled off the trucks at the factory or store, filled during the week by factory or store personnel, and transported once a week by Richard's large roll-off trucks to the farm dump, then returned for the next week's trash.

As the operation increased in size over the years and as civilization spread in the direction of the farm, environmentalists became interested in Richard's operation. The state was brought in and inspected the premises and the operation in 1979, determining that Richard's business was necessary and safe if certain precautions were taken. Richard was obligated to put a clay cap on the old dump and to install clay walls around the dump to prevent the leakage of leachate into the surrounding area. A new dump could be opened if it was operated according to the then-current regulations. The regulations at that time required that clay walls be built around the area, drainage ditches be installed, and the material be covered each day with a layer of dirt. This procedure was followed, and Richard was issued the proper permits by the Pollution Control Agency. His business prospered.

One April day in 1984, some fishermen who were fishing in one of the fine streams in a valley near Richard's dump discovered several dead fish floating about. The fish that they caught had no fight in them and in general looked sick. Naturally, the dump became a prime suspect. The village health department inspected the dump, found nothing out of order, and called the state Pollution Control Agency. It was suspected that toxic material had been deposited in the dump and that some of the drums had deteriorated, allowing their toxic contents to seep into the surrounding area and, eventually, into the stream. Concern arose about the safety of the drinking water in the area, especially for those who relied on well water.

Upon being questioned by the agency, Richard denied having any knowledge of toxic matter or even of drums being deposited in the dump by his operators. However, he admitted that pollution by his operation was possible because he never knew what went into the roll-off containers that came from the industries and stores. Naturally, when asked about the problem, representatives of the industries involved denied such allegations. They said that no records had been kept concerning what the industries threw away, or when, but the representatives were sure that any toxic material was handled according to all federal, state, and local regulations.

Several test borings were made in the dump, with no toxic material being located. This finding was anticipated because a considerable number of tests were needed to locate a relatively few leaky drums in such a large area.

Finally, the town convinced the Pollution Control Agency to close Richard's dump and operation. When served with the closing papers, Richard decided to take some time off and investigate the law on his own before seeking the services of his attorney.

Richard gathered together his Search Process Flow Chart, 4″ x 6″ cards, a pen, and the CORP rule, hopped into his pickup truck, and drove to the county law library some twenty-five miles away. The CORP rule was used to help him find effective words for his legal research (C for course of action, O for object involved, R for restitution sought, and P for parties). The first thing Richard did was to make a card listing the facts of the situation as he currently saw them (Fig. 92).

After checking the facts he had written, Richard looked at his copy of the Search Process Flow Chart, and started thinking of words to use in searching the legal material (Step 1). *Environment, trash, garbage,* and *leachate,* were the search words that came immediately to mind. Then he picked up a copy of the *Minnesota Digest* published by West and opened it to the Outline of the Law. Quickly reviewing the CORP rule for the areas of interest, he ran through the outline and added the word *injunction* to his list. The list of Digest Topics in the same volume contributed *health and environment, negligence, nuisance,* and *water and water courses.*

In Step 2 (jurisdiction) Richard decided that he would first consider the pollution issue as a problem for Minnesota, but he kept in mind the possibility

8/8/84
Richard   (Unilateral Dump Closing by State)   Richard
Facts: On 250 acres of a farm in Minnesota, Richard entered the
trash disposal business. At the time, a considerable amount of trash
had been disposed of in a swale over the years. Business grew
rapidly. Weekly, Richard picked up industrial containers and dumped
them in the same area used to dispose of local and household trash.
An inspection of the premises in 1979 by the state Pollution Control
Agency resulted in a clay wall being constructed around the area
then in use and a clay cap being placed over it. A new dumping area
was established, proper drainage installed, and clay walls built to
prevent the leakage of leachate. The operation continued under a
license from the agency.
     Dead fish were discovered in a stream below the dump, tests were
made for toxic material at the dump site, and no toxins were found.
The dump owner denied having any knowledge of disposing of toxic
material in his dump, and representatives of industries using his
services denied disposing of such material in Richard's roll-offs. The
village persuaded the Pollution Control Agency to have the dump
closed.

Fig. 92.   Dump Closing Fact Card

8/8/84
Richard   (Unilateral Dump Closing by State)   Richard
Issue: Can the Pollution Control Agency of Minnesota close a trash
dump suspected of polluting streams without a hearing?

Fig. 93.   Dump Closing Issue Card

that jurisdiction might also include the federal government. Minnesota was
chosen first because Richard was a resident of Minnesota, and the property
involved was located in Minnesota, as was the village that was causing him the
problem. He decided to bypass Step 3 (obtain a general overview from texts
or from a legal encyclopedia) because he was positive that he would find the
information he needed in the Minnesota statutes. Richard then addressed the
important point of framing an issue to be searched (Step 4). He placed the issue
on another card (Fig. 93).

     Step 5 led Richard to statute and case finders, and here he decided to start
with the statutes; after all, he realized, he was regulated by them. The word he
felt would be most productive was *environment,* so he picked up Volume 45
of the *Minnesota Statutes Annotated*—the general index covering the letters *D*
through *K*. The index of this 1962 publication did not include the word *environment.* Turning to the pocket part in the back of the volume, however,
Richard found that there the term took up almost a full page of the index. Not
finding what he was specifically looking for, he noted that most of the items

listed fell under Section 116, "Pollution Control Agency." He then made a card for relevant items in the index for future reference (Fig. 94).

Returning the index to the shelves, he searched the spines of the volumes until he located one indicating that it covered Sections 110 through 119. Richard returned to his desk and began Step 6—checking the statutes and entering them on a card (Fig. 95).

Richard recalled that one always had to consider administrative regulations in areas where an agency was empowered by statute to enforce the policies established by legislative enactments. Having learned that the Pollution Control Agency in Minnesota was granted such authority in the statutes he uncovered in his research, Richard decided to investigate whether the agency had pro-

---

8/8/84

Richard   (Unilateral Dump Closing by State)   Richard
45 Minn. Stat., Index D–K.
    Environment
    Sec. 116 Pollution Control Agency
    Sec. 116.06 Definitions

Fig. 94. Minn. Stat. Index Card

8/8/84

Richard   (Unilateral Dump Closing by State)   Richard
Minn. Stat., Sec. 116, Pollution Control Agency
    Sec. 116.06 Definitions
    Subd. 10 Solid Waste. (This includes the material Richard was dumping.)
    Sec. 106.091. This section states, in summary, that Richard must give the agency any information he has and allow it to examine his records and to have access to the premises.
    Sec. 116.11, Emergency Powers. According to the pocket part, this section was amended on August 1, 1983, and the important information states:
    "If there is imminent and substantial danger to the health and welfare of the people of the state or any [individual] of them, as a result of the pollution of air, land, or water, the agency may by emergency order direct the immediate discontinuance or abatement of the pollution without notice and without a hearing.... The Agency order ... shall remain effective until notice, hearing, and determination pursuant to other provisions of law, or, in the interim, as otherwise ordered. A final order of the agency in these cases shall be appealable...." No cases were found under the annotations in the original volume or in the pocket parts. Library references are Health and Environment 28, C.J.S., Health and Environment, Sec. 21.

Fig. 95. Minn. Stat., Sec. 116, "Pollution Control Agency" Card

mulgated any regulations that might be relevant to his problem. He referred to the latest edition of *Minnesota Rules,* which compiled the administrative rules of all state agencies that were officially published by the state of Minnesota. The last volume of the multi-volume set contained tables and a subject index. He looked under the term *Pollution Control Agency* in the index but found no listings that appeared promising. After verifying this fact by glancing at the rules themselves, he decided that there were no administrative regulations that applied to his particular problem.

Richard knew that another possible avenue for research in a heavily regulated subject field was the use of looseleaf services. He therefore reviewed the latest edition of *Legal Looseleafs in Print* to determine whether there were any services that would be helpful to him. He discovered that quite a few services bore on environmental law in general or on more specific aspects of the topic, but none dealt directly with Minnesota. He concluded that he was better off stopping his research at that point rather than pursuing possibly marginally related materials and that he should visit his lawyer.

Richard took the library references to his lawyer to give him a lead. Richard had already discovered that he was in trouble, and he wanted to present what information he already had to his lawyer. It was important to his business that this matter be settled as soon as possible because Richard needed to scurry around and locate a temporary place to dump his material. There was no need to follow Step 6 or Step 7 because the annotations indicated that no cases decided in Minnesota covered these points. Step 9 called for the assembling of a report, for Richard's own clarification and for his attorney's.

The lawyer would be able to size up the legal aspects of the case. Once the legal issues were resolved, however, the problems not covered by law had to be addressed. These involved the practicality of pursuing and the financial ability to pursue the issue to the desired conclusion. Having the law on one's side, Richard knew, did not necessarily mean that one had the power to enforce it.

Law Library Research Report

Title: Unilateral Dump Closing by State

Requested by: Richard

Submitted by: Richard

Date Submitted: August 10, 1984

Statement of Facts   On 250 acres of a farm in Minnesota, Richard entered the trash disposal business. At the time, a considerable amount of trash had been disposed of in a swale over the years. Business grew to include the servicing of stores and industrial plants. Weekly, Richard picked up the containers and dumped them in the same area used to dispose of local and household trash. An inspection of the premises in 1979 by the state Pollution Control Agency suggested that a clay wall be constructed around the area then in use and that a clay cap be placed over it. A new dumping area was established and was properly drained and surrounded by a clay wall to prevent the leakage of leachate, and the operation continued under a license from the agency.

Shortly thereafter, dead fish were discovered in a stream below the dump, tests were made at the dump site for toxic material, and no toxins were found. The dump owner—Richard—denied having any knowledge of disposing of toxic material in his dump, and representatives of industries using his services denied disposing of such material in his roll-offs. The village persuaded the Pollution Control Agency to have the dump closed.

Question Presented   Can the Pollution Control Agency of Minnesota close a trash dump suspected of polluting streams without a hearing?

Brief Answer   The state of Minnesota acting through its Pollution Control Agency may close any operation that is creating an imminent danger to its citizens through the pollution of the ground, water, or air, immediately and without a hearing.

Discussion   According to Minn. Stat., Sec. 116.11, Emergency Powers (of the Pollution Control Agency), amended on August 1, 1983,

> If there is imminent and substantial danger to the health and welfare of the people of the state or any [individual] of them, as a result of the pollution of air, land, or water, the agency may act by emergency order and direct the immediate discontinuance or abatement of the pollution without notice and without a hearing. . . . The Agency order . . . shall remain effective until notice, hearing, and determination pursuant to other provisions of law, or, in the interim, as otherwise ordered. A final order of the agency in these cases shall be appealable. . . .

No cases were found under the annotations in the original volume or in the pocket parts. Library references are Health and Environment ⟨key⟩ 28, C.J.S., Health and Environment, Sec. 21.

Bibliography

(Note: The looseleaf materials listed below may set forth the best overview and provide the most up-to-date information. They are not completely described here because the services are tremendously expensive for individuals to purchase, the titles identify the topics, their formats are relatively similar, and most of these materials can be found in law libraries.

If a book cannot be found in your library or in the nearest law library, ask your librarian if it can be obtained through interlibrary loan.)

Bacon, Lawrence S., and Michael Wheeler. *Environmental Dispute Resolution.* New York: Plenum, 1984.

Brown, Sanford M., and Theodore R. Forrest. *Environmental Health Law.* Westport, Conn.: Praeger, 1984. Includes bibliography.

Energy Controls. (P-H) Looseleaf.

Energy Users Report. (BNA) Looseleaf.

Environmental Law Reporter. (Environmental Law Inst.) Looseleaf.

Findlay, Roger W., and Daniel A. Farber. *Environmental Law in a Nutshell.* St. Paul, Minn.: West, 1983.

Firestone, David B., and Frank C. Reed. *Environmental Law for Non-Lawyers.* Ann Arbor, Mich.: Ann Arbor Science, 1983.

Food Drug Cosmetic Law. (CCH) Looseleaf.

Grad, Frank P. *Environment Law: Sources and Problems.* 3d ed. New York: Matthew Bender & Co., 1985. Includes indexes. Kept up to date with pocket supplements.

————. *Treatise on Environmental Law.* 5 vols. New York: Matthew Bender & Co., 1973. Covers pollution control, NEPA, land use planning and land use controls, public lands and conservation, and international aspects of environmental protection. A separate volume contains primary source material such as statutes and administrative regulations, policies, and standards. In looseleaf for updating.

Green, Mark, and Norman Waitzman. *Business War on the Law: An Analysis of the Benefits of Federal Health/Safety Enforcement.* Rev. 2d ed. Washington, D.C.: Corporate Accountability Research Group, 1981. Gives a rationale for regulations, discussing cost-benefit analysis, cost of regulations, and alternatives. With footnotes and appendix. Updated for the Reagan years.

Hazardous Materials Transportation. (BNA) Looseleaf.

Hazardous Waste Regulation Handbook: A Practice Guide to RCRA and Superfund. Rev. ed. New York: Executive Enterprises, 1985.

Mandelker, Daniel R. *Environment and Equity: A Regulatory Challenge.* New York: McGraw-Hill, 1981. An examination of conceptual and legal problems involving environmental land use controls, including state constitutional provisions, coastal management, environmental impact statements, and low income housing. Includes figures, chapter notes, and index.

————. *NEPA Law and Litigation: The National Environmental Policy Act.* Wilmette, Ill.: Callaghan & Co., 1984. In looseleaf for updating.

Miller, Jeffrey G., and Environmental Law Institute. *Citizen Suits: Private Enforcement of Federal Pollution Control Laws.* New York: Wiley Law Pubns., 1987. Includes bibliography and index. Kept up to date with pocket supplements.

Moss, Elaine, ed. *Land Use Controls in the United States: A Handbook on the Legal Rights of Citizens.* New York: Dial Wade, 1977. Sets forth for citizens what they must do to control the use of land. Explains laws and programs, including in each chapter a section on citizen action. Contains tables, chapter notes, and index.

Noise Regulations Report. (CCH) Looseleaf.

Nuclear Regulations Report. (CCH) Looseleaf.

Pollution Control Guide. (CCH) Looseleaf.

Rau, John G., and David C. Wooten. *Environmental Impact Analysis Handbook.* New York: McGraw-Hill, 1980. Provides specific tools and techniques used to assess and predict the environmental impact of projects. Covers concepts, socioeconomic impact analysis, air quality analysis, methodology, examples, noise impact analysis, energy impact analysis, water quality impact analysis, and vegetation and wildlife impact analysis. With chapter references and index.

Robinson, Nicholas A. *Environmental Regulation of Real Property.* New York: Law Journal Seminars Pr., 1982. Contains bibliographical references and index. In looseleaf for updating.

Schwartz, Mortimer D. *Environmental Law: A Guide to Information Sources.* Detroit: Gale, 1977. A bibliography of environmental law, covering the legal process, pollution control, and conservation of resources. With appendixes, author index, title index, and subject index.

Skillern, Frank F. *Environmental Protection: The Legal Framework.* Colorado Springs, Colo.: Shepard's/McGraw-Hill, 1981– . Includes bibliographies and index. Kept up to date with pocket supplements.

Stever, Donald W. *Law of Chemical Regulation and Hazardous Waste.* New York: Clark Boardman, 1986. In looseleaf for updating.

Truitt, Thomas H. et al. *Environmental Audit Handbook: Basic Principles of Environmental Compliance Auditing.* Washington, D.C.: Executive Enterprises, 1981. A guide for people faced with first-time environmental compliance audits, giving step-by-step procedures. Includes appendixes, table of authorities, and index.

Worobec, Mary Devine. *Toxic Substances Controls Primer: Federal Regulation of Chemicals in the Environment.* 2d ed. Washington, D.C.: Bureau of Natl. Affairs, 1986.

Administrative Law

The writers of the Constitution were very concerned with individual freedoms and went to great lengths to insure these freedoms for future generations. The Constitution is written in such a way that it gives the federal government enumerated powers, reserving all others to the states or to the people. Enumerated powers exist only in areas where if states acted separately they would be ineffective and create confusion. All laws, however, restrict someone's freedom to some extent, and the power to enact laws breeds the desire for more power.

The previous sections of this book all deal with laws, or restrictions of some type on some people, e.g., regulations of marriage, property, actions, and environment. This vast extension of federal control over people, however, is the result either of legal fiction or of very broad interpretations of certain aspects of the Constitution while ignoring other aspects. An example of the first instance is the extension of the role of the federal government into the field of health and welfare, based upon the theory advanced in *U.S. v. Sutter*, 127 F. Supp. 109 (D.C., Cal.) that the state is an entity organized for the purpose of government and is required to defend itself from destruction, and to that end, its citizens must be well and able bodied. An example of a very broad interpretation of the Constitution can be found in the control Congress and the courts have taken over people's lives by interpreting anything one does by mail, telephone, or telegraph to be interstate commerce even if such activity concerns strictly local matters. The interpretation seems to be that bigger is better in government but not in business.

The Advisory Commission on Intergovernmental Regulations, with Abraham D. Beame serving as chairman, was established by the federal government to examine the operations of the federal government, its relationships with local governments, and federal involvement in selected functions. The first volume of the report was published in 1980 and was titled *The Federal Role in the Federal System: The Dynamics of Growth*. It states on page 2,

> The most noted characteristics of the federal government are:
>
> (1) great growth since 1930;
>
> (2) assumption of new roles for providing social benefits, managing the economy, protecting the environment, and pursuing other

innovative goals so that now it is involved in virtually every function of government;

(3) the dynamic growth of the federal aid system in the past two decades;

(4) the mounting burden of federal regulations, paperwork, and intrusion into the activities of virtually every individual, business, nonprofit corporation, and state and local government.

These trends add up to a very real shift of governmental responsibilities in the United States toward national government and away from state and local governments and private power centers. This centralization tendency has placed the national government:

(a) directly in charge of an increased proportion of the nation's gross national product;

(b) in a position to affect an even larger proportion of the economy indirectly;

(c) at the center of a complex intergovernmental system that now makes almost all of the nation's 80,000 units of government interdependent.

Regulatory and administrative agencies are established by Congress and are delegated the authority to make rules and regulations in the field within which they operate. These agencies frequently are also given the power to hear and to settle disputes arising from statutes and their regulations. The regulatory agencies issue rules and regulations to carry out the particular function Congress has given the agencies. They also issue orders and licenses covering matters that fall within their jurisdiction. Additionally, they issue non-binding opinions and interpretations of statutes and regulations. Some agencies make decisions concerning controversies involving statutes and regulations, and enforce penalties stemming from violations of them. However, before any of the agencies' rules and regulations become effective as law, they must be published in the *Federal Register (Fed. Reg.)*. The material is codified yearly by subject matter into fifty titles of the *Code of Federal Regulations (C.F.R.)*. (See "Where It Is Recorded" for a complete discussion of the *Fed. Reg.* and the *C.F.R.*)

Introduction to Research Problem

One area of government that affects a large segment of the population of the United States is the Veterans Administration. It administers all of the benefits and handles all of the problems veterans and their dependents and survivors have concerning or springing from the veterans' military service. Veterans are entitled, in varying degrees, to pensions, disability benefits, hospitalization and nursing home care, special housing, burial benefits, and insurance. Veterans also may be provided with training and rehabilitation, GI loans for housing, and specially equipped automobiles. The Veterans Administration is a huge organization—one with unusual powers.

38 U.S.C., Section 211 covering the Veterans Administration states, ". . . the decisions of the Administrator on any question of law or fact under any law administered by the Veterans Administration providing benefits for veterans

and their dependents or survivors shall be final and conclusive and no other official or any court of the United States shall have power or jurisdiction to review any such decision by an action in the nature of mandamus or otherwise." Few agencies have such complete control over their findings of facts and law.

For background material on the tools used in legal research, review the section titled "Where It Is Recorded"; and for an example of the use of these tools in a legal research problem, see "How to Find It." See the Glossary for unfamiliar terms and Appendix A for abbreviations.

The legal explanations and the issues selected here are not comprehensive due to space limitations. Should the researcher become interested in a legal problem not covered by the background material, by the introduction, or by the research problem, he or she should note the question, and, using the procedures suggested in this book, perform his or her own legal research to discover the answer.

Research Problem

The research tools used in this problem consist of the Search Process Flow Chart, the CORP rule, statutes, administrative regulations as found in the *C.F.R.*, newsletters, and indexes.

John came out of the army with malaria and finally was awarded a 10 percent disability under "Old Cases with Moderate Disability" as set forth in the table found in 38 C.F.R. 4.88(a). His entitlement had grown to fifty-eight dollars a month by 1982. He also at one time received a GI loan on a house that he later sold. Five years later, the purchaser defaulted on the loan and let it go under foreclosure, leaving a balance due of $9,783.21. Suddenly John discovered that his disability check was not being deposited in his bank account under the direct deposit agreement he had executed. John contacted the Veterans Administration, but workers there did not know why John was not receiving his check; they said they would look into the matter and call him. Three months later, John called the Veterans Administration and was told that his disability compensation was discontinued because the Veterans Administration was using it as a setoff against the $9,783.21 owed them when his mortgage loan was foreclosed.

John wrote the agency a letter stating that, first, the loan was no longer his obligation because he had sold the house and another party had assumed the loan and agreed to pay the mortgage, and, second, the amount could not be correct because the balance was only $7,500 when John transferred the loan. The Veterans Administration responded six weeks later, writing that the amount was correct, that the difference was due to the accumulated interest and charges incurred before the foreclosure, and that John had not obtained a release from his obligation to the government before the sale.

John called his attorney and explained his predicament. The attorney told John that he could be of little assistance in John's case and that he could not afford to take on the Veterans Administration. Under 38 U.S.C. 3404(c)(2), attorneys are limited to a ten-dollar (formerly three-dollar) fee. However, the attorney told John, if John wished to look into the matter himself, he should know that the Veterans Administration is governed by 38 U.S.C. 1 et. seq., and the agency's regulations are found in Volume 38 of the *C.F.R.* The attorney did tell John that the decisions of the Administrator cannot be appealed because 38 U.S.C. 211 prohibits it.

John was a bit miffed, and he was angry enough—even for a measly fifty-eight dollars a month—to go after his rights. Index cards in hand, John marched to the Columbia University Law School library to do the necessary research.

In addition to the cards, John also took with him his copy of the Search Process Flow Chart and the CORP rule. He found the CORP rule to be useful in generating relevant search words under the following categories: *C* for course of action, *O* for object involved, *R* for restitution, and *P* for parties.

Finding a convenient desk, John sat down, reviewed his material, and decided to make up a fact card from which he could work (Fig. 96).

Checking his Search Process Flow Chart (Step 1), John was instructed to construct a word list that might help him in his research. Using the CORP rule, he came up with *setoff* and *Veterans Administration*. Not wishing to rely on his memory, he also examined the Outline of the Law and the Digest Topics in the West digests. From the Outline of the Law, John added *United States* and *administrative law and procedure* to his list. The Digest Topics, on the other hand, did not seem helpful. Thus, he ended up with the following list of search words: *administrative law and procedure, setoff, United States,* and *Veterans Administration*. The most promising of these, and the one he decided to research first, was *Veterans Administration*.

Step 2 (jurisdiction) was not too difficult in this case. The Veterans Administration is part of the federal government, so John's jurisdiction was federal.

John decided to skip Step 3 (conduct a general overview using an encyclopedia or text) because he believed he would be examining statutes and administrative law procedures in statute books and other government records.

This brought him to Step 4, the framing of the issue. After thinking a bit, John entered his issue on a card (Fig. 97).

Looking in the index of the *U.S.C.A.* as his attorney suggested (Step 5) had produced for John the first reference above. After glancing at 38 U.S.C.A.,

---

5/13/82

John   (Setoff Against V.A. Disability)   John

Facts: John has a 10 percent V.A. disability payment, which ceased arriving in January, 1982. In 1960 he took out a thirty-year 7-1/2 percent GI loan for $20,000. In 1977 he sold the house subject to the loan, neglecting to obtain a release from the Veterans Administration. The Veterans Administration set off the balance on the loan against his disability payments because the agency foreclosed on the loan in 1981, claiming that John owed a balance of $9,783.21 on the loan.

John disputes the amount and wonders about the lacking release and about whether or not Section 211 prohibiting appeals from the Administrator's decisions is valid in his situation.

Fig. 96.   V.A. Disability Setoff Fact Card

5/13/82
John   (Setoff Against V.A. Disability)   John
Issue: If a veteran sells a house subject to a GI loan without obtaining a release from his obligation to the Veterans Administration,
can that agency collect, by setoff against his VA disability allowance,
the balance due from him when the purchaser defaults, the property
is foreclosed, and the proceeds are insufficient to cover the balance
of the loan?
x 38 U.S.C., Sec. 1817, Release from liability under guaranty.
x 38 C.F.R., Sec. 36.4285, Subrogation and indemnity.

Fig. 97.   V.A. Disability Setoff Issue Card

5/13/82
John   (Setoff Against V.A. Disability)   John
38 U.S.C.A. 1817: (a) (pocket part) Upon application of veteran and
the transferee, the Administrator shall issue a release to the veteran
if examination shows that (1) the loan is current, (2) purchaser is
(A) obligated by contract to assume full liability for repayment, and
(B) qualifies from credit standpoint.
   (b) If a veteran disposes of property without receiving a release
and a default occurs, resulting in liability of veteran to the Veterans
Administration, the Administrator may issue a release of the veteran's financial obligation if it was disposed of in such a manner
and subject to such conditions that the Administrator would have
issued a release if the veteran had applied. Failure of transferee to
assume by contract all obligations shall bar release only when no
transferee is legally liable to the Administrator for the debt.

Fig. 98.   38 U.S.C.A. 1817(a) Card

5/13/82
John   (Setoff Against V.A. Disability)   John
38 C.F.R. 36.4285: Repeats 38 U.S.C. 1817

Fig. 99.   38 C.F.R. 36.4285 Card

Sec. 1817, he turned to the pocket parts (Step 6) and found an amendment
dated November 3, 1981, from which he took the following notes (Fig. 98).

   John turned to 38 C.F.R. 1 et seq. and came upon the following section
in the Table of Contents, which he investigated and entered on another card
(Fig. 99).

In looking at 38 U.S.C.A., Sec. 1817, John decided that the loan was current at the time of sale, the purchaser had obligated himself in the deed of transfer to pay the loan (the deed specifically stated, "subject to the mortgage . . . which the purchaser assumes and agrees to pay"), and the purchaser met the credit standards because the bank that made the original mortgage checked the purchaser's ratings and agreed that he was acceptable. Therefore, under Section 1817(b), the Administrator *may* relieve the veteran, but in John's case he did not.

If John could get his case into court, could he convince the court that the Administrator's ruling was capricious, an abuse of discretion, and not in accordance with the facts? John located a reference to the finality of decisions of the V.A. Administrator, 38 U.S.C. 211 (Step 5), by using the general index to the *U.S.C.A.* Since this reference seemed to be relevant to the question he was researching, John proceeded to review that section, using the *U.S.C.A* and returning to Step 6. He entered his findings on a card (Fig. 100).

Matters sounded bad for John. This reference appeared to cover all bases and indicated that whatever the Administrator decided was final. However, John found some interesting cases in the notes of 38 U.S.C.A. 211 (Step 7). John therefore made cards on several of the notes that might be helpful (Step 6). This example shows only one of them, which is checked off on the card to indicate that it has been examined. The pocket part under note 76 entitled "Setoffs" revealed the deMagno case (Fig. 101).

This case was of some encouragement to John, but he still had a long way to go, and without the benefit of counsel. It had been pointed out to John that the Veterans Administration's boards are composed predominantly of attorneys and that they have well-staffed legal services available at all times. In spite of this fact, the Veterans Administration makes it almost impossible for a veteran to have legal help by limiting the veteran's lawyer's fees to ten dollars. John's next step was to approach one of the veterans' organizations for assistance. Frequently, their offices can be found in the same government building that houses the local office of the Veterans Administration. These organizations

---

5/13/82

John   (Setoff Against V.A. Disability)   John

38 U.S.C.A. 211: "Decisions by the Administrator . . . (a) On and after Oct. 17, 1940, except as provided in Sections 775, 784 [insurance] and as to matters arising under Chapter 37 of this title [pay] the decisions of the administrator on any question of law or fact under any law administered by the Veterans' Administration providing benefits for veterans and their dependents or survivors shall be final and conclusive and no other official or any court of the United States shall have power or jurisdiction to review any such decision by an action in the nature of mandamus or otherwise."

x deMagno v. United States, 636 F.2d 714 (1980)

Fig. 100.   38 U.S.C.A. 211 Card

5/13/82

John   (Setoff Against V.A. Disability)   John
deMagno v. United States, 636 F.2d 714 (1980). The case involved a
widow with insurance benefits and survivorship benefits from the
Veterans Administration. Benefits were discontinued by the Veterans Administration, allegedly due to fraudulent statements she gave
in an unrelated incident (the court found no evidence of fraud). The
court said on page 727: "We conclude that when the VA takes
affirmative action against an individual whether by bringing an
action to recover on an asserted claim or by proceeding on its
common-law right of set off, the validity of the underlying basis of
the action becomes open to judicial scrutiny."

Fig. 101.   deMagno v. United States Card

will represent all veterans free even if a veteran does not belong to the organization. By turning his problem over to such an organization, John received
aid and advice from people working in the field, and representation before the
board. To assist the organization, John made up a law library research report
to take with him on his first visit.

Once the legal issues have been resolved, however, problems not covered
by law must be addressed. These involve the practicality of pursuing and the
financial ability to pursue the issue to the desired conclusion. Having the law
on one's side does not necessarily mean that one has the power to enforce it.

Law Library Research Report

Title: Setoff against Veterans' Disability Benefits

Requested by: John

Submitted by: John

Date Submitted: June 16, 1982

Statement of Facts   John has a 10 percent VA disability payment, which
stopped arriving in January 1982. In 1960 he took out a thirty-year 7-1/2 percent
GI loan for $20,000. In 1977 he sold the house subject to the loan, neglecting
to obtain a release from the Veterans Administration. The Veterans Administration set off the balance on the loan against John's disability payments because
the agency foreclosed on the loan in 1981, claiming that John owed a balance
of $9,783.21 on the loan.

Question Presented   If a veteran sells a house subject to a GI loan and
does not obtain a release from his obligation to the Veterans Administration,
can that agency collect, by setoff against his V.A. disability allowance, the
balance due when the purchaser defaults, the property is foreclosed, and the
proceeds are insufficient to cover the balance of the loan?

Brief Answer   The Veterans Administration may not set off a claim it
has against a veteran against the veteran's disability allowance without the possibility of that agency's action being reviewed by the courts.

Discussion   The conditions under which a veteran may be released from his obligation on a mortgage to the Veterans Administration are clearly set forth in 38 U.S.C. 1817 as follows:

> 38 U.S.C. 1817: (a) (pocket part) Upon application of veteran and the transferee, the Administrator shall issue a release to the veteran if examination shows that (1) the loan is current, (2) purchaser is (A) obligated by contract to assume full liability for repayment, and (B) qualifies from credit standpoint.
>
> (b) If a veteran disposes of property without receiving release from the Veterans Administration and a default occurs, resulting in liability of veteran to the Veterans Administration, the Administrator may issue a release if it was disposed of in such a manner and subject to such conditions that the Administrator would have issued a release if the veteran had applied. Failure of transferee to assume by contract all obligations shall bar release only when no transferee is legally liable to the Administrator for the debt.

The decisions made by the Administrator of the Veterans Administration are final, as provided for in 38 U.S.C.A. 211, set forth below:

> 38 U.S.C.A. 211: Decisions by the Administrator . . . (a) On and after Oct. 17, 1940, except as provided in Sections 775, 784 [insurance] and as to matters arising under Chapter 37 of this title [pay] the decisions of the administrator on any question of law or fact under any law administered by the Veterans Administration providing benefits for veterans and their dependents or survivors shall be final and conclusive and no other official or any court of the United States shall have power or jurisdiction to review any such decision by an action in the nature of mandamus or otherwise.

However, in cases where the Veterans Administration attempts to set off its claim against a veteran's benefits, the actions of the Veterans Administration may be reviewed by the courts. See *deMagno v. United States*, 636 F.2d 714 (1980). The case involved a widow having insurance benefits and survivorship benefits from the Veterans Administration. These benefits were discontinued by the Veterans Administration, allegedly due to fraudulent statements the widow gave in an unrelated incident (the court found no evidence of fraud). The court said on page 727: "We conclude that when the VA takes affirmative action against an individual whether by bringing an action to recover on an asserted claim or by proceeding on its common-law right of set off, the validity of the underlying basis of the action becomes open to judicial scrutiny."

Bibliography

(Note: The looseleaf materials listed below may set forth the best overview and provide the most up-to-date information. They are not completely described here because the services are tremendously expensive for individuals to purchase, the titles identify the topics, their formats are relatively similar, and most of these materials can be found in law libraries.

If a book cannot be found in your library or in the nearest law library, ask your librarian if it can be obtained through interlibrary loan.)

Administrative Law. (Pike and Fisher) Looseleaf.

Barnum, John W. et al. *Effective Washington Representation.* New York: Law & Business/ Harcourt, 1980. Contains articles covering the strategies and techniques to be used before agencies, departments, and Congress. Includes notes and speaker biographies.

Bornfield, Arthur E. *State Administrative Rule Making.* Waltham, Mass.: Little, 1986.

Craine, Judie, ed. *The Federal Register: What It Is and How to Use It.* Washington, D.C.: Off. of the Fed. Reg., 1980. Gives historical background and samples of *Fed. Reg.* documents and *C.F.R.* documents as well as aids; includes telephone information and assistance numbers, the Federal Regulations Act, the Administrative Procedure Act, depository libraries, Govt. Printing Off. bookstores and distribution centers, the *United States Government Manual,* and more. With index.

Davis, Kenneth Culp. *Administrative Law Treatise.* 2d ed. 5 vols. San Diego, Calif.: K. C. Davis, 1978– . Considered the standard in the field.

Edles, Gary J., and Jerome Nelson. *Federal Regulatory Process: Agency Practices and Procedures.* New York: Law & Business/Harcourt, 1981– . Gives a general overview of administrative law; covers agency powers, rulemaking, adjudication procedures, judicial review, freedom of information act, statutes, and some specific agencies. With subject index and case index. In looseleaf for updating.

Federal-State Reports, Inc. Rules and Regulations. Arlington, Va.: Federal-State Reports, 1979. A state-by-state review of administrative procedure acts, considering the procedures for rulemaking, for emergency rulemaking, for rule adoptions, and for legislative review.

Gellhorn, Ernest, and Barry B. Boyer. *Administrative Law and Process in a Nutshell.* 2d ed. St. Paul, Minn.: West, 1981.

Jacobini, H. B. et al. *Research Essentials of Administrative Law.* Pacific Palisades, Calif.: Palisades Pub., 1983. Summarizes the main themes of American administrative law, instructing users on legal briefs, glossaries, and annotated surveys. Written for use in developing research papers. Contains tables, glossary, bibliography, and index.

Mashaw, Jerry L. *Due Process in the Administrative State.* New Haven, Conn.: Yale Univ. Pr., 1985.

Medicare & Medicaid Guide. 4 vols. Chicago: Commerce Clearing House. Contains accurate and authoritative information. Vol. 1 includes coverage, exclusions, cost, topical index, case table, and finding list. Vol. 2 includes audits, physicians, forms, requirements for payment, disagreements, administration, and appeal. Vol. 3 covers federal Medicaid, state programs, laws, and regulations. Vol. 4 considers Medicaid regulations and includes a cumulative index, topical index to new developments, new developments, and last Report Letter. In looseleaf for updating.

Mezines, Basil J., Jacob A. Stein, and Jules Gruff. *Administrative Law.* 6 vols. New York: Matthew Bender & Co., 1977– . In looseleaf for updating.

Modjeska, Lee. *Administrative Law: Practice and Procedure.* Rochester, N.Y.: Lawyers Cooperative/Bancroft-Whitney, 1982. Includes bibliographical references and index. Kept up to date with pocket supplements.

Rosenbloom, David H. *Public Administration and Law.* New York: Marcel Dekker, 1983. An attempt to study law within the context of public administration, reviewing the rise of the "American Administrative State," the place of the judicature, and citizens as clients, as bureaucrats, as captives of the system, and as antagonists of the Administrative State. With figures, chapter references, and index.

White, Lawrence J. *Reforming Regulations: Processes and Problems.* Englewood Cliffs, N.J.: Prentice-Hall, 1981. Gives background and enters the area of new-style social regulations of smog, coal, vehicles, chemical production, dumps, electronic mail, gasoline, and conglomerate mergers. With index, tables, and chapter notes.

Taxation

The ancient Sumerian civilization, considered the first organized society and extinct since the third century B.C., established the first system of taxation. The income from this original tax appears to have come mainly from customs duties imposed upon the importation of goods.

A tax is a sum of money that is used by a government for its own operations or for some public purpose. In the United States, tax is assessed by the legislative branch of the government on its citizens. It is not a voluntary payment to the state but rather a contribution to the upkeep of the state enforced by the state. The amount of tax to be raised is regulated only by what the government feels it needs.

The power to tax rests upon necessity and does not depend upon Constitutional grants or the consent of the owners of property. Therefore, governments have inherent taxing powers to raise the funds that are needed for their operations. Constitutional provisions with respect to taxes are in the form of limitations on the legislative power to tax and not in the form of a grant of power. Such Constitutional limitations on taxing power must be expressed positively in the Constitution and cannot be inferred or derived as a conclusion from facts or premises. Tax legislation must also be positive and not inferred. Because the legislature is the branch of government that has the power to tax, it may delegate that power to political subdivisions. Thus states may delegate the power to levy and collect taxes for specific local purposes to counties, cities, villages, towns, and districts.

The power to tax is as extensive as the range of subjects that are considered to be within the scope of the government. The subjects for which taxes intended for public use may be raised are generally absolute, unless those subjects are limited by a constitution. Taxes extend to all persons, businesses, and property within the jurisdiction of the state. It is, however, against public policy to raise taxes faster than the money may be needed, and it is also improper to levy them in excess of the amount required.

State taxes, and the power of the states to tax, do not depend upon the federal government or its Constitution. Federal and state policies concerning taxes may differ, but states may not interfere with the exercise of the taxing rights of the federal government. Within a state, property that is owned by a foreign government or by the United States of America is not subject to taxation by the state. Other tax exemptions are based upon public policy. Such exemptions may be used to encourage industry to settle in a designated area or to support schools, charities, or churches, for instance.

The limits of the taxing power depend upon the needs of the state; and unless restricted by a constitution, the taxing power is valid for any public purpose. This power cannot, however, be used to impose non-tax burdens. Legislatures may not use the excuse of taxation as a subterfuge to accomplish a forbidden goal. However, it has been held that the taxing power may be used to accomplish purposes other than that of merely raising revenue, in order to fairly distribute the burden of regulations and controls. The mere fact that a tax is unfair and unjust does not invalidate the tax unless there are constitutional restraints covering the subject area. While it is not essential that a tax be uniform and equal, the principle is that taxes should be as uniform and equal as possible. Taxation without representation does not apply to individuals; it applies to political communities. Therefore, representation in the political body voting upon tax measures is sufficient.

Revenue raised incidentally through non-tax legislation is not considered a tax (e.g., fees to cover the cost of certain operations, such as the licensing of occupations). A tax is also to be distinguished from assessments made by a governing body for specific purposes against only the beneficiaries of a project, such as the installation of water lines, sewer mains, or sidewalks. Fines, forfeitures, or property taken by eminent domain is also excluded from the definition of a tax. It is not the label given to legislation that makes that legislation a tax. If the purpose of a law is to raise revenue, however, that law is a tax; otherwise it fits into some other category.

A tax cannot be considered a debt because it is not a contractual obligation. It is, however, a liability, and as such may by legislation be transformed into a debt. Because the tax is not a debt, it cannot be set off against any claim the taxpayer may have against the state. This fact can cause problems for people working for the state, such as contractors working under state contracts. Situations frequently arise where such a contractor is not paid on time by the state, yet the contractor must meet all tax payments to the state even if the money must be borrowed.

Unless the statutes so stipulate, taxes do not draw interest. However, most states and the federal government now provide for interest to be charged on overdue taxes after a certain specified date, as well as for interest to be paid to taxpayers who have overpaid their taxes.

Governments are necessary to carry out certain general purposes, to provide protection, to provide a forum for settling disputes, and to regulate activities. Taxes are raised to support all of these activities. To be valid, a tax need not benefit a specific individual; a tax is sufficient if it provides a general benefit to the citizens. Inherent in the power to tax is the power to destroy businesses. Unless prohibited by a constitution, a legislature may set any rate or amount of tax, and being excessive alone does not make a tax unlawful. However, the current trend is to strike down taxes that are confiscatory.

Generally, taxes are direct, or ad valorem taxes, i.e., imposed directly upon the property according to its value. Indirect taxes are placed on a privilege of doing something, such as running a franchise or having a right, and are generally passed on to the consumer as part of the cost of the product, thereby being hidden from view. For a listing of the variety of taxes, see the Glossary.

Double taxation means taxing the same property twice for the same purpose in the same time span while other property in the tax district is taxed only once. Double taxation is permissible unless it is prohibited by a constitution. Such taxation is not favored, however, and is avoided whenever possible. Taxing different interests in the same property is not an act of double taxation; therefore, it is not double taxation to tax the owner of real estate and also to levy an occupancy tax upon the lessee. A real estate tax is the only tax that is required to be based on value; other specific taxes may be imposed in a fixed sum for each article or item of property within a given class without consideration of that item's value.

A levy is an official action of a legislature whereby that body determines and declares that a tax of a certain amount or percentage of value shall be imposed on some object. State legislatures in the absence of constitutional restrictions have levying power, and they may expressly confer the right to levy as well as to collect taxes to counties, cities, villages, towns, and districts.

Tax assessors are elected or appointed to assess property within the jurisdiction of the taxing body and must meet the qualifications set forth in state statutes. An assessment is the official estimate of the value of the property within the taxing body's jurisdiction. Assessors must comply with the law concerning their assessing of land. A valid assessment is necessary to the validity of and for the collection of taxes. Minor irregularities, however, do not invalidate an assessment.

An assessment roll lists all of the taxable property and the persons who own taxable property in a jurisdiction in accordance with statutory directions; such a roll is usually needed to make an assessment valid. The roll must list and describe the property. In common law, the tax rolls are open to public inspection, but statutes now may restrict or prohibit this right.

States also may impose income taxes upon all of the income of their residents whether that income was earned within or outside of the state, but some states by statute provide for apportioning such income for tax purposes. The income of foreign corporations and of non-residents earning income within the state may also be taxed by a state. The method of collecting the states' fair share of income tax from the larger multi-national corporations is being argued in the courts to this day. The income tax cannot discriminate between individuals of the same class, but it may establish various levels of taxation.

Inheritance, succession, and estate taxes are within the jurisdiction of the state within which the property is located at the time of the owner's death. These taxes are generally imposed on the property of those domiciled in the state at the time of death and may include intangible personal property outside of the state as well. A state may impose such a tax on the property of a non-resident only if that property is within the state at the time of the non-resident's death. Real estate is taxed by the state within whose boundaries it lies. Tangible personal property may be taxed by the state within which it is located, even if the decedent was a non-resident. Intangible property may be taxed by (1) the state of the domicile of the deceased, (2) the state with jurisdiction over the property at the time of death, (3) the state with jurisdiction over persons whose relationships are the source of the intangible property, (4) the states with jurisdiction over persons who have extended benefits or protection to the intangible property. As a result of all these conditions, the cumulative taxes imposed following the death of an individual may exceed the value of the estate.

Introduction to Research Problem

Unincorporated businesses are taxed in various ways. Some jurisdictions tax such associations as partnerships, while others treat them as corporations for tax purposes. Although they must file a tax return, partnerships do not themselves pay income taxes. The taxes are passed directly on to the partners as part of their income and are reported on each partner's personal income tax form. Corporations, however, do pay taxes on their incomes; and when corporations declare dividends, these dividends are considered income to stockholders, who must include the dividends as income on their individual income tax forms.

Congress passed the first income tax in 1894. A two percent tax was imposed on income over $4,000, and four percent, on corporate income. This act was declared un-Constitutional by the Supreme Court in *Pollock v. Farmers' Loan and Trust* 157 U.S. 429 and 158 U.S. 601 (1895). The Sixteenth Amendment to the Constitution in 1913 officially gave Congress the power to establish an income tax. The first tax under this amendment imposed a one percent charge on net income above $3,000 for single taxpayers, one percent on net income above $4,000 for married taxpayers, and a one percent surtax on income above $20,000, graduated to six percent on incomes above $500,000. This structure contrasts greatly with the current taxing schedule now used by the federal government.

Closely held corporations—those with few shareholders and those controlled by one or only a few persons—at times run into difficulty with the Internal Revenue Service (IRS) due to the control that may be exerted over the corporation by these few stockholders. As a result, claimed corporate expenses may be reclassified by the IRS as personal and charged to the individual as a dividend instead of being a tax deductible expense for the corporation.

For background material on the tools used in legal research, review the section titled "Where It Is Recorded"; and for an example of the use of these tools in a legal research problem, see "How to Find It." For unfamiliar terms, see the Glossary. See Appendix A for abbreviations.

The legal explanations and the issues selected here are not comprehensive due to space limitations. Should the researcher become interested in a legal problem not covered by the background material, by the introduction, or by the research problem, he or she should note the question, and, using the procedures suggested in this book, perform his or her own legal research to discover the answer.

Research Problem

The research tools used in this problem consist of the Search Process Flow Chart, the CORP rule, a looseleaf service, statutes, reporters, and citators.

Antonio came to the United States with his parents as a four year old and settled in Burlington, Vermont. Being poor, the family lived down by the railroad tracks, where young Antonio gathered coal to heat their apartment in the winter. He was a bright, ambitious youngster and by the age of seven knew the language well. He watched the older children in the neighborhood appear from nowhere and rush to the bakery wagon for their stolen feast of pastry as the baker made his deliveries to stores and restaurants. One day, Antonio approached the baker and suggested that if he would teach Antonio the baking trade, he, Antonio, would ride the delivery wagon with the baker and keep the gangs from looting the goods. His offer was accepted, and in a few years, Antonio had gained considerable knowledge about making dough.

A neighboring bakery came up for sale, and at age seventeen, Antonio struck a deal with the seller. His business prospered, so he bought out his old employer, incorporated in 1962 with a capitalization of $40,000, and saved his money. He married, and his wife worked with him in the office and store. His two sons worked for Antonio for ten years, although they were not listed on the payroll. He gave them an allowance and put the rest of what they received as pay aside for their future. True to his word, as soon as the boys married, Antonio purchased houses for them, each in the $45,000 range. He also started purchasing stocks from his friendly broker, Amerigo, in fairly large blocks in the late 1960s, some jointly with his wife, Rosa, and in smaller amounts for each son. By 1978 each son had a stock inventory of approximately $150,000, and Antonio and Rosa had a stock inventory of some $250,000.

Someone evidently became jealous, because one day Antonio was invited to explain to the Internal Revenue Service how he had accumulated such sums of money when his income tax returns seemed to indicate that he could not have saved that much from his reported income. The IRS concentrated on the last six years of business activity, claiming that Antonio's savings had all been siphoned off during that period of time and that he now owed deficiency taxes for those years totaling $400,000, plus penalties amounting to another $200,000. The IRS had arrived at the figures by using the "Net Worth Method" of reconstructing Antonio's income for the period and determined that he had received constructive dividends sufficient to increase his taxes by the above amount during the six years.

Antonio and Rosa were shaken by the amount that the IRS claimed they owed. The couple saw no way they could possibly pay such a large sum. They therefore took the problem to their old friend and accountant, Enrico, and explained it to him. They could not account for the extra sums above those stated in their tax returns, and even after extensive questioning, they could give no satisfactory explanation of where they obtained the money for the stocks and houses they purchased for their sons or for the stocks they held themselves.

Joseph, Enrico's nephew, was given the task of searching the law on the subject, so he collected his Search Process Flow Chart, his CORP rule, and some 4" x 6" cards, and listed the facts on an index card (Fig. 102).

Joseph reviewed the CORP rule: C for course of action, O for object involved, R for restitution, and P for parties. The CORP rule was used to help him locate key words to be used in his examination of the law.

Retiring to the rather extensive library kept by his Uncle Enrico, Joseph settled down at a table and considered Step 1 on the flow chart (the creation

3/3/81

Enrico   (Constructive Dividends)   Antonio

Facts: Antonio went into business for himself at age 17 and incorporated his bakery business in 1962 with a capitalization of $40,000. His two sons worked in the business for ten years but never received a salary. Antonio gave them an allowance instead. In the late 1960's, Antonio started purchasing stocks for each son and larger amounts for himself and his wife, Rosa. When the sons married, he purchased a $45,000 house for each. By 1978 each son had an inventory of stocks amounting to about $150,000, and Antonio and Rosa jointly owned stocks amounting to about $250,000. Neither the records of the corporation, Antonio, nor the couple's personal tax returns could explain how they managed to accumulate such large sums of money. The Internal Revenue Service, upon investigating, reconstructed their income for the last six years using the Net Worth Method, crediting all of the increases to constructive dividends (i.e., money that Antonio had diverted from the corporation to his own use over that period of time), and came up with a tax deficiency on the couple's individual income taxes during the period totaling $400,000 and a penalty of $200,000.

Fig. 102.   Constructive Dividends Fact Card

of a word list to be used in the search). He had been given the terms *constructive dividends, Net Worth Method,* and *income tax.* Reaching for a West digest, Joseph turned to the Outline of the Law to look for additional terms and to insure against a lapse of memory. He located *corporations, internal revenue,* and *taxation,* and then he continued looking in the digest at the Digest Topics. There he found *dividends* and added that term to his list. Taxation was too large an area to be of help. Examining the remainder of his list, Joseph decided that he should start with *internal revenue,* then *income tax,* and, under that term, *constructive dividends.*

Step 2 presented no difficulty. Joseph was definitely concerned with federal jurisdiction, and here his concern was limited further to the Internal Revenue section regarding income taxes. Step 3 (conduct a general overview using a text or an encyclopedia) was passed over because Joseph was reasonably familiar with the area under study. He therefore concentrated next on Step 4, the framing of an issue, which he put on another card (Fig. 103).

Step 5 was to locate a statute or case in the statute and case finders. Joseph decided to use the handy *Federal Tax Coordinator 2d,* a multi-volume looseleaf publication of the Research Institute of America (RIA). The "How to Use" section in the front of the first volume, which also contained an index, indicated that he could use a topical approach to the subject matter. The topical index listed where the volume and section numbers of the topic were found. The other usual research methods were also available; for instance, if he knew the proper section of the Internal Revenue Code, Joseph could have used the code table to find the appropriate section in the *Fed. Tax Coord. 2d.* He decided to use the topical index and looked for *constructive dividends.* He found this term listed within the following volumes and sections: "Generally—F 1000, 1600

```
                              3/3/81
Enrico                (Constructive Dividends)              Antonio
Issue: Are constructive dividends to be charged against a stockholder
of a corporation when his or her income is reconstructed using the
Net Worth Method and the stockholder can give no accounting of
where he or she received his or her wealth?
x  Federal Tax Coordinator 2d (RIA)
```

Fig. 103.   Constructive Dividends Issue Card

```
                              3/3/81
Enrico                (Constructive Dividends)              Antonio
Fed. Tax Coord. 2d, Vol. F, Sec. 1657
   A taxpayer who diverts corporate checks for his or her personal
use with no intent to borrow the funds or to repay them realizes a
constructive dividend.
      Pizzarelli, TC Memo 1080-118
```

Fig. 104.   Fed. Tax Coord. 2d, Vol. F, Sec. 1657 Card

et seq."; "Allocation of Income—G 4008"; and "Exclusion from Gross Income—F 1054, 1055." Checking the "Detailed Reference Table" in Volume F, he saw "Diversion of Corporate Funds—1657."

Looking at this section, Joseph learned that a taxpayer who diverts corporate checks for his or her personal use with no intent to borrow the funds or to repay them realizes a constructive dividend. Following Step 6, he put this information on a card (Fig. 104).

This finding did not seem good for Antonio's case. Joseph therefore began to rethink the case and decided that maybe he jumped ahead of himself. Before he researched *constructive dividends* further, he decided that it might be advisable to find out just what *dividends* meant. Returning to Step 5, Joseph ran down the general index under the "Dividends" heading and noted that under the subheading "Capital Gains," there was a section (F 1001) covering "Ordinary Income Versus Capital Gains." Joseph realized that there was a considerable tax difference between an item being treated as income and as a capital gain. If Antonio could consider the increase in net worth a capital gain, he might save a considerable sum in taxes. Returning to Step 6, Joseph checked this possibility and entered his findings on another card (Fig. 105).

Now Joseph had a code reference, i.e., a primary source of the law; and although he might not be able to reduce Antonio's obligation to zero, it sounded as if he might be able to establish that the amount claimed by the IRS as constructive dividends was in fact only partly dividend, a portion of it being a return of capital to the extent of Antonio's basis of capital, and the remainder being treated as a capital gain.

3/3/81

Enrico   (Constructive Dividends)   Antonio

Fed. Tax Coord. 2d, Vol. F, Sec. 1001

"Aside from such cases . . . a corporate distribution is treated in this manner: (1) Dividend. The portion which is dividend is included in gross income. (2) Reduction of Basis (return of capital). The portion of the distribution which is not dividend—for instance, in the absence of sufficient corporate earnings and profits—is first applied against and reduces the adjusted basis of the stock of the stockholder. (3) Excess over Basis. Once the portion of the distribution which is not a dividend has reduced the stockholder's adjusted basis of his stock to zero, any remaining excess over the adjusted basis is treated as a capital gain from the sale or exchange of property."

x Code Sec. 301(c)(1), Code Sec. 301(c)(2), Code Sec. 301(c)(3)

Fig. 105.   Fed. Tax Coord. 2d, Vol. F, Sec. 1001 Card

3/3/81

Enrico   (Constructive Dividends)   Antonio

26 U.S.C.A., Sec. 301(c)(1), Amount constituting dividends.

That portion of the distribution which is a dividend (as defined in Sec. 316 [26 U.S.C.A. Sec. 316]) shall be included in gross income.

(2)   Amount applied against basis.

That portion of the distribution which is not a dividend shall be applied against and reduce the adjusted basis of the stock.

(3)   Amount in excess of basis.

(A)   In general, except as provided in subparagraph (B), that portion of the distribution which is not a dividend, to the extent that it exceeds the adjusted basis of the stock, shall be treated as gain from the sale or exchange of property.

(B)   . . .

x Simon v. Commissioner, 248 F.2d 869 (C.A. 8, 1957)

x DiZenzo v. C.I.R., 348 F.2d 122 (C.A. 2, 1965)

Fig. 106.   26 U.S.C.A., Sec. 301(c)(1) Card

Joseph indicated the code references on the "Fed. Tax Coord." card; checked them off, indicating that he had looked at each reference; and then turned to the *U.S.C.A.* (Step 6). The spines of these volumes indicated that Title 26 contained the Internal Revenue Code, Sections 301 through 400. The information found was entered on another card (Fig. 106).

Step 7 indicated that if new references were found while the researcher was examining the information in Step 6, he or she should return to Step 6 for the newly discovered material. So Joseph returned the *U.S.C.A.* to the shelf and took down 248 F.2d to look at the Simon case, which he put on its own card (Fig. 107).

After making the entry on the card, Joseph wanted to make sure that there had been no judicial changes in the interpretation of this case since the decision. This he did by checking *Shepard's Citations* (Step 8) for the case 248 F.2d 869. Finding nothing, he checked the card to indicate that he had completed the task. Next, he turned to Step 6 for the other case he found in *U.S.C.A.* and entered it on another card (Fig. 108).

There being no new references to check (Step 7), Joseph moved on to Step 8 and Shepardized 348 F.2d 122, again finding nothing. He checked *Shepard's Citations* on the card, indicating that this step was completed.

It appeared fortunate for Antonio that his parents had settled in Vermont and that he had built his business there. Some jurisdictions in the country had decided such cases in favor of the Internal Revenue Service, which claimed that the entire amount should be considered constructive dividends. In some other

---

3/3/81

Enrico   (Constructive Dividends)   Antonio

Simon v. Commissioner, 248 F.2d 869 (8th Cir. 1957)

VanOlsterhout, J., stated on page 867, "The diversions of corporate earnings and assets in our present case should be treated and taxed as ordinary income only to the extent that corporate earnings ... are available for dividend payments. To the extent that the distribution is not a dividend, the distribution is to be treated as a return of capital to the extent of the cost of the stock, and as capital gain as to the excess, if any, as provided for in Sec. 115(D)."

x Shepardized through Jan. 1981.

Fig. 107.   Simon v. Commissioner Card

3/3/81

Enrico   (Constructive Dividends)   Antonio

DiZenzo v. Commissioner, 348 F.2d 122 (2d Cir. 1965)

Lumbard, C.J., applied 26 U.S.C. 301 to the case, affirming that the interpretation given in the Simon case will be followed by the Second Circuit decisions. Assets diverted from a corporation by a stockholder will be treated as dividend income to the stockholder to the extent of corporate earnings, as a return of capital to the extent of the basis of the stock owned, and as capital gains regarding any excess. In reviewing the history of such cases, Judge Lumbard noted that the Sixth Circuit and the Third Circuit have decided otherwise, but the Eighth Circuit has decided as he has above, while the Fifth Circuit and the Seventh Circuit tend in the same direction.

x Shepardized through Jan. 1981.

Fig. 108.   DiZenzo v. Commissioner Card

parts of the country, no decision had been made by the circuit courts concerning the applicability of 26 U.S.C. 301 to such cases. This information emphasized the fact that circuit courts do not decide cases uniformly, and until the Supreme Court states its position, the law in this area will remain inconsistent throughout the United States. Things now looked better for Antonio because earlier circuit court cases in his jurisdiction had been decided favorably to his position.

Once the legal issues were resolved, the problems not covered by law needed to be addressed. These involved the practicality of pursuing and the financial ability to pursue the issue to the desired conclusion. Joseph knew that having the law on one's side did not necessarily mean that one had the power to enforce it.

Glancing again at his Search Process Flow Chart, Joseph found that the final step was to make a report (Step 9), which he did in the form of a Law Library Research Report.

Law Library Research Report

Title: Constructive Dividends

Requested by: Enrico

Submitted by: Joseph

Date Submitted: March 5, 1981

Statement of Facts   Antonio went into business for himself at age seventeen and incorporated the business in 1962 with a capitalization of $40,000. His two sons worked in the business for ten years but never received a salary, only an allowance. In the late 1960s, Antonio started purchasing stocks for each son; and when the sons married, he purchased a $45,000 house for each. By 1978 each son had an inventory of stocks amounting to about $150,000, and Antonio and his wife, Rosa, jointly owned stocks amounting to about $250,000. Neither the records of the corporation, Antonio, nor their personal tax returns could explain how they had managed to accumulate such large sums of money. The Internal Revenue Service, upon investigating, reconstructed their last six years of income using the Net Worth Method, i.e., crediting all of the increases to "constructive dividends" as money that Antonio had diverted from the corporation to his own use over that period of time. The IRS came up with a tax deficiency on the couple's individual income taxes during the period totaling $400,000 and a penalty of $200,000.

Question Presented   Are constructive dividends to be charged against a stockholder of a corporation when his or her income is reconstructed using the Net Worth Method and the stockholder can give no accounting of where he or she received his or her wealth?

Brief Answer   In the case of a stockholder in a corporation who has diverted funds from the corporation to his or her own use, only the portion of the diverted funds arising from corporate earnings and assets may be treated as constructive dividends. To the extent that the distribution is not a dividend, it shall be treated as a return of capital to the extent of the adjusted basis of the stock. Any remaining distribution shall be treated as capital gains.

Discussion   The *United States Code* defines what shall constitute dividends, return of capital, and capital gains as follows:

> 26 U.S.C., Sec. 301(c)(1), Amount constituting dividends.
> That portion of the distribution which is a dividend ... shall be included in gross income.
> 26 U.S.C., Sec. 301(c)(2) Amount applied against basis.
> That portion of the distribution which is not a dividend shall be applied against and reduce the adjusted basis of the stock.
> 26 U.S.C., Sec. 301(c)(3) Amount in excess of basis.
> (A) In general, except as provided in subparagraph (B), that portion of the distribution which is not a dividend, to the extent that it exceeds the adjusted basis of the stock, shall be treated as gain from the sale or exchange of property.

26 U.S.C., Sec. 301(c)(1) through (3) has been interpreted by the courts. In our jurisdiction, the Second Circuit Court of Appeals, in the case of *DiZenzo v. Commissioner*, 348 F.2d 122 (2d Cir. 1965) Lumbard, C.J., applied 26 U.S.C. 301 to the case, affirming that the interpretation given in the Simon case will be followed by the Second Circuit decisions. Assets diverted from a corporation by a stockholder will be treated as dividend income to the stockholder to the extent of corporate earnings, as a return of capital to the extent of the basis of the stock owned, and as capital gains regarding any excess. In reviewing the history of such cases, Judge Lumbard noted that the Sixth Circuit and the Third Circuit have decided otherwise, but the Eighth Circuit has decided as he has above, while the Fifth Circuit and the Seventh Circuit tend in the same direction.

In the case of *Simon v. Commissioner*, 248 F.2d 869 (8th Cir. 1957) referred to by Chief Justice Lumbard, above, VanOlsterhout, J., stated on page 867, "The diversions of corporate earnings and assets in our present case should be treated and taxed as ordinary income only to the extent that corporate earnings ... are available for dividend payments. To the extent that the distribution is not a dividend, the distribution is to be treated as a return of capital to the extent of the cost of the stock, and as capital gain as to the excess, if any, as provided for in Sec. 115(D)."

Bibliography

(Note: The looseleaf materials listed below may set forth the best overview and provide the most up-to-date information. They are not completely described here because the services are tremendously expensive for individuals to purchase, the titles identify the topics, their formats are relatively similar, and most of these materials can be found in law libraries.

If a book cannot be found in your library or in the nearest law library, ask your librarian if it can be obtained through interlibrary loan.)

Advanced Legal Education, Hamline Univ. School of Law. *Legal Research for Practicing Attorneys: Researching Taxation.* St. Paul, Minn.: Advanced Legal Education, Hamline

Univ. School of Law, 1979. Covers primary sources, secondary sources, researching statutory changes, and legislative history. Gives recommended citation forms. Includes table of contents.

Bittker, Boris I. *Federal Taxation of Income, Estates, and Gifts.* 4 vols. Boston: Warren, Gorham, & Lamont, 1981. Provides complete coverage, including history, structure, exclusions, foreign income, trusts, partnerships, corporations, non-profit organizations, accounting methods, and tax practices and procedures. Includes index volume, appendixes, notes, and examples. With cumulative supplements.

————, and James S. Eustice. *Federal Income Taxation of Corporations and Shareholders.* 4th ed. Boston: Warren, Gorham, and Lamont, 1979.

Commerce Clearing House Editorial Staff. *Federal Estate and Gift Tax Reporter.* Chicago: Commerce Clearing House, 1983. Gives complete coverage of estate and gift taxes, with comments. How to use this reporter explained in Volume 1. In multi-volume looseleaf.

Daily Tax Report. (BNA) Newsletter.

Due, John F., and John L. Mikesell. *Sales Taxation, State and Local Structure and Administration.* Baltimore, Md.: Johns Hopkins Univ. Pr., 1983. Traces developments; gives forms and yields of state taxes; and examines structures, rates, exemptions, audit programs, use taxes, and local government sales taxes. With index, selected bibliography, tables, and notes.

Federal Income Tax Regulations. (CCH) Looseleaf.

Federal Tax Citator. (P-H) Looseleaf.

Federal Tax Compliance Manual. (CCH) Looseleaf.

Federal Tax Coordinator 2d. (Research Inst. of America) Multi-volume looseleaf.

Federal Tax Guide. (CCH) Looseleaf.

Federal Tax Library. (P-H) Looseleaf.

Hartman, Paul J. *Federal Limitations on State and Local Taxation.* Rochester, N.Y.: Lawyers Cooperative/Bancroft-Whitney, 1981. Discusses and analyzes developments in Constitutional and federal legislative limitations on state and local taxing powers. Includes cumulative pocket parts, index, table of cases, and notes.

Hellerstein, Jerome R. *State Taxation.* Boston: Warren, Gorham, & Lamont, 1983. A basic tool for dealing with statutory and constitutional issues arising under taxes of the various states. With index, table of cases, notes, and tables.

Kostelanetz, Boris, and Louis Bender. *Criminal Aspects of Tax Fraud Cases.* 3d ed. Philadelphia, Pa.: Amer. Law Inst.-Amer. Bar Assn. Committee on Continuing Professional Educ., 1980. Provides information concerning how a tax fraud case is approached through the criminal justice system, covering the arsenal of power of the IRS, proofs, investigative techniques used, rights of the taxpayer, third parties, protections, conferences, prosecution, indictment, trial, and sentencing. With index; table of cases; table of statutes; rules and regulations; and chapter notes.

McNutly, John K. *Federal Estate and Gift Taxation in a Nutshell.* 3d ed. St. Paul, Minn.: West, 1983. Introduction to gift tax, estate tax, generation skipping tax, jointly owned property and community property, life insurance, annuities, powers of appointment, deductions, marital deductions and split gifts, credits, liability for payment, and fundamentals of estate planning. Includes Table of Cases, Table of Internal Revenue Code Sections, Table of Revenue Rulings, and Index.

————. *Federal Income Taxation of Individuals in a Nutshell.* 3d ed. St. Paul, Minn.: West, 1983. Covers definition of income and deductions, and how income is taxable. Contains index, Table of Internal Revenue Code Sections, Table of Cases, Outline, Table of Treasury Regulations, and Table of Revenue Rulings.

Meldman, Robert E., and Thomas Mountin. *Federal Taxation: Practice and Procedure.* Chicago: Commerce Clearing House, 1986.

Mertens, Jacob. *The Law of Federal Income Taxation.* Wilmette, Ill.: Callaghan & Co., 1942– . Kept up to date with annual supplements.

Penniman, Clara. *State Income Taxation.* Baltimore, Md.: Johns Hopkins Univ. Pr., 1980. Traces the development of state income taxes, showing the statutory policy and administrative provisions, management resources, and processing. With index, selected bibliography, notes, tables, and charts.

Posin, Daniel Q. *Federal Income Taxation of Individuals and Basic Concepts in the Taxation of all Entities.* St. Paul, Minn.: West, 1983. Begins with the history, policy, and structure of taxation and continues through income, deductions, exemptions, tax planning, computation of tax liability, credits, and tax practice and procedure. Contains index, appendixes, table of cases with parallel citations, Table of Internal Revenue Code Sections, Table of Treasury Regulations, Table of Revenue Rulings, and table of articles and books cited.

Rabkin, Jacob, and Mark H. Johnson. *Federal Income, Gift, and Estate Taxation.* Albany, N.Y.: Matthew Bender & Co., 1974– . In looseleaf for updating.

Rasch, Joseph. *Handling Federal Estate and Gift Taxes.* 4th ed. 3 vols. Rochester, N.Y.: Lawyers Cooperative/Bancroft-Whitney, 1984. Kept up to date with pocket supplements. Includes index.

Richmond, Gail Levin. *Federal Tax Research: Guide to Materials and Techniques.* 3d ed. Mineola, N.Y.: Foundation Pr., 1987.

Robinson, Gerald J. *Federal Income Taxation of Real Estate.* 4th ed. Boston: Warren, Gorham, & Lamont, 1984. Gives background of law, with creative planning for real estate transactions, including residential, landlord and tenant, mortgages, financing, sales, and conversions. Includes cumulative tables and index. Kept up to date by annual supplements.

Saltzman, Michael I. *IRS Practice and Procedure.* Boston: Warren, Gorham, & Lamont, 1981. Kept up to date with pocket supplements.

Willis, Arthur B., John S. Pennell, and Philip F. Postewait. *Partnership Taxation.* 3d ed. 3 vols. Colorado Springs, Colo.: Shepard's/McGraw-Hill, 1981– . In looseleaf for updating.

Contracts

$\mathbf{A}$ contract is an agreement or promise, the breach of which is remedied by an action of law. A contract needs (1) competent parties, (2) mutual agreement, (3) a subject matter, (4) legal consideration, and (5) mutual obligations. Under the Uniform Commercial Code, a contract is the total of the legal obligations resulting from an agreement as affected by the code and other laws.

Contracts may arise out of various situations. The clearest form of contract is a written one that spells out in detail the parties' mutual agreements and obligations. If the contract is unclear in any aspect, parol, or oral, evidence may be given regarding the intent of the parties. Contracts other than bills of exchange, promissory notes, those concerning the transfer of real estate, and those required by law to be in writing may be oral. Many contracts are strictly oral; and as long as they contain all of the elements of a contract, they are valid. Therefore a contract can be partly written and partly oral, and unless required to be in writing, the contract is perfectly valid. Contracts can be specifically agreed upon by the parties, or they may be inferred, i.e., exist by the actions of the parties. If the parties act as if a contract has been made between them, an enforceable contract may be inferred.

The first requirement of a contract is that it must be made between competent parties. A person may be considered incompetent if he or she is insane, unable to understand the terms of a contract, or under the legal age required to make a binding contract.

The second requirement, mutual agreement, relates to the first requirement because there can be no real agreement with an insane person or with someone who is unable to understand the terms of the contract. However, a person who is unable to contract because of tender years might make a contract, repudiate it, and in some situations keep the benefits that have accrued as a result of the contract. There are even situations, discussed in greater detail in Part 2 "Children," where those under age are held to their contracts.

The third requirement, that there must be a subject matter, implies that without a subject matter there is nothing to discuss, bargain for, or contract for. The subject matter need not be tangible, such as goods to be traded. The promise of an action to be performed now or in the future may be the subject matter of a contract. The actions required by the contract must be possible to perform and must be legal.

The fourth requirement, legal consideration, is the factor needed to make a promise enforceable. A consideration is something of value, possibly tangible, possibly the promise to perform an act at a future date, or perhaps a promise *not* to do something. Promises to do something a person is already legally obligated to perform, or past considerations, are not sufficient considerations for a contract. A mere moral obligation, unless connected with a legal obligation, is not considered sufficient consideration for a contract.

The fifth requirement, mutual obligations, means that each party must be obliged to do something, e.g., make a purchase or sale, pay money, perform or refrain from performing certain acts.

Contracts are generally the result of bargaining between parties. A bargain is an agreement between parties to exchange promises or to exchange a performance for the fulfillment of some kind of promise. Each party acquires some right from the other, and each is obligated to the other. The law imposes upon the parties the duty to keep their contracts. The terms of a contract may be established through bargaining between the parties; but once the terms are established, they are enforceable by an action of law. The most important part of the contract is the intention of the parties involved as established by the writing of the contract, by the words spoken, or even by the actions of the parties. For a contract to exist based only upon the actions of the parties, the intent of the parties must be fairly inferred from their actions. Unless a promise given is enforceable by law, the agreement between the parties does not result in a contract. A void contract is no contract at all (i.e., it cannot be enforced), and thus it has no effect. Therefore, an agreement to perform some illegal act does not result in a contract. A misunderstanding of an existing or past fact by both parties concerned also may void a contract. However, a unilateral error in itself is not sufficient to void a contract, nor is a person's failure to read a contract before signing it. A contract produced by the fraud of one party is invalid and may be avoided. A voidable contract, on the other hand, is one in which one of the parties has the legal option to avoid the contract. To avoid such a contract, the party must specifically disclaim the contract.

An implied contract to pay the reasonable cost of some service may exist if the recipient knows of the acts to be performed for his or her benefit and does not object. If the performer does not intend to be paid, however, no contract arises from the completion of the acts. Generally, a mere request that someone perform services for another does not create a contract to pay for the services, unless there is some indication otherwise. The loaning of money to someone creates an implied contract that the loan will be repaid. Persons living together as a family and performing services for each other do not generally create a contract to pay for such services; however, since the Marvin case in California, this concept may be weakening.

A bilateral contract exists when both parties have bound themselves by some obligation to the other. A unilateral contract would be in the form of an agreement to make a contract. One party to the unilateral contract states that he or she will perform a certain act provided that the other party does a specified thing. Once the "thing" is done, the contract is made and the person doing the thing is entitled to enforce the contract.

Technically, contracts by their nature are executory; once the execution of the terms has been accomplished, the contract no longer exists. In law, however, an executory contract is considered to be one in which the parties are bound to do some act, while an executed contract is considered to be one in which one of the parties has completed his or her part of the bargain.

More than a mere proposal is required to create a contract. An initial proposal, even if accepted by the other party, does not create a contract because such proposals are considered preliminary negotiations. A proposal in this sense is an offer for consideration and discussion. If both parties understand that no contract shall exist until the signing, then the formal signing of a document by both parties is required to produce a contract. If the parties do not have such an understanding, a contract may be created before the actual creation of a written instrument if all of the conditions are agreed upon, there is nothing left to be settled, and it is agreed that these conditions should be reduced to a written instrument.

Contracts are generally created by a process of bargaining, i.e., through an offer, a counter offer, and finally an acceptance. The offer must be certain and definite and not a mere expression of interest. A counter offer, counter proposal, or conditional offer destroys the original offer and creates in its own right a new offer to be accepted or rejected. An offer may be made generally, as in newspapers, in magazines, on the radio, or on television. If the offer is made without consideration, it may be withdrawn at any time. An offer once rejected cannot later be accepted to create a contract; the rejection cancels the offer. An attempt to accept a rejected offer can at most be a counter offer.

The acceptance must be made by someone who is entitled to accept the offer, without qualifications, and it must be communicated to the offerer in order for the agreement to become a contract. If the mails are used as a means of communication, the post office is considered the agent of the parties; and if the offer is accepted, the contract is made when the acceptance is placed in the mail.

An option is an agreement by a person, for a consideration, to perform an act for a set price within a limited time, leaving the right to exercise the option to the other party. This type of contract is frequently used in the purchase of real estate.

Written contracts frequently state the jurisdiction governing the contract. If not stated, then the jurisdiction will be governed by the law of the jurisdiction intended by the parties, if such jurisdiction can be determined; otherwise jurisdiction will be determined by the jurisdiction within which the contract is executed. If the performance of the contract is to be in a jurisdiction other than the one where the contract is executed, and the governing jurisdiction is not stated, authorities differ as to the controlling law.

Introduction to Research Problem

For some time, there have been concerns about contracts that for one reason or another appear most unfair or unconscionable. When faced with such a problem, the courts have been inclined to torture it into an existing legal concept, sometimes to the point of almost ignoring the facts of the case or inventing theories and facts to prevent unfair results. This situation has festered to the point that it has finally found a voice as a recognized portion of contract law. The Uniform Commercial Code, Section 2–302 now provides that if a clause in a contract is found to be unconscionable, the court may refuse to enforce the contract, or may enforce the remainder of the contract, or may limit the unconscionable clause. The principle is to prevent oppression and unfair surprise, not to distribute the allocation of risk because of superior bargaining power. The term *unconscionable* is not defined; therefore, in those jurisdictions that have adopted this section of the code, the judiciary must determine the limits of the term. So far the cases appear to have been divided into three groups. The first group defines as unconscionable those situations where there is a lack of a meaningful choice by one of the parties during the formation of the contract. The second group consists of those cases where the price is deemed excessive. The third group involves situations in which one of the parties (usually the seller) expands his or her own remedies or unduly limits the remedies of the other party. The doctrine does not appear to apply in cases where both parties to the transaction are business people because, being familiar with business transactions, they are left to their own devices.

Courts also have made a distinction between "substantive unconscionability" and "procedural unconscionability." Substantive unconscionability results from an undue harshness in the contract's terms. The contract is written in such a manner that one party has all the advantages, and the other, none. Procedural unconscionability involves the contract-forming process's focusing on high pressure tactics, fine print in contracts, misrepresentation, or unequal bargaining positions.

Some courts claim that both substantive and procedural unconscionability must be combined in various degrees before the courts will declare a contract, or a clause of a contract, void as unconscionable. It has been suggested in other jurisdictions that a sliding scale for evaluating each situation individually should be applied; thus, if there exists either gross substantive or procedural unconscionability, very little of the other will be needed to declare the contract or certain clauses void as unconscionable.

For background material on the tools used in legal research, review the section titled "Where It Is Recorded"; and for an example of the use of these tools in a legal research problem, see "How to Find It." See the Glossary for unfamiliar terms and Appendix A for abbreviations.

The legal explanations and the issues selected here are not comprehensive due to space limitations. Should the researcher become interested in a legal problem not covered by the background material, by the introduction, or by the research problem, he or she should note the question, and, using the procedures suggested in this book, perform his or her own legal research to discover the answer.

Research Problem

The research tools used in this problem consist of the Search Process Flow Chart, the CORP rule, an encyclopedia, a uniform code, statutes, reporters, and citators.

Nick was born in Pure Air, Missouri. He had two brothers and two sisters, and the family was always poor. His older brother had a job with a trucking company in Chillicothe; and when Nick reached the age of sixteen, he quit school and joined his brother. Although Nick had little formal training, he learned the business rapidly, and in his late twenties, he took over the management of the company. As he worked his way up, Nick became aware of the vast possibilities in the field. Profits could be made not only from trucking but from leasing equipment to other companies. This situation was especially attractive to the lessee since the tax laws were advantageous to those leasing equipment. Such individuals were allowed to write the entire lease off as a business expense, while the company that purchased its own equipment could write off depreciation only.

As a sideline to his prospering trucking business, Nick purchased a fleet of trucks to lease to others. He secured contracts with several big companies in New York, Chicago, Philadelphia, and Miami, renting trucks to them for hauling their products, newsprint, beer, steel, livestock, etc. He worked out a system by which the lessees picked out the equipment they wished to use, and Nick purchased the trucks and in turn leased them to the operators.

One day while he was doing business in Miami Beach, Nick entered the bar at the Fontainbleau and struck up a conversation with a gentleman named Ronald from Blue Springs, Missouri, who was just starting up a soft drink distribution business in the Kansas City area. Ronald had recently completed a course in business and was anxious to put his knowledge to work. During the course of their conversation, Ronald mentioned that even though the money he had inherited gave him some capital, he would be heavily in debt before he even started. Naturally, Nick suggested that Ronald should lease trucks, then he would have the equipment he needed, and the cost involved could be entirely written off each year as an expense. Nick told Ronald that if he would pick out the trucks he needed, Nick would purchase them and in turn rent them to Ronald. They agreed to meet in St. Louis, where Nick frequently purchased new trucks from a friendly dealer, and Ronald could pick out his trucks. Nick would handle matters from there.

After Ronald had picked out six trucks, both men agreed that Nick would fly his private plane to Kansas City, where they could review the standard contract Nick's attorney would prepare for Ronald to go over and, if acceptable, sign.

Upon returning to Chillicothe, Nick put in his order for the specified six trucks at $15,000 each. He then told his attorney that he had a "live one" in the Kansas City area, gave him the details, and instructed him to draw up one of the company's usual favorable leasing agreements, covering the six specific trucks at $1,000 per month per truck for a period of five years. Seymour, the attorney, took this to mean that the contract should be drawn as usual so that it favored Nick, and the resulting contract reflected this belief. The lease was written to cover six trucks for a period of sixty months, with a monthly payment of $1,000 per truck, or $6,000 per month. At the end of the term, Ronald could purchase the trucks for $1.00 each if he so desired.

Along with the usual language, the lease, dated March 15, 1983, contained the following terms in large print:

That the lessee represents that the lessee has selected the equipment leased hereunder prior to having requested the lessor to purchase the same for leasing to the lessee, and lessee agrees that the lessor has made and makes no representations or warranties of whatsoever nature, directly or indirectly, express or implied, as to the suitability, durability, fitness for use, merchantability, condition, quality, or otherwise of any such unit. Lessee specifically waives all rights to make claim against the lessor herein for breach of any warranty of any kind whatsoever and as to lessor, or lessor's assignees, lessee leases the equipment "as is." Lessor and lessor's assignees shall not be liable to lessee for any loss, damage, or expense of any kind or nature caused directly or indirectly by any unit leased hereunder, or the use or maintenance thereof, or the failure of operation thereof, or the repairs, service, or adjustment thereto, or by any delay or failure to provide any thereof, or by any interruption of service or loss of use thereof, or for any loss of business or damages whatsoever and howsoever caused.

Lessor, lessor's successor, or lessor's assignee shall have no obligation to install, test, adjust, or service the equipment. . . . No defect or unfitness of the equipment shall relieve lessee of the obligation to pay rent or of any other obligation under this lease. This is a non-cancelable lease for the term indicated above. Any default of any of the terms of this contract shall automatically make the full balance of the total rent under this contract immediately due and payable. This contract shall be interpreted under the laws of Missouri.

Three of the trucks acted up from the beginning; the rest apparently were late starters, but eventually Ronald had trouble with them all. Nick felt sorry for Ronald and sent mechanics to Blue Springs as a friendly gesture, but eventually Nick gave up and told Ronald that he could do no more. Ronald would have to take care of the equipment as per the contract.

Eventually, Ronald stopped paying the monthly rent. Nick thereupon sued for the balance due on the entire contract, and Ronald's attorney responded that the contract should be set aside as unconscionable on the grounds that the lessor took advantage of the inexperience of the lessee, the price was excessive for the value received, and the lessor had relieved himself of all the normal obligations of a lessor. Nick fumed and thought, what could be unconscionable about the contract? The contract was almost like all the rest of the ones he had made concerning his leasing business. Seymour was instructed to prepare a proper case and to proceed. Seymour's son, Meyer, had just been admitted to practice law in Missouri; so Meyer, as the newest member of the firm, was assigned the job of researching the law. His instructions were to report on unconscionable contracts in the state of Missouri and to indicate the application of those principles to the present case.

First, Meyer looked over the contract and saw that it was to be interpreted according to Missouri law. Reading over the entire contract, he found nothing unusual; it appeared to be about the same as all the other "boiler plate" contracts he had seen in the office concerning Nick's leasing operations.

Second, remembering the CORP rule from his law school days, Meyer reviewed that rule: C for course of action, O for object, R for restitution, and P for parties. He kept this rule in mind as he looked for key legal words during his research. Next, Meyer looked for a copy of the Search Process Flow Chart to guide him through the process of finding the primary law involved in the case, i.e., statutes or cases.

After checking the Search Process Flow Chart, Meyer entered the facts of the case as gathered from the information he had received, as well as from the copy of the contract, using 4″ x 6″ cards (Fig. 109).

Step 1 of the Search Process Flow Chart reminded Meyer to establish a list of words to use in examining the available legal material. These words would lead him to the primary sources of the law (i.e., statutes and cases) involving his problem. *Contracts* and *unconscionable contracts* came immediately to mind after Meyer reviewed the facts. Not wanting to miss any words that might prove useful, he turned to the Outline of the Law found in a West digest. He repeated the CORP rule while searching for pertinent legal terms. Under the heading "Contracts," he found and listed *implied and constructive contracts.* Under the section entitled "Actions for Particular Forms or Special Relief," he located *debtor and creditor* and *specific performance.* Turning next to the Digest of Topics in the same digest volume, he located *product liability* and *vendor and purchaser.* Looking over his list of terms, Meyer mused to himself that the doctrine of unconscionability possibly covered a variety of other legal topics and was itself possibly ill defined. The words that appeared

---

6/2/84

Seymour   (Unconscionable Contract)   Nick

Facts: Nick, from Chillicothe, Missouri, met Ronald, from Blue Springs, Missouri, in Miami and convinced him that Ronald should rent trucks from Nick for his soft drink distribution business. The parties met in St. Louis at the office of a truck dealer, where Ronald picked out six trucks he wished Nick to purchase for him to rent. A contract was drawn up for the rental of six trucks over a period of sixty months, the rent on each truck to be $1,000 per month. The contract was drawn up by Nick's attorney, but neither party was represented by an attorney at the signing of the lease. Nick purchased the trucks for $15,000 each. Pertinent terms of the contract, dated March 15, 1983, appeared in large print and eliminated any warranties and waived the lessee's right to make any claims against the lessor for any warranty. The contract stated that the lessee took the goods "as is." The lessee agreed that the lessor was under no obligation to install, test, adjust, or service the equipment, although the lessee was required to pay the full amount specified under the lease regardless of any defaults of the lessor. Upon any default by the lessee, the entire balance immediately became due and payable.

Shortly after delivery, the trucks started breaking down. Nick, the lessor, sent mechanics to see if the problem could be solved, but finally he gave up, stating to Ronald that the lessee had to comply with the terms of the contract. Ronald, the lessee, stopped paying the rent, whereupon Nick, the lessor, sued under the contract for his full balance of the rent due. The lessee responded that the contract should be set aside as unconscionable on the grounds that the lessor took advantage of the inexperience of the lessee, the price was excessive for the value received, and the lessor had wrongly relieved himself of all the normal obligations of a lessor.

Fig. 109. Unconscionable Contract Fact Card

to be most promising from those he had gathered were the ones he originally started with: *contracts* and, under this, *unconscionable contracts*.

Step 2 concerned jurisdiction. Rereading the contract convinced Meyer that the case's jurisdiction was Missouri; both parties resided and did business in Missouri, and the contract specifically stated that its terms should be interpreted under the laws of Missouri.

Not being familiar with unconscionable contracts, Meyer decided to follow the advice set forth in Step 3 (using a text or encyclopedia for a general overview). He discovered that there was no legal encyclopedia that dealt exclusively with Missouri law, so he chose to obtain background information through *American Jurisprudence 2d*. (Had there been an encyclopedia available for Missouri, he would have used it since he was interested only in the Missouri law on the subject and could have saved considerable time in not having to peruse cases from many other jurisdictions.) He looked in the general index of *Am. Jur.2d* under "Contracts" and ran down the list of terms until he came to *unconscionable*. This term referred him to the main heading "Unconscionable," under which he found "Commercial Code, unconscionable course of dealing and use of trade, Comm. Code, Sec. 28" and "Contracts, legality in general, Contracts, Sec. 192." Checking the latter, Meyer entered his findings on a card (Fig. 110).

After much thought, Meyer proceeded to Step 4 (the framing of issues) and reduced his notes to construct the following issue (Fig. 111).

The U.C.C. and *Missouri Statutes* were added to the issue card to be checked during Step 5 (finding cases and statutes). In order to locate the text of the U.C.C., Meyer referred to the multi-volume set entitled *Uniform Laws Annotated*. He knew that all the uniform acts drafted by the National Con-

---

6/2/84
Seymour   (Unconscionable Contract)   Nick
17 Am. Jur.2d, Contracts, Sec. 192 (1964), Improvident, oppressive, or unconscionable agreements.

In the absence of fraud, mistake, or oppression, the courts are not interested in the wisdom or impolicy of contracts and agreements voluntarily entered into. It has been stated almost without limitation that parties are bound by the agreements they make. Courts have held that if a contract is unconscionable, although void of fraud, the court will give relief according to what a person is entitled to and not according to what is stated in the contract. Situations unreasonably restricting the liberty of a person to earn a living, affecting the public or the rights of third parties, enabling one party to oppress third persons, or charging extortionate rates of interest will bring relief.

The pocket part quotes the Restatement of Contracts 2d, Sec. 208 and the Uniform Commercial Code (U.C.C.), Sec. 2-302. Under the digest of cases involving unconscionability, there are none listed in Missouri fitting the present situation.

Fig. 110.   Am. Jur.2d, Contracts, Sec. 192 (1964) Card

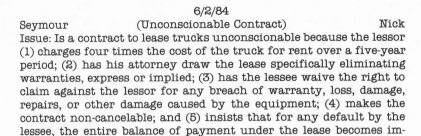

6/2/84

Seymour   (Unconscionable Contract)   Nick

Issue: Is a contract to lease trucks unconscionable because the lessor (1) charges four times the cost of the truck for rent over a five-year period; (2) has his attorney draw the lease specifically eliminating warranties, express or implied; (3) has the lessee waive the right to claim against the lessor for any breach of warranty, loss, damage, repairs, or other damage caused by the equipment; (4) makes the contract non-cancelable; and (5) insists that for any default by the lessee, the entire balance of payment under the lease becomes immediately due and payable?

x U.C.C., Sec. 2-302
x Mo. Stat.

Fig. 111.   Unconscionable Contract Issue Card

ference of Commissioners on Uniform State Laws were published in this set, along with official comments, cross-references, and notes of decisions. He used the *Directory of Uniform Acts and Codes* (published separately on an annual basis in a pamphlet format) and found from the alphabetically arranged list of acts that the Commercial Code was located in Volumes 1 through 3A of the set. The spines of these volumes showed which sections were contained in each—Section 2-302 was in Volume 1. Meyer removed Volume 1 of the *Uniform Laws Annotated* from the shelves, turned to Section 2-302, and made a note of its contents on a card (Fig. 112). He also saw that there was an extensive list of law review commentaries on this section and made a mental note to go back to these if he needed further information later in his research.

The above cases gave Meyer something to work on, although only one case from Missouri was found. Before checking these cases, he decided to check the Missouri statutes to see if this particular portion of the U.C.C. was included. Meyer thus continued his search, under Step 5, for cases and statutes. Looking in the general index of *Vernon's Annotated Missouri Statutes*, Meyer found in the pocket part a reference to the U.C.C. under Section 400.1-101 and "Unconscionable Contract or Clause" under Section 400.2-302. He looked at Section 400.2-302 and, following Step 6, entered it on a card (Fig. 113).

The Missouri statute concerning unconscionable contracts appeared to have been taken word for word from the U.C.C., and, again, the only Missouri case referred to was the Funding Systems case. This brought Meyer to Step 7, which directed him to return to Step 6 and to examine new cases discovered. This he did and checked the case found under both the U.C.C.Ann. and the *Missouri Statutes*. He summarized his findings on another card (Fig. 114).

After entering the case on the card, Meyer continued to Step 8, Shepardizing the case to discover any new decisions involving his problem. This information he noted on the Funding Systems case card (Fig. 114) and checked it off to indicate that he had performed the task. He decided not to further pursue case law through the *Missouri Digest* and the *Missouri Digest 2d* because he now understood that unconscionability in contract law is a concept

6/2/84

Seymour   (Unconscionable Contract)   Nick

Uniform Laws Annotated, Sec. 2-302(1) (1976). "If the court as a matter of law finds the contract or any clause of the contract to have been unconscionable at the time it was made, the court may refuse to enforce the contract, or it may enforce the remainder of the contract without the unconscionable clause, or it may so limit the application of any unconscionable clause as to avoid any unconscionable result.

"(2) When it is claimed or appears to the court that the contract or any clause thereof may be unconscionable, the parties shall be afforded a reasonable opportunity to present evidence as to its commercial setting, purpose, and effect to aid the court in making the determination." No Missouri cases found under the annotations.

Pocket part for use in 1984.

6. Test of Unconscionability, generally.

x Funding Systems Leasing Corp. v. King Louis Internat'l, Inc.,
        597 S.W.2d 624 (Mo. 1979)

13. Lease Provisions.

Eastern Oil Co., Inc. v. Burroughs Corp., 625 F.2d 1291 (Fla. 1980)

All-State Leasing Corp. v. Top Hat Lounge, Inc., 649 P.2d 1250
        (Mont. 1982)

TransAmerican Leasing Co. v. Three Bears, Inc., 568 S.W.2d 472
        (Tex. 1979)

O. J. & C. Co. v. General Hospital Leasing, Inc., 278 S.W.2d 877
        (Tex. 1979)

Bogatz v. Case Catering Corp., 383 N.Y.S.2d 535 (1976)

Fig. 112.   Uniform Laws Annotated, Sec. 2-302(1) (1976) Card

6/2/84

Seymour   (Unconscionable Contract)   Nick

Mo. Ann. Stat., Sec. 400.2-302(1) (Vernon 1965). "If the court as a matter of law finds the contract or any clause of the contract to have been unconscionable at the time it was made, the court may refuse to enforce the contract, or it may enforce the remainder of the contract without the unconscionable clause, or it may so limit the application of any unconscionable clause as to avoid any unconscionable result.

"(2) When it is claimed or appears to the court that the contract or any clause thereof may be unconscionable, the parties shall be afforded a reasonable opportunity to present evidence as to its commercial setting, purpose, and effect to aid the court in making the determination."

No helpful cases in the volume.

Pocket part for use in 1984.

x Funding Systems Leasing Corp. v. King Louis Internat'l, Inc.,
        597 S.W.2d 624 (Mo. 1979).

Fig. 113.   Mo. Ann. Stat., Sec. 400.2-302(1) (Vernon 1965) Card

based on legislative enactments and not on the common law. Any relevant cases would necessarily have emanated from the statute creating this theory in Missouri (Sec. 400.2-302) and would consequently have been listed in the annotated code, which he had already examined. (Ordinarily he would have looked in the digest when researching a question of contract law, since this subject is generally based on the common law.) He had looked at the only case discovered and had found that it did not apply, and so he stated this fact in his remarks.

There remained only Step 9, the making of a report, which Meyer did in the form of a Law Library Research Report.

6/2/84

Seymour   (Unconscionable Contract)   Nick
Funding Systems Leasing v. King Louis Internat'l, 597 S.W.2d 624
(Mo. 1979)

The case involved the leasing of automated radio equipment for a radio station by International Good Music, Inc. (IGM), one of the parties to this situation, to King Louis International, Inc. (King Louis), with "boiler plate" clauses in the lease very similar to those in the present case. The lease stated that "said lease shall be interpreted and all rights and liabilities of the parties here determined in accordance with the laws of New York." Therefore, although the case was decided in a Missouri court by a Missouri judge, it interpreted New York law. King Louis acknowledged that the disclaimers appeared in the lease in large print, but the company attempted to avoid the disclaimers therein on the grounds that they were unconscionable. New York has accepted the "Leff Test" of unconscionability, which states that there must be both procedural and substantive unconscionability. Substantive unconscionability consists of there being undue harshness in the contract's terms. Procedural unconscionability is involved with the formation of the contract itself, focusing on high pressure tactics, fine print, misrepresentation, and unequal bargaining positions. Both forms of unconscionability must be present to find a contract unconscionable; however, there may be a balancing between them or a sliding scale between them; and if there exists gross procedural unconscionability, then not much is needed in the form of substantive unconscionability, and vice versa.

Wasserstrom, J., on page 634 stated that King Louis would have had a strong case of substantive unconscionability if the agreement had deprived the company of all warranty rights. He found that the lease did not do this. On page 635, he stated that in the King Louis case, with regard to finding procedural unconscionability, it is ". . . flatly impossible to do so with respect to the aspect of procedural unconscionability. There can be no claim of surprise on the part of King Louis in light of the very prominent and conspicuous nature of the written disclaimer on the face of the lease agreement." He found no economic coercion, high pressure tactics, or inequality of position.

x Shepardized through May 1984.

Fig. 114.   Funding Systems Leasing v. King Louis Internat'l Card

Once the legal issues were resolved, the problems not covered by law had to be addressed. These involved the practicality of pursuing and the financial ability to pursue the issue to the desired conclusion. Meyer knew that having the law on one's side did not necessarily mean that one had the power to enforce it.

Law Library Research Report

Title: Unconscionable Contract

Requested by: Seymour

Submitted by: Meyer

Date Submitted: June 2, 1984

Statement of Facts   Nick, from Chillicothe, Missouri, met Ronald, from Blue Springs, Missouri, in Miami Beach and convinced Ronald that he should rent trucks from Nick for his soft drink distribution business. The parties met in St. Louis at the office of a truck dealer, where Ronald picked out six trucks he wished Nick to purchase for him to rent. A contract was drawn up for the rental of six trucks over a period of sixty months, the rent on each truck to be $1,000 per month. The contract was drawn up by Nick's attorney, but neither party was represented by an attorney at the signing of the lease. Nick purchased the trucks for $15,000 each. Pertinent terms of the contract, dated March 15, 1983, appeared in large print and eliminated any warranties and waived the lessee's right to make any claims against the lessor for any warranty. The contract stated that the lessee took the goods "as is." The lessee agreed that the lessor was under no obligation to install, test, adjust, or service the equipment, although the lessee was required to pay the full amount specified under the lease regardless of any defaults of the lessor. Upon any default by the lessee, the entire balance immediately became due and payable.

Shortly after delivery, the trucks started breaking down. Nick, the lessor, sent mechanics to see if the problem could be solved, but he finally gave up, informing Ronald, the lessee, that he had to comply with the terms of the contract. The lessee stopped paying the rent and responded that the contract should be set aside as unconscionable on the grounds that the lessor took advantage of the inexperience of the lessee, the price was excessive for the value received, and the lessor had wrongly relieved himself of all the normal obligations of a lessor.

Question Presented   Is a contract to lease trucks unconscionable because the lessor (1) charges four times the cost of the truck for rent over a five-year period; (2) has his attorney draw the lease specifically eliminating warranties, express or implied; (3) has the lessee waive the right to claim against the lessor for any breach of warranty, loss, damage, repairs, or other damage caused by the equipment; (4) makes the contract non-cancelable; and (5) insists that for any default by the lessor, the entire balance of payment under the lease becomes immediately due and payable?

Brief Answer   There is no clear answer to the question in Missouri, but the indications are that the terms of the contract are not unconscionable.

Discussion   The question of unconscionable contracts is covered in Missouri by Mo. Rev. Stat., Sec. 400.2-302(1) (1965), wherein the court stated that if, as a matter of law, the court finds the contract or any clause of the contract to have been unconscionable at the time it was made, the court may refuse to enforce the contract. The wording of the statute exactly follows U.C.C., Sec. 2-302. No case has interpreted the statute as it involves Missouri law. The only case decided in Missouri involving this section was an interpretation of the laws of the state of New York, *Funding Systems Leasing v. King Louis Internat'l,* 597 S.W.2d 624 (Mo. 1979). The case involved the leasing of automated radio equipment for a radio station by International Good Music, Inc. (IGM), one of the parties to the action, to King Louis International, Inc. (King Louis), with "boiler plate" clauses in the lease very similar to those in the present case. The lease stated that "said lease shall be interpreted and all rights and liabilities of the parties here determined in accordance with the laws of New York." King Louis acknowledged that the disclaimers appeared in the lease in large print, but the company attempted to avoid the disclaimers therein on the grounds that they were unconscionable. New York has accepted the Leff Test of unconscionability, which states that there must be both procedural and substantive unconscionability. Substantive unconscionability consists of there being undue harshness in the contract's terms. Procedural unconscionability is involved with the formation of the contract itself, focusing on high pressure tactics, fine print, misrepresentation, and unequal bargaining positions. Both forms of unconscionability must be present to find a contract unconscionable; however, there may be a balancing between them or a sliding scale between them; and if there exists gross procedural unconscionability, then not much is needed in the form of substantive unconscionability, and vice versa.

Wasserstrom, J., on page 634 stated that King Louis would have had a strong case of substantive unconscionability if the agreement had deprived the company of all warranty rights. He found that the lease did not do this. On page 635, he stated that in the King Louis case, with regard to finding procedural unconscionability, it is ". . . flatly impossible to do so with respect to the aspect of procedural unconscionability. There can be no claim of surprise on the part of King Louis in light of the very prominent and conspicuous nature of the written disclaimer on the face of the lease agreement." He found no economic coercion, high pressure tactics, or inequality of position.

This case has been Shepardized through May 1984.

There are no real indications whether Missouri will follow the lead of New York in accepting the Leff Test and make a distinction between substantive and procedural unconscionability.

U.C.C. Ann., Sec. 2-302(1) (1976) lists cases from a variety of jurisdictions that involve this problem, but these opinions do not lead to a consensus. Should Nick's present case proceed to trial, cases from other jurisdictions must be examined to locate the trend of decisions in the country, the jurisdictions with the best thought out decisions, and those that will carry the most persuasive authority. Those listed in the U.C.C. are as follows:

Eastern Oil Co., Inc. v. Burroughs Corp., 625 F.2d 1291 (Fla. 1980)

All-State Leasing Corp. v. Top Hat Lounge, Inc., 649 P.2d 1250 (Mont. 1982)

TransAmerican Leasing Co. v. Three Bears, Inc., 568 S.W.2d 472 (Tex. 1979)

O. J. & C. Co. v. General Hospital Leasing, Inc., 278 S.W.2d 877 (Tex. 1979)

Bogatz v. Case Catering Corp., 383 N.Y.S.2d 535 (1976)

Bibliography

(Note: The looseleaf materials listed below may set forth the best overview and provide the most up-to-date information. They are not completely described here because the services are tremendously expensive for individuals to purchase, the titles identify the topics, their formats are relatively similar, and most of these materials can be found in law libraries.

If a book cannot be found in your library or in the nearest law library, ask your librarian if it can be obtained through interlibrary loan.)

Calamari, John D., and Joseph M. Perillo. *The Law of Contracts.* 3d ed. St. Paul, Minn.: West, 1987.

Corbin, Arthur L. *Corbin on Contracts.* 8 vols. St. Paul, Minn.: West, 1950– . Kept up to date with pocket supplements and revised volumes.

Deutch, Sinai. *Unfair Contracts.* Lexington, Mass.: Lexington Bks., 1977. An exhaustive study of the doctrine of unconscionability in contracts, how it developed, and to what extent it has developed in U.S. law. Includes bibliography, table of cases, index, and chapter notes.

Elias, Stephen. *Make Your Own Contract.* Berkeley, Calif.: Nolo Pr., 1986. Includes sample forms.

Felsenfield, Carl, and Alan Siegel. *Writing Contracts in Plain English.* St. Paul, Minn.: West, 1981. A step-by-step process by a lawyer and a communicator showing how legal contracts can be written in plain, understandable English. Contains index, appendixes, notes, and forms.

Friedman, Jane M. *Contract Remedies in a Nutshell.* St. Paul, Minn.: West, 1981. Covers common-law and equitable remedies for breach of contract, contracts, remedies of the buyer and seller, contractual control over remedies, and remedies for mistake and unconscionability. Includes index, table of references to the Uniform Commercial Code, and official comments.

Hunter, Howard O. *Modern Law of Contracts.* Boston: Warren, Gorham, & Lamont, 1986– . Kept up to date with a cumulative annual supplementary pamphlet.

Neubert, Christopher, and Jack Withiam. *How to Handle Your Own Contracts: A Layman's Guide to Contracts, Leases, Wills, and Other Legal Agreements.* Rev. ed. New York: Greenwich House, 1984.

Schaber, Gordon D., and Claude D. Rohover. *Contracts in a Nutshell.* 2d ed. St. Paul, Minn.: West, 1984. Covers contracts from the offer through acceptance, consideration, statute of frauds, defenses, capacity, mistake, misrepresentation, duress, undue influence, unconscionability, public policy, third party beneficiaries, assignment, interpretations, parole evidence, performance, discharge, and remedies. With contract questions and index.

Stockton, John M. *Sales in a Nutshell.* 2d ed. St. Paul, Minn.: West, 1981. Covers definitions and subject matter, formation of contracts, statute of frauds, parole evidence, documents of title, performance, title, risk of loss, warranties, repudiation, breach, excuses, and seller's and buyer's remedies. With index, table of cases, table of references to U.C.C. provisions, and comments.

Williston, Samuel. *A Treatise on the Law of Contracts.* 3d ed. 22 vols. Prepared by Walter H. E. Jaeger. Rochester, N.Y.: Lawyers Cooperative/Bancroft-Whitney, 1957– . Kept up to date with pocket supplements.

Civil Rights

In common law, a person who serves the general public is required to serve anyone requesting his or her service without discrimination. This rule applies to such servicers as common carriers and innkeepers. Proprietors of private enterprises can serve anyone they please and can refuse to serve others. Civil rights, as these laws have become known, are dependent upon the Constitution and upon various statutes. Civil rights are variously defined, but basically they consist of those rights given to persons by constitutions and laws, and enforced by law. If there is no provision for enforcement, no right exists. Civil rights consist of those laws giving privileges to individuals that, if trespassed upon by another individual, allow the trespassed upon individual to seek redress through civil action in court. Civil rights have a basis only in the constitutions and laws that maintain and organize the government. If an imagined civil right is not defined in a constitution or statute and is not enforceable by law, it is not a civil right. Civil rights include such items as the right to property, marriage, legal protection, freedom of contract, trial by jury, freedom from interference with a person's lawful conduct and actions, suffrage, and the enjoyment of the guarantees provided under federal and state constitutions and statutes.

Civil rights are not the same as natural rights. Natural rights exist without statutes and constitutions. However, such natural rights may be limited by constitutions and statutes. Natural rights are frequently called civil liberties and are in the nature of restraints upon government, thus providing immunities for citizens.

Citizens of the United States have a variety of rights, and those rights are often confused and ill-defined. Political rights are the rights of citizens to participate in the establishment and management of the government.

Civil rights have been of great concern since the beginning of the United States. Article 6, Clause 2 of the Constitution provides that:

> This Constitution, and the laws of the United States which shall be made in pursuance thereof; and all Treaties made, or which shall be made, under the authority of the United States, shall be the supreme law of the land; and the judges in every State shall be bound thereby, any thing in the Constitution or laws of any State to the contrary notwithstanding.

With memories of ill treatment at the hands of the British, the Founding Fathers wished to establish a system in which the government was formed for the sole purpose of governing and in which the rights of the individual citizens remained predominant. The Constitution was immediately modified by the first ten amendments, frequently referred to as the "Bill of Rights." Without these essential amendments, which made clear the predominant position of the citizens, it is doubtful if the Constitution would have been ratified.

Amendment I provides for freedom of religion, speech, press, petition, and assembly.

Amendment II provides for the bearing of arms.

Amendment III forbids the quartering of soldiers in homes in peacetime without the consent of the owners, and in wartime except in the manner prescribed by law.

Amendment IV prohibits unreasonable searches and seizures.

Amendment V requires a grand jury indictment for capital crimes; due process of law before depriving a person of life, liberty, or property; and just compensation for the taking of property for public use. It also prohibits double jeopardy.

Amendment VI establishes the right of speedy and public trial, and trial by jury.

Amendment VIII prohibits excessive bail or fines, and cruel and unusual punishment.

Amendment IX provides that the enumeration in the Constitution of certain rights shall not deny other rights retained by the people.

Amendment X reserves for the states or for the people all powers not delegated to the United States by the Constitution.

The Civil War brought about the next flurry of civil rights actions with the passage of Amendment XIII to the Constitution, which eliminated slavery and involuntary servitude. The amendment also gave Congress the authority to enforce these rights through legislation, which Congress did with the passage of the Reconstruction Civil Rights Act. The provisions of the act are found in the Civil Rights Act of 1870 (42 U.S.C., Sec. 1981) and in the Civil Rights Act of 1866 (42 U.S.C., Sec. 1982), which follow:

42 U.S.C., Sec. 1981. Equal Rights Under the Law.

All persons within the jurisdiction of the United States shall have the same right in every State and Territory to make and enforce contracts, to sue, be parties, give evidence, and to the full and equal benefit of all laws and proceedings for the security of persons and property as is enjoyed by white citizens, and shall be subject to like punishment, pains, penalties, taxes, licenses, and exactions of every kind, and to no other.

The above section applies to racial discrimination only and has no effect on sexual discrimination or on discrimination on the basis of national origin. The following section concerns still more rights:

42 U.S.C., Sec. 1982. Property Rights of Citizens.

All citizens of the United States shall have the same right, in every State and Territory, as is enjoyed by white citizens thereof to inherit, purchase, lease, sell, hold, and convey real and personal property.

Amendment XIV to the Constitution, Section 1 prohibited the states from abridging the privileges or immunities of citizens of the United States; from depriving any person of life, liberty, or property without due process of law; and from denying any person within the jurisdiction of the state equal protection of the law. This amendment was directed specifically at the states, but it protected citizens residing therein as citizens of the United States only, not as citizens of the state. Acting under this amendment, Congress passed 42 U.S.C., Section 1983, which gave any injured party a process for redress.

42 U.S.C., Section 1985 makes it a federal crime to conspire to interfere with an officer in the performance of his or her duties; to obstruct justice; to intimidate parties, witnesses, or jurors; or to deprive persons of their rights or privileges. 42 U.S.C. Section 1987 provides for the arrest and imprisonment of individuals for the violation of the statutes.

42 U.S.C., Section 2000a prohibits discrimination or segregation in places of public accommodation, so long as such places remain open to the public. The facility must provide full and equal enjoyment of goods, services, facilities, advantages, privileges, and accommodations without discrimination or segregation on the basis of race, color, religion, or national origin. Restaurants and theaters are affected only if their operation affects commerce. If food or movie reels move in interstate commerce, or if they serve interstate travelers, they affect commerce and thereby become subject to the prohibition.

42 U.S.C., Section 2000a-2 prohibits the deprivation of, interference with, or punishment for the exercising of any of the rights or privileges, as set forth above, and 42 U.S.C., Section 2000a-3 allows court action for preventive relief when there are reasonable grounds to believe that such illegal actions are about to take place. 42 U.S.C., Section 2000b provides for actions by the Attorney General to intervene to see that preventive relief is provided, and 42 U.S.C., Section 2000b-2 allows individuals to sue if they are discriminated against in any facility covered by the subchapter.

The right to an education is not a federal civil right, but the opportunity for an education, when provided by a state, must be made available on equal terms. 42 U.S.C., Section 2000c-8 provides the right to sue for relief if one's rights are adversely affected by discrimination in public education, and 42 U.S.C., Section 2000d continues this protection to cover discrimination on the basis of race, color, or national origin involving federally assisted programs. 42 U.S.C., Section 2000d-6 declares a uniform policy of nondiscrimination in schools of local educational agencies as follows:

> 42 U.S.C., Sec. 2000d-6. Policy of United States as to application of nondiscrimination provisions in schools of local educational agencies.
>
> (a) It is the policy of the United States that guidelines and criteria established pursuant to title VI of the Civil Rights Act of 1964 and Section 1812 of the Elementary and Secondary Education Amendments of 1966 dealing with conditions of segregation by race, whether de jure or de facto, in the schools of the local educational agencies of any State shall be applied uniformly in all regions of the United States whatsoever the origin or cause of such segregation.

Continuing into fair housing, 42 U.S.C., Section 3601 declares that it is the policy of the United States to provide, within Constitutional limitations, fair housing throughout the United States, and Section 3604 covers discrimination in the sale or rental of housing. Section 3605 prohibits discrimination in financing housing, Section 3606 covers brokerage services, while Section 3607 exempts religious organizations and private clubs not open to the public. Section 3010 provides for enforcement of the statutes by the government, and Section 3612 allows private persons to sue.

Other sections of the federal statutes are involved in discrimination also. 18 U.S.C., Section 241 imposes fines and imprisonment for conspiring to deprive any citizen of the free exercise of any rights or privileges secured by the Constitution or laws of the United States, while Section 242 makes such action illegal if done under color of law. "Under color of law" is a shorthand phrase equivalent to "under color of any statute, ordinance, regulation, custom, or usage." Section 234 prohibits the exclusion of jurors on account of race or color, and Section 245 protects a variety of activities from discriminatory actions whether or not such actions are done under color of law.

Native Americans are not covered under any of the above statutes because the Constitution of the United States does not apply to any Native American tribe. However, Congress has the power to enact legislation concerning such tribes, and under 25 U.S.C., Section 1302 Congress has prohibited Native American tribes from restricting freedom of religion, speech, or press, or the right of petition and assembly. Included in the section are also limitations on searches and seizures, double jeopardy, testifying against oneself, taking private property without just compensation, excessive bail or fines, and cruel and unusual punishment. A person also may not be denied a speedy trial and must have equal protection of the law. Section 1303 gives Native Americans the privilege of the writ of habeas corpus.

Older workers now have protection under 29 U.S.C., Section 621. Congressional statement of findings and purpose, which provides the following:

(a) The Congress hereby finds and declares that
   (1) in the face of rising productivity and affluence, older workers find themselves disadvantaged in their efforts to retain employment, and especially to regain employment when displaced from jobs;
   (2) the setting of arbitrary age limits regardless of potential for job performance has become a common practice, and certain otherwise desirable practices may work to the disadvantage of older persons;
   (3) the incidence of unemployment, especially long-term unemployment with resultant deterioration of skill, morale, and employer acceptability is, relative to the younger ages, high among older workers; their numbers are great and growing; and their employment problems grave;
   (4) the existence in industries affecting commerce, of arbitrary discrimination in employment because of age, burdens commerce and the free flow of goods in commerce.
(b) It is therefore the purpose of this chapter to promote employment of older persons based on their ability rather than age; to prohibit arbitrary age discrimination in employment; to help employers and workers find ways of meeting problems arising from the impact of age on employment.

Introduction to Research Problem

In common law, no civil right of employment exists. Such rights are brought about only by constitutions and statutes in the federal and state governments. Employment is included in the list of items protected by federal statutes, and 29 U.S.C., Section 206 establishes a minimum wage for all those engaged in commerce and also prohibits sex discrimination in employment. Much controversy has arisen over the definition of sex discrimination, including problems of promoting women to higher levels of employment and of pay scales for women that differ from pay scales for men who do the same job. Most recently, this controversy has shown up in the request for comparable wages for comparable jobs.

Remember, for background material on the tools used in legal research, review the section titled "Where It Is Recorded"; and for an example of the use of these tools in a legal research problem, see "How to Find It." For unfamiliar terms, see the Glossary. See Appendix A for abbreviations.

The legal explanations and the issues selected here are not comprehensive due to space limitations. Should the researcher become interested in a legal problem not covered by the background material, by the introduction, or by the research problem, he or she should note the question, and, using the procedures suggested in this book, perform his or her own legal research to discover the answer.

Research Problem

The research tools used in this problem consist of the Search Process Flow Chart, the CORP rule, statutes, reporters, and citators.

Rosie grew up on a Texas ranch, finished high school, and obtained a job with a firm named Construction Co., which specializes in building federal highways. Her job is that of a flag person, the one who directs traffic around construction, allows the traffic to flow one way at a time, and stops all traffic when construction equipment blocks the roadway. Rosie's job requires her to be outside in all sorts of weather, mental alertness, some judgment, but not much physical effort. It also entails a certain amount of danger, some to herself but more to the travelers on the highway and to the other construction workers. She works mostly with Carrie, who handles the same job but at the other end of the construction project. They communicate by walkie-talkie radios to coordinate the flow of traffic and to keep things running smoothly. The pay scale for this job, negotiated between the contractor and the union, is $4.95 per hour, up from the $2.25 Rosie earned when she started work several years ago. Neither the contract nor the job description makes any mention of the sex of the person required for the job. The hours are the same as those of the rest of the construction crew.

After hours, the single members of the crew gather at a local pub for a couple of beers, talk, and relaxation before going home. Rosie has become quite friendly with Jake, who holds a job as a laborer and works with the asphalt-laying crew. His job is to accompany the machine, clear away obstructions in its path, and shovel asphalt and gravel, as required, to produce a sound base for the asphalt. His job also requires shoveling asphalt, as required, to fill in holes before rolling the asphalt, and fixing up the gutters on the side. The job requires considerable physical exertion, not much training or judgment, and some danger, mainly to Jake. Neither the contract nor the job description makes any mention of the sex of the person required for the job. Jake's pay scale for this job is set by union contract at $6.28 per hour. Rosie and Jake naturally talk about their jobs, and the more they talk, the more Rosie feels that she should receive wages comparable to those of Jake.

In checking, Rosie discovers that all of the flag persons are female, but there are no female laborers. She sits down to draw up a list comparing the jobs as follows:

JOB COMPARISONS—FLAG PERSON AND LABORER

Rosie, Flag Person	Jake, Laborer
Employer: Construction Co.	Construction Co.
Project: federal road building	federal road building
Hours: 8 hrs. a day, 5 days a week	8 hrs. a day, 5 days a week
Pay: $4.95 per hr.	$6.28 per hr.
Conditions: outdoor work; dusty or muddy work	outdoor work; hot, dusty, or muddy work
Responsibility: to self, co-workers, and travelers	to self
Danger: to co-workers, self, and travelers	to self
Personnel: all flag persons female	all laborers male

Rosie and Carrie call a meeting of the female flag persons, they outline what they have discovered, and they ask if the others will join them in requesting that their job be considered comparable to that of a laborer, entitling them to the same pay and benefits. About three-quarters of the women agree to go along with this plan if doing so doesn't cost too much; on $4.95 per hour, the women don't have much money to spare for legal expenses.

Rosie has a high school chum who is married to Willie Smart, a lawyer. Willie works with a local branch of the American Civil Liberties Union (ACLU). After hearing the story, he tells Rosie that he will look into her case and will let her know if he thinks it would be worthwhile to ask the ACLU to aid Rosie and her colleagues.

Willie is going to have to do the research on this one himself and on his own time because his work at the ACLU does not allow him time to work on other matters during office hours. Unless Willie can convince the ACLU that Rosie's is a cause they should consider, he is on his own. He considers Rosie's case good experience and therefore does not mind the long hours he will have to put in on her behalf. The first thing he does is to write up the facts as he sees them on a 4″ x 6″ index card (Fig. 115).

The next evening after work, Willie enters the quite extensive library of the ACLU, taking with him his Search Process Flow Chart and 4″ x 6″ cards. The chart will be used to economize his efforts and to keep him on track while he does his research. He also reviews the CORP rule: C for cause of action, O

```
                            2/3/84
Rosie                 (Comparable Wages)              Rosie et al.
Facts: Rosie works with Construction Co., which specializes in build-
ing federal highways. Her job is that of a flag person. Jake, a laborer,
works with the asphalt-laying crew. Neither the contract nor the
job description makes any mention of the sex of the persons required
for these jobs. The jobs are compared below:
              Job Comparisons—Flag Person and Laborer
        Rosie, Flag Person                    Jake, Laborer
Employer, Construction Co.           Construction Co.
Project, federal road building       Federal road building
8 hrs. a day, 5 days a week          8 hrs. a day, 5 days a week
Pay, $4.95 per hr.                    $6.28 per hr.
Outdoor work                         Outdoor work
Dusty or muddy work                  Hot, dusty, or muddy work
Responsibility to self, co-          Responsibility to self
    workers, and travelers
Danger to co-workers, self,          Danger to self
    and travelers
All flag persons female              All laborers male
```

Fig. 115.   Comparable Wages Fact Card

for object involved, *R* for restitution, and *P* for parties. He will use the CORP rule to assure himself that he has found all of the useful search words.

Step 1 on the chart advises Willie to make a list of words to be used in his legal research. Working as he does for the American Civil Liberties Union, he thinks of two words to begin with, *civil rights* and *comparable wages*. Taking a volume of *West's Federal Practice Digest 2d* from the shelf, he skims through the Outline of the Law to see if there are other words he should consider. Here he locates *labor relations*. Then, turning to the Digest of Topics in the same volume, he attempts to complete his list. Finding nothing new, he jots down his list, which consists of *civil rights, comparable wages,* and *labor relations.* Although the problem may involve labor relations, Willie feels that the focus will be on civil rights and on comparable wages, so he picks these terms to examine first.

Step 2 of the chart concerns jurisdiction. Remembering that most of the material he has been working with is on the federal level and reviewing the facts as presented, Willie concludes that the jurisdiction will be federal. This means that he will be searching for Constitutional provisions, federal statutes, and federal cases.

He decides to skip Step 3 (review a textbook or encyclopedia) because he is fairly familiar with the background of the law involving civil rights as a result of his job. This step brings him to the framing of the issue (Step 4), which he enters on a card (Fig. 116).

Willie knows that this is a fairly new concept and recalls that for such "cutting edge" legal theories it often is a good idea to consult sources of recent commentary, usually in the form of legal periodical articles. Such articles will often provide information about new cases or statutes that would otherwise be

```
                              2/3/84
Rosie                  (Comparable Wages)                Rosie et al.
Issue: Is the job of a flag person on a construction job comparable
to that of a laborer on a construction job, so as to require the
payment of equal wages for the two positions?
```

Fig. 116. Comparable Wages Issue Card

difficult to find. These articles are often looked to by courts that are struggling with novel theories of liability. Willie quickly locates several articles about comparable worth by using recent issues of the *Index to Legal Periodicals* and discovers that this concept arises out of the Equal Pay Act of 1963 and the Civil Rights Act of 1964, Title VII. Step 5 on the chart leads him to the statute finders, and for these he uses the general index of the United States Code. The version available to Willie in the library is the *United States Code Annotated (U.S.C.A.)*; and since he knows the popular name of the statute he is looking for (i.e., Equal Pay Act of 1963), he uses the "Popular Name Table" that is included with the general index. He finds the act listed as Title 29, Section 206. Taking 29 U.S.C.A. from the shelf, Willie finds Section 206; and running through the table of contents for this section, he comes across Section 206(d)(1). Following Step 6 on his chart, he reads the section and enters that information on a card (Fig. 117).

Following the text of the statute, Willie finds sections intended as aids to researchers, covering such items as historic notes, cross-references, library references, the Code of Federal Regulation references, references, and notes on decisions, which are divided into "I General" and "II Sex Discrimination 61-93." Under "Sex Discrimination," there is a subdivision index, which, when checked, indicates that Section 66 considers "Comparability, equality, or identity of work performed generally." Rosie's case is in Texas, and Texas is within the jurisdiction of the Fifth Federal Judicial Circuit, currently along with Louisiana and Mississippi. The Fifth Circuit until 1980 included the above states plus Alabama, Georgia, and Florida. Therefore, Willie is mainly interested in cases decided either in the Fifth Circuit or by the Supreme Court. He knows that cases decided in the former Fifth Circuit involving the states of Alabama, Georgia, and Florida should also be included in the research, especially because many of the judges from the old Fifth Circuit still serve in the new Fifth Circuit. Cases from other circuits would not be precedents but might prove persuasive in case no decisions in Rosie's jurisdiction are located. Under "References and Notes on Decisions, II Sex Discrimination 66, Comparability, equality, or identity of work performed, generally," Willie finds the following notes and cases: "Application of Subsec. (d) of this section is not restricted to identical work. *Brennan v. Prince William Hospital Corp.*, C.A.Va. 1974, 503 F.2d 282, cert. den. 420 U.S. 973."

This is a Virginia case in the Fourth Circuit, but it did go to the Supreme Court, which refused to hear the case. The reasons for refusal may be many

2/3/84

Rosie   (Comparable Wages)   Rosie et al.

29 U.S.C.A. 206(d)(1). "No employer having employees subject to any provisions of this section shall discriminate, within any establishment in which such employees are employed, between employees on the basis of sex by paying wages to employees in such establishment at a rate less than the rate at which he pays wages to employees of the opposite sex in such establishment for equal work on jobs the performance of which requires equal skill, effort, and responsibility, and which are performed under similar working conditions, except where such payment is made pursuant to (i) a seniority system; (ii) a merit system; (iii) a system which measures earnings by quantity or quality of production; or (iv) a differential based on any other factor other than sex: Provided, That an employer who is paying a wage rate differential in violation of this subsection shall not, in order to comply with the provisions of this subsection, reduce the wage rate of any employee."

x Brennan v. Prince William Hospital Corp., C.A.Va. 1974, 503 F.2d
        282, cert. den. 420 U.S. 973
x Brennan v. City Stores, Inc., C.A.Ala. 1973, 479 F.2d 235
x Hodgson v. Golden Isles Convalescent Homes, Inc., C.A.Fla. 1972,
        468 F.2d 1256
x Hill v. J. C. Penney Co., Inc., C.A.Tex. 1982, 688 F.2d 370
x Marshall v. Dallas Independent School District, C.A.Tex. 1979, 605
        F.2d 191
x Schulte v. Wilson Industries, Inc., D.C.Tex. 1982, 547 F.Supp. 324
x Hodgson v. Madison, D.C.La. 1972, 344 F.Supp. 843

Fig. 117.   29 U.S.C.A. 206(d)(1) Card

and may not be stated, so the case's validity as a precedent in the Fifth Circuit may be suspect but will be noted by Willie as possibly worth investigating.

When Congress enacted equal pay provision of subsec. (d) of this section, it substituted the word "equal" for "comparable" to show that jobs involved should be virtually identical, that is, they should be very much alike or closely related to each other and restrictions were meant to apply only to jobs that are substantially identical or equal. *Brennan v. City Stores, Inc.*, C.A.Ala. 1973, 479 F.2d 235, rehearing denied 481 F.2d 1403. This case is from the former Fifth Circuit and must be given considerable weight. "For Subsec. (d)(1) of this section to be applicable, there must be substantial identity of job functions, and not merely comparable skill and responsibility. *Hodgson v. Golden Isles Convalescent Homes, Inc.*, C.A.Fla. 1972, 468 F.2d 1256." This case is also from the former Fifth Circuit and must be considered.

Under the pocket part, Willie finds other cases, including federal district court cases in both Texas and Louisiana, and some cases from the Fifth Circuit, which he notes to examine but does not copy the entire listing. They are as follows:

Hill v. J. C. Penney Co., Inc., C.A.Tex. 1982, 688 F.2d 370
Marshall v. Dallas, C.A.Tex. 1979, 605 F.2d 191

Schulte v. Wilson Industries, Inc., D.C.Tex. 1982, 547 F.Supp. 324
Hodgson v. Madison, D.C.La. 1972, 344 F.Supp. 843

These cases are entered on the card covering 29 U.S.C.A. 206(d)(1) (Fig. 117) and are checked off as Willie examines them. Step 7 instructs him to return to Step 6 for the new cases he has found. For those he wishes to use, he makes separate cards (Fig. 118), as specified in Step 6.

Step 8 is taken care of by the Shepardizing process, so Willie can now proceed to Step 6 for the next case (Fig. 119).

Step 8 is taken care of by the Shepardizing process, so Willie can now proceed to Step 6 for the next case (Fig. 120).

Step 8 is taken care of by the Shepardizing process, so Willie again can proceed to Step 6 for the next case (Fig. 121).

Step 8 has been performed by the Shepardizing process, so Willie proceeds to Step 6 for the next case (Fig. 122).

Willie notes that he has found a new case to examine—the Corning Glass Works case—and Step 7 reminds him that he must investigate this case later. Step 8 has been performed by the Shepardizing process, so Willie can now proceed to Step 6 for the next case (Fig. 123).

Step 8 has been taken care of by the Shepardizing process, so again Willie proceeds to Step 6 for the next case (Fig. 124).

Willie, having entered on the cards the cases he has found in the notes of *U.S.C.A.* concerning the subject, reviews his cards. He finds that in one case (*Marshall v. Dallas,* above), there is a reference to another case decided by the Supreme Court. This fact alerts him to Step 7 of the chart, which instructs him

---

2/3/84

Rosie   (Comparable Wages)   Rosie et al.
Brennan v. Prince William Hospital Corp., 503 F.2d 282 (5th Cir.Va. 1974), cert. den. 420 U.S. 973

   Butzner, J., after stating that the Equal Pay Act must be applied on a case-by-case basis because of the unique factual situations, decided that although one of the most common grounds for justifying wage differentials is an assertion that male employees perform extra tasks, this assertion may not be allowed to mask the existence of wage discrimination based on sex. He found that the positions of hospital aids and orderlies showed no difference in skill, effort, or responsibility. He found no substantial extra work accounting for the difference in the wage scales. The tasks of each are not identical, but the basic routine tasks are equal. When jobs are substantially equal, a minimal amount of extra skill, effort, or responsibility cannot justify wage differentials. The application of 29 U.S.C. 206(d)(1) is not restricted to identical work.

   This is a Virginia case, 4th Circuit, but it did go to the Supreme Court, which refused to hear it.

x Shepardized through Jan. 1984; no case changed results.

Fig. 118. Brennan v. Prince William Hospital Corp. Card

to return to Step 6 for any new cases he finds and to examine them. Willie does this task and enters the Corning Glass Works case on a card (Fig. 125).

No new cases having been found, Willie can proceed to Step 9 and make a report of his findings. This he will do in the form of a Law Library Research Report.

Once the legal issues are resolved, the problems not covered by law must be addressed. These involve the practicality of pursuing and the financial ability to pursue the issue to the desired conclusion. Willie knows that having the law on one's side does not necessarily mean that one has the power to enforce it.

2/3/84

Rosie   (Comparable Wages)   Rosie et al.
Brennan v. City Stores, Inc., 479 F.2d 235, 238 (5th Cir. Ala. 1973)
   Tuttle, J., stated, "When Congress enacted the Equal Pay Act it substituted the word 'equal' for 'comparable' to show that the jobs involved should be virtually identical, that is, they would be very much alike or closely related to each other. The restrictions in the act were meant to 'apply only to jobs that are substantially identical or equal.' While the standard of equality is clearly higher than mere comparability, yet lower than absolute identity, there remains an area of equality under the act the metes and bounds of which are still indefinite."
   This case is from the former Fifth Circuit and must be given considerable weight.
x Shepardized through Jan. 1984, mentioned in seven cases, and
      followed in one case from the 5th Cir.; no cases changed results.

Fig. 119.   Brennan v. City Stores, Inc. Card

2/3/84

Rosie   (Comparable Wages)   Rosie et al.
Hodgson v. Golden Isles Convalescent Homes, Inc., 468 F.2d 1256
(5th Cir. Fla. 1972)
   The Court stated on page 1258: "By substituting the term 'equal work' for 'comparable work,' which was originally suggested, Congress manifested its intent to narrow the applicability of the Act. . . . It is not merely comparable skill and responsibility that Congress sought to address, but a substantial identity of job functions."
   This case is from the former Fifth Circuit and must be given considerable weight.
x Shepardized through Jan. 1984 and mentioned in one case; no
      case changed results.

Fig. 120.   Hodgson v. Golden Isles Convalescent Homes, Inc. Card

Law Library Research Report

Title: Comparable Wages
Requested by: Rosie
Submitted by: Willie Smart
Date Submitted: February 5, 1984

Statement of Facts   Rosie works with Construction Co., which specializes in building federal highways. Her job is that of a flag person, the one who directs traffic around the construction, allows the traffic to flow one way at a time, and stops all traffic when construction equipment blocks the roadway. Jake, a laborer, works with the asphalt-laying crew. Neither the contract nor the job description makes any mention of the sex of the person required for either job. The comparison of the jobs is as follows:

JOB COMPARISONS—FLAG PERSON AND LABORER

Rosie, Flag Person	*Jake, Laborer*
Employer: Construction Co.	Construction Co.
Project: federal road building	federal road building
Hours: 8 hrs. a day, 5 days a week	8 hrs. a day, 5 days a week
Pay $4.95 per hr.	$6.28 per hr.
Conditions: outdoor work; dusty or muddy work	outdoor work; hot, dusty, or muddy work
Responsibility: to self, co-workers, and travelers	to self
Danger: to co-workers, self, and travelers	to self
Personnel: all flag persons female	all laborers male

2/3/84

Rosie   (Comparable Wages)   Rosie et al.
Hill v. J. C. Penney Co., Inc., 688 F.2d 370 (5th Cir. Tex. 1982)
   A female seamstress was paid much less than an alleged male supervisor (Carter) in a department consisting of two people. The male supervisor was also responsible for hiring, evaluating (oral input), and determining when to ship out excess work in overload situations. Evaluations of him did not mention him as a supervisor, nor was he rated on the standard form for supervisors but on the same form used to rate seamstresses.
   Garza, J., on page 374 characterized Carter's position as supervisor as simply an illusionary designation, i.e., he was a figurehead. His nominal position involved no real added responsibility. On page 376, the court affirmed the district court's determination that J. C. Penney Co., Inc., violated the Equal Pay Act (29 U.S.C. 206(d)(1)) in not paying the seamstress wages equal to those of Carter.
x Shepardized through Jan. 1984; no cases found altering this interpretation.

Fig. 121.   Hill v. J. C. Penney Co., Inc. Card

Question Presented   Is the job of a flag person on a construction job comparable to that of a laborer on a construction job, so as to require the payment of equal wages for the two positions?

Brief Answer   Although some similarities exist in the positions of flag person and laborer, and there are indications that comparable wages for comparable jobs are acceptable, the jobs must be something more than comparable but not necessarily equal. In view of the cases found in the Fifth Circuit, it

---

2/3/84

Rosie   (Comparable Wages)   Rosie et al.

Marshall v. Dallas, 605 F.2d. 191 (5th Cir. Tex. 1979)

In a school district, Helpers 1 had a year-round job of heavy custodial work, while Helpers 2 did light custodial work for nine months of the year. Some of the work involved was done by both classes of helpers, e.g., cleaning classrooms, etc.

Wisdom, J., on page 196 quoted from Corning Glass Works v. Brennan, 417 U.S. 188 (1974): "This court has formulated the following equality standard: When Congress enacted the Equal Pay Act, it substituted the word 'equal' for 'comparable' to show that the jobs involved should be virtually identical, that is, they would be very much alike or closely related to each other.' The restrictions in the Act were meant to 'apply only to jobs that were substantially identical or equal.' " Wisdom, J., found that the jobs of Helper 1 and Helper 2 were not comparable.

x Shepardized through Jan. 1984; no cases found altering this interpretation.

Fig. 122.   Marshall v. Dallas Card

2/3/84

Rosie   (Comparable Wages)   Rosie et al.

Schulte v. Wilson Industries, Inc., 547 F.Supp. 324 (D.C. Tex. 1982)

The company hired male employees for the same position held by a female employee for greater pay than she received and gave raises quicker to the male employees. The employee hired to assist her had little experience; she trained him, and he received initially a pay higher than hers. No valid reasons were given by the company for the wage disparity.

McDonald, J., on page 338 stated that the work need not be identical but substantially equal. He found that the Equal Pay Act had been violated.

x Shepardized through Jan. 1984; no cases found altering this interpretation.

Fig. 123.   Schulte v. Wilson Industries, Inc. Card

would appear that the jobs would not be considered comparable because of their dissimilarity.

Discussion   29 U.S.C., Section 206(d)(1) prohibits the payment of different wages based on sex for "equal work on jobs the performance of which requires equal skill, effort, and responsibility, and which are performed under similar working conditions. . . ."

The Supreme Court has looked at this issue, and in the case of *Corning Glass Works v. Brennan*, 417 U.S. 188 (1974), found that the payment of higher wages to night shift inspectors than to day shift inspectors doing the same job

---

2/3/84

Rosie   (Comparable Wages)   Rosie et al.
Hodgson v. Madison, 344 F.Supp. 843 (5th Cir. La. 1972)
    Male orderlies were paid twenty to forty cents more per hour than female nurses' aids. Patient care by both was almost identical. Orderlies performed some manual tasks that aids did not, up to two hours per shift.
    West, J., on page 847 found that the added labor did not consume a significant amount of the orderlies' time and did not merit more pay than the aids received.
x Shepardized through Jan. 1984; no cases found altering this interpretation.

Fig. 124.   Hodgson v. Madison Card

2/3/84

Rosie   (Comparable Wages)   Rosie et al.
Corning Glass Works v. Brennan, 417 U.S. 188 (1974)
    Night shift inspectors were paid more than day shift inspectors. The 2d Cir. held that the practice violated 29 U.S.C., Sec. 206(d)(1), and the 3d Cir. in a like case held that the practice did not violate the act.
    The union contract established a plant-wide pay differential for day and night workers; and under this contract, night inspectors were paid more than day inspectors. Night inspectors were traditionally male; day inspectors, female. The differential was kept because women would perform the same work for lower wages than the men.
    The court found that the situation was not cured when females were allowed to bid for the night inspectors' jobs; women were still left on the day shift in lower paying jobs, doing the same work.
x Shepardized through Jan. 1984; no cases found altering this interpretation.

Fig. 125.   Corning Glass Works v. Brennan Card

was contrary to 20 U.S.C., Section 206(d)(1) when the day shift consisted of predominantly females, and the night shift, males. The Court found that the only reason for the disparity in wages was the fact that women would work at a lower wage during the day than the men would. The fact that women were allowed to bid for the night inspectors' positions did not change the situation, for it left the day shift still predominantly female.

The Supreme Court refused to hear a Fourth Circuit case in which it was decided that the tasks of female nurses' aids were sufficiently equal to those of male orderlies to require equal pay under the act. It found that the tasks of each were not identical but that the basic routine of the tasks was equal; and when jobs are substantially equal, a minimal amount of extra skill, effort, or responsibility cannot justify wage differentials. *Brennan v. Prince William Hospital Corp.*, 503 F.2d 282 (4th Cir. 1974).

A case arising in a federal district for Louisiana also found that a twenty- to thirty-cent-per-hour wage differential between male orderlies and female nurses' aids was contrary to the act because the patient care provided by both was almost identical. The orderlies performed some manual tasks that the aids did not, up to two hours per shift. The judge found that the added labor did not consume a significant amount of the orderlies' time and did not entitle them to more pay than the aids received. *Hodgson v. Madison*, 344 F.Supp. 843 (D.C.La. 1972).

In a recent federal district court in Texas, the question of comparable wages arose. A company hired male employees for the same position held by a female employee for greater pay than she received, and it gave raises quicker to the male employees. The employee hired to assist her had little experience; she trained him, and he received initially a pay higher than hers. No valid reasons were given by the company for the wage disparity. It was decided that the work need not be identical but substantially equal. In this case, the Equal Pay Act had been violated. *Schulte v. Wilson Industries, Inc.*, 547 F.Supp. 324 (D.C. Tex. 1982).

The Fifth Circuit Court has also spoken on this subject. In *Brennan v. City Stores, Inc.*, 479 F.2d 235 (5th Cir., Ala. 1973) Tuttle, J., stated, "When Congress enacted the equal pay provision of Subsec. (d) of this section, it substituted the word 'equal' for 'comparable' to show that the jobs involved should be very much alike or closely related to each other and restrictions were meant to apply only to jobs that are substantially identical or equal." He continued that while the standard of equality is clearly higher than mere comparability, yet lower than absolute identity, there remains an area of equality under the act the metes and bounds of which are still indefinite.

In a Florida case presented to the Fifth Circuit, it was stated that, "by substituting the term 'equal work' for 'comparable work,' which was originally suggested, Congress manifested its intent to narrow the applicability of the Act.... It is not merely comparable skills and responsibilities that Congress sought to address, but a substantial identity of job functions." *Hodgson v. Golden Isles Convalescent Homes, Inc.*, 468 F.2d 1256 (5th Cir. Fla. 1972).

In a Texas case, *Marshall v. Dallas*, 605 F.2d 191 (5th Cir. Tex. 1979), a school district hired Helpers 1 for a year-round job of heavy custodial work, while Helpers 2 did light custodial work for nine months of the year. Some of the work involved was done by both classes of helpers, e.g., cleaning classrooms, etc. Wisdom, J., on page 196 quoted from *Corning Glass Works v. Brennan*, 417 U.S. 188 (1974): "This court has formulated the following equality standard: When Congress enacted the Equal Pay Act, it substituted the word 'equal' for 'comparable' to show that the jobs involved should be virtually identical, that is, they would be very much alike or closely related to each other. The restrictions in the Act were meant to apply only to jobs that were substantially identical or equal." The judge found that the jobs of Helper 1 and Helper 2 were not comparable.

In a recent Texas case from the Fifth Circuit, *Hill v. J. C. Penney Co., Inc.*, 688 F.2d 370 (5th Cir. Tex. 1982), a female seamstress was paid much less than an alleged male supervisor (Carter) in a department consisting of two people. The male supervisor was also responsible for hiring, evaluating (oral input), and determining when to ship out excess work in overload situations. Evaluations of him did not mention him as a supervisor, nor was he rated on the standard form for supervisors but on the same form used to rate seamstresses. His position as a supervisor was characterized as being simply an illusionary designation, i.e., he was a figurehead. His nominal position involved no real added responsibility.

Bibliography

(Note: If a book cannot be found in your library or in the nearest law library, ask your librarian if it can be obtained through interlibrary loan.)

Abernathy, M. Glenn. *Civil Liberties Under the Constitution.* 4th ed. Columbia, S.C.: Univ. of South Carolina Pr., 1985.

Abraham, Henry J. *Freedom and the Court.* 4th ed. New York: Oxford Univ. Pr., 1982. Considers the Supreme Court's role in solving issues regarding the relationship between basic liberties and the judicial process, the Bill of Rights, due process, freedom of expression, religion, race, and gender. Includes bibliographic note, appendixes, general index, name index, case index, notes, and tables.

ADEA. Compiled by the Commission on Legal Problems of the Elderly, Amer. Bar Assn. Washington, D.C.: Commission on Legal Problems of the Elderly, 1983. A summary of the most significant decisions relative to the Age Discrimination in Employment Act.

Adler, Allan, ed. *Litigation Under the Federal Freedom of Information Act and Privacy Act.* 10th ed. Washington, D.C.: Center for Nat'l. Security Studies in Cooperation with the Freedom of Info. Clearing House, 1985. A reference manual for attorneys and related professionals covering the Freedom of Information Act, agency records, administrative process, exemptions from the act, and the Privacy Act. With appendix.

Antieau, Chester J. *Federal Civil Rights Acts—Civil Practice.* 2d ed. 2 vols. Rochester, N.Y.: Lawyers Cooperative/Bancroft-Whitney, 1980. Complete, up-to-date coverage of civil legislation under the Federal Civil Rights Act. With index and notes. Cumulative pocket part.

Baer, Judith A. *Equality Under the Constitution.* Ithaca, N.Y.: Cornell Univ. Pr., 1983. An examination of equality under the Constitution, including age, disability, and gay rights. Contains bibliography, general index, index of cases, and notes.

Chamberlin, Bill F., and Charlene J. Brown, eds. *The First Amendment Rediscovered.* New York: Longman, 1982. Encourages research in the First Amendment, both historical and empirical. Covers the role of the states, the meaning of freedom of the press, and the First Amendment. Includes subject index, case index, appendix, and notes.

Cook, Joseph G., and John L. Sobieski. *Civil Rights Actions.* 3 vols. New York: Matthew Bender & Co., 1983– . With bibliographical references and index. In looseleaf for updating.

Coutner, Richard C. *The Supreme Court and the Second Bill of Rights.* Madison, Wis.: Univ. of Wisconsin Pr., 1981. Covers the 13th, 14th, and 15th Amendments to the Constitution, and the restraints they place on the states. With notes on sources, notes, index of cases, and general index.

Curtis, Michael Kent. *No State Shall Abridge: The 14th Amendment and the Bill of Rights.* Durham, N.C.: Duke Univ. Pr., 1986.

Equal Employment Advisory Council. *Comparable Worth.* Washington, D.C.: Equal Employment Advisory Council, 1981. Contains discussions by various authorities representing government, academia, and industry, on the comparable worth theory of wages. Includes tables.

Free Press Fair Trial. Amer. Soc. of Newspaper Eds./Amer. Newspaper Pubs. Assn. Foundation, 1982. An analysis of the historic and legal precedents concerning the First Amendment. With footnotes.

Freilich, Robert H., and Richard G. Carlisle. *Sword and Shield: Section 1983: Civil Rights Violations: The Liability of Urban, State, and Local Government.* Chicago: Amer. Bar Assn., 1983.

Guidebook to the Freedom of Information and Privacy Acts. 2d ed. Compiled by Justin D. Franklin and Robert F. Bouchard. New York: Clark Boardman, 1986. An explanation of how to use the FOIA and Privacy Act to obtain government data and business data. Includes a state-by-state listing of freedom of information statutes. Includes text of the acts, bibliography, and index. In looseleaf for updating.

Hermann, Michele G. *Search and Seizure Checklist.* 2d ed. New York: Clark Boardman, 1982. A quick reference and outline of 4th Amendment law, covering search, seizure, arrest, search warrant requirements, vehicle stop and searches, luggage, inventory, plain view, consent, mail, electronic surveillance, institutions, and interrogations.

Jones, Augustus J., Jr. *Law, Bureaucracy, and Politics.* Washington, D.C.: Univ. Pr. of America, 1982. An analysis of legislative efforts to overcome and redress racial discrimination and inequities, specifically examining the actors and dynamics involved in implementing Title VI of the Civil Rights Act of 1964. With index, bibliography, tables, and list of tables.

LaFave, Wayne R. *Search and Seizure.* 3 vols. St. Paul, Minn.: West, 1978. Covers the exclusionary rule, probable cause, search warrants, seizure and search of persons and personal effects, entry, vehicles, consent, stop and frisk, inspections, and administration of the exclusionary rule. Includes index, notes, and tables of statutes. With pocket parts.

Livernash, E. Robert, ed. *Comparable Worth: Issues and Alternatives.* Washington, D.C.: Equal Employment Advisory Council, 1980. A comprehensive analysis of the concept of equal pay for jobs of comparable worth, with articles addressing economic, social, and legal aspects of the concept. Contains table of cases, supplemental readings, notes, and figures.

Misner, Robert L. *Speedy Trial, Federal and State Practice.* Charlottesville, Va.: Michie Co., 1983. Covers the 6th Amendment in federal courts by circuits, the Speedy Trial Act of 1974, and Constitutional, statutory, and procedural rights to a speedy trial in the states and in the District of Columbia. With pocket parts, appendixes, table of cases, index, and notes.

Morgan, Richard E. *The Law and Politics of Civil Rights and Liberties.* New York: Knopf, 1985.

Nahmod, Sheldon H. *Civil Rights and Civil Liberties Litigation: The Law of Section 1983.* 2d ed. Colorado Springs, Colo.: Shepard's/McGraw-Hill, 1986.

Newman, Edwin S., and Daniel S. Moretti. *Civil Liberty and Civil Rights.* 7th ed. Legal Almanac Series. New York: Oceana, 1987.

Nimmer, Melville. *Nimmer on Freedom of Speech.* New York: Matthew Bender & Co., 1984– . Includes bibliographical references and index. In looseleaf for updating.

O'Brien, David M. *Privacy, Law, and Public Policy.* New York: Praeger, 1979. Presents the Privacy Doctrine the Supreme Court has drawn from the 1st, 4th, 5th, and 9th Amendments, covering privacy as a concept and as a political idea, the Constitution, personal disclosures, and privacy and public policy. With selected bibliography, index to Supreme Court cases, name and subject index, notes, and figures.

Overbeck, Wayne, and Rick D. Pullen. *Major Principles of Media Law.* New York: Holt, 1982. An attempt to clarify and summarize the major principles of media law, covering the tradition of freedom, restraints, libel and slander, privacy and publicity, mass communications as private property, fair trial–free press, newsgatherers' privilege and contempt of court, freedom of information, obscenity and the First Amendment, broadcasting and cable, advertising, monopoly, and the student press. Contains appendixes, index, and chapter summaries.

Pepper, William F., and Florynce R. Kennedy. *Sex Discrimination in Employment.* Charlottesville, Va.: Michie Co., 1981. Written for students or practitioners concerning sex discrimination in employment; covers Title VII of the Civil Rights Act of 1964 (Equal Employment Opportunity Act), giving history and background, summary of provisions, procedures, affirmative action, remedies, and relief. With index and forms.

Richey, Charles R. *Manual on Employment Discrimination and Civil Rights Actions in the Federal Courts.* Rev. ed. Washington, D.C.: Fed. Judicial Ctr., 1984. Includes bibliographical references. In looseleaf for updating.

Spurrier, Robert L. *Rights, Wrongs, and Remedies: Section 1983 and Constitutional Rights Vindication.* Port Washington, N.Y.: Assoc. Faculty Pr., 1986. Includes bibliographical references and index.

Vieira, Norman. *Civil Rights in a Nutshell.* St. Paul, Minn.: West, 1978.

Way, H. Frank. *Criminal Justice and the American Constitution.* North Scituate, Mass.: Duxbury, 1980. Presents due process of law, covering rules of law and discretionary power, principle of legality, arrest, search and seizure, self incrimination, grand jury indictment, bail, plea bargaining, double jeopardy, attorneys, trial by jury, trial rights, sentencing, and legal rights of prisoners. Contains the Constitution of the United States, table of cases, index, and notes.

IV · Business Organizations

Business Structures

The simplest form of business structure is the sole proprietorship, in which a person goes into some sort of business all by him- or herself. This type of business structure probably started with the development of specialization when a person found out that he or she could produce something better than a neighbor could. A person could then trade produced goods with a neighbor for what needed goods that neighbor could best produce.

A modern example of a sole proprietorship is Milton, who has decided to open a corner grocery store. He must first obtain the store—by purchase or by lease—and then obtain the necessary permits to operate the store as well as permits to supply such popular items as beer, cigarettes, and lottery tickets. His store must be inspected by the health department and probably by a variety of other city departments as well before Milton will be allowed to open it for business. He must set up the store as an efficient unit with shelves, coolers, racks, and counters, and stock it with merchandise from various suppliers. He must also get an employer's identification number from the federal government even if he has no employees other than himself. He will need help with insurance, financing, banking, deliveries, credit, accounting, advertising, waste disposal, legal services, protection, and much more even before he opens his door to make the first sale. Life is so much more complicated now than in the past that one can no longer just open a store and start in business. Nowadays, one must first comply with regulations. All of these things Milton must do himself or hire someone else to do them for him. He is solely responsible for everything that must be done, and he alone must bear the burden of the loss if he fails. However, he does have a chance at the American Dream, the opportunity to make a profit and to keep that portion of profit that is not taken by taxes.

Another fairly simple method of doing business is to operate through agents. Agency started out as a simple concept of doing business but has now developed into a vast and complex world of its own. Agency may have developed from the old doctrine of "master and slave," in which the master, or principal, frequently expanded operations by sending a talented servant, or agent, to perform certain specific tasks for him or her. From these situations, the law evolved and made agency a contract. This was done in order to accommodate the problems created, thus resulting in the rules of agency, which make the principal responsible for the acts of the agent if the agent works within the bounds of the contract. If the agent works as directed, the agent is not held personally responsible for his or her actions. An agency contract may be oral or written, but it must be in writing, sealed, and acknowledged if the acts to be performed by the agent require the writing, sealing, and acknowledging of instruments, such as deeds, mortgages, and certain leases. Unless the task of the agent requires the exercise of judgment, the agent may hire subagents. Agents must be loyal to the principal, act in good faith, and keep the principal informed of their activities. Should a conflict of interest arise between the position of the principal and that of the agent, the principal should be notified immediately. Confidences are to be kept, and the agent may not benefit from a transaction made for the principal beyond the agreed upon remuneration.

Because it is a contract, the principal-agent relationship is not one sided. The principal has the obligation to disclose to the agent any facts that might cause a loss to the agent were the agent not informed. The agent, upon completion of the assigned task, is due the compensation agreed upon in the agency contract. Should any liability befall the agent while acting under the instructions of the principal, he or she is entitled to reimbursement. Third parties cannot hold an agent responsible if the acts fall within the agency contract; the third party must instead look to the principal. The theory of the principal's liability is based upon the belief that one who does an act through another is deemed by law to be doing it himself or herself.

In a very broad sense, all employees are agents of a sort, although this area is now basically covered by employer-employee relationships and labor negotiations. An agent may be any legal entity, including partnerships and corporations. Most self-employed individuals are acting as agents when they fix someone else's household appliance, repair another person's car, or act as another individual's lawyer or accountant, the person doing the hiring being the principal. People frequently deal with agents: insurance agents, automobile agencies, talent agents, agents for professional athletes, etc.

Another common-law method of doing business is to form an association. An association consists of two or more individuals joined together by a contract—either written or unwritten—for the accomplishment of certain objectives, the concern here being for business objectives. The common-law association has no legal status outside of the contract, so it cannot hold property—real or personal—and cannot sue or be sued. It exists only through its members; and in common law, any action must be taken by or against all of them. This situation can cause great confusion, so many states have passed statutes governing certain aspects of associations. For example, New York State has passed statutes simplifying court actions by and against associations. Except where authorized by statute, the courts are very reluctant to interfere in any way with the internal organization and operation of associations. Associations organized for profit are generally governed by the law of partnership, and the legal effect can make each associate individually liable for debts contracted by other associates in the name of the association, or jointly and severally liable on contracts. In non-commercial associations, the liability of the associates is governed by the law of agency; therefore, to be held liable, the member must have assented to the contract involved. For tax purposes, an association is one of the miscellaneous business organizations that are collected under the partnership tax return.

The next organizational form a business can take is the partnership. A partnership is an association of two or more individuals (which may include corporations or other partnerships) who carry on a business as co-owners. In most jurisdictions, partnerships are entirely a creature of the legislature; and most jurisdictions have adopted the Uniform Partnership Act, with local variations. So whenever one talks of forming a partnership, the first place to turn is to the statutes. In a partnership, all partners are agents of the partnership for the purpose of carrying on its business. Real property as well as personal property can be held by a partnership in its name, and any partner may convey the property in the partnership's name. All partners are jointly and severally liable for partnership obligations, which means that anyone claiming against the partnership has the right to claim against any one of the partners or against all of them. Upon dissolution, the partnership is not terminated until all of the then existing business of the partnership is completed. In the past, any change in the makeup of a partnership caused its dissolution. However, most statutes now provide for the continuation of partnerships when one partner dies, one partner resigns, or new partners are added. Partnerships as such do not pay income taxes; however, they are required to file an informational tax form, 1065. Schedule K of this form lists the partners' share of the income, credits, deductions, etc., and each partner must use this schedule in filing his or her individual tax return. Each partner should also receive a copy of schedule K-1, which gives the above information.

Another type of business organization with limited popularity is the business trust, frequently called the "Massachusetts Business Trust." In this arrangement, a trust agreement is drawn up that gives trustees certain powers to operate a business for the benefit of the beneficiaries. This type of agreement has been used in situations where incorporation was not allowed but in which limited liability was desired. The beneficiaries, who may or may not include the trustees, receive trust certificates indicating their interest in the trust. The business is run by the trustees, and the whole operation is outlined in the trust agreement. Any profits from the trust are taxed as if it were a corporation, and the beneficiaries receive dividends as voted by the trustees. The need for this type of organization has diminished with changes in corporation law that now allow doctors, attorneys, and other professionals to incorporate in what is called the "Professional Corporation." The tax laws have also been changed to provide for what is popularly called a "Chapter S Corporation," which allows certain closely held corporations to be taxed as partnerships, with the entire profits and losses being taxed directly to the individual shareholders.

Corporations are the final structure for doing business, and they range from the small shop on the corner to large multi-national corporations with worldwide business. A corporation is another creature of the legislature. A corporation has its exact powers and duties granted to and imposed upon it by the legislature of the state in which it is incorporated and by any other state in which it does business. As with partnerships and business trusts, certain papers must be filed with the state for a business to be incorporated. The corporation, once formed, is considered a person able to own and convey property, make contracts, and generally operate in its own name. In addition to the state statutes, the corporation is governed by its own charter outlining the basic formation of the corporation. Under the charter, bylaws are passed and accepted by the shareholders. A corporation is set up as a democracy, i.e., the stock owners elect the board of directors, and, generally, the directors choose the corporation's officers. The officers do the actual running of the business, while the board of directors directs the policies and aims of the corporation. Corporations by their nature generate a tremendous amount of paperwork, either for their own control and information or as directed by some governmental body. All levels of government demand reports from corporations, and most governments collect taxes from corporations. The corporation, being treated as a person, files its own corporate income tax return and pays a tax on any profits. The stockholders receive a return on their investment in the form of dividends that are declared by the board of directors and that are paid when the board decides. These dividends, when received, are taxed by the various levels of government as income to the individual stockholders.

More than one class of stock may be authorized by the corporate charter. Common stock involves the investor in the full ownership of the corporation, although an individual's liability is limited to the amount he or she has invested. The common stockholders, as owners, are the last in line to collect if the corporation fails. Preferred stock usually pays a set dividend that must be met before any dividends can be declared for the common stockholders. Also, when it comes to final distribution, the preferred stockholders are paid off before the common stockholders. A great variety of other preferences may be written into the stock issue to make it attractive. Sometimes the stock issue is written with a conversion privilege, which allows the preferred stockholder to trade the stock for common stock at a set price. This issue is called convertible preferred stock.

Corporations may not always be able to raise all the money they need by issuing stock, or they may not wish to dilute the equity of the stockholders, so they borrow money and issue bonds as an indication of their debt. These bonds also come in a variety of colors, some of which are unsecured and are called debentures. Other bonds are secured by certain property owned by the corporation or perhaps by a claim on the future earnings of the corporation. Here also preferences are given; some preferences even give the bondholders power over future borrowings or the right to elect members of the board of directors under stated conditions.

Introduction to Research Problem

No matter what organizational setup a business uses, the aim is the same—to earn a profit. Size does not make a business good or bad; being large just adds to the complications of operation and increases paperwork and non-productive activity. However, size also allows greater pressures to be exerted because of increased financial assets and ideally paves the way to earning more money. Corporations can be large, but there are also very large trusts, partnerships, limited partnerships, associations, and individual proprietorships operating successful businesses. The decision concerning the type of organization to establish depends upon many factors, both legal and practical. There also comes a time in the growth of a business when its owner(s) should consider a change in structure to increase efficiency, and these judgments come under the heading of "business risks."

A main consideration for changing the organizational setup of a business is taxes. The federal income tax structure treats different business organizations differently. Two stores selling identical merchandise may be taxed differently because one is organized as a corporation and the other as a partnership.

For background material on the tools used in legal research, review the section titled "Where It Is Recorded"; and for an example of the use of these tools in a legal research problem, see "How to Find It." For unfamiliar terms, see the Glossary. See Appendix A for abbreviations.

The legal explanations and the issues selected here are not comprehensive due to space limitations. Should the researcher become interested in a legal problem not covered by the background material, by the introduction, or by the research problem, he or she should note the question, and, using the procedures suggested in this book, perform his or her own legal research to discover the answer.

Research Problem

The research tools used in this problem consist of the Search Process Flow Chart, the CORP rule, looseleaf services, and statutes.

Mr. Grunt and his wife, after a successful career in the big city, decided that they no longer wanted to be part of the rat race and would instead go into hog farming. To do this, they purchased forty acres of land in the hills of Tennessee. They sold off the house and five acres of land in exchange for enough money to pay for the entire purchase price, moved a mobile home onto the remaining land, built a farrow house, fenced in enough land to contain their pigs, and started their hog raising business. The object was to breed the sows, raise the piglets as starter pigs, and then sell the latter to other farmers who did not want to go through the breeding and piglet raising stages.

The business grew slowly. Mrs. Grunt had always been interested in real estate, and when the couple saw an advertisement in the local paper offering repossessed homes, they looked into the offer. It looked as if they could make money by purchasing a house, fixing it up, and either renting or selling it. This they did and repeated the process. Between raising the hogs and refurbishing the houses, the Grunts felt the need for a computer, which they purchased with the help of one of their sons, who worked with computers. Their other three children expressed an interest in the entire operation, so the couple decided to incorporate and included the four children as stockholders. For a few years thereafter, the business showed a net operating loss (NOL).

Three years later, while talking with his attorney at a closing of one of the couple's real estate sales, Mr. Attorney mentioned that they might be able to avoid the double taxation on corporate dividends if they formed a Subchapter S Corporation. He explained that such corporations were taxed as partnerships and that the individual stockholders paid the taxes, not both the stockholders and the corporation. Mr. Grunt said that the idea sounded good, that he would look into it, and that he would let Mr. Attorney know if he and his wife wanted to go ahead with such a plan. Mr. Attorney gave the couple a copy of the Search Process Flow Chart to aid them in their research.

The Grunts picked up their copy of the Search Process Flow Chart and headed for the law library. They also took along some 4″ x 6″ cards and a copy of the CORP rule to direct their thinking along legal lines. *C* stood for cause of action, *O* for object, *R* for restitution, and *P* for parties.

After finding a secluded section of the library, Mr. and Mrs. Grunt decided to list on a card the facts of their situation to clarify their thoughts and problems (Fig. 126).

The facts having been stated, the couple looked at their copy of the Search Process Flow Chart. Step 1 instructed them to form a word list to use in their search. They thought of the obvious terms given to them by Mr. Attorney: *corporations* and *Subchapter S Corporations*. For Step 2 (jurisdiction), they knew they were involved in Tennessee law in forming their corporation or in converting the corporation to a different form. However, they were involved mainly with federal tax laws when it came to transferring the NOL from the old Grunt Corporation to a Subchapter S Corporation. This tax transfer possibility was predominant in their minds. The NOL would be just too much to give up, so the couple decided to concentrate on this aspect of the problem, saving the technical changeover until later if needed. Therefore, the jurisdiction was federal.

The couple then thought about Step 3. It did not seem likely that they would need much general information, so the use of an encyclopedia or a textbook was bypassed. The law library had a roomful of federal tax material. Probably everything needed could be found there. So Mr. and Mrs. Grunt skipped Step 3. This brought them to Step 4, the framing of the issues involved, or a statement of their problem. They stated their problem of saving the NOL if they changed to a Subchapter S Corporation. They put this fact on an issue card as follows (Fig. 127).

At this point, the Grunts decided to vary the search process a bit and to combine Step 5 with Step 3 by using the Prentice-Hall *Federal Tax Service,*

4/24/84

Mr. & Mrs. Grunt   (Subchapter S Corporation)   Grunts

Facts: Mr. & Mrs. Grunt moved to the country, where they purchased a farm to be used as a pig farm. They are also involved in purchasing distressed property, improving it, and renting or selling it. A corporation was formed that included their children as stockholders. The Grunt Corporation has a net operating loss (NOL) that can be used under the Internal Revenue Code to offset past profits and/or used to offset future profits of the corporation, thereby reducing the tax burden.

Three years after the formation of the corporation, it was suggested that the couple convert to a Subchapter S Corporation to avoid double taxation—first on the corporation, and then on the individuals as stockholders. Mr. & Mrs. Grunt wonder if they will be able to carry the NOL forward to the new Subchapter S Corporation.

Fig. 126.   Subchapter S Fact Card

```
                              4/24/84
Mr. & Mrs. Grunt    (Subchapter S Corporation)            Grunts
Issue: If the Grunt Corporation is changed to a Subchapter S Cor-
poration, will it be able to transfer its NOL to the new corporation?
```

Fig. 127. Subchapter S Issue Card

one of the looseleaf services covering taxes. It consisted of several volumes, and Volume 1 contained the general index. Before checking the index, the couple decided to investigate the front of the volume and found a section covering "How to Look Up a Question." This section informed them that if they knew the code section, or key word, it could be located on the backbone of the binders. By turning to the proper tab, the couple would find a topical table of contents, listing topics by paragraph numbers. The paragraph numbers were located at the bottom of the pages; the page numbers, found at the top of the pages, were used mainly for filing.

The Grunts did not know the proper code section, so they read on and discovered that the index was an extensive subject matter index which led them to the proper paragraph. Opening the index to "Subchapter S Corporation," they were referred to "S Corporations," which in turn listed some three pages of topics along with the topics' section numbers. Rechecking the instructions, the couple learned that the Internal Revenue Code sections were identified in boldface print in the index, the regulations were italicized, and other material was listed in regular print. This arrangement made it easy for the Grunts to pick out the code sections, the regulations, and the informative text.

Under S, the first subject was "S Corporations," with topics arranged alphabetically thereunder. Going through the list, Mr. and Mrs. Grunt came to the heading "Net Operating Loss," which was followed by the following paragraph numbers: 16,141(b); 16,144(g); 16,144.40; 16,150; 33,348.55; 33,377.10; 33,393–33,397; 33,413–33,419; 33,423; and 33,426.10.

The couple made a note of these sections, returned the index to the shelf, and picked up the volumes containing the 16,000's and the 33,000's (Step 6). Checking paragraphs 16,141(b), 16,144(g), and 16,144.40 produced nothing helpful. However, paragraph 16,150 covered their subject, so the couple put their findings on a card (Fig. 128).

The two new paragraphs mentioned were then checked out (Step 7), and Paragraph 18,501 et seq. was found to be of no help with the Grunts' particular question. However, Paragraph 33,348.55 was helpful and thus was placed on a card of its own (Fig. 129), in accordance with Step 6.

The reference to Section 1317(b) was a reference to the Internal Revenue Code, and the couple wanted to check this point in its original language. So they put an x in front of the section, indicating that it was to be checked, and continued with Step 6. The Grunts found the section of the U.S.C.A. with "Internal Revenue Code" printed on the spines and came to a volume containing Sections 1031 through 2000. Turning to Section 1317(b), the Grunts found that it was entitled "Electing Small Business Corporation." This section had no

---

4/24/84

Mr. & Mrs. Grunt   (Subchapter S Corporation)   Grunts
Federal Taxes, Sec. 16,150

"S Corporations are not entitled to a NOL for any year the election is in effect, since the loss is passed through to the stockholders."

x   Federal Taxes, Paragraph 18,501 et seq., Predecessor and Successor Corporations.

x   Federal Taxes, Paragraph 33,348.55, How to Handle Net Operating Losses.

Fig. 128.   Federal Taxes, Par. 16,150 Card

4/24/84

Mr. & Mrs. Grunt   (Subchapter S Corporation)   Grunts
Federal Taxes, Paragraph 33,348.55, How to Handle Net Operating Losses

"An S Corporation cannot deduct a carry forward or carry back loss arising in a year in which it was taxable as a C Corporation."

x   Paragraph 1317(b)

Fig. 129.   Federal Taxes, Par. 33,348.55 Card

4/24/84

Mr. & Mrs. Grunt   (Subchapter S Corporation)   Grunts
26 U.S.C.A. 1371(b), Pocket Part for use in 1984, No carryover between C year and S year

"(1) From C year to S year. No carry forward, and no carry back, arising for a taxable year for which a corporation is a C Corporation may be carried to a taxable year for which such corporation is an S Corporation."

Fig. 130.   U.S.C.A. 1371(b) 1984 Pocket Part Card

answer for their question, so they turned to the cumulative annual pocket part for use in 1984, which was in the pocket in the back of the volume. There they found a revision of the code and made a card for the section of interest to them (Fig. 130).

The Grunts had found the answer in its primary source, although they admitted that it was not the answer they had wanted. They might have to carry on the C Corporation in its present form until it used up its NOL, and then possibly start another corporation for some of their future activities. To keep this information for reference and to show it to their attorney, the Grunts made up a Law Library Research Report (Step 9).

Once the legal issues were resolved, the problems not covered by law had to be addressed. These involved the practicality of pursuing and the financial ability to pursue the issue to the desired conclusion.

Law Library Research Report

Title: Subchapter S Corporation, NOL

Requested by: Mr. & Mrs. Grunt

Submitted by: Mr. & Mrs. Grunt

Date Submitted: April 26, 1984

Statement of Facts   Mr. & Mrs. Grunt moved to the country, purchased a farm, and started raising pigs. They also purchased distressed property, improved it, and rented or sold it. A corporation was formed that included their children as stockholders. The Grunt Corporation has a net operating loss (NOL) that can be used under the Internal Revenue Code to offset past taxes and/or used to offset future profits of the corporation.

Three years after the formation of the corporation, it was suggested that the couple convert to a Subchapter S Corporation to avoid double taxation— first on the corporation, and then on the individuals as stockholders. Mr. & Mrs. Grunt wonder if they will be able to carry the NOL forward to the new Subchapter S Corporation.

Question Presented   If the Grunt Corporation is changed to a Subchapter S Corporation, will it be able to transfer its NOL to the new corporation?

Brief Answer   When one changes from a C Corporation to an S Corporation, the accumulated NOL may not be transferred to the S Corporation.

Discussion   The topic in question is covered under 26 U.S.C.A. 1371(b), Pocket Part for use in 1984, No carry over between C year and S year, as follows:

"(1) From C year to S year. No carry forward, and no carry back, arising for a taxable year for which a corporation is a C Corporation may be carried to a taxable year for which such corporation is an S Corporation."

Bibliography

(Note: The looseleaf materials listed below may set forth the best overview and provide the most up-to-date information. They are not completely described here because the services are tremendously expensive for individuals to purchase, the titles identify the topics, their formats are relatively similar, and most of these materials can be found in law libraries.)

If a book cannot be found in your library or in the nearest law library, ask your librarian if it can be obtained through interlibrary loan.)

Adams, Paul. *The Complete Legal Guide for Your Small Business.* New York: Wiley, 1982. Gives basic principles of contract law with hints and forms for drawing up very basic agreements for small businesses. With index.

Business Organizations. New York: Matthew Bender & Co., 1963– . A multi-volume set by various authors, with volumes covering a variety of topics, including types of business organizations. Describes tax planning, federal securities laws, and corporate acquisitions and mergers. In looseleaf for updating.

Cheeseman, Henry R. *The Legal and Regulatory Environment of Business.* New York: Macmillan, 1985.

Corley, Robert Neil, and O. Lee Reed. *Fundamentals of the Legal Environment of Business.* New York: McGraw-Hill, 1986.

Corporation Law Guide. (CCH) Looseleaf.

Corporation Service. (P-H) Looseleaf.

Diamond, Michael R., and Julie L. Williams. *How to Incorporate: A Handbook for Entrepreneurs and Professionals.* New York: Wiley, 1987. Includes sample incorporation forms and other related corporate agreements, along with step-by-step explanations of how to complete them. Considers when to use standard incorporation and when to use an alternative, such as Subchapter S Corporations or partnerships.

Fletcher, William Meade. *Fletcher Cyclopedia of Law of Private Corporations.* 20 vols. Revised by Morton S. Wolf. Chicago: Callaghan & Co., 1931– . Provides complete coverage of corporation law in twenty volumes. Includes notes and Vol. 29 index. Kept up to date with cumulative pocket parts.

Hagen, Willis W., and Gordon H. Johnson. *Digest of Business Law.* 2d ed. St. Paul, Minn.: West, 1979. Covers in expanded outline form various legal aspects of business laws and regulations, contracts, guaranty, employment and agency, partnerships, corporations, personal property, bailment, sales, commercial paper, bankruptcy, real estate, mortgages, wills, estates, and trusts. Includes chapter cross-index and table of contents.

Haynsworth, Harry J. *Organizing a Small Business Entity.* Philadelphia: Amer. Law Inst.-Amer. Bar Assn., 1986.

———. *Selecting the Form of a Small Business Entity.* Philadelphia: Amer. Law Inst.-Amer. Bar Assn., 1985. Kept up to date with pocket supplements.

Henn, Harry G., and John R. Alexander. *The Law of Corporations and Other Business Enterprises.* 3d ed. St. Paul, Minn.: West, 1983.

Jacobs, Arnold S. *Manual of Corporate Forms for Securities Practice.* New York: Clark Boardman, 1983. Volume 9 covers questions to be asked of officers, directors, and stockholders; checklists; standard documents; certificates; bylaws; etc. Looseleaf.

Klein, William A., and John C. Coffee. *Business Organizations and Finance. Legal and Economic Principles.* 2d ed. Mineola, N.Y.: Foundation Pr., 1986. An easy-to-read outline of business organizations, economic elements, and legal principles for the bright but untutored student. Covers sole proprietorships, partnerships, corporations, investment devices, valuation, and financial strategies. With references, table of cases, tables, and index.

Meiners, Roger E., and Al H. Ringleb. *The Legal Environment of Business.* St. Paul, Minn.: West, 1982. A textbook on how the legal regulatory system works and its effect on business. Contains index, appendixes, and figures.

Norton, Joseph Jude. *Regulation of Business Enterprise in the U.S.A.* New York: Oceana, 1983– . In looseleaf for updating.

Professional Corporation Guide. (P-H) Looseleaf.

Reuschlein, Harold Gill, and William A. Gregory. *Handbook on the Law of Agency and Partnership.* St. Paul, Minn.: West, 1979. Covers agency, partnerships, and other unincorporated business units, such as sole proprietorships and business trusts. With footnotes, appendixes, table of cases, and index. Annual cumulative pocket part supplements.

Ross, Martin J., and Jeffrey S. Ross. *New Encyclopedic Dictionary of Business Law—with Forms.* 2d ed. Englewood Cliffs, N.J.: Prentice-Hall, 1981. An easy-to-use dictionary of legal terms, expanded with explanations of legal principles, forms, checklists, brief discussions, and illustrations.

Steffen, Roscoe T. *Agency—Partnership in a Nutshell.* St. Paul, Minn.: West, 1977. Covers the scope, definitions, relationships, transactions, torts, contracts, and forms of enterprises. Includes table of cases, appendixes, and index.

Steward, David O., ed. *Representing Small Business.* New York: Wiley, 1986.

Whitman, Douglas, and John William Gergacz. *The Legal Environment of Business.* 2d ed. New York: Random, 1988. Includes bibliographies and index.

Wolfe, Arthur D., and Frederick J. Naffziger. *The Law of American Business Organizations: An Environmental Approach.* New York: Wiley, 1984.

Labor Relations

Early common law considered it a criminal conspiracy for workers to join together to demand increased wages or to enforce demands by striking. This strict rule was relaxed later so that joining together to improve working conditions was not criminal, but concerted action against an employer made workers subject to civil liability for a civil conspiracy. Concerted labor activity was considered a tort and was justified only if the objects and methods used were legal. In the late nineteenth century, some courts came to the conclusion that what a person could do legally as an individual concerning his or her working conditions, he or she could also do jointly with others as long as the objective was a legal one and the means used to accomplish the ends were legal.

Labor relations cases involve three parties: employees, management, and the public. The federal government derives its power to regulate labor relations involving interstate commerce from its Constitutional authority to regulate commerce between the states and between the United States and foreign countries. The concept of interstate commerce has been expanded by the courts so that it now includes any business, no matter how local in nature, that uses the telegraph, telephone, television, radio, or mails in conducting any part of its business. Therefore, a local merchant is involved in interstate commerce if he or she mails a letter via the United States Postal Service. States also have the power to regulate employee–employer relationships under the states police powers. When the interests of the public become involved, the rights of employers and employees are subject to reasonable restrictions placed upon them by the states. This power is included in the right of the states to regulate public welfare, health, and safety within their respective boundaries. This right has been interpreted to give states very broad powers in these areas.

In areas where the federal government has acted under its own power to regulate interstate commerce, its right has superseded the right of states to so act. However, in areas where the federal government may intervene but has not, the states still control their own labor activities.

A labor union is a group of workers joined for the purpose of securing for themselves favorable conditions of wages, hours, and terms of employment through united action. Generally, labor and management may contract freely with each other. In the case of *U.S.-N.L.R.B. v. International Woodworkers of America, Local Union No. 13-433, A.F.L.-C.I.O.,* 264 F.2d 649 (C.A.9, 1959), cert. denied 361 U.S. 861, the judge stated in Paragraph 5 on page 658: "The right to enjoy the blessings of life, liberty and the pursuit of happiness is founded on the right to work. Deprived of that right, man becomes a groveling animal. This being true, it follows that every statute, decision, contract, rule or decree impinging upon that right should be carefully scrutinized and as carefully construed." These rights are not unrestricted; the state legislatures retain the right to license certain occupations, thereby restricting membership in those occupations.

The National Labor Relations Act of 1935, known as the Wagner Act, and the Labor Management Relations Act of 1947, known as the Taft-Hartley Act, Chapter 29 U.S.C. 141 et seq., provide for the uniform administration of labor relations in the public interest by public authority. The Transportation Act of 1920 established the Railroad Labor Board to settle controversies between the railroads and their employees. In 1926 the act was repealed and replaced with the Railway Labor Act, which encouraged settlements and provided methods of enforcing awards. A 1934 act imposed restrictions on carriers to prevent their interference with employees' organizations and created the Railroad Adjustment Board. A 1936 act extended the previous act's coverage to all common carriers. The policy of the statute is to foster self-government in the railroad industry concerning its labor relations, and the statute encourages reliance on peaceful negotiations instead of strikes and work stoppages. The Rehabilitation Act of 1973 established a program to furnish vocational and rehabilitation services, to promote the hiring of the handicapped, and to promote employment opportunities for the disabled in the public and private sectors, including the construction and improvement of rehabilitation facilities and the construction of barrier-free public facilities. The Comprehensive Employment and Training Act of 1973 (CETA) established procedures for providing job training and employment opportunities for the economically disadvantaged, unemployed, and underemployed, and for assuring that such training led to maximum employment opportunities and the enhancement of self-sufficiency through a flexible and decentralized system of combined federal, state, and local programs. 29 U.S.C. 621 et seq., the Age Discrimination in Employment Act, promotes the employment of the older worker on the basis of ability rather than age. It allows recovery of damages for anyone aggrieved by a discriminatory practice on the part of an employer. To make a prima facie case, it must be shown that:

(1) the employee is within the age group intended to be protected;
(2) he or she was requested to leave against his or her will;
(3) his or her work was satisfactory; and
(4) he or she was replaced by someone younger.

Some states also have right-to-work statutes that prohibit discrimination against a worker based on the worker's union or non-union status, thereby eliminating closed shops. Unless the legislature shows an intent to include public employees, such employees are not considered to be affected by these statutes.

The National Labor Relations Act and the Labor Management Relations Act are remedial in nature and not punitive. They confer no private rights and were created only to protect the interests of the public by creating public procedures for public ends (i.e., through the furtherance and maintenance of industrial peace). The board acts on behalf of the public and not on behalf of the individual victims, although a secondary objective may be the giving of relief to the victim.

29 U.S.C. 158 (a)(1) makes it an unfair labor practice for an employer to interfere with, restrain, or coerce employees in the exercise of their rights (1) of self-organization, (2) to form and join, or to assist labor organizations, (3) to bargain collectively through representatives of their own choosing, or (4) to engage in other concerted activity for the purpose of collective bargaining or other mutual aid or protection. Workers have the right to combine and exert economic pressures on employers for reasons concerning working conditions, provided that the employees' actions are lawful, peaceful, and within the limits of their contract. Workers also have the right to strike for legitimate purposes. An employer may not discriminate against a worker because of his or her union membership or activity. It is also illegal for an employer to favor one union over another. Within the workplace, peaceful picketing is legal. Some boycotts may also be legal. It is not legal, however, for workers to seize the property of the employer or to obstruct access to the business.

Labor contracts may cover a variety of subjects, including wages, hours, seniority, holidays, vacations, discharges, severance pay, grievance procedures, arbitration procedures, no-strike provisions, union shops, non-discrimination clauses, transfer provisions, shutdowns, relocations, benefits and welfare, sickness and accident, most-favored-nation clauses, renewals, and many other areas that can be tortured into the terms "wages, hours, and conditions of employment." Striking employees are generally considered employees during the course of the strike.

It is an unfair labor practice for either party to refuse to bargain collectively in good faith on a mandatory subject (e.g., wages, hours, or working conditions) or to refuse to execute an agreement once reached. Collective bargaining between employer representatives and union representatives is an attempt to make an agreement concerning wages, hours, and other conditions of employment. Statutes require that the bargaining must be in good faith; this condition may even include the furnishing of certain information by either or both parties on matters relating to the issues. However, there is no duty to reach an agreement. Closed shops, union shops, and union security provisions are valid unless they are prohibited by statute. However, a union cannot have a closed shop and refuse membership to those currently employed in the shop, and it cannot demand the discharge of a non-union employee while refusing that employee membership. The Labor Management Relations Act in effect forbids a closed shop agreement and strictly regulates union shop agreements. Agency shops, where non-union workers may either join the union or pay the union a sum equivalent to the union dues, are permissible.

Workers have the right to combine and exert economic pressures on an employer for reasons concerning working conditions if such action is lawful and peaceful, and if it is not a breach of the employees' contract. Workers also have the right to strike for legitimate purposes, and lockouts on the part of management are not necessarily illegal. Peaceful picketing is permissible in the vicinity of the workplace. Boycotts also may be legal under certain conditions yet not under others, depending upon the interpretation of the pertinent statutes.

An employer must provide a reasonably safe place of employment and reasonably safe machinery for the use of the employees. These conditions are regulated either by federal statutes or by state laws. Regulatory bodies are frequently given authority by statute to make the necessary reasonable rules and regulations governing workplaces and machinery.

Some states protect the individual right of political activity by workers, making it unlawful for an employer to interfere with the free expression of workers' political beliefs and activities.

When it becomes impossible for labor and management to reach an agreement, they may at least agree to arbitration. It is the function of the mediation, arbitration, and conciliation machinery of the statute to adjust and alleviate disputes. The National Labor Relations Board (N.L.R.B.) has the power to enforce any rights that come under collective bargaining agreements, but it may not control or shape the bargaining negotiations, make contracts, dictate terms, or compel agreement or concessions.

Introduction to Research Problem

An employer must recognize the representative and the exclusive bargaining agent of the employees, provided that the union represents a majority of the employees. When a question arises concerning the proper bargaining unit, the N.L.R.B. has exclusive jurisdiction. Supervisory employees should not be included within the unit made up of subordinate employees; the N.L.R.B. has the power to determine who are the supervisory employees. Professionals may not be included in a unit of non-professionals unless a majority of the professionals vote in favor of inclusion.

Remember, for background material on the tools used in legal research, review the section titled "Where It Is Recorded"; and for an example of the use of these tools in a legal research problem, see "How to Find It." See the Glossary for unfamiliar terms and Appendix A for abbreviations.

The legal explanations and the issues selected here are not comprehensive due to space limitations. Should the researcher become interested in a legal problem not covered by the background material, by the introduction, or by the research problem, he or she should note the question, and, using the procedures suggested in this book, perform his or her own legal research to discover the answer.

Research Problem

The research tools used in this problem consist of the Search Process Flow Chart, the CORP rule, looseleaf services, and administrative agency reports.

John, with his technical skills and knowledge in the computer field, is considered a professional. He is looking forward to moving up to a management position; and indeed, his boss has suggested several times that it would be a good move for John and that he would be welcome on the management team. The plant had been non-union, but it had neglected to keep up with the wages and other benefits available in competing plants. Six months ago, the plant was unionized. Although John could have bettered his wages and benefits by changing to another company, the jump-to-management carrot kept him in place. He was familiar with company operations, and he felt that he should stick with the devil that he knew rather than take a risk with another company.

As union activities heated up among the laborers in John's plant, he began to show an interest in unions. He attended several meetings and learned about the labor movement, the history of the union involved, and, naturally, the wonderful things the union had done in other plants and companies. When John asked the shop steward what could be done for John in his own position, he was told that unless the professionals voted to join with the laborers, the union could not represent them. The steward went on to explain what the union had done for professionals in other shops who had voted to join it. The steward hinted that the combined power of laborers and professionals would cause tremendous gains in wages, benefits, vacations, and working conditions. John began talking with the other professionals. He figured that if he did move up to management, the labor experience would be helpful. Moreover, he would have a better "in" with the workers, and it would be easier to manage satisfied workers.

Naturally, management heard of John's activity, and his boss called him in for a little talk. He explained to John that as soon as John became a part of management, he changed sides; and anything John had done for labor up till then, labor would immediately forget and consider him a traitor and an enemy. Labor–management disputes were adversary activities, said John's boss; and in such a situation, John could not remain friendly with the people subordinate to him. Besides, an attempt at such friendliness might injure his very good chance at joining the management team.

John thought matters over, decided that his ideas and beliefs would benefit everyone—both labor and management—and then pursued his activity with the union. Two weeks later, Amos, a team-playing co-worker who lacked John's technical ability and organizational talent, was appointed manager of John's department. On the way out of the shop that day, John sought out the friendly shop steward, Joe, and invited him out for a couple of beers. Over drinks, John told his story. Joe advised him that there was nothing the union could do because it could not represent the professionals without a vote of the professionals. However, Joe added, it might be worthwhile to consider charging the company with discrimination in promotions due to John's union activity. It had been some time since Joe had done any legal research, but he told John that he personally, not as a union representative, would look into the matter for John because he felt that John deserved the promotion and that John was actually being discriminated against because of his friendliness toward the union. Joe then promised to turn over the results of his examination to John in the form of a law library research report for him to review and to take to his attorney for appropriate action.

Although the particular plant Joe works in is located in New York State, the company has other plants throughout the country and thus is obviously engaged in interstate commerce. The company also deals with a large international labor union. So the first thing Joe does is to make up the fact card (Fig. 131).

3/18/79

John   (Promotion Discrimination)   John

Facts: John has worked for XPD Electronics as a professional engineer for a period of years and was told that he was being seriously considered for a promotion into management. He has also become acquainted with the labor movement, friendly with a shop steward, and interested in having the professional engineers join the union representing the rank-and-file employees. He was told by his boss that his "friendliness toward the union might jeopardize his promotion possibilities." John nonetheless continued his union activity. Two weeks later, Amos, another engineer, was appointed to a management position over John, who was better qualified. 29 U.S.C. 159(b)(1) prohibits the inclusion of professional employees with a bargaining unit of rank-and-file employees unless a majority of such professional employees vote for inclusion in the unit.

Fig. 131.   Promotion Discrimination Fact Card

Looking at the Search Process Flow Chart, Joe finds that he should create a Word List of Search Terms to help him in identifying the legal problem. Using the CORP rule, Joe comes up with the words *Promotion, union activity,* and *discrimination.* Knowing he shoud not rely entirely upon his own memory, Joe then goes to the county law library, where he takes out one of West's Digests and reviews the Outline of the Law found in each volume. He runs across *labor relations.* Not having gained much, he continues to the Digest Topics in the same volume. He finds nothing new, so his list of search words consists of *discrimination, labor relations, promotion,* and *union activity.* He feels that his best bet is to look first under *labor relations* and then under this topic for *promotion, discrimination* and *union activity.*

Step 2 (jurisdiction) causes Joe to think for a few minutes. The plant and job are all within the state; however, it is a large manufacturing company with plants in several states. Moreover, Joe's union is a large international union, and labor relations having anything to do with interstate trade come under federal labor legislation. Therefore, Joe decides on federal jurisdiction.

Step 3 concerns conducting a general overview of the subject by using a textbook or an encyclopedia. Labor is a large area of law, and there are probably good looseleaf services that are completely up to date, so Joe decides to use the looseleaf room of the library for starters.

Framing the issue is the concern of Step 4, and this gives Joe something else to think about. Reviewing the above facts, he comes up with an issue and places it on a card (Fig. 132).

Proceeding with Step 5, Joe first checks the *Labor Law Reporter* (published by Commerce Clearing House). He looks at the volume containing the general index, where he discovers a section titled "How to Use This Reporter." Here he learns that if he has a case name and citation, he can turn to the Case Table and find a digest of the case or a full report, as well as summaries of related decisions. If Joe knows a statute or a National Labor Relations Board regulation, he can turn to the finding list covering statutes and regulations, which will direct

```
                              3/18/79
  John                 (Promotion Discrimination)                 John
  Issue: Is it a discriminatory action for someone in management to
  suggest to a professional employee that his or her friendliness toward
  the labor union might injure his or her chance at promotion to a
  supervisory position?
```

Fig. 132.   Promotion Discrimination Issue Card

him to the proper section covering the statute or regulation that interests him. Having neither of these, he can turn to the topical index. The publisher uses a paragraph numbering system, and paragraph numbers are located at the bottom of each page. If Joe finds his topic in the topical index, the index will refer him to the volume section in which that topic is discussed.

Joe also discovers that the library has the Labor Relations Reporter (published by Bureau of National Affairs or BNA). This reporter interests him, so he continues with Step 5 by turning to that publication's "How to Use" section. There he finds that he can do his research by subjects. The references he finds indicate which section of the series he should use: *LR* for labor relations, *LA* for labor arbitration, and *FEP* for fair employment practices. Looking at the remaining volumes of the *Labor Relations Reporter* Joe sees that the spine of each volume identifies a particular section. He is instructed to use the "Labor Relations, Arbitration, and Fair Employment Practices Index," which he finds listed on Tab(A), "General LRR-FEP-LA." Checking his word list, Joe feels that his problem will come under "Fair Employment Practices." Looking for *discrimination*, he finds the heading "Discrimination Against Employees," and further on, "Supervisory Jobs, Promotions, etc." Under "Supervisory Jobs," he discovers references in the index to "LRX 498" (Labor Relations Expeditor), which is designed to provide quick answers. Following this reference, he sees "LR 42.301, 52.56, LA 102.03, and FEP cases 215.781." Checking first the LRX 498 (found at the top of the page), he finds "Section 5, Seniority and Supervisor Positions (LA 102)," which provides no help. Continuing on, Joe runs across "Section 9, Unfair Labor Practices, liability for damages," which states "Thus a promotion or promise of promotion [in order] to wean an employee away from the union may draw an N.L.R.B. cease and desist order (LR 50.54, 50.777)." And a little further on, Joe sees "Refusal to consider an employee applicant because of his concerted activity during his employment is held discriminatory. *Pacific American Shipowners Association*, 1952, 29 L.R.R.M. 1376." This sounds like the case he is looking for.

Climbing the library stairs to the floor that houses the *Labor Relations Reference Manual (L.R.R.M.)*, a Bureau of National Affairs publication, Joe finds that Volume 29 contains a table of cases (Step 6). Using this table, he locates the case of *Pacific American Shipowners Association*, 98 N.L.R.B. 99 (1952), and sure enough, it is listed on page 1376. Turning to this page, Joe reads the case and puts the information on a card (Fig. 133).

```
                                   3/18/79
John                      (Promotion Discrimination)              John
Pacific American Shipowners Association, 98 N.L.R.B. 99, 29 L.R.R.M.
1376 (1952)
     "To refuse to accord an actual employee the normal consideration
for promotion to a higher position, albeit that of supervisor, based
on protected concerted activity during such employment, would
clearly be a violation of the rights of nonsupervisory employees."
x  Shepardize
```

Fig. 133. Pacific American Shipowners Association Card

Joe feels that there is no need for Step 7 because he has found nothing new; and upon Shepardizing the case (Step 8), he finds nothing that might change the results of his examination. He realizes that statutes are often very significant in the area of labor law, especially given the number of federal legislative enactments that have occurred during the twentieth century, but he decides not to pursue this avenue at this time. Joe has not come upon the mention of any relevant statute in the research he has done to date, so he thinks it may be unlikely that such a statute exists. In any case, he knows that John's attorney has access to both the *United States Code Annotated* and the *United States Code Service* (each with an extensive general index that provides subject access to all laws passed by Congress that are currently in force); therefore, John's attorney can investigate the federal statutes him- or herself. The only remaining step is for Joe to make a report of his findings for John to review with his attorney (Step 9).

Joe knows that once the legal issues are resolved, the problems not covered by law must be addressed. These involve the practicality of pursuing and the financial ability to pursue the issue to the desired conclusion. Having the law on one's side, Joe realizes, does not necessarily mean that one has the power to enforce it.

Law Library Research Report

Title: Promotion Discrimination

Requested by: John

Submitted by: Joe

Date Submitted: March 20, 1979

Statement of Facts   John has worked for XPD Electronics as a professional engineer for a period of years and was told that he was being seriously considered for a promotion into management. He has also become acquainted with the labor movement, friendly with a shop steward, and interested in having the professional engineers join the union representing the rank-and-file employees. He was told by his boss that his "friendliness toward the union might jeopardize his promotion possibilities." John nonetheless continued his union activity. Two weeks later, Amos, another engineer, was appointed to a management position over John, who was better qualified. 29 U.S.C. 159(b)(1) prohibits the inclusion of professional employees with a bargaining unit of rank-and-file employees unless a majority of such professional employees vote for inclusion in the unit.

Question Presented   Is it a discriminatory action for someone in management to suggest to a professional employee that his or her friendliness toward the labor union might injure his or her chance at promotion to a supervisory position?

Brief Answer   For management to suggest to an employee that his or her continued association with the union might jeopardize his or her opportunity to be promoted to a management position can be considered an unfair labor practice.

Discussion   "To refuse to accord an actual employee the normal consideration for promotion to a higher position, albeit that of supervisor, based on protected concerted activity during such employment, would clearly be a violation of the rights of nonsupervisory employees." *Pacific American Shipping Association,* 98 N.L.R.B. 99, 29 L.R.R.M. 1376 (1952). No changes found upon Shepardizing.

Bibliography

(Note: The looseleaf materials listed below may set forth the best overview and provide the most up-to-date information. They are not completely described here because the services are tremendously expensive for individuals to purchase, the titles identify the topics, their formats are relatively similar, and most of these materials can be found in law libraries.

If a book cannot be found in your library or in the nearest law library, ask your librarian if it can be obtained through interlibrary loan.)

American Labor Arbitration. (P-H) Looseleaf.

Bartosic, Florian, and Roger C. Hartley. *Labor Relations Law in the Private Sector,* 2d ed. Philadelphia: Amer. Law Inst., 1986. An analysis of labor relations in the private sector, covering union legality, techniques, bargaining agents, regulations and economic weapons, administration of agreements, laws, and employee rights. Includes subject index, table of cases, and text of Labor Management Relations Act, as amended.

Bulmer, Charles, and John J. Carmichael, Jr., eds. *Employment and Labor Relations Policy.* Lexington, Mass.: Lexington Bks., 1980. Includes articles covering full employment policy, equal employment opportunity, occupational safety and health, labor law reform, and unionization of the public sector. Also includes an examination of the Humphrey-Hawkins Act, Manpower Training Programs, CETA, workmen's compensation, and public sector unionism. Contains name index, subject index, figures, tables, chapter notes, and chapter references.

Collective Bargaining Negotiations & Contracts. (BNA) Looseleaf.

Construction Labor Reports. (BNA) Looseleaf.

Daily Labor Report. (BNA) Looseleaf.

EEOC Compliance Manual. (CCH) Looseleaf.

Elkouri, Frank, and Edna Asper Elkouri. *How Arbitration Works.* 4th ed. Washington, D.C.: BNA Bks., 1985.

Employment Practice Guide. (CCH) Looseleaf.

Employment Safety and Health Guide. (CCH) Looseleaf.

Fair Employment Practice Series. (BNA) Looseleaf.

Feerick, John D., Henry P. Baer, and Jonathan P. Arfa. *N.L.R.B. Representation Elections: Law, Practice, and Procedure.* 2d ed. Clifton, N.J.: Law & Business/Harcourt, 1985.

Feldacker, Bruce S. *Labor Guide to Labor Law.* Reston, Va.: Reston, 1980. A comprehensive study of labor law in the private sector from the point of view of labor. For law students, union officials, and other interested parties. Explains legal citations, federal regulations, collective bargaining, union rights, strikes, picketing, antitrust laws, enforcement of collective bargaining agreements, membership, and federal and state regulations. Includes statutory appendix, the Labor Management Relations Act, the Labor Management Reporting and Disclosure Act, and the Civil Rights Act. With index, figures, and a review of questions and answers.

Gould, William B. *A Primer on American Labor Law.* 2d ed. Cambridge, Mass.: MIT Pr., 1986. Written for labor management representatives, general practice lawyers, students of labor laws, and others involved in or interested in labor dispute resolutions. Includes background information, the National Labor Relations Act, unfair labor practices, collective bargaining, and dispute resolution.

Jagelski, Jeanne M. *Doing Research in Federal Labor Law.* Washington, D.C.: Library of Congress, 1978. A guide for law students and non-labor law practitioners in beginning legal research. Broadly covers Congress, the courts, and the executive branch, focusing on private and public sectors of labor–management relations, fair employment practices, and labor standards. Contains a bibliography that is divided into three sections: General Works, Specialized Works, and Legislative Histories.

Labor Arbitration Report. (BNA) Looseleaf.

Labor Relations Reporter. (BNA) Looseleaf.

Ledvinka, James. *Federal Regulations of Personnel and Human Resource Management.* Boston: Kent Pub., 1982. Based on the premise that there are principles of federal regulation and that they are understandable and predictable. Gives a regulatory model and covers equal employment opportunity; sex, race, and other discrimination; the Occupational Health and Safety Act; OSHA; pensions; retirement; and unemployment. Contains case index, subject index, chapter notes, and exhibits.

Leslie, Douglas L. *Labor Law in a Nutshell.* St. Paul, Minn.: West, 1986.

McGuiness, Kenneth C., and Jeffrey A. Norris. *How to Take a Case Before the N.L.R.B.* 5th ed. Washington, D.C.: BNA Bks., 1986.

Morris, Charles J., ed. *The Developing Labor Law.* Washington, D.C.: BNA Bks., Looseleaf.

Occupational Safety & Health Reporter. (BNA) Looseleaf.

Policy and Practice Series. (BNA) Looseleaf.

Retail/Services Labor Report. (BNA) Looseleaf.

Schlei, Barbara Linderman, and Paul Grossman. *Employment Discrimination Law.* 2d ed. Washington, D.C.: BNA Bks., 1983. A comprehensive casebook and research tool, covering sexual harassment, comparable worth, and age discrimination.

Union Labor Report. (BNA) Looseleaf.

Westin, Alan F., and Stephan Sailsbury, eds. *Individual Rights in the Corporation.* New York: Pantheon, 1980. A reader on employees' rights, covering liberty and work, limiting employer prerogatives, employee bill of rights, free expression on the job, privacy in the workplace, fair procedures, rights of participation, and the right to information. With bibliography, index, list of editors and contributors, and notes.

White Collar Report. (BNA) Looseleaf.

Workmen's Compensation Law Reports. (CCH) Looseleaf.

Commercial Law

Commerce has been of interest to the world since the dawn of history. People began to communicate and to trade with one another; and as communication and trading grew, so grew the customs associated with these activities. The customs of the marketplace varied from area to area so that a tradesperson had to learn these various rules as his or her trading horizons expanded. This fact applied not only to geographic areas but also to the manufacture and transfer of specific goods. Different customs were established for a trader in local goods than for a trader in international goods, for example, and the maker of nails had different standards than the maker of silverware. Eventually, uniform laws were established for various trades and trading practices in order to make it easier for merchants to deal with each other. Nevertheless, complicated transactions still required a variety of rules.

To bring some sort of order out of this confusion in commerce, various uniform codes or laws were proposed. In the United States these consisted of the Uniform Negotiable Instrument Law (1896), the Uniform Sales Act (1906), the Uniform Bill of Lading Act (1909); the Uniform Stock Transfer Act (1909), the Uniform Conditional Sales Act (1918), and the Uniform Trust Receipts Act (1933).

Given the list of proposed acts above, it is clear that a single commercial transaction could easily involve several of the individual statutes. For instance, the sale of goods could involve a contract to sell them, the actual transfer of the goods, the payment, bank collection, a security transaction for the balance of the payment, shipping, storing, warehousing, and more.

The Uniform Commercial Code (U.C.C.) is divided into ten articles. Parts of the U.C.C. involve technical areas for which most people have little concern. However, other parts are very much woven into our daily lives.

Part I of Article I, the introductory article, covers the construction, application, and subject matter of the act. Part II gives the general definitions of some forty-six terms and the principles for interpreting the act.

Article II which is in seven parts, covers the law of sales and supersedes the older Uniform Sales Act.

Commercial paper, with the exclusion of investment securities, money, and documents of title, is the topic of Article III. This article is of interest to those issuing and accepting loans of various types.

Article IV covers bank deposits and collections. This area naturally concerns banks and their relationships with other banks; however the article also covers relationships between banks and their customers. Any business or individual interested in the interrelationships of banks or in how banks should deal with customers should check the state statutes for this article.

Of special interest to business people who require credit for the purchase of goods located either nearby or in a foreign country is Article V, which covers letters of credit. Letters of credit allow businesses to request their banks to honor certain drafts or other demands for payment upon the completion of certain preconditions. Without such assurances, sellers might very well be reluctant to extend credit to an unknown buyer.

Article VI takes up the problem of bulk transfers. Bulk transfers are described as ". . . any transfer in bulk and not in the ordinary course of the transferor's business of a major part of the materials, supplies, merchandise or other inventory of an enterprise . . ." Such transfers do not include security agreements, assignments for the benefit of creditors, or sales under judicial process. The article requires certain notices to be given before any such transfer, a stipulation that is intended to protect creditors of the transferor.

Business people engaged in transferring their goods from one place to another are frequently concerned with Article VII. This article covers warehouse receipts, bills of lading, and other documents of title.

Those who issue securities, as well as investors in the stock market, should take notice of Article VIII, which concerns investment securities. This article sets forth the duties, obligations, and rights of the parties involved, i.e., those issuing securities, those acting as their agents, and those purchasing securities.

The area touching the general public the most is covered in Article IX, which deals with secured transactions, sales of accounts, contract rights, and chattel paper. This area supersedes any conditional sales act and chattel mortgage act and involves individuals who purchase everyday household goods on credit. The article also outlines responsibilities of all parties upon the assignment of the security interest created.

The final article, Article X, is a short technical article that gives the effective date of the article and recommends that upon the U.C.C.'s enactment, certain other acts be repealed. Generally, it is recommended that upon the enactment of a uniform commercial code, any existing uniform negotiable instruments acts, uniform warehouse receipts acts, uniform sales acts, uniform bills of lading acts, uniform stock transfer acts, uniform conditional sales acts, and uniform trust receipts acts be repealed. Also, any act regulating bank collections, bulk sales, chattel mortgages, conditional sales, factor's liens, assignment of accounts receivable, farm storage of grain, and other similar commercial activities should be looked at carefully for conflicts and possibly, repeal.

Introduction to Research Problem

Most states have adopted some of these proposed model acts with local variations, and two states have adopted all of them. (For statutory references to the Uniform Commercial Code in each state, see Appendix B.) Work was started on the Uniform Commercial Code in 1942 and was completed in 1951. The object of this act was to bring together in one instrument the various rules governing commercial transactions, thereby eliminating the need to refer to numerous pieces of legislation for a single transaction. The U.C.C. was enacted first in Pennsylvania in 1953 and now has been passed in all states except Louisiana. As with all uniform acts promulgated by the National Conference of Commissioners on Uniform State Laws, the Uniform Commercial Code becomes the law of a particular jurisdiction only when the code has actually been enacted by the legislature of the state in question. Although it is a uniform act, conditions vary in each state; therefore, each state has adapted the code to local conditions, enacting those provisions that are appropriate for a particular state and either amending or omitting the other sections. Thus, the U.C.C. as adopted in one state may not be exactly the same as that in another state. It must be remembered that any discussion of the code here is general and based upon the Uniform Commercial Code as it was developed by the American Law Institute and the National Conference of Commissioners on Uniform State Laws and as it has been amended over the years. In working in an individual state, it is essential that the statutes and cases of that state be examined during the research process.

For background material on the tools used in legal research, review "Where It Is Recorded"; and for an example of the use of these tools in a legal research problem, see "How to Find It." See the Glossary for unfamiliar terms, and Appendix A for abbreviations.

The legal explanations and the issues selected here are not comprehensive due to space limitations. Should the researcher become interested in a legal problem not covered by the background material, by the introduction, or by the research problem, he or she should note the question, and, using the procedures suggested in this book, perform his or her own legal research to discover the answer.

Research Problem

The research tools used in this problem consist of the Search Process Flow Chart, the CORP rule, statutes, reporters, and citators.

Walter worked for Chip Co. for several years, and during that time progressed from a production line worker up through the ranks to become the manager of one of the plants that manufactured computer chips in Silicon Valley, California. He was passed over for the next position, Vice President, and therefore decided to go into business for himself. Together with several friends, Walter collected enough capital to rent a factory in Denver, Colorado. He purchased the necessary machinery and began production under the name of Walter Chips, Inc.

While this process was going on, Walter wandered about the country contacting users of computer chips and managed to land several orders, one from Pluto Computers, Inc. in Trinidad, Colorado. After Walter delivered several batches of chips to his customers, business started humming.

One day in May 1984, Pluto Computers, Inc. wrote Walter a letter requesting a large number of chips, giving minute specifications as well as the number of chips desired, and stating that the chips were to be shipped by Flying Chips Airlines in November 1984. The chips would be paid for in December 1984. This was a large order, and there were prospects of repeat business, so Walter, as president of Walter Chips, Inc., wrote back stating that the order was accepted, delivery would be made in accordance with Pluto Computers, Inc.'s instructions, and December 1984 payment was acceptable.

The chips were a bit unusual, so Walter Chips, Inc. began immediately to produce them. By August 1, 1984, all the chips had been manufactured, packed, addressed, and set aside in the company's warehouse, awaiting the shipment date.

On September 15, 1984, Pluto Computers, Inc. wrote Walter Chips, Inc. canceling the order. Walter Chips, Inc. at this point had a considerable investment in the chips; and because the chips were a special order, the company could not sell them to anyone else. A letter went back to Pluto Computers, Inc. on September 20, 1984, stating that Walter Chips, Inc. could not cancel the order and that the chips would be shipped according to the contract.

True to their word, Walter Chips, Inc. on November 7, 1984, shipped the chips via Flying Chips Airlines and sent an invoice by mail. When Pluto Computers, Inc. received the invoice on November 10, 1984, the company immediately wrote Walter Chips, Inc. that it would refuse the chips when they arrived. Sure enough, when Flying Chips Airlines attempted to deliver the chips, the order was refused. The chips have remained in the warehouse of Flying Chips Airlines ever since.

Flying Chips Airlines now wishes to discuss with the owner of the chips the possibility of getting them out of the warehouse and, incidentally, of paying for the airline's services. The company therefore asks its bright young law librarian to do preliminary research on the question of who owns the chips.

Taking the Search Process Flow Chart, the librarian settles down at a desk in the library. In addition to the cards and the chart, the librarian also keeps in mind the CORP rule: C for cause of action, O for object involved, R for restitution, and P for parties. The librarian uses this rule to organize the search for legal words that will lead the librarian to the relevant laws to be examined. After reviewing the facts, the librarian makes out the fact card (Fig. 134).

At this point, the librarian checks the Search Process Flow Chart as a guide and looks at the CORP rule. Step 1 instructs the librarian to make a list of search words. The librarian immediately thinks of *contract* and *breach of contract*. But to be sure that no important terms are missed, the librarian goes through the Outline of the Law in a West digest. Under the heading "Contracts," the librarian picks up *vendor and purchaser*. Also in the same digest are the Digest Topics, which lead the librarian to *commerce, manufacturers, shipping, tender,* and *warehousemen*. The most likely words to start with appear to be *commerce* and *contract*.

Step 2 concerns jurisdiction. Since the transaction took place within the state of Colorado, most likely Colorado has jurisdiction.

11/21/84

Airlines   (Chip Ownership)   Airlines

Facts: In May 1984 Pluto Computers, Inc. of Trinidad, Colorado, wrote
to Walter Chips, Inc. of Denver, Colorado, requesting the production
of a large number of chips for its computers, giving minute specifications and the number of chips desired, and stating that the chips
were to be shipped by Flying Chips Airlines in November 1984 and
would be paid for in December 1984. The chips were unique, requiring unusual work not usually done by Walter Chips, Inc.

Walter Chips, Inc. wrote back accepting the order, delivery date,
and payment terms. Walter Chips, Inc. began production immediately
and by August 1, 1984, had the chips all manufactured, packed,
addressed, and set aside in its warehouse.

On September 15, 1984, Pluto Computers, Inc. wrote to Walter
Chips, Inc. canceling the order. Walter Chips, Inc. could not sell the
chips to anyone else because they were a special order. A letter was
immediately sent to Pluto Computers, Inc. stating that Walter Chips,
Inc. could not cancel the order and that the chips would be shipped
according to the contract.

Walter Chips, Inc. on November 7, 1984, shipped the chips via
Flying Chips Airlines, and an invoice was mailed. When Pluto Computers, Inc. received the invoice on November 10, 1984, the company
immediately wrote to Walter Chips, Inc. that it would refuse the
chips when they arrived. When Flying Chips Airlines attempted to
deliver the chips, the order was refused. The chips have remained
in the warehouse of Flying Chips Airlines ever since.

Fig. 134. Chip Ownership Fact Card

11/21/84

Airlines   (Chip Ownership)   Airlines

Issue: Who owns the chips that were shipped, in accordance with a
contract, by Walter Chips, Inc. of Denver, Colorado, to Pluto Computers, Inc. of Trinidad, Colorado, the delivery having been refused
by Pluto Computers, Inc.?

x Colorado Revised Statutes

Fig. 135. Chip Ownership Issue Card

Step 3 suggests conducting an overview of the subject by checking a
textbook or an encyclopedia. This step is skipped, since the librarian expects
to find all the necessary information in the statutes.

Step 4 calls for the librarian to make up the question involved, or to frame
the issue. This the librarian does and puts the information on a card (Fig. 135).

Next, the librarian checks the 1983 index of the *Colorado Revised Statutes*
and looks for *commerce* (Step 5). There the librarian finds the heading "Com-

mercial Code." Glancing down the long alphabetical list of topics thereunder, the librarian runs across the heading "Title," which is what is needed to answer the question, who owns the chips? Under the heading "Title" is the subheading "Passing of title, Sec. 4-2-401."

Returning the index to the shelf, the librarian looks at the spine of the 1973 *Colorado Revised Statutes Annotated* and finds that Volume 2 entitled "Commerce 1, Titles 4 to 6" covers the needed sections. Turning to Section 4-2-401, "Passing of Title," the librarian reads through the rules listed (Step 6) and makes a card for the important section (Fig. 136).

Looking in the *Colo. Rev. Stat. Ann. Cumulative Supplement* for 1983 found in the pocket part of the volume, the librarian finds no annotations that would alter the present situation and makes a note of this fact on the card above.

The librarian realizes that in situations where no relevant case law has been found in the jurisdiction in question, it is often advisable to check whether cases on that legal point have been decided elsewhere. This advice is especially true in the case of a uniform law such as the Uniform Commercial Code because it is often the case that other jurisdictions have enacted identical provisions to those passed in the forum jurisdiction. Although such cases would not be mandatory authority on a court, they could be highly persuasive when the statute has not been yet interpreted by the state's own judiciary. The librarian also is aware of a particularly useful tool for this sort of research when the U.C.C. is involved, the *Uniform Commercial Code Reporting Service*. The digest that accompanies this set allows direct access by code section to cases from all jurisdictions, and the cases themselves are published in the reporter volumes of the service. Nevertheless, the librarian recognizes that such research can be done later if it is determined to be necessary.

This information brings the research up to date, so the librarian now skips to Step 9 and makes a report.

Once the legal issues have been resolved, the problems not covered by law must be addressed. These involve the practicality of pursuing and the financial ability to pursue the issue to the desired conclusion. Having the law on one's side does not necessarily mean that one has the power to enforce it.

11/21/84
Airlines   (Chip Ownership)   Airlines
Colo. Rev. Stat. Ann., Sec. 4-2-401(4) (1973)
    "A rejection or other refusal by a buyer to receive or retain the goods, whether or not justified, or a justified revocation of acceptance vests title to the goods in the seller. Such revesting occurs by operation of law and is not a 'sale.' "
    There are no annotations to this section to date.

Fig. 136. Colo. Rev. Stat. Ann., Sec. 4-2-401(4) (1973) Card

Law Library Research Report

Title: Chip Ownership

Requested by: Flying Chips Airlines

Submitted by: Law Librarian

Date Submitted: November 22, 1984

Statement of Facts   In May 1984 Pluto Computers, Inc. of Trinidad, Colorado, requested of Walter Chips, Inc. of Denver, Colorado, the production of a large number of chips for its computers, giving minute specifications and the number of chips desired, and stating that the chips were to be shipped by Flying Chips Airlines in November 1984 and would be paid for in December 1984. The chips were unique, requiring unusual work not usually done by Walter Chips, Inc.

Walter Chips, Inc. accepted the conditions, delivery date, and payment schedule. Walter Chips, Inc. began production immediately and by August 1, 1984, had the chips all manufactured, packed, addressed, and set aside in its warehouse. On September 15, 1984, Pluto Computers, Inc. canceled the order. Walter Chips, Inc. informed Pluto Computers, Inc. on September 20, 1984, that Walter Chips, Inc. could not cancel the order and that the chips would be shipped according to the contract.

Walter Chips, Inc. on November 7, 1984, shipped the chips via Flying Chips Airlines, and an invoice was mailed. When Pluto Computers, Inc. received the invoice on November 10, 1984 the company immediately wrote to Walter Chips, Inc. that it would refuse the chips when they arrived. When Flying Chips Airlines attempted to deliver the chips, the order was refused. The chips have remained in the warehouse of Flying Chips Airlines ever since.

Question Presented   Who owns the chips that were shipped, in accordance with a contract, by Walter Chips, Inc. of Denver, Colorado, to Pluto Computers, Inc. of Trinidad, Colorado, the delivery being refused by Pluto Computers, Inc.?

Brief Answer   The chips are still owned by Walter Chips, Inc. of Denver, Colorado, by operation of law under the *Colo. Rev. Stat. Ann.*, Sec. 4-2-401(4) (1973) because they have been refused by Pluto computers, Inc.

Discussion   Under the *Colo. Rev. Stat. Ann.*, Sec. 4-2-401(4) (1973), a portion of the Uniform Commercial Code, the situation above is covered by the following quote:

"A rejection or other refusal by a buyer to receive or retain the goods, whether or not justified, or a justified revocation of acceptance vests title to the goods in the seller. Such revesting occurs by operation of law and is not a 'Sale.' "

The 1983 pocket part supplement has been examined, and there are no annotations to this section to date.

Bibliography

(Note: The looseleaf materials listed below may set forth the best overview and provide the most up-to-date information. They are not completely described here because the services are tremendously expensive for individuals to purchase, the titles identify the topics, their formats are relatively similar, and most of these materials can be found in law libraries.

If a book cannot be found in your library or in the nearest law library, ask your librarian if it can be obtained through interlibrary loan.)

Anderson, Ronald A. *Anderson on the Uniform Commercial Code.* 3d ed. 9 vols. Rochester, N.Y.: Lawyers Cooperative/Bancroft-Whitney, 1981– . An exhaustive study of the code, also covering non-code areas. More broadly described as "commercial law under the code." Covers all local variations and appellate cases reported, and all federal cases, opinions of referees in bankruptcy, and attorneys general. Kept up to date with pocket supplements.

Bankruptcy Law Reports. (CCH) Looseleaf.

Beutel, Frederick K., and Milton R. Schroeder. *Bank Officer's Handbook of Commercial Banking Law.* 5th ed. Boston: Warren, Gorham, & Lamont, 1982. For bankers, law students, lawyers, or other interested individuals. Contains information regarding ordinary legal problems arising in the regular course of banking. Gives an overview of the nature and regulation of banking, commercial paper, duties of a bank to its customers, secured transactions, bankruptcy, and special consumer credit regulations. With list of tables, table of abbreviations, table of cases, notes, and index.

Braucher, Robert, and Robert A. Riegert. *Introduction to Commercial Transactions.* Mineola, N.Y.: Foundation Pr., 1977. A clear statement of the background information needed to understand the setting in which commercial transactions take place, based on the Uniform Commercial Code. Includes tables, forms, notes, index to forms, index to terms, table of cases, table of statutes, and general index.

Clark, Barkley. *The Law of Bank Deposits, Collections, and Credit Cards.* 2d ed. Boston: Warren, Gorham, & Lamont, 1981– . Includes bibliographical references and index. Kept up to date with paperbound supplement.

————. *The Law of Secured Transactions Under the Uniform Commercial Code.* Boston: Warren, Gorham, & Lamont, 1980– . Includes bibliography and index. Kept up to date with paperbound supplement.

Cohen, Arnold B., and Mitchell W. Miller. *Consumer Bankruptcy Manual.* Boston: Warren, Gorham & Lamont, 1985. Includes forms and index. Kept up to date with cumulative supplements.

Federal Banking Law Reports. (CCH) Looseleaf.

Meiners, Roger E., and Al H. Ringleb. *The Legal Environment of Business.* St. Paul, Minn.: West, 1982. Written for business students needing an awareness of law. Covers the regulatory process, consumer protection, investor protection, environmental law, antitrust law, management and labor, and industrial regulations. With appendixes, glossary, index, and figures.

Reiley, Eldon H. *Guidebook to Security Interests in Personal Property: A Comprehensive. One-Volume Guide to the UCC's Article 9.* 2d ed. New York: Clark Boardman, 1986.

Squillante, Alphonse M., and John R. Fonseca. *The Law of Modern Commercial Practices.* Rev. ed. 2 vols. Rochester, N.Y.: Lawyers Cooperative/Bancroft-Whitney, 1980. Provides complete and up-to-date coverage of commercial law, giving background and focusing on the U.C.C. and consumer product warranties. Updated with pocket parts.

Stone, Bradford. *Uniform Commercial Code in a Nutshell.* 2d ed. St. Paul, Minn.: West, 1984. A condensation of the some seven hundred pages of the text and comments of the code, using the wording of the code as much as possible. Includes relevant citations and examples.

Trade Regulations Reports. (CCH) Looseleaf.

Treister, George M. et al. *Fundamentals of Bankruptcy Law.* Philadelphia: Amer. Law Inst.-Amer. Bar Assn., 1986.

Uniform Commercial Code Reporting Service. Wilmette, Ill.: Callaghan & Co., 1965– . A looseleaf service with bound reporter volumes and accompanying digest.

White, James J., and Robert S. Summers. *Handbook of the Law Under the Uniform Commercial Code.* 2d ed. St. Paul, Minn.: West, 1980. Accepted as the standard one-volume treatise in the field of U.C.C. law.

Copyright, Patent, Trademark, Tradename

Copyright

Each of the above areas is intended to give legal protection to individuals for their own work or creations. A copyright is the legal recognition of the right of an author to control the benefits of his or her authorship. Three theories of copyright law exist: (1) that the law is for the sole protection of the author, (2) that the law is for the benefit of the public and is intended to stimulate creative writing, and (3) both of the above. In the late 1400s, Venice, Italy, granted monopolies the right to print and publish books. Publishers paid for the right to publish books. The state thus received revenue from, and had censorship over, the printing of books.

In England, the Statute of Anne (1710) set forth a new principle; it granted the author protection, but only for the limited time of twenty-eight years. Most of Europe took a different view; and at the Berne Convention for the Protection of Literary and Artistic Works (1886), the theory was established that a copyright should primarily benefit the author, and protection should be as broad and for as long as possible. In 1952 the Universal Copyright Convention gave protection to the author only to the extent needed to encourage creative writing.

The Constitution of the United States worded this protection as follows: "To promote the progress of science and the useful arts by securing for limited times, to authors and inventors the exclusive right to their respective writings and discoveries." In 1790 Congress enacted the first federal copyright statute following the guidelines of the Statute of Anne. In addition to these Constitutional and statutory rights, authors had common-law copyright protection for their unpublished works.

The copyright laws are covered in 17 U.S.C., Sections 101 et seq. For the first time since 1909, these laws were extensively revised in 1976, with the changes becoming effective in 1978. The revisions have created considerable confusion, especially in the area of copying in libraries, schools, television, and movies. Copyright protects the following: (1) literary works; (2) musical works, including accompanying words; (3) dramatic works, including accompanying music; (4) pantomimes and choreographic works; (5) pictorial, graphic, and sculptural works; (6) motion pictures and other audiovisual works; and (7) sound recordings; all as set forth in 17 U.S.C. 102.

243

Section 104 protects unpublished works and continues the protection upon publication if (1) at that time the author is a national or resident of the United States, or a national or resident of a foreign nation that is a party to a copyright treaty to which the United States is also a party, or the person is stateless; (2) the work is first published in the United States or in a foreign nation that is a party to the Universal Copyright Convention; or (3) the work is published by the United Nations or its agencies, or by the Organization of American States; or (4) the work comes within the scope of a presidential proclamation. Publications of the United States government are not protected by copyright; however, the government can purchase, or have transferred to it, copyrights, according to Section 105.

Under Section 108, it is not an infringement of a copyright for libraries (A) to reproduce no more than one copy, or to distribute such copy, if (1) the distribution is made without profit, (2) the copy is included in collections of the library open to the public, and (3) the reproduction includes a notice of copyright; and (B) to make copies for replacements and security, for preservation of material, or for interlibrary loans. Also, certain performances for teaching or for religious ceremonies and the like are exempt under Section 110.

According to Section 201, the ownership of a copyright vests in its author, unless the work is done for hire; in the latter case, the copyright vests in the author's employer. In collective works, unless the copyright to an article is transferred, the right still remains with the author. The copyright can be transferred; however, the transfer of the object in which the work is embodied does not constitute a transfer of the copyright.

Section 203 considers the termination of transfer rights, and Section 204 states that a transfer of the copyright by an author must be in writing and signed. Section 205 requires that the transfer of ownership be recorded with the U.S. Copyright Office.

Section 301 deals with the changes in the law after January 1, 1978. After that date, all rights, whether created before or after that date, published or unpublished, are governed exclusively by 17 U.S.C. 101 et seq. In the field of copyrights, federal copyright laws pre-empt state laws and cut off all common-law rights. Existing rights are considered, however, and Section 302 gives them a span extending for the life of the last surviving author plus fifty years. Anonymous and pseudonymous works and works for hire are treated differently. They are protected for seventy-five years from the first publication, or one hundred years from their creation, whichever comes first. Any person having a proprietary interest in a copyright may record with the U.S. Copyright Office a statement that the author is living on a particular date. If nothing is recorded indicating that the author is living, there is a presumption of death after seventy-five years from publication, or one hundred years from the creation of the work, whichever comes first, and the copyright expires.

Section 303 covers works created before January 1, 1978, but not published or copyrighted or in the public domain, and continues their protection through the year 2002, or longer if the work comes under Section 302. If the work is published before December 31, 2002, protection will not then expire before December 31, 2027. Subsisting copyrights in their first term as of January 1, 1978, according to Section 304, continue for twenty-eight years from the date originally secured. In the case of posthumous works; periodical, cyclopedic, or other composite works; works of a corporate body (other than an assignee or licensee of individual authors); or works by an employee for hire, these copyrights are entitled to be renewed for a period of forty-seven years when the continuation is applied for one year before the expiration of the original copyright. If the copyright is not so registered, then it will expire twenty-eight years from the date of the first copyright. Those copyrights in a renewal term subsisting between December 31, 1976, and December 31, 1977, for which a renewal has been made between those dates, are extended for seventy-five years beyond the date originally secured.

Sections in the 400's cover notices, errors, procedures, and evidence. For example, a notice including the words *copyright,* or *Copr.,* or a *c* enclosed in a circle must be placed on the material. Phonorecords use an *r* enclosed in a circle, the year of publication, and the name of the owner; and this information must appear on the surface of the record or on the label. Works that include copies of the original works of the United States Government must identify those portions. The omission of the notice on copies of the work does not necessarily invalidate the copyright, but it may limit the liability for an innocent infringement. The owner of the work must deposit two copies in the U.S. Copyright Office within three months of publication for the use of the Library of Congress, and the owner may register his or her claim with the U.S. Copyright Office. Section 409 outlines the above procedure. If the work is registered within five years of the first publication, this is prima facie evidence of the validity of the copyright. The work must, however, be registered before the commencement of an infringement suit.

The sections in the 500's deal with violations and rights. If the rights of a copyright owner are violated, the owner can sue the violator for infringing upon the copyright. The court can issue an injunction prohibiting the violator from performing the injurious act, can order the impounding of the infringing articles, and can even order their destruction. The owner can recover the actual damages incurred plus the additional profits made by the infringer, or an amount stated in the statutes. Costs of the suit and attorney's fees can be assessed against any party except the United States. If the infringement is willful and for gain, criminal penalties consisting of a fine not to exceed $10,000 and/or one year in prison can be imposed for the first offense, and $50,000 and/or two years in prison, for subsequent offenses. If a copyright notice is fraudulently placed on a copy, or a copyright notice is removed from a copy, the fine is not more than $2,500. There is a three-year criminal statute of limitations, starting from the time the cause of action arose, and a three-year civil statute of limitations, starting from the time the claim accrued. In the criminal action, all goods, plates, etc., seized are forfeited to the United States.

The 600 sections deal with the manufacture, importation, and public distribution of materials not made in the United States. The 700's concern the operations of the U.S. Copyright Office, and the 800's outline the establishment and operations of the Copyright Royalty Tribunal.

Patents

The grant of a patent is the exclusive grant by a government authorizing a person to manufacture and deal with the patented product for a limited time.

The history of patents parallels that of copyrights; and in the United States, a patent is the right to exclude others from making, using, or selling the invention for a set period of years.

Article 1, Section 8 of the Constitution allows Congress to promote the progress of science and useful arts by securing for inventors the exclusive right to their discoveries for limited times. Under this article, the Congress has enacted 35 U.S.C. 1 et seq., Patents. The first sections of this code deal with the establishment of the U.S. Patent Office and its proceedings, practices, and fees. Section 100 deals with definitions, and Section 101 states,

> Whoever invents or discovers any new and useful process, machine, manufacture, or composition of matter, or any new and useful improvement thereof, may obtain a patent therefor, subject to the conditions and requirements of this title.

Section 102 states that an inventor is entitled to the patent, unless (a) the invention was known or used in this country, or patented or described in printed publications of this or a foreign country before application was made for the patent; or (b) the invention was patented or described in a printed publication in a foreign land, or in public use or sale in this country more than one year before application was made; or (c) the invention has been abandoned; or (d) the invention was first patented in a foreign country twelve months before the application was filed in the United States; or (e) there exists a previously granted patent to another person covering the identical patent; or (f) the alleged inventor did not invent the item; or (g) there was filed, before the invention was made, a claim by another inventor who had not abandoned the invention, suppressed it, or concealed it. The invention is not patentable if at the time it was invented the invention would have been obvious to a person having ordinary skills in the art, according to Section 103.

Sections 111 through 122 outline the steps for applying for a patent, including the written specifications, drawings, and models required, and the oath that the applicant is the first inventor. The examination of the patent by the U.S. Patent Office is covered in Sections 131 through 135, and court reviews are covered by Sections 141 through 146. Sections 151 through 153 cover the issuance of the patent upon approval and payment of the fee. A variety of patents is also provided for; patents of plants are covered in Sections 161 through 164, and design patents, in Sections 171 through 173.

Certain patents may adversely affect the security of the United States and are therefore suppressed. Compensation for the confiscation of such patents by the United States is provided for in Sections 181 through 188.

The rights of the owner of a patent can be assigned, but the assignment must be in writing and must be recorded in the U.S. Patent Office within three months of the assignment. The rights and remedies of the owner are covered in Sections 270 through 299. Anyone making, using, or selling a patented invention, or anyone who induces an infringement or sells a component knowingly without the permission of the patent owner infringes on the patent. The owner has a remedy by civil action for the infringement; and the court can grant injunctions and award damages adequate to compensate for the infringement, but the award must not be less than a reasonable royalty for the use made by the infringer, plus interest and cost. There is an additional remedy for the infringement on a design patent; the liability is to the extent of the total profit, but not less than $250. In exceptional cases, the court can award attorney's fees to the prevailing party. The statute of limitations for filing such a complaint is six years.

A patent, once issued, is presumed valid, and the burden of proof of invalidity, is upon the person claiming the patent's invalidity. This can be done by the alleged infringer's claiming that he or she is not infringing on the patent, that there is no liability for the infringement if an infringement did occur, or that the patent is unenforceable. Also, the alleged infringer can claim that the patent is invalid on any of the grounds set forth in Part II, which includes patentability, applications, examinations, issue of the patent, etc. In addition, invalidity can also be claimed for the inventor's failure to comply with Section 112 (35 U.S.C. 112, Specifications) or with Section 152 (35 U.S.C. 251, Re-issue of defective patents). Also, the alleged infringer can claim as a defense any other fact or act that is made a defense by this title (35 U.S.C. 1 et seq.).

Falsely marking articles as "patented" or advertising articles falsely as "patented," or marking articles "patent applied for" or "patent pending" when no application for a patent has been made can incur a fine of not more than $500 for each offense. The 300 sections deal with citations to existing art, requests for re-examinations of patents, the Patent Cooperation Treaty, and patents made with federal aid.

Trademarks and Tradenames

Trademarks and tradenames have a background in history and in common law. Artisans took great pride in their work and created designs that they implanted on their work to distinguish it from the work of others. One still sees in some areas of this country the imprint, or brass plate, placed in cement sidewalks by the proud makers. A slightly different use of the mark is indicated in the branding of cattle by ranchers in order to identify their cattle from that of their neighbors. In common law, the trademark is directly associated with the goods of a manufacturer and is also used in advertising; in such a case, the goods must be in existence before any claim to the trademark's exclusive use can be made.

The Trademark Act, incorporated in 15 U.S.C. 1051 et seq., was passed to allow owners of distinguishing marks to sue for the deceptive and misleading use of such marks in commerce and to protect owners from unfair competition. This act provides that the owners of a trademark used in commerce can register it by filing a written application, a drawing of the mark, three specimens or facsimiles of the mark as actually used, paying a fee, and complying with the rules and regulations.

Section 1052 states that no trademark will be refused registration unless (a) it is immoral, deceptive, or scandalous; (b) it consists of the flag or coat of arms of the United States, a state, a municipality, or a foreign nation; (c) it consists of the name, portrait, or signature of a living person without his or her consent, or of a deceased president of the United States during the life of the widow except by her consent; (d) it resembles another trademark that has not been abandoned; or (e) it consists of a mark that, when applied to goods, is merely descriptive or deceptively misdescriptive. Service marks can also be registered under Section 1053, and collective marks or certification marks, under Section 1054.

Section 1058 makes the mark good for twenty years, with a provision for cancelation within six years thereafter unless an affadavit is filed showing that the mark is still in use. The registration of the mark can be renewed if an affidavit is filed one year before the expiration of the first twenty-year term. The mark is assignable with the sale of the business in which it was used. Anyone damaged by the issuance of a mark can file for its cancelation. Notice of the mark is given by including the phrase "Registered in the U.S. Patent Office," or the phrase "Reg. U.S. Pat. Off.," or an *R* enclosed in a circle.

The registration of a mark is prima facie evidence of the owner's exclusive right to use the mark. The court can give injunctive relief for an infringement of the mark, and the plaintiff is entitled to the defendant's profits, to damages, and to the costs of the suit. The court can also order the destruction of the infringing marks, along with the paraphernalia connected therewith.

The Commission can make rules and regulations concerning the use and registration of marks, and can establish the procedures for enforcing these rules. Decisions of the Commission are appealable to the federal district courts for review.

Introduction to Research Problem

The Constitution of the United States gives to authors and producers of creative works the exclusive right to use such works for a limited time. However, the definition of *creative works* has evoked much litigation.

Section 106 of 17 U.S.C. gives the copyright owner the exclusive right to (1) reproduce the work; (2) prepare derivative works based on the copyrighted material; (3) distribute copies by sale, lease, or otherwise; (4) perform the work publicly; and (5) display the work publicly.

Section 107 gives certain people the right to use copyrighted material for the purpose of criticism, comment, news reporting, teaching, scholarship, or research without being considered to infringe upon the rights of the owner. Any other use of copyrighted material is considered illegal and may subject the user to a claim in court by the owner or to criminal proceedings.

Remember, for background material on the tools used in legal research, review "Where It Is Recorded"; and for an example of the use of these tools in a legal research problem, see "How to Find It." For unfamiliar terms, see the Glossary. See Appendix A for abbreviations.

The legal explanations and the issues selected here are not comprehensive due to space limitations. Should the researcher become interested in a legal problem not covered by the background material, by the introduction, or by the research problem, he or she should note the question, and, using the procedures suggested in this book, perform his or her own legal research to discover the answer.

Research Problem

The research tools used in this problem consist of the Search Process Flow Chart, the CORP rule, statutes, reporters, and citators.

Alice's former tenant in Hawaii, the pyrophoric Zora, finally left her lodging and found a small fenced-in ranch near Merizo, Guam. Here, in January 1980, she and some associates formed Zora Films and went into the filmmaking business, but they found it extremely difficult to make a profit. In desperation, they eventually decided to enter the pornographic market, where they had been told there were fortunes to be made.

Zora and her associates had found success in marketing their first three copyrighted films. The fourth film was already finished and copyrighted when the authorities of their small village raided their studio. The authorities made a copy of the fourth film to be used in court as evidence of pornography against Zora Films.

Zora stormed the village attorney's office, demanding the return of the copied film and claiming that the village had violated her copyright rights by copying the film. Zora threatened to sue. The attorney puffed on his pipe and told her that her films were pornographic and therefore were not protected in any way by the copyright law. Zora returned home and asked her friend Abraham to check this claim out.

Before retiring that evening, Abraham decides to write the facts of the situation on a card (Fig. 137). This will save him time at the library and will give him plenty of time to work quietly.

Abraham takes himself to the law library in Agana early the next morning, clutching his 4″ x 6″ index cards, a new pen, a copy of the Search Process Flow Chart, and some scribbled notes on the CORP rule (C for cause of action, O for object involved, R for restitution, and P for parties) to aid him in thinking up a list of legal words for use in searching out his answer.

5/29/83

Zora   (Copyright of Pornographic Material)   Zora Films

Facts: In 1980 Zora and associates formed a film company, Zora Films, and purchased several acres of land near Merizo, Guam. The area was fenced in and was used for the production of films. The company eventually started producing pornographic films, the first three of which were very successful. In all, four films were copyrighted. The village raided the ranch and made copies of the fourth film to be used as evidence. Zora claimed that in copying the film the village had violated the copyright law, and she therefore threatened to sue. The village attorney claimed that the village had a perfect defense—obscene material could not be copyrighted.

Fig. 137. Copyright Fact Card

Going over the case on the bus, he uses the CORP rule and thinks of some words (Step 1). *Copyright* seems like a good start. *Pornography* is a likely bet also. The lawyer had mentioned *obscenity*, so that word is added to Abraham's list. Upon reaching the library, he settles down with one of West's digests and patiently goes through the Outline of the Law found therein. He finds *theaters and shows* but doesn't believe that these words will help. Nevertheless, he writes them down anyway. He also finds *Copyright and intellectual property;* as these words are an extension of *copyright*, they are substituted for just plain *copyright*. Not satisfied with the list, Abraham continues to the Digest of Topics, also found in the digest, but he finds nothing new. Reviewing the facts and the CORP rule, Abraham notices a fine point; the attorney's statement referred to a defense of the case being brought by Zora against the village (*R* for restitution, or a defense). He therefore includes *defense* in his list.

The word list (Step 1) now consists of *copyright and intellectual property, defense, obscenity, pornography,* and *theaters and shows.* Abraham feels that the best chance he has to answer the question is to start with *copyright and intellectual property* and to look under those terms for *pornography* and *obscenity.*

Looking back at his Search Process Flow Chart, Step 2 (jurisdiction) causes him to think a bit. Zora Films is being hauled into the local court on a charge of making pornographic films. This would be a criminal charge involving the local Guam laws. But that is not the question Abraham has been asked to answer. Zora wants to know whether, if she sues the village, the village can defend its actions by claiming that the material copied is pornographic and obscene and cannot be copyrighted. Copyright comes under federal jurisdiction, so Abraham decides that his question will be answered in the federal statutes and cases.

Abraham is inclined to skip Step 3 (the use of a textbook or an encyclopedia) for the time being because he feels that a direct look at the statutes involved may be more productive. He can return to the encyclopedia later if necessary. So he proceeds to Step 4 (framing the issue). This step is fairly easy, for he has been given only one question, which he writes on a card (Fig. 138).

The first book Abraham takes from the shelf is the general index of the *United States Code Annotated* (Step 5). Here *copyright* is shown as being in Title 17. He finds nothing under the subject concerning either pornography or obscenity, nor are these issues covered in the supplementary pamphlet (1972–1982). Returning the index and removing 17 *U.S.C.A.* (1977), which has *Copy-*

```
                            5/30/83
Zora            (Copyright of Pornographic Material)     Zora Films
Issue: In a suit for copyright infringement, is it a valid defense that
the material is pornographic and obscene, and thereby not subject
to being copyrighted?
x  U.S.C.
```

Fig. 138. Copyright Issue Card

right on its spine, Abraham looks at the table of contents. Section 101 contains definitions. To be sure he knows what he is talking about, Abraham enters some of these definitions on a card (Fig. 139), in accordance with Step 6.

Returning to Step 5, Abraham turns to the index in the back of Title 17 and looks for *defenses*. He is referred to the heading "Infringement, this index." Under this topic in the index, he first finds "General, Sec. 501" but nothing more specific from his word list. Advancing to Step 6, Abraham turns to Section 501 and makes a card for his findings (Fig. 140), including the information located in the alphabetical breakdown under "Notes and Decisions."

5/30/83

Zora   (Copyright of Pornographic Material)   Zora Films
17 U.S.C.A., Sec. 101, Definitions

"Motion Pictures—Audiovisual works consisting of a series of related images which, when shown in succession, impart an impression of motion, together with accompanying sound, if any. . . .

"Audiovisual Works—Consisting of a series of related images which are intrinsically intended to be shown by the use of machines or devices such as projectors, viewers, or electronic equipment, together with accompanying sound if any, regardless of the nature of the material objects, such as films or tapes, in which the works are embodied."

"Sec. 102. Copyright protection subsists in accordance with this title, in original works of authorship fixed in any tangible medium of expression, now known or later developed, from which they can be perceived, reproduced, or otherwise communicated, either directly or with the aid of a machine or device. Works of authorship include the following categories: . . . (6) motion pictures and other audiovisual works. . . ."

Fig. 139.   17 U.S.C.A., Sec. 101 Card

5/30/83

Zora   (Copyright of Pornographic Material)   Zora Films
17 U.S.C.A. 501, Infringement

"(a) Anyone who violates any of the exclusive rights of the copyright owner as provided by Sections 106 through 118, or who imports . . . is an infringer of the copyright."

Notes and Decisions: Defenses, Generally 338. Nothing helpful in main volume.

Pocket Part, Note 338: "Obscenity is not a defense to copyright infringement claim. Jartech Inc. v. Clancy, C.A.Cal. (1982) 666 F2d 403, certiorari denied 103 S.Ct. 58, 59, 175, rehearing denied 103 S.Ct. 477."

Fig. 140.   17 U.S.C.A., Sec. 501 Card

Following Step 7, Abraham returns to Step 6, checks the Jartech case, and makes a card for this important case (Fig. 141).

After Shepardizing the Jartech case for this particular point (Step 8) and finding nothing, Abraham goes to the final stage (Step 9), making up a report of his findings. This he does in the form of a Law Library Research Report.

Once the legal issues have been resolved, the problems not covered by law must be addressed. These involve the practicality of pursuing and the financial ability to pursue the issue to the desired conclusion. Having the law on one's side does not necessarily mean that one has the power to enforce it.

Law Library Research Report

Requested by: Zora

Submitted by: Abraham

Date Submitted: May 30, 1983

Statement of Facts   In 1980 Zora and associates formed a film company, Zora Films, purchased several acres of land near Merizo, Guam. The fenced-in area was used for the production of films. Zora Films successfully produced pornographic films, all of which were copyrighted. The village raided the ranch and made copies of the last film so that the village could use it in a trial against Zora Films et al. Zora claimed that in copying the film the village had violated the copyright law, and therefore she threatened to sue. The village attorney claimed that the village had a perfect defense—obscene material could not be copyrighted.

Question Presented   In a suit for copyright infringement, is it a valid defense that the material is pornographic and obscene, and thereby not subject to being copyrighted?

5/30/83

Zora   (Copyright of Pornographic Material)   Zora Films
Jartech Inc. v. Clancy, 666 F.2d 403 (9th Cir. 1982)
    Muecke, C.J.: "The Constitution authorizes the granting of copy-rights 'to promote the Progress of Science and useful Arts,' U.S. Const., Art. 1, Par. 8, Cl. 8. In response, Congress has authorized the copyrighting of 'original works of authorship.' 17 U.S.C., Par. 102 (1976). The Council argues that Congress may not grant copyright protection to obscenity as that would defy the Constitutional mandate of promoting the progress of science and the useful arts . . . 'There is nothing in the Copyright Acts to suggest that the courts are to pass upon the truth or falsity, the soundness or unsoundness, of the views embodied in copyrighted work.'. . . Pragmatism further compels a rejection of an obscenity defense. . . . Obscenity is a community standard which may vary to the extent that controls thereof may be dropped by the state altogether."
x Shepardized: 695 F.2d 1175 found to be on another point.

Fig. 141. Jartech Inc. v. Clancy Card

Brief Answer   In an action for copyright infringement, the fact that the material in question is pornographic and obscene is not a valid defense.

Discussion   Motion pictures are among the original works that can be protected by a copyright. According to 17 U.S.C.A., Section 102, states: "Copyright protection subsists in accordance with this title, in original works of authorship fixed in any tangible medium of expression, now known or later developed, from which they can be perceived, reproduced, or otherwise communicated, either directly or with the aid of a machine or device. Works of authorship include the following categories: . . . (6) motion pictures and other audiovisual works. . . ."

Anyone making a copy of the work without permission is an infringer. 17 U.S.C.A. 501, Infringement states: "(a) Anyone who violates any of the exclusive rights of the copyright owner as provided by Sections 106 through 118, or who imports . . . is an infringer of the copyright."

Notes and Decisions under 17 U.S.C.A. 501: Defenses, Generally 338. Pocket Part, Note 388: "Obscenity is not a defense to copyright infringement claim. Jartech Inc. v. Clancy, C.A. Cal. (1982) 666 F2d 403, certiorari denied 103 S.Ct. 58, 59, 175, rehearing denied 103 S.Ct. 477."

In an action against an infringer upon a copyright, it is not a defense that the material is obscene.

Jartech Inc. v. Clancy, 666 F.2d 403 (9th Cir. 1982):

> Muecke, C.J.: The Constitution authorizes the granting of copyrights "to promote the Progress of Science and useful Arts," U.S. Const., Art. 1, Par. 8, Cl. 8. In response, Congress has authorized the copyrighting of "original works of authorship." 17 U.S.C., Par. 102 (1976). The Council argues that Congress may not grant copyright protection to obscenity as that would defy the Constitutional mandate of promoting the progress of science and the useful arts. . . . "There is nothing in the Copyright Acts to suggest that the courts are to pass upon the truth or falsity, the soundness or unsoundness, of the views embodied in copyrighted work.". . . Pragmatism further compels a rejection of an obscenity defense. . . . Obsenity is a community standard which may vary to the extent that controls thereof may be dropped by the state altogether.

This case was Shepardized to date, and no new cases on this point were discovered.

Bibliography

(Note: The looseleaf materials listed below may set forth the best overview and provide the most up-to-date information. They are not completely described here because the services are tremendously expensive for individuals to purchase, the titles identify the topics, their formats are relatively similar, and most of these materials can be found in law libraries.

If a book can not be found in your library or in the nearest law library, ask your librarian if it can be obtained through interlibrary loan.)

BNA's Patent, Trademark, & Copyright Journal. Washington, D.C.: BNA Bks., 1982– . Weekly. Reports the latest information affecting copyrights, patents, and trademarks, including Congressional bills, court actions, and Copyright Office doings. Includes table of cases.

Burge, David A. *Patent and Trademark Tactics and Practices.* 2d ed. New York: Wiley, 1984.

Chickering, Robert B., and Susan Hartman. *How to Register a Copyright and Protect Your Creative Work.* New York: Scribner, 1980. A guide to the copyright registration process, with general information covering the most frequently asked questions. With forms, appendixes, and index.

Chisum, Donald S. *Patents.* 6 vols. New York: Matthew Bender & Co., 1978– . The focus is on substantive patent law relating to questions of patentability, validity, and infringement. In looseleaf for updating.

Copyright Law Reports. (CCH) Looseleaf.

Heller, James S., and Sarah K. Wiant. *Copyright Handbook.* Amer. Assn. of Law Libraries Pub. Series, no. 23. Littleton, Colo.: Fred B. Rothman, 1984.

Johnston, Donald F. *Copyright Handbook.* 2d ed. New York: Bowker, 1982. Covers areas of the main features of the law, with elaboration on works protected, legal rights, transfer rights, length of protection, advantages of registration, remedies for infringement, fair use, and library reproductions. Includes list of cases, tables, notes, appendixes and index.

Lawrence, John Shelton, and Bernard Timberg, eds. *Fair Use and Free Inquiry.* Norwood, N.J.: Ablex, 1980. A comprehensive study of copyright law, including fair use, impact on scholars, publishers, educational resource institutions, audiovisual centers, duplications, creators, producers, and distributors, and unauthorized use. Contains notes, illustrations, cases, bibliography, and index.

Lipscomb, Ernest B. *Lipscomb's Walker on Patents.* 3d ed. 11 vols. Rochester, N.Y.: Lawyers Cooperative/Bancroft-Whitney, 1984. Long considered the standard treatise in the field.

McCarthy, J. Thomas. *Trademarks and Unfair Competition.* 2d ed. 2 vols. Rochester, N.Y.: Lawyers Cooperative/Bancroft-Whitney, 1984.

Miller, Arthur R., and Michael H. Davis. *Intellectual Property: Patents, Trademarks, and Copyright in a Nutshell.* St. Paul, Minn.: West, 1983.

Nimmer, Melville B. *Nimmer on Copyright.* Rev. ed. 4 vols. New York: Matthew Bender & Co., 1978– . Recognized as the most authoritative work in the field. In looseleaf for updating.

Patton, Warren L. *An Author's Guide to the Copyright Law.* Lexington, Mass.: Lexington Bks., 1980. An easy-to-read guide covering all necessary subjects, including permission, duration, infringement, ownership, transfer, and licenses. With appendixes and index.

Rose, Gerald. *Patent Law Handbook.* New York: Clark Boardman, annually. Serves as a point of reference and immediate entry into the current patent law. Covers the Supreme Court, statutes, the Patent and Trademark Office, and practice and litigation procedures. Includes appendixes, notes, subject index, and case index.

Rosenberg, Peter D. *Patent Law Fundamentals.* 2d ed. New York: Clark Boardman, 1980. Defines and explains the rights and duties of the public and patentees and is directed toward professionals and newcomers to the area. Also relates the principles of patent law that are considered indispensable to an understanding of the system. With notes, appendixes, table of cases, and index. Updated by looseleaf insertions.

Tseng, Henry P. *New Copyright U.S.A.* Columbus, Ohio: AMCO Internat'l, 1979. A guide for teachers and librarians in the area of copyright law. Provides a very readable review of the law, covering subject matter, duration, infringement, teachers and librarians, and photocopying. Contains notes, appendixes, bibliography, table of cases, and index.

U.S. Patent Quarterly. (BNA) Looseleaf.

V · Concerns of the Elderly

Final Distribution

The receipt of real estate from an ancestor by operation of law has always been considered a privilege and not a right; and inasmuch as such a privilege is provided for by law, it is not a natural privilege. Such descents are governed by statutes passed by state legislatures and consist of sets of arbitrary rules that take into consideration those nearest to the deceased in relationship, i.e., the family and relations. The right to the inherited property comes into existence at the date of the owner's death, and the operation of the law is defeated only by the existence of a valid will. Heirs inherit real estate.

The transfer of property from parents to children upon the death of the parents has existed since biblical times. English law, which was based on the federal system of tenure and obligation, incorporated the feudal system into the transfer of real estate upon death. The invasion of England by Rome brought the civil law to England and has had considerable influence upon the law of descent. One point of English common law gives the eldest male preference over younger males, and all males are given preference over females. This condition has been changed in the United States, and the civil law of Rome has become the basis for U.S. laws of descent. In almost all states, however, both the common law and the civil law have been superseded by statutes.

Just as descent involves real estate, distribution concerns itself with personal property left by a decedent who has no will. Next of kin and distributees take personal property. The personal property is distributed as ordered by the court. In general, both descent and distribution are governed by the law of the domicile of the deceased, if the property is located in that domicile. Real estate located in jurisdictions other than that of the deceased is governed by the laws of the state within whose boundaries it is located.

The order in which the distributees take personal property is set forth in the statutes of each state. In general, personal property is left first to descendents, secondly to ascendents, and lastly to collaterals. Subject to the rights of a surviving spouse, children will take such property by descent to the exclusion of all others. However, this order may be disturbed by various equitable considerations; for example, it is generally agreed that a person should not be allowed to profit from the commission of a felony. Therefore, a person who

257

causes the death of another may be prohibited from taking the deceased's property by distribution or by descent.

To all but those involved in these problems on a daily basis, the differences between descent and distribution tend to become blurred. Statutes in general make the wife a statutory heir, and she takes a share of her husband's estate, both real and personal, upon his death. In common law, a husband takes all of his deceased wife's property. The interests of a spouse are now governed by statutes, which generally give a husband and a wife approximately the same rights.

No one is an heir of a living person; therefore, until death, a person may dispose of his or her property as he or she sees fit. Immediately upon the owner's death, real estate descends to the heirs so that there is no gap in the title. On the other hand, personal property goes to the administrator of the estate and is then distributed as directed by the court.

Dower and curtesy rights are of ancient origin, arising out of the common law. Dower was the legal right a wife acquired in the estate of her husband and was the right to use during her lifetime one-third of her husband's real estate. To clear her interest, she had to release her rights in any deed given by her husband. The husband could not dispose of his real estate by will and deprive his wife of her dower interest. The husband was presumed to know of his wife's rights and was presumed to make his will with these rights in mind. In theory, dower was intended to provide sustenance for the man's widow and children upon his death.

Curtesy, on the other hand, was a life estate of the husband in the real estate of his wife; but curtesy only arose upon the birth of a live child capable of inheriting. Therefore, curtesy required (1) a marriage, (2) ownership of real estate by the wife, and (3) the live birth of a child capable of inheriting.

In most jurisdictions, both common-law dower and curtesy have been replaced by statutes that vary from state to state. Frequently, the wife is allowed to elect statutory dower rights upon waiving the will within a certain period of time after her husband's death or within the statutory time allowed for probating the will. Statutory dower generally sets off a fee interest in a portion of the husband's real estate. Statutory curtesy in some states gives the husband a one-third life estate in the wife's real estate, while in other states he may receive a fee interest.

Administrators are appointed by the court to administer the affairs of a deceased person who has no will. Administrators are charged with collecting the assets of the estate; paying taxes, the expenses of administration, and all debts; and, finally, distributing the remainder of assets to those individuals entitled to them under the law. Any creditor can compel an administration if one is not filed by the heirs or distributees. Executors, on the other hand, are nominated in the decedent's will to carry out the terms of the will and to dispose of the decedent's property according to the terms of the will.

Should a person die with no estate, there is no need to file for either an administration or a proof of will. Some states have provisions for small estates; and for those estates that qualify, this situation provides a quick and inexpensive method of probate. If only real estate is left, and there is a will, the will should at least be filed in the probate or other proper court so that the proper owner can be ascertained. Statutes usually allow anyone who is capable of making a will to qualify as administrator or executor. Administrators are appointed by the court according to the order of kinship set forth in the statutes unless otherwise agreed upon by the parties involved.

Executors and administrators are under the supervisory jurisdiction of the court and may be required to file a bond to insure the proper performance of their duties. They are personally liable for any waste or conversion of the property under their control. One of the first duties is to see to the proper burial of the deceased. The executors and administrators must, after collecting the assets, have an appraisal made of the property and must include the property in the inventory at its fair market value. If the will permits, the executor may sell real estate held in the estate; otherwise an executor or an administrator may sell the decedents' real estate only upon the order of the court. In most jurisdictions, an executor or an administrator may sell personal property without a court decree, for these individuals are considered as acquiring legal title to the personal property.

When the legal affairs have been completed, all assets collected, costs, taxes, and expenses paid, and distribution made to those entitled, an accounting must be made by the executor or the administrator. If an accounting is not filed, the court can order its filing upon the application of any interested party.

A will is an instrument in which a person makes a disposition of his or her property that will take effect upon that individual's death. A codicil is a supplement to a will, making changes in it by adding to or subtracting from the will, and must follow the same formalities as required for the execution of a will.

The right to dispose of property by will is not a natural right; therefore, the statutes of each jurisdiction must be examined to determine their requirements. To dispose of property by will, a testator generally must have sufficient mental capacity to (1) understand the nature and purpose of what is being done, (2) understand the extent of his or her holdings, (3) know and remember those most naturally holding a claim of remembrance (wife, children, etc.), (4) understand how the property is being disposed of, and (5) understand the consequences of such disposition. The right to take property under a will is also subject to state regulation. Confidential advisers (e.g., accountants, attorneys, bankers, priests, etc.) may take anything under a will, but a subscribing witness may not unless there are sufficient other witnesses to the will to establish the will without them.

A person may make a valid contract to leave property in a particular way in his or her will. Unless prohibited by local statutes, such contracts may be oral. The contract must be assented to mutually, and there must be consideration. The consideration can be either a benefit to the promisor or a detriment to the promissee. Thus, a long string of court cases claiming a share of various estates exists based upon oral promises to leave something in a will.

No particular form or words are required for a will as long as the will complies with the pertinent statutes. Most usually, a will must be in writing, be clear enough to determine what the testator intended, and be executed as required by the statutes. This last requirement includes signing, witnessing by the required number of attesting witnesses, and subscribing (writing the witnesses' name on the will) by the statutory number of disinterested parties at the request of the testator. Some states require publication, or the declaration to the witnesses that the instrument is the decedent's last will. The will must be signed in the presence of the witnesses, or the signature must be acknowledged by the testator to the witnesses as being the testator's own signature.

Some states allow holographic or olgraphic wills (i.e., written entirely in the testator's handwriting). Generally, such wills must be dated and signed, but witnesses may not be required.

Inheritance and transfer taxes play a large role in the distribution of larger estates, and the reduction of taxes is always a concern. However, taxes should not be the primary concern. The first consideration should be the distribution of the property in the manner desired by the testator. There are a variety of devices to accomplish both the proper distribution of the proceeds and the reduction of taxes; these devices include trusts, corporations, life estates, joint holdings, delayed vesting of interests, generation skipping trusts, and more. However, such devices are so complex and complicated, especially when taking into consideration their tax consequences, that they usually require the services of both attorneys and accountants to complete a satisfactory disposition.

One method of reducing the tax burden on the transfer of property, while accomplishing the desired results, is the judicious use of trusts. Trusts began in the English civil law courts and expanded into the chancery courts. In early English law, a system of "Feoffment to Use" developed in land ownership. This system allowed one person to hold the legal title to real estate, not for his or her own use and benefit, but for the use and benefit of another. This procedure freed the property from the rigid formality required under the feudal tenure and common-law in existence in England at the time. The system was so helpful that at one time a large portion of England was held for the use of another. Abuses of this system caused the passage of the Statute of Uses, which eliminated intermediate estates of the feoffee and converted certain "uses" into legal estates, brought the uses within the jurisdiction of the common-law courts, and established legal methods of transferring real estate. Certain uses, not falling within the jurisdiction of the statute, developed into the modern law of trust.

While the formation of a trust requires few formalities and can be used for any purpose not contrary to law, modern uses have added complexities that go beyond the comprehension of most laypeople. A trust is used to separate the burden of owning property from the enjoyment of the benefits derived from the property. A trust is a legal contract between a person or persons (beneficiaries) owning the equitable (beneficial) interests in the property and a person owning the legal title to the property (trustee). The trustees have certain legal duties and obligations under the trust agreement that can be enforced in court. In the United States, the jurisdiction over trusts fell to the equity courts, which now have exclusive jurisdiction in this area unless usurped by constitutions or statutes.

A variety of trusts are recognized, but here we will consider only express trusts created either in wills, in which case the trust will come into existence upon the death of the settlor (testamentary trusts), or in trust instruments created by a person during his or her lifetime that will continue in effect after that person's death (inter vivos, or living, trusts). Both of these trusts are used to conserve wealth and to pass it on from one generation to another. Trusts are in the nature of gratuitous transfers of property. Testamentary trusts must comply with state statutes covering wills, while inter vivos trusts must comply with the state statute of frauds. A statute of frauds requires that certain things must be put in writing to be enforceable in court. An inter vivos trust is not a public record and thus is not open to public inspection. Such a trust may provide that the settlor may revoke the trust during his or her lifetime, or it may provide that the trust is irrevocable. The trust may also provide for current income to be paid to named beneficiaries, including the settlor. The trust may be so written that upon the occurrence of certain events, such as the death of a beneficiary, the income or property will be transferred to others. A revocable trust may be established that appoints a certain person trustee and that allows the settlor to observe if the trustee is performing satisfactorily. The settlor may also observe the reactions of the beneficiaries; and if things are not developing in a desired way, the trust may be revoked. A settlor may also give a person the power to appoint others to receive benefits from the trust. The inter vivos trust creates immediate beneficial interests for the beneficiaries; but if it is a revocable trust, the beneficiaries' interests are subject to being divested if the trust is revoked. The inter vivos trust does not avoid death taxes.

A person of modest means may find trusts helpful. For example, a pour-over trust may be established that will receive designated property under a will, as well as insurance benefits, upon the death of the settlor. In this case, the trustee, in his or her official capacity as trustee, will be named the beneficiary under the will or in the insurance policy.

Some states recognize the so-called spendthrift trust or a limited version of it. This type of trust is frequently established for the benefit of an individual who is incapable of handling his or her own affairs. The trust is written in such a way as to prevent or hinder creditors of the beneficiary from claiming the funds before the funds are distributed to the beneficiary.

Introduction to Research Problem

The Rule Against Perpetuities gives trusts a limited existence that consists of not more than the stated "lives in being" at the time the trust is created plus twenty-one years. The lives in being must be actual individuals and must be listed in the instrument as limiting the existence of the trust. The time limit of twenty-one years allows for all listed lives in being to reach legal age. At the end of such a period, the property held in trust must be vested absolutely in a person, free of all trust restrictions and controls. This rule is intended to prevent the tying up of great wealth for an unlimited time. It is felt that public policy requires the periodic rejuvenation of the wealth-gathering ability of individuals. The human mind, naturally, is constantly attempting to circumvent such restrictions, and sharp lawyers earn their keep by finding the methods and means to accomplish their clients' desired aims. Each state has variations on the above rule, so state statutes must be investigated whenever a legal problem involves this rule.

Remember, for background material on the tools used in legal research, review the section titled "Where It Is Recorded"; and for an example of the use of these tools in a legal research problem, see "How to Find It." For unfamiliar terms, see the Glossary. See Appendix A for abbreviations.

The legal explanations and the issues selected here are not comprehensive due to space limitations. Should the researcher become interested in a legal problem not covered by the background material, by the introduction, or by the research problem, he or she should note the question, and, using the procedures suggested in this book, perform his or her own legal research to discover the answer.

Research Problem

The research tools used in this problem consist of the Search Process Flow Chart, the CORP rule, an encyclopedia, statutes, digests, law review articles, and a restatement of laws.

Sally died on June 10, 1980, and the proceeds of her estate were duly transferred to the Edward and Sally Family Trust. The trust made quarterly payments of the income to Edward until his death on January 10, 1984. At that time, the West Mesa Trust Company as trustee of the Edward and Sally Family Trust ascertained that John, age thirty-four, was alive and living in New York with his second wife, Josephine, age forty, who had provided him with no heirs. John's children with his former wife Jane, ages thirteen, eleven, and nine, all lived with their mother, Jane, in California. Each beneficiary was provided with a copy of the trust agreement and was informed that his or her payment from the trust could be expected to arrive quarterly.

The trust provided that the income should be paid to the survivors of Edward and Sally as long as they lived, then to John and any children of John. Upon the death of the last survivor of John and his children, the balance was to be paid to the Society for the Preservation of Old Attorneys of Mesa, Arizona (SPAM).

John didn't like the trust one bit. He didn't mind sharing the income with his children, but he couldn't see any reason why SPAM should be entitled to the remainder of the estate. He figured that if there were some way to break the trust, he as the only heir of his parents would take the property free of the trust, and then he could care for his own children without SPAM receiving anything.

This research project sounded a bit over John's head, but he had done a bit of legal research himself on various problems and decided to undertake the project so that he would be able to talk intelligently to an attorney should he decide to act upon his thoughts. The first thing John does is to make up a card covering the facts as he sees them (Fig. 142).

John picks up his Search Process Flow Chart, which tells him that before starting a research project he should find appropriate words to use in his search (Step 1). He thinks of *trust* and then goes blank. Recalling the CORP rule gives John areas in which to search for words: C for cause of action, O for object involved, R for restitution sought, and P for parties. With this rule in mind, he locates a recent West digest and goes through the seven headings in the Outline of the Law. There he finds *life estates* and *wills*, both things, and *reformation of instruments*, which falls under C for cause of action. Following the Outline of the Law is a listing of Digest Topics. Not wishing to miss any possible avenue of research, John looks over the topics and adds to his list the word *perpetuities*. The most promising word for a beginning appears to be trusts.

8/11/84
John   (Trust Validity)   John & Children

Facts: John, now age 34, and Jane were married in 1969. John left Jane and their three children, now ages 13, 11, and 9, and settled in New York. After being divorced by Jane in California, John married Josephine, now age 40. There are no children born of the union of John and Josephine.

John's parents, Edward and Sally, who lived in Mesa, Arizona, made pour-over wills, placing their assets upon their death in the hands of the West Mesa Trust Company as trustee for the Edward and Sally Family Trust dated November 3, 1979. The trust provides for the payment of income quarterly to the survivor of Edward and Sally; and upon the death of the last survivor of Edward and Sally, the income is to be divided among John and any children of John. Upon the death of the last survivor of John and his children, the balance of the trust is to be turned over to the Society for the Preservation of Old Attorneys of Mesa, Arizona (SPAM). Sally died on June 10, 1980. Edward died on January 10, 1984.

Fig. 142.   Trust Validity Fact Card

Referring to his chart (Step 2) reminds John that he should consider what court will have jurisdiction over any actions so that he will be able to narrow his examination to works covering that specific jurisdiction. His parents lived in Arizona when the trust and the wills were created. The West Mesa Trust Company is an Arizona corporation, doing business in Arizona. He thus concludes that any action taken will be decided under the laws of Arizona.

Step 3 tells John that for a general overview of the law on any subject, he can consult a textbook or an encyclopedia. He turns to *American Jurisprudence 2d* and looks under the heading "Trusts." Under the "Scope of Topic" subheading, he finds nothing that looks helpful in solving his current problem. This fact suggests that there may be a better word to examine. So, continuing, he browses through the section titled "Treated Elsewhere," which only adds to his confusion. Finally, under "Also Treated Elsewhere," John finds another word on his list under the heading "The Rule Against Perpetuities and Restraints on Alienation as Affecting Trusts (Am. Jur.2d, Sec. 61, Perpetuities and Restraints on Alienation)." This discovery spurs his thinking. Maybe the trust is invalid as a restraint on alienation of property; and if so, the trust may be voided, thus collapsing the entire scheme and leaving his parents' estate entirely to John as the sole heir.

Taking down 61 *Am. Jur.2d,* John turns to "Perpetuities and Restraints on Alienation" and looks through the section titled "Scope of Topics." He learns that the article covers the rule against perpetuities, including statutory provisions restricting the suspension of the power of alienation, and the related doctrine barring restraints on alienation of property. It seems as if John is on the right track. His parents' trust seems to him to tie up the property too long. Under Section 6, he finds that the rule prohibits the creation of future interests or estates that may not become vested within lives in being at the effective date of the instrument creating the future interest, plus a period of gestation, plus twenty-one years. "Lives in being" refers to any natural person living at the time the instrument takes effect; for a testamentary trust, this would be the date of death of the testator. Section 9 informs John that the rule is a positive mandate of law to be obeyed, irrespective of intention. This information he places on a card (Fig. 143).

With this information in mind, John sees that Step 4 asks him to frame his issue. Reviewing the facts and what he has found in *Am. Jur.2d*, he wonders about the part of the trust that states ". . . upon the death of the last survivor of John and his children. . . ." What children? Is the trust limited to the children he already has, or does it include any children that he might bring into the world later? After all, he is still a young man! If the trust includes any children he might have later, this fact might violate the rule, because measuring the term of the trust by the life of a child born several years after Edward's death certainly would not allow the vesting of the property within lives in being, plus a period of gestation, plus twenty-one years. These thoughts he puts into the issue card (Fig. 144).

Continuing to Step 5 (statute and case finders), John decides to check the *Arizona Statutes* because there has been an indication that some states have changed the Rule Against Perpetuities by statutes. Looking in the general index of the *Arizona Revised Statutes Annotated* under "Perpetuities," John locates "Common Law Rule Against, 33-216." Checking this statute, he places his findings on a card (Fig. 145), in accordance with Step 6.

8/11/84

John   (Trust Validity)   John & Children
61 Am. Jur.2d, Perpetuities and Restraints on Alienation
    "Sec. 6. The Rule Against Perpetuities prohibits the creation of future interests or estates which may not become vested within 'lives in being' at the effective date of the instrument creating the future interest, plus a period of gestation, plus twenty-one years."
    "Sec. 9. The rule is a positive mandate of law to be obeyed irrespective of intention."

Fig. 143.   61 Am. Jur.2d, Perpetuities Card

8/11/84

John   (Trust Validity)   John & Children
Issue: Does a trust instrument drawn by "A" providing that the trust shall terminate upon the death of the last survivor of his son "B" and the children of "B" violate the rule against perpetuities?

Fig. 144.   Trust Validity Issue Card

8/11/84
John   (Trust Validity)   John & Children
Ariz. Rev. Stat. Ann., Sec. 33-216 (1974), Rule Against Perpetuities
"The common-law rule known as the Rule Against Perpetuities
shall hereafter be applicable to all property of every kind and nature
and estates and other interests therein, whether personal, real, or
mixed, legal or equitable by way of trust or otherwise."
Library References: x Perpetuities 🗝 1
                    C.J.S., Perpetuities, Sec. 1 et seq.
Notes and Decisions: Lowell v. Lowell, 29 Ariz. 138, 240 P. 280 (1925).
When the Arizona Rule Against Perpetuities, which was adopted
from Wisconsin, had previously been construed by the highest court
of Wisconsin, such construction was also adopted.
Law Review Commentaries: x Perpetuities in Arizona,
                    1 Ariz. L. Rev. 225
                    Power of Appointment,
                    8 Ariz. L. Rev. 276

Fig. 145.   Ariz. Rev. Stat. Ann., Sec. 33-216 (1974) Card

The library reference gives John a key number to use in the West Digest System (Perpetuities 🗝 1) and a reference to C.J.S., Perpetuities, Sec. 1 et seq. There is nothing specific about how the rule will be applied in Arizona and not much in the way of cases for positive law. John decides to check the first law review article, returning him to Step 3, in order to get a general overview of the Arizona law on perpetuities. His findings, naturally, are entered on another card (Fig. 146).

John now sees the reason for the statute passed in 1963, Ariz. Rev. Stat. Ann., Sec. 33-261 (1974). It returned the Rule Against Perpetuities to its original common-law concept instead of carrying forward the changes made in the New York statute copied by Michigan, which in turn was copied by Wisconsin, and finally copied by Arizona. This statute made the same rule applicable to both real and personal property, thereby saving considerable confusion in its application. John decides that it would be helpful if he could find a case in point under the new 1963 statute. Finding no Arizona digest, he starts with the *Seventh Decennial Digest*, a general digest that covers both state and federal cases for the years 1956 through 1966. Here he looks either for federal cases involving Arizona law or for Arizona cases. Federal cases are listed first, followed by the states in alphabetical order.

Taking down the volume covering perpetuities (Step 5 again), the first thing he finds is a section indicating the sections included. He learns that the volume covers estates inalienable beyond the time allowed by law; restrictions under either common-law rules or statutes; the creation of future contingent estates; and the application of such restrictions to a variety of things, including trusts. The analysis lists the key numbers, 🗝 1, being the nature of the rule against the remoteness of limitations. 🗝 4(3) considers the vesting of an estate at the death of the testator, or within the permissible period. 🗝 4(10) covers limitations to unborn persons or to heirs of the decedent. 🗝 4(15)

8/11/84

John   (Trust Validity)   John & Children
1 Ariz. Law Rev. 225, Richard R. Powell, Perpetuities in Arizona
(1959)
    "Thus as a result of six landmark cases stretching over a span of
a century and a half, the permissible period under the common-law
Rule Against Perpetuities became crystallized at (a) lives of 'persons
in being' when the limitation spoke . . . ; plus (b) a period of twenty-
one years; plus (c) such period of gestation as might be called for
by the circumstances of the person affected. This is the permissible
period stated and discussed in Section 374 of the Restatement of the
Law of Property. This is the period still used in most of the United
States. This is the period governing in Arizona all dispositions of
personal property. . . ."
    The author found only eleven decisions in Arizona to 1959 in-
volving the Rule Against Perpetuities. None of them are relevant to
the present case. Mr. Powell urged the adoption of the old common-
law Rule Against Perpetuities instead of the one in existence in
1959, which was borrowed from Wisconsin, which in turn borrowed
it from Michigan, which also borrowed it from New York. The New
York rule, carried down to Arizona, provided one rule for personal
property and a different one for real estate.

Fig. 146.   1 Ariz. Law Rev. 225 Card

8/11/84

John   (Trust Validity)   John & Children
American Digest System from 1963, covering Perpetuities
🗝 4(3), 🗝 4(10), 🗝 4(15)
7th Dec. Dig., 🗝 4(15), Trust Estates. x Olivas v. Board of National
Missionaries of Presbyterian Church, United States of America, 405
P.2d 481
8th Dec. Dig., nothing
Gen. Dig., Sixth Series, Number 1 through Number 26 (1984), nothing

Fig. 147.   American Digest System, Perpetuities Card

talks of trust estates. John decides that he should look for Arizona cases under
"Perpetuities," key numbers 4(3), 4(10), and 4(15). Listing this information on
a card (Fig. 147), he proceeds.
    Moving on to Step 6, John checks the only case he has found in Arizona,
*Olivas v. Board of National Missionaries of Presbyterian Church, United States
of America,* 405 P.2d 481 (1965), only to discover that the case involved a
charitable trust and therefore does not enlighten his problem a bit.
    Remembering the law review article by Powell in 1 Ariz. Law Rev. 225
and that it referred to the *Restatement of the Law of Property,* John decides

to investigate the restatement. The *Restatement of the Law,* produced by the American Law Institute, is a recognized and accepted secondary authority on American law and has been cited numerous times in court decisions. This work's stated purpose is "to preserve an orderly restatement of the general common law of the United States, including in that term not only the law developed solely by judicial decision, but also law that has grown from the application by the courts of statutes that were generally enacted and were in force for many years."

Evidently, there are no relevant cases in Arizona since the 1963 statute was passed but the restatement can at least give John a respectable secondary authority. This procedure may fall between Step 3 and Step 5, but it certainly is useful (Fig. 148).

John sits back and studies the information he has found. He is still a young man and may have children born in the future. If children are born in the future, and the trust states that such children are a portion of the class whose lives measure the term of the trust, the "what might happen" approach puts the vesting well beyond the permissible time for vesting. If the "wait and see" approach is applied, the waiting period will be the remainder of John's life; and if he lives another twenty-one years, the trust will be invalid because he still might produce children more than twenty-one years after the effective date of the trust, the date of his father's death. If John dies before that time, the trust will be valid. It seems a bit speculative that the staid courts of Arizona will decide thus with these facts presented to them.

This brings John to Step 9 (making a report). Even though John has done the research for himself, the report will help to crystallize his thoughts; and should he decide to consult an attorney, John will be able to discuss the problem intelligently and to present the attorney with something from which to work.

John knows that once the legal issues are resolved, the problems not covered by law must be addressed. These involve the practicality of pursuing and the financial ability to pursue the issue to the desired conclusion. Having the law on one's side, John realizes, does not necessarily mean that one has the power to enforce it.

8/11/84

John   (Trust Validity)   John & Children
Restatement of the Law, Second
   Property, 2d, Vol. 1 (1983)
   p. 12. Introductory Note. Points out two different approaches.
(1)   The property must be certain to vest within the period of the
      rule (the "what might happen" approach).
(2)   The property in fact vests within the period of the rule (the
      "wait and see" approach).
The "what might happen approach" has been adopted by the major-
    ity of the courts.

Fig. 148.   Restatement of the Law, Second, Property Card

Law Library Research Report

Title: Trust Validity
Requested by: John
Submitted by: John
Date Submitted: August 15, 1984

Statement of Facts   John, now age thirty-four, and Jane were married in 1969. John left Jane and their three children, now ages thirteen, eleven, and nine, and settled in New York. After being divorced by Jane in California, John married Josephine, now age forty. There are no children born of the union of John and Josephine.

John's parents, Edward and Sally, who lived in Mesa, Arizona, made pour-over wills, placing their assets upon their death in the hands of the West Mesa Trust Company as trustee for the Edward and Sally Family Trust dated November 3, 1979. The trust provides for the payment of income quarterly to the survivor of Edward and Sally; and upon the death of the last survivor of Edward and Sally, the income is to be divided among John and any children of John. Upon the death of the last survivor of John and his children, the balance of the trust is to be turned over to the Society for the Preservation of Old Attorneys of Mesa, Arizona (SPAM). Sally died on June 10, 1980. Edward died on January 10, 1984.

Question Presented   Does a trust instrument drawn by "A" providing that the trust shall terminate upon the death of the last survivor of his son "B" and the children of "B" violate the rule against perpetuities?

Brief Answer   Apparently this situation has not presented itself to the Arizona Supreme Court for decision. There are two points of view, the "what might happen" view, and the "wait and see" view. Under the "what might happen" view, the trust would appear to violate the Rule Against Perpetuities. Under the "wait and see" view, there is still a strong possibility that the trust would violate the rule.

Discussion   The statute involved was passed in 1963, Ariz. Rev. Stat. Ann., Sec. 33-261 (1974), and merely states that:

The Common Law Rule known as the Rule Against Perpetuities shall hereafter be applicable to all property of every kind and nature and estates and other interests therein, whether personal, real, or mixed, legal or equitable by way of trust or otherwise.

There are no Arizona cases since 1963 that address the problem at hand under the new statute. However, the recent *Restatement of the Law of Property* may shed some light on the current thinking on the subject. The *Restatement of the Law, 2d,* Property, Vol. 1 (1983), on page 12 points out two different approaches:

(1) The property must be certain to vest within the period of the rule (the "what might happen" approach).

(2) The property in fact vests within the period of the rule (the "wait and see" approach).

The "what might happen approach" has been adopted by the majority of the courts.

Bibliography

(Note: The looseleaf materials listed below may set forth the best overview and provide the most up-to-date information. They are not completely described here because the services are tremendously expensive for individuals to purchase, the titles identify the topics, their formats are relatively similar, and most of these materials can be found in law libraries.

If a book can not be found in your library or in the nearest law library, ask your librarian if it can be obtained through interlibrary loan.)

Bogert, George Taylor. *Trusts.* 6th ed. St. Paul, Minn.: West, 1987. An outline of the basic theories and rules relating to private trusts. With index and table of cases.

Casner, A. James. *Estate Planning.* 4th ed. 6 vols. Boston: Little, 1980. Provides complete and up-to-date coverage of estate planning, including wills, taxation, trusts, and gifts. Weighted heavily in the area of taxation. Covers statutes on descent and distribution in each state, which determine how a person may leave his or her estate. With supplement.

Cooper, George. *A Voluntary Tax?* Washington, D.C.: Brookings, 1979. A description of how the rich avoid transfer taxes. With figures and index.

Dacey, Norman F. *How to Avoid Probate—Updated!* New York: Crown, 1980. Outlines probate procedures, gives forms for probate and trust matters, and suggests methods of avoiding probate. Includes table of contents and glossary.

Dukeminier, Jessie, and Stanley M. Johnson. *Family Wealth Transactions: Wills, Trusts, and Estates.* 2d ed. Boston: Little, 1978. A coursebook covering estates, trusts, future interests, and estate planning, for law students. Includes index, table of cases, table of citations to the Uniform Probate Code, and appendixes.

Estate Planning Library. (P-H) Looseleaf.

Estate Planning & Taxation Coordinator. (Research Inst. of America) Looseleaf.

Inheritance Estate and Gift Tax Reports. (CCH) Looseleaf.

Kahn, Arnold D. *Family Security Through Estate Planning.* 2d ed. New York: McGraw-Hill, 1983. Covers legal and tax rules, planning, and the effective use of an attorney's time. Appendixes cover a worksheet, federal estate and gift tax rates, and inheritance and estate tax tables for all states, the District of Columbia, and Puerto Rico. Includes a glossary of legal and tax terms. With index.

Kess, Sidney, and Bertil Westlin. *New Planning Operations and Pitfalls Under the 1981 Economic Recovery Act.* Chicago: Commerce Clearing House, 1981. An analysis of the act with regard to estate planning. With index.

———, et al. *CCH Estate Planning Guide.* 5th ed. 4 vols. Chicago: Commerce Clearing House, 1983. Covers strategies, forms, planning aids, articles, and estate planning review. In looseleaf.

Lynn, Robert J. *Introduction to Estate Planning in a Nutshell.* 3d ed. St. Paul, Minn.: West, 1983. Examines the use of trusts, settlors, trustees, pour-over wills, spendthrift trusts, termination of trusts, and sprinkling or spraying trusts. Includes index, and table of cases.

Scott, Austin Wakeman, and William F. Fratcher. *The Law of Trusts.* 4th ed. Boston: Little, 1987. Gives complete coverage of the law of trusts. Includes index, table of cases, and table of statutes.

Tax Management: Estates, Gifts, Trusts. (BNA) Looseleaf.

Warren, Gorham, & Lamont, Inc. *Estate Planning.* New York: Warren Gorham, & Lamont, bimonthly. Contains articles, notes, and comments covering the major changes in the field of estate planning.

Zaritsky, Howard M., and Martha Altschuller Zaritsky. *New Estate Planning Handbook with Forms and Tables.* Englewood Cliffs, N.J.: Prentice-Hall, 1980. Emphasis placed on tax aspects of estate planning. Contains index, appendix, table of cases, and table of revenue rulings and procedures.

Insurance

Insurance has been described as a contract whereby for a fee, one party agrees to pay a fixed sum to another party for a specified loss by specific perils on a stated subject. There is a trend to call this contract "assurance" when it covers life, and "insurance" when the risk covers property. The terms are probably being split in this manner because insurance is defined as insuring against a risk, while assurance—a more soothing term—denotes confidence and certainty, and is more likely to make a person feel better about dealing with his or her own death in a positive frame of mind, that of protecting loved ones.

A form of our present mutual insurance is found in ancient Greek, Roman, Chinese, Teutonic, Hebrew, and early Christian societies. Mutual insurance associations were formed for the mutual benefit of the members and probably arose out of the custom and usage evolved from shipping, or marine, insurance. Marine insurance was in existence at least in the tenth century and was imported into England from Venice and from other Italian seaports. The first English statute concerning insurance was passed in 1601.

The contract between the insurer and the insured is called a policy. The money paid for the insurance coverage is the premium. The company issuing the insurance policy is the insurer, while the person purchasing the policy is called the owner, and the person whose life is insured is called the insured. An indemnity policy insures against loss or damage to property, indemnifying the owner to the extent of the coverage; while a liability policy insures against the liability for loss or damage and protects the owner against such liability only to the extent of the policy. For a description of other types of insurance, see the Glossary under "Insurance."

Insurance policies can be written to cover almost any imaginable event, including accidents, burglary, robbery, theft, casualty, collision, confiscation (issued to mortgagees of automobiles), conversion, embezzlement, credit, cyclone and tornado, disability, fidelity, fire, group guaranty (against want of integrity, fidelity, or insolvency of employees or persons in a position of trust), industrial (sometimes called people's life, emphasized by Prudential in the early days as a family insurance, usually with just enough coverage for funeral expenses, with the premiums being collected weekly), liability (for injuries sustained by others or for injury to the property of others), etc.; and now even broader risks are covered.

Automobile insurance policies can cover a variety of hazards for different premiums. Some states have what is called a statutory insurance, which is a minimum that must be carried on all automobiles registered in the state. There also are choices covering bodily injury; property damage; medical payments; a comprehensive coverage that may include glass, etc.; collision; and towing and labor. Most of the above can be purchased with varying amounts of coverage, and some, with adjustable amounts of deductibility. A deductible amount means that the insurance company will pay the cost of repairs or damages, less the amount of the deductible so that if the entire bill comes to one thousand dollars, for example, and the policy has a one-hundred-dollar deductible clause covering the risk involved, the insurance company will pay only nine hundred dollars. Many states by statute now have the controversial no-fault insurance, in which the owner of the automobile insures with his or her own insurance company to cover his or her own losses from accidents; and the statutes, except for limited situations, prohibit lawsuits for automobile accidents and the inflated claims of "conscious pain and suffering."

Insurance in the United States is regulated by the states through their legislative bodies, administrative agencies, and court systems, and not by the federal government. A statement in *Paul v. Virginia*, 75 U.S. 168 at 183 (1869), "Issuing a policy of insurance is not a transaction in commerce," saved the insurance industry from federal regulations. The insurance industry has fought tooth and nail to keep its moneymaking operations within the sphere of the states. This is so in spite of the fact that there may be advantages to dealing with only one governing body instead of more than fifty-two. So an insurance company must meet the regulations of the state within which it is organized, as well as the regulations of each state within which it wishes to sell insurance.

Life insurance was created to provide protection for families of insured persons upon the latter's death. Life insurance did not meet universal approval and was prohibited in France because of the belief that it would lead to the premature death of the insured. England sanctioned life insurance, however, and the concept was carried over from English law to American law. Life insurance is one of the major ingredients in the financial planning of business-people and is used to insure funds to buy out heirs of deceased partners or corporate officers in closely held companies, to protect against the loss of key personnel, and as perks for various employees.

Insurance companies collect and examine information that is needed to fix premiums that are sufficient to cover their projected losses, required surpluses, and expenses. Most life insurance companies, being mutual companies, do not figure their earnings in profits, but instead redistribute at least a portion of their excesses to the policyholders. The collection of premiums from many people with the anticipation of having to pay off on only a limited number of fatalities a year enables insurance companies to spread the risks and to keep costs to a minimum.

One of the earliest types of insurance was term insurance, whereby for a low premium the insurance company issued a life policy giving a guaranteed benefit upon death and covering a limited number of years. At the end of the period, the insurance expired. A new policy could be purchased at a reasonable price up to a certain age, then the premiums rose sharply. To smooth out the premium, and to add some value to the policy, the whole life policy came into existence in England in the eighteenth century. This plan built a savings plan into the policy. Payments and death benefits remained equal throughout the life of the policy. The owners of the policies were overcharged in the beginning, the excess being invested. A small portion of the earnings on the excess was credited to the savings part of the policies and created the cash surrender value. The companies incurred tremendous profits on the investments, and with an increase in inflation, people began switching from whole life to term insurance and investing the savings themselves.

When the volume of enlightened policyholders increased sufficiently, the insurance industry became concerned and thought up new ways of keeping their customers happy, even if doing so included increasing the savings part of their whole life policy. This was done by shifting the risk factor of the investment to the policyholder, while keeping control of the insurance and the investments.

The variable insurance policy has a constant premium and carries the regular insurance portion of the whole life policy, but it changes the investment portion. In this case, the policyholder is given a voice in the investments. The usual choice is among several mutual funds. Any cash value and additional death benefits will vary depending upon the investment programs the policyholder selects.

The universal policy allows the policyholder to alter both the premium paid and the death benefits. The interest on the cash value changes with the rates obtainable in the marketplace.

The latest variation is the universal variable policy, which combines parts of both the variable policy and the universal policy. This plan allows the policyholder to change the premium and the death benefit. The cash value and additional death benefits will vary according to the performance of the investment program selected by the policyholder.

With insurance policies taking on an investment vehicle as part of their package, the question arises as to the nature of the newer policies. Are such policies insurance, based primarily on the old insurance values of conservatism and protection, or are they investments, based upon the performance of the market? And if they are investments, does this fact then bring the policy under the supervision of the Securities and Exchange Commission? The best answer to date appears to be that the insurance portion of the policies comes under the supervision of each state within whose boundaries the policies operate, and the investment portion of the policies is involved in interstate commerce and thus falls under the jurisdiction and regulation of the S.E.C.

Introduction to Research Problem

Fire insurance is intended to cover the owner, lessee, or mortgagee for any loss, which is specifically stated in the policy, to the property caused by fire. Insurance policies are necessarily complex in order to cover all the necessary exceptions, because the courts are inclined to interpret policies in favor of the insured. This situation results from the tremendous resources available to insurance companies to write policies in their favor, in contrast with the limited knowledge of individual policy purchasers.

One major area excluded from all policies is arson. The policies will not pay a person for any damages to his or her own property if the individual sets fire to the property. This situation gets a bit complicated when the property is owned by two or more individuals, and one of them has arson in mind.

For background material on the tools used in legal research, review "Where It Is Recorded"; and for an example of the use of these tools in a legal research problem, see "How to Find It." See the Glossary for unfamiliar terms and Appendix A for abbreviations.

The legal explanations and the issues selected here are not comprehensive due to space limitations. Should the researcher become interested in a legal problem not covered by the background material, by the introduction, or by the research problem, he or she should note the question, and, using the procedures suggested in this book, perform his or her own legal research to discover the answer.

Research Problem

The research tools used in this problem consist of the Search Process Flow Chart, the CORP rule, encyclopedias, reporters, citators, and digests.

Back in Section 2, we left Joe with John's model airplane. As it turned out, John never followed up on his claim to the plane, but their friendship did cool considerably. This situation bothered Joe, and he often discussed it with his wife, Sandra. But as time went on and Joe's interest in model airplanes increased, he started a sports shop specializing in airplanes, especially the newer remote-controlled computerized ones. The business grew gradually until, in 1979, Joe left his job with a large farm equipment distributor and purchased a small shop in suburban College Park, near the William B. Hatsfield Atlanta International Airport. He took the building in the name of Joe and Sandra, husband and wife, tenants by the entirety. The property was promptly insured against the usual fire and theft by the Provincial Protection Insurance Association, a Georgia corporation, for $97,500, covering the cost of the property and the stock on hand. The policy was issued in the names of "Joe and Sandra, husband and wife."

By early 1981, Joe had built the business up and asked Sandra to help him. She had no interest in the business and told him so. She intended to keep her teaching job. So Joe hired Sylvia. Sandra became suspicious of the amount of time Joe spent at the store, especially when Sylvia was working evenings. Joe assured Sandra that there was nothing going on between Sylvia and him, but jealousy has a nasty habit of feeding on itself. It began eating away at Sandra, ruined the couple's home life, and interfered with Sandra's teaching. Finally Sandra exploded; and on September 10, 1983, she set fire to the shop, causing a total loss to Joe.

Joe put in a claim for the loss. Provincial Protection Insurance Association declined to honor the claim, stating that inasmuch as the policy was issued to Joe and Sandra as husband and wife, they were jointly insured, and the fraud committed by Sandra was attributed to the joint owner, Joe. Therefore, he could not recover his loss. Joe was upset; his marriage was on the rocks, his wife faced criminal charges of arson, his business was destroyed, and now the insurance company refused to settle with him. Without the settlement, Joe could not go back into business.

In desperation, Joe calls his old friend, John, and tells him the story. John, still a bit miffed about his old airplane, is cool but does sympathize with Joe. John explains how he had gone to the law library several times to look up his rights himself, and he suggests that Joe do the same before visiting a lawyer. John promises to mail Joe a copy of a chart he has and to outline how Joe should approach the research.

A few days later, Joe receives some notes and a copy of the Search Process Flow Chart from John. He reviews them, obtains some 4″ x 6″ index cards, and heads for the law library in Atlanta. After locating a table near the Georgia law books, Joe first sets forth the facts as he sees them on one of the cards (Fig. 149).

Looking at the Search Process Flow Chart, Joe sees that Step 1 instructs him to make up a word list of search words to use in his research. Thinking through the CORP rule (C for cause of action, O for object, R for restitution, and P for parties), Joe decides that his situation will involve O for the insurance, and P for parties, which include himself, Sandra, and the insurance company, and possibly R for restitution, or the money he wishes to obtain from the insurance company. Useful words that come to mind are *fire insurance, husband and wife,* and *arson.* Wanting to be sure that he has not overlooked any useful search words, Joe follows John's advice and looks in a current *Georgia Digest* for the Outline of the Law. Here he finds *property.* Next he goes through the Digest Topics in the same digest, and it yields *indemnity.* The problem centers on an insurance claim, so Joe decides to start with *insurance.*

Checking his chart, Joe follows Step 2 and considers the jurisdiction. He really doesn't know whether the jurisdiction is federal or state; so looking ahead to Step 3 (obtaining a general overview from a textbook or an encyclopedia), Joe decides to look in the nearby encyclopedia *Corpus Juris Secundum (C.J.S.)* under "Insurance" for the answer to both questions. In the contents under "Insurance," he finds "II. What Law Governs, Sec. 50–54." The first thing he

---

2/2/84

Joe   (Insurance Claim)   Joe

Facts: Joe and Sandra, as husband and wife, tenants by the entirety, purchased a store in College Park, Georgia, and placed fire insurance for $97,500 on the building and its contents. Sandra, in a disturbed frame of mind, set fire to the building, causing a total loss of both building and contents. Joe put in a claim for the damages, but the insurance company refused to pay on the grounds that the couple had jointly insured the property, one of the co-owners burned it, and the fraud was attributable to both; therefore, Joe could not collect on his losses.

Fig. 149.   Insurance Claim Fact Card

finds is the statement, "Policies of insurance have been said to be local trans-actions and to be governed by local law, 41." Checking note 41, Joe finds more help: "The interpretation and legal effect of policies of insurance entered into by the inhabitants of Georgia, who are sued upon them in its courts, are pe-culiarly matters of local concern. Pink v. A.A.A. Highway Express, 62 S.Ct. 241, 247, 314 U.S. 201, 86 L.Ed. 152, affirming 13 S.E.2d 373, 191 Ga. 502, 137, 137 A.L.R. 957, certiorari granted 61 S.Ct. 1096, 313 U.S. 555, 85 L.Ed. 1517, and rehearing denied 62 S.Ct. 477, 314 U.S. 716, 86 L.Ed. 570." This information seems to settle the first question; the jurisdiction is Georgia. Joe makes a note to check this case and to enter it on a card later.

Joe notes that "Insurance" spans three volumes of *C.J.S.* and realizes that he cannot possibly read all of these. So he goes through the section headings. Looking under "XVII. Right to Proceeds," he sees "A. Fire Insurance, Sec. 1140–1153." Opening the volume containing these sections, he finds a further breakdown in the listing of contents and sees that Section 1142 covers "Husband and Wife." This section turns out to be of little help. It merely states that if one spouse takes out insurance on joint property, that spouse is entitled to the proceeds; and if the couple take the policy out jointly, they are both entitled to the proceeds. Joe's question is whether or not his wife's arson affects his right to recover on his losses from the insurance company. So he goes back to the contents of the title on insurance. Studying the contents more carefully, he finds "XIII. Risks or causes of loss, Sec. 753–896," and under this, "D. Fire Insurance, Sec. 807–823." Further on under this heading he finds, "3. Limitations as to cause of loss, Sec. 817–823." This information narrows his search con-siderably, so he looks in 45 *C.J.S.* Locating Section 817, Joe browses through the volume to Section 822, which covers "Negligence or Misconduct." Here, under "Property owned by several persons," Joe learns that when property is jointly owned, an innocent owner cannot recover on the policy when a co-owner willfully sets the property on fire. Under note 59, he finds cases from Massachusetts, Pennsylvania, and Wisconsin. Turning to the 1983 pocket part, he finds no Georgia cases. He is beginning to feel that he really does have a problem. The problem may be that the question has not been presented to the Georgia court. Before returning the volumes to the shelf, Joe looks under "Li-brary Reference" found under some sections in the pocket parts to see if he can pick up a West key number. If he can find a West key number, he may be able to investigate the West Digest Series for up-to-date cases.

Joe finds none under Section 822, but under Section 818 he finds "Insur-ance 🔑 422"; and under Section 824, he finds "Insurance 🔑 433." Think-ing that he may find help in this area, he makes a note to check these digest sections, focusing on key numbers 422 through 433.

His Search Process Flow Chart tells Joe that Step 4 calls for the framing of an issue. After careful consideration, Joe frames the issue and enters it on a card (Fig. 150).

Joe considers Step 5 (examine statute and case finders). He decides to use case finders because the insurance policy is a contract between the parties and would most likely be interpreted by the courts. Before starting this process, Joe decides to clean up the loose ends caused by the Pink case above. He locates the case in the U.S. Reports and enters it on a card (Fig. 151).

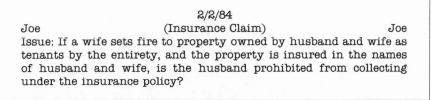

2/2/84
Joe   (Insurance Claim)   Joe
Issue: If a wife sets fire to property owned by husband and wife as
tenants by the entirety, and the property is insured in the names
of husband and wife, is the husband prohibited from collecting
under the insurance policy?

Fig. 150.   Insurance Claim Issue Card

2/2/84
Joe   (Insurance Claim)   Joe
Pink v. A.A.A. Highway Express, 314 U.S. 201 (1941)
    In a suit in Georgia to enforce contributions under a New York
insurance contract, Stone, C.J., stated on page 211, "The interpretation and legal effect of policies of insurance entered into by the
inhabitants of Georgia, who are sued upon them in its courts, are
peculiarly matters of local concern."

Fig. 151.   Pink v. A.A.A. Highway Express Card

For case finders (Step 5), Joe turns to the *Georgia Digest* under "Insurance"
and looks at the key numbers, starting with 422, which he suspected above
might be helpful. Here he finds " 🔑 429 Wrongful Acts of Insured." The
library reference given here is to *C.J.S.*, Insurance, Sec. 791 et seq., 822. This
information reinforces Joe's belief that he has hit the right area, so he looks at
the cases under "Insurance 🔑 429." The case of *Merchants Ins. Co. v.
Lilgemont, Inc.*, 84 F.2d 685 (1936) catches his eye because it states that the
fraud of one of two or more persons hiring another to burn the property will
not defeat the insurance in view of the innocent person's interest, the insurer's
remedy being a subrogation suit in damages against the insured's rights. On the
other hand, the case of *Sandersville Oil Mill Co. v. Globe & Rutgers Fire Ins.
Co.*, 124 S.E. 728, 32 Ga. App. 722 (1924) states that when practically the entire
stock of a corporation is owned by one stockholder whose relationship to the
minority stockholders is such as to fuse their interests with his, and to constitute
his acts their own, the corporation cannot recover on a policy for loss sustained
by his incendiary act.

    Turning to the pocket part under "Insurance 🔑 429," Joe locates the
case of *Richards v. Hanover Ins. Co.*, 299 S.E.2d 561, 250 Ga. 613 (1983),
which is remarkably similar to his own situation. Joe makes up a card for the
digest and lists the three cases on the card (Fig. 152).

    Step 6 on the flow chart instructs Joe to check the above cases; and in
looking them over, he decides to look at the most recent, which appears to be
close to his own situation. This case is entered on a 4″ x 6″ card (Fig. 153).

2/2/84

Joe   (Insurance Claim)   Joe

Georgia Digest, Insurance 429, Wrongful Acts of Insured

Merchants Ins. Co. v. Lilgemont, Inc., 84 F.2d 685 (1936)

Sandersville Oil Mill Co. v. Globe & Rutgers Fire Ins. Co., 124 S.E.2d
    728, 32 Ga. App. 722 (1924)

x Richards v. Hanover Ins. Co., 299 S.E.2d 561, 250 Ga. 613 (1983)

Fig. 152.   Georgia Digest, Insurance Card

2/2/84

Joe   (Insurance Claim)   Joe

Richards v. Hanover Ins. Co., 250 Ga. 613 (Jan. 1983)

　　Smith, J., reported a unanimous decision in the case, which involved a husband and a wife purchasing a homeowner's insurance
policy, the husband later burning the house, and the wife suing to
recover her losses. The case is one of first impression in Georgia,
and other jurisdictions appear to be divided. Most older cases deny
recovery to an innocent co-insured spouse on the grounds that those
holding property jointly have a joint obligation to refrain from
defrauding the insurance company, and the fraud of one becomes
the fraud of the other. An increasing number of jurisdictions have
focused on the duties under the contract instead of on property
rights. This court considered it a case of contract of insurance. The
court looked at the contract and found that it designated both Mr.
and Mrs. Richards as the "Named Insured" and excluded coverage
for destruction caused by the acts of the insured. The contract did
not state whether the Richards' rights and obligations were joint or
several. In this case, the court applied the rules of construction
concerning insurance contracts, which state that (1) any ambiguity
in the contract is to be construed strictly against the insurer as the
drafter of the contract, (2) any exclusion from coverage sought to
be invoked by the insurer is also strictly construed, and (3) insurance contracts are to be read in accordance with the reasonable
expectations of the insured. The court found for Mrs. Richards.

Fig. 153.   Richards v. Hanover Ins. Co. Card

Joe bypasses Step 7 because the Richards case is recent and seems to cover
Joe's situation. He does not Shepardize (Step 8) the Richards case in order to
look for more recent cases on the subject because he feels that his lawyer will
do that at the proper time. This brings him to Step 9 (the report). Joe prepares
a library report in order to be sure that his thinking has been proper and as a
basis for a talk with his attorney.

Joe knows that once the legal issues have been resolved, the problems
not covered by law must be addressed. These involve the practicality of pursuing
and the financial ability to pursue the issue to the desired conclusion. Having

the law on one's side, Joe realizes, does not necessarily mean that one has the power to enforce it.

Law Library Research Report

Title: Insurance Claim
Requested by: Joe
Submitted by: Joe
Date Submitted: February 2, 1984

Statement of Facts   Joe and Sandra, as husband and wife, tenants by the entirety, purchased a store in College Park, Georgia, and placed fire insurance for $97,500 on the building and its contents. Sandra set fire to the building, causing a total loss of both building and contents. Joe put in a claim for the damages, but the insurance company refused to pay on the grounds that the couple had jointly insured the property, one of the co-owners burned it, and the fraud was attributable to both; therefore, Joe could not collect on his losses.

Question Presented   If a wife sets fire to property owned by husband and wife as tenants by the entirety, and the property is insured in the names of husband and wife, is the husband prohibited from collecting under the insurance policy?

Brief Answer   In Georgia an innocent spouse will be able to recover his or her damages under a fire insurance policy issued to both husband and wife when the other spouse set fire to the premises, unless recovery is specifically excluded in the contract of insurance.

Discussion   The older cases appear to hold in favor of the insurance company and deny coverage on the basis that the joint owners owe a duty to the insurance company not to defraud the company, and any such act by one joint owner will be imputed to the innocent owners.

The more recent cases appear to have decided such situations on the basis of insurance contract law instead of on property law, and many have found in favor of the insured. Smith, J., took this approach in the case of *Richards v. Hanover Ins. Co.*, 250 Ga. 613 (Jan. 1983) and reported a unanimous decision.

The case involved a husband and a wife purchasing a homeowner's insurance policy, the husband later burning the house, and the wife suing to recover her losses. The case is one of first impression in Georgia, and other jurisdictions appear to be divided. This court considered it a case of contract of insurance. The court looked at the contract and found that it designated both Mr. and Mrs. Richards as the "Named Insured" and excluded coverages for destruction caused by the acts of the insured. The contract did not state whether the Richard's rights and obligations were joint or several. In this case, the court applied the rules of construction concerning insurance contracts, which state that (1) any ambiguity in the contract is to be construed strictly against the insurer as the drafter of the contract, (2) any exclusion from coverage sought to be invoked by the insurer is also strictly construed, and (3) insurance contracts are to be read in accordance with the reasonable expectations of the insured. The court awarded Mrs. Richards her share of the insurance proceeds.

Bibliography

(Note: The looseleaf materials listed below may set forth the best overview and provide the most up-to-date information. They are not completely described here because the services are tremendously expensive for individuals to purchase, the titles identify the topics, their formats are relatively similar, and most of these materials can be found in law libraries.

If a book can not be found in your library or in the nearest law library, ask your librarian if it can be obtained through interlibrary loan.)

American Bar Association, Committee on Property Insurance Law. *Annotations to the Home-owner's Policy.* Chicago: Amer. Bar Assn., 1980. Follows the form of the policy, giving state-by-state cases, with annotations on various policy actions. Looseleaf.

Appleman, John Alan, and Jean Appleman. *Insurance Law and Practice with Forms.* St. Paul, Minn.: West, 1981. Provides complete coverage of types of contracts, risks, misrepresentation, incontestability, loss clauses, exposure to danger, transportation risks, disability, specific losses, hospitalization and medical expenses, property insurance, casualty insurance, uninsured motorists, commercial insurance, procedures, and forms. Includes index, table of cases, and notes. A multi-volume set updated with pocket parts.

Automobile Insurance Law Reports. (CCH) Looseleaf.

Burke, D. Barlow. *Law of Title Insurance.* Boston: Little, 1986. Includes table of cases and index. Kept up to date with pocket supplements.

Couch, George J. *Couch Cyclopedia of Insurance Law.* 2d ed. Edited by Ronald A. Anderson. Rochester, N.Y.: Lawyers Cooperative/Bancroft-Whitney, 1984. Provides complete insurance coverage with origin and history, investigating various kinds of insurance. Includes forms, table of cases, index, and notes. A multi-volume set updated with pocket parts.

Dobbyn, John F. *Insurance Law in a Nutshell.* St. Paul, Minn.: West, 1981. An overview of the entire insurance field in plain English.

Fire and Casualty Insurance Law Reports. (CCH) Looseleaf.

Fisher, Emeric, and Peter Swisher. *Principles of Insurance Law.* New York: Matthew Bender & Co., 1986.

Insurance Guide. (P-H) Looseleaf.

Jerry, Robert H. *Understanding Insurance Law.* New York: Matthew Bender & Co., 1987. Includes bibliography and index.

Life-Health and Accident Insurance Law Reports. (CCH) Looseleaf.

Long, Rowland H. *The Law of Liability Insurance.* 4 vols. New York: Matthew Bender & Co., 1966– . In looseleaf for updating.

Schermer, Irvin E. *Automobile Liability Insurance.* 2d ed. 2 vols. New York: Clark Boardman, 1981– . With index. In looseleaf for updating.

Windt, Allan D. *Insurance Claims and Disputes: Representation of Insurance Companies and Insureds.* New York: McGraw-Hill, 1982. Gives answers to problems routinely arising in insurance disputes. Contains index, case index, and table of statutes. Updated by pocket parts.

Pensions

One of the oldest records of a pension system is found in the Roman Empire. Here personal pensions were given to disabled soldiers for military service. The system expanded into areas of Europe that were at one time controlled by the Roman Empire. From the concept of disability military pensions, the system expanded to include public pensions established by governments for disabled government workers. From this point, the pension systems became corrupt and developed into arbitrary grants from monarchs to favored individuals. In the sixteenth century, the corrupt nature of public pensions in France reached a level that had to be reduced to prevent a fiscal crisis. Pensions were being granted to loyal servants, past ministers of state, generals, officers, nobles, members of the representative assembly in exchange for votes, men of letters and distinguished talent, favorites of the king, and courtesans. The awards were frequently for huge sums, discretionary, arbitrary, and subject to no rules. Some individuals received more than one pension, and a system of hereditary rights in pensions developed. There were even some secret pensions, for secret purposes, naturally.

This entire system was swept away by the French Revolution, and a new system was established to cover state and local pensions. Pensions were then given to incapacitated or injured public employees, or to those who had sacrificed to serve society, after long years of faithful service and only according to set rules. The new system was later expanded to include the dependents of pensioners. The French system of regulated pensions spread to other European countries and eventually reached England in the last quarter of the nineteenth century. The extension of the system to include civilian public employees arose due to pressure from employee organizations. With the rise of the industrial revolution, industrial countries such as England experienced pressure to establish pension systems for workers in private industry. These systems were based more on contributions by the beneficiaries than on contributions from the employers, and benefits were definitely set according to the worker's pay and length of service. Pension funds grew to cover the necessary payments, and the idea of compulsory contributions grew. The rising demands on the funds required, finally, that industries adopt actuarially funded systems.

Soon the theory arose that pensions should be considered deferred wages of the employees, due employees because of the destruction of their wage-earning ability, and that the employer should contribute to pensions on the same basis as they contributed to depreciation of equipment. People wear out, as do machines, and must be replaced, the thinking went. Following this line of thought, the German government in 1889 established an old-age system for its public employees. Industry, faced with this problem, used pensions to eliminate old and disabled workers, and to allow for faster promotion of younger, more aggressive workers. The trend turned away from strict disability and toward retirement due to old age, or due to the attainment of a certain age rather than the completion of a certain number of years spent working for the same employer. The inclusion of savings plans and insurance options became popular, and the idea of portability of pensions splashed across the scene.

All this activity in Europe naturally had an effect on pension systems in the United States. Only in the United States have military pensions ever been paid to citizens who sustained no service-connected injuries. However, the pension systems that grew in the early days of our history seldom provided safeguards for the pension rights of employees. Because of the turnover of the work force and the service requirements needed to obtain a pension, only a relatively small number of workers ever received pension rights. Investigations of pension funds in the United States found that a majority of such funds were either underfunded or unfunded.

The Pension Reform Act (Employee Retirement Income Security Act of 1974, Public Law 93-406, 29 U.S.C., Sec. 1101 et seq.) was an attempt to deal with the many problems associated with pensions. This act had an impact on both labor law and tax law, being partly enforced by the Labor Department and partly by the Treasury Department. The act established minimum standards for participating in pension funds, for the vesting of pension interests in employees, and for funding the plans. It also set forth the duties of pension plan fiduciaries under employee benefit plans, established certain responsibilities, and limited investments in qualified employer securities and real estate. In addition, the statute established the Pension Benefit Guaranty Corporation to administer the plan, the insurance provisions of the plan, and the termination procedures.

Employers are not required to provide pension plans, but unions frequently see to it that such plans are included in collective bargaining agreements. If such a plan is provided by an employer, certain standards must be met. To qualify, a plan must meet the minimum vesting standards. These include the provision that each participating employee will have non-forfeitable rights to normal retirement benefits when he or she reaches the normal retirement age, in the accrued benefits derived from the contribution each has made to the plan. These accrued benefits are to be derived from employer contributions under one of three schedules. The schedules provide for (1) a ten-year vesting, or 100 percent vesting after ten years of participation by the employee; or (2) a five- to fifteen-year vesting, twenty-five percent after five years, plus five percent for each year from the fifth to the tenth year, when benefits are to be at least fifty percent, and an additional ten percent for each year thereafter to the maximum of 100 percent vesting after fifteen years of participating service; or (3) the Rule of forty-five to fifty percent, providing for vested interest in pensions for employees leaving the service of a company with a qualified plan after five years of service, if his or her age and years of service exceed forty-five, plus ten percent for each additional year up to 100 percent, to be received after completing ten years of participating service.

Minimum funding standards also were established, but these standards exempted profit-sharing plans, stock bonus plans, plans funded entirely with individual insurance contracts, plans established by governments, church plans unless they elect to be included, plans to which the employer does not contribute, fraternal and society plans, and employee-established benefit plans. If the funding is found to be deficient, the employer can be charged a five percent excise tax on the amount of each year's accumulated deficiency.

The fiduciaries of these qualifying funds are required to discharge their duties solely in the interests of the participating beneficiaries. The duties of the fiduciary are to defray expenses; provide benefits; use the care, skill, prudence, and diligence of a prudent person; diversify investments; and minimize the risk of large losses, all of which are to be set forth in each plan. Criminal penalties are provided for breach of fiduciary duties.

Certain transactions between the plan and disqualified persons are prohibited. Disqualified persons, or parties in interest, are described as:

(1) a fiduciary, or
(2) a person providing service to the plan, or
(3) an employer whose employees are covered under the plan, or
(4) an employee organization with members covered under the plan, or
(5) the owner (either direct or indirect) of fifty percent of:
    (a) the voting power of stock, or
    (b) capital interest in or profits of a partnership, or
    (c) the beneficial interest of a trust or estate, or
(6) a member of a family of a fiduciary, or a provider of services to the plan, or
(7) a corporation, partnership, trust, or estate with fifty percent or more of the combined voting power of, capital interest in, or profits in such entity dealing with a plan, or,
(8) officers, directors, or individuals with power or responsibilities like officers or directors, or with ten percent or more shares in the company providing the plan, or who are highly compensated employees of said company.

If a prohibited transaction takes place, the plan can maintain its status, but an excise tax is placed upon the disqualified person. Prohibited acts include.

(1) selling, exchanging, or leasing property between the plan and a disqualified person, or
(2) lending money to such person, or
(3) furnishing goods, services, or facilities between a plan and such a person, or
(4) transferring to or for the use or benefit of such person income or assets of the plan, or
(5) an act by a disqualified person who is a fiduciary, whereby he or she deals with the income or assets of the plan for his or her own interests, or

(6) receiving consideration for his or her own account by a disqualified person who is a fiduciary, from any party dealing with the plan in a transaction involving income or assets of the plan.

Introduction to Research Problem

The Pension Benefit Guaranty Corporation was established in the Department of Labor for the purpose of encouraging contributions to pension plans and is charged with making payments, maintaining the insurance fund, and keeping the fund liquid. The act applies only to tax-qualifying plans that meet its requirements for a period of five years, and excludes individuals. Termination insurance is provided for vested basic benefits if the plan is in effect for sixty months, and increased benefits provided by amendments to plans are included only if the amendment has been in effect for sixty months. The guarantee is only to the extent that it does not exceed the actuarial value of benefits in the form of a life annuity, payable monthly at age sixty-five and equal to the lesser of (1) one-twelfth of participants' average compensation during the highest paid consecutive five years, or (2) 750 times the fraction in which the numerator is the Social Security average base in effect during the year the plan terminated, and the denominator is $13,200.

Benefits are assured if the participant's rights are fully vested, the vested benefits are fully insured, and the funds are safeguarded and insured by the Pension Benefit Guaranty Corporation. If the participant is partially vested, he or she will receive such partial interest.

Even today, with the possibility of being 100 percent vested after only ten years of continuous employment, many employees end up with no vested benefits due to constant job changes. Still another danger crosses the horizon for the working person. Even though he or she is covered by a retirement plan, the plan may not be as beneficial as once thought. In the June 25, 1984, issue of *Business Week,* an article appeared indicating that companies are reaping large benefits by terminating overfunded pension plans, purchasing annuities to cover the vested interests of their employees, and pocketing the balance, all done according to the law. Between 1981 and 1983, it was reported that 162 companies had taken this path, with some ninety more considering such action. Other companies are considering reducing contributions to their plan and revising their actuarial assumptions to reflect current economic trends. A recent news flash indicates that the Great Atlantic and Pacific Tea Co. has served notice that it intends to terminate its company pension plan and return about $275 million in surplus assets to the company. The near future in this area appears interesting for lawyers.

Remember, for background material on the tools used in legal research, review "Where It Is Recorded"; and for an example of the use of these tools in a legal research problem, see "How to Find It." For unfamiliar terms, see the Glossary. See Appendix A for abbreviations.

The legal explanations and the issues selected here are not comprehensive due to space limitations. Should the researcher become interested in a legal problem not covered by the background material, by the introduction, or by the research problem, he or she should note the question, and, using the procedures suggested in this book, perform his or her own legal research to discover the answer.

Research Problem

The research tools used in this problem consist of the Search Process Flow Chart, the CORP rule, digests, reporters, and citators.

As time went by, John, whom we left in New York back in Section 4, lost interest in crusading for union rights. Things had gone quite well for him, even though he did not join the management team of XPD Electronics and Amos had advanced to the office of Vice-President in Charge of Efficiency. John held a highly respected position—as high as he could go without becoming a part of management—had his choice of vacations, and was looked up to by everyone in the plant. He became disenchanted with the union and eventually gave up his union membership. The union, however, had obtained considerable benefits, including a pension plan paying liberal monthly benefits after ten years' service, upon retirement at age sixty-five. The plan also provided for early retirement if agreed upon by both the worker and the employer. In addition, upon an individual's retirement, the company had agreed with the union to continue paying that individual's premiums on life insurance, as well as medical and health benefits.

As John reached his later years, he began to think about retirement, talked with the office the company had established to help workers with their retirement plans, and collected all the information he could. He was seriously considering retiring early.

However, business slacked off in his division, the parent company began cutting the work force, and, finally, upon the recommendation of Amos—the Efficiency Vice-President—the company decided to sell the division. The purchaser, ABComputers, wanted to obtain this division to help build its ABC computer. ABComputers was a bit worried, however, about the inflated benefits the workers received and about the generous pension plan. The problem was discussed among XPD Electronics, the union representing the workers in John's division, and the pension trustees. A tentative agreement was reached whereby (1) the division would be sold, (2) vested benefits earned would be continued through XPD Electronics, (3) ABComputers would establish its own retirement plan, which would exclude early retirement provisions, and (4) ABComputers would not continue the policy of paying premiums on the life insurance as well as on the medical and hospital insurance of the retirees. If this agreement could not be accomplished, ABComputers was not interested in the purchase, and XPD Electronics would have to close down the division entirely.

When XPD Electronics announced the deal in cooperation with the union, many of the employees were upset. Union meetings were held to discuss the situation, but everything all boiled down to the fact that if the employees did not take the deal along with the reduction in retirement benefits, there would be no sale, and the employees would be out of a job. Many employees felt as John did, that they had been betrayed by the union and that they had interests in the retirement plan that could not be taken away from them. In the Golden Chips Bar and Grill that evening, a lively discussion took place, and several employees asked John if he would look into their rights. His reputation as a legal researcher had spread, and he was quite happy to accommodate this request.

Collecting his 4″ x 6″ cards, a pencil, and his Search Process Flow Chart, John takes off for the law library of the New York University Law School. His first task is to establish the facts of the situation as he can re-create them from the evidence. He puts these facts on a card (Fig. 154).

Turning to his Search Process Flow Chart, John sees that Step 1 is to develop a list of words to aid him in researching his problem. He thinks over the CORP rule; *C* stands for cause of action, *O* for an object involved, *R* for the restitution desired, and *P* for the parties involved. Under *O* for things, John comes up with *pensions, retirement,* and *benefits.* Not wanting to rely on his memory alone, he looks in *West's New York Digest* for the Outline of the Law. From this outline, he gleans the additional terms *employer's liability, labor relations,* and *master and servant.* He takes one further step, and looking at the Digest Topics in the same volume, he finds no new terms.

Step 2 brings John to the consideration of jurisdiction. This matter confuses him a bit because both companies are headquartered in New York, he and his fellow workers work in New York, and there will be no relocation after the sale. On the other hand, both companies are engaged in interstate commerce, so maybe this fact brings them under federal jurisdiction. John will hold his decision on this item until later, after he learns a bit more about the subject.

7/5/84

John   (Retirement Benefits)   Employees

Facts: The workers in the engineering division of XPD Electronics, which was being sold to ABComputers, had all worked for XPD Electronics for eleven or more years. They were enrolled in the retirement plan, which provided them with a retirement at age 65, the actual vested benefits depending upon the amount contributed by the employer and the employees to their accounts over their years of employment with the company and upon their wages. This amount was not forfeitable. The plan provided that after ten years of employment, the right to retirement benefits was fully and 100 percent vested in the employee. Yearly contributions were made by both the employer and the employee, and the fund was handled by a board of trustees completely independent of the company. The company also provided an early retirement plan if both the employer and employee agreed to it. In addition, this package provided for the continuation of the company's payment of premiums on such life insurance, medical insurance, and health insurance as was being covered at the time of retirement.

In the proposed sale of the division to ABComputers, the buyers, sellers, union, and trustees for the retirement fund all agreed that the early retirement plan and the insurance premium benefits would be eliminated from the retirement package for those workers staying with the engineering division after the sale.

Fig. 154. Retirement Benefits Fact Card

Step 3 suggests that John look in a textbook or in an encyclopedia for a general background of the subject. Since he lacks an adequate background in this field, he knows that the success of his research may well depend upon his completing this step before going any further. He chooses to look in 70 *C.J.S.*, revised in 1987, which contains a newly written title, *Pensions and Retirement Plans and Benefits*. Using the detailed table of contents provided at the beginning of this title, he sees that Part VIII (Secs. 111–114) concerns the subject of "Merger, Transfer, and Termination of Plans in General." This information seems relevant, so John reviews these sections thoroughly. Unfortunately, the material does not seem to address John's specific problem, but at least he now feels more secure in his general understanding of pension-related issues. Thus, he goes on to Step 4, the framing of the issue. He places his issue on a card (Fig. 155).

Step 5 leads John to the statute and case finders. He decides to look for cases, since, if he can find one involving his problem, it will lead him to both the jurisdiction involved and a solution to the problem. Checking his word list, John picks out *pensions* and proceeds to the *Ninth Decennial Digest*. This unit of the American Digest System contains cases from all jurisdictions, including federal courts in case the proper jurisdiction is federal, and is the most up-to-date and complete unit of the System. Looking at the first page under the heading "Pensions," John sees that the subjects excluded and covered by other topics include "Employer's Pension and Benefit Funds." The cross-reference provided instructs him to see "Master and Servant."

Taking this lead, John looks under "Master and Servant" in the digest, and here under "Wages and Other Remuneration" ⟨key⟩ 78.1, he sees "Pensions, Benefits, and Relief Funds in General."

Picking up 23 *General Digest, Sixth Series* and turning to "Master and Servant ⟨key⟩ 78.1(1)," John finds reference to the case *American Progressive Life and Health Insurance Co. of New York v. Corcoran*, 715 F2d 784. The note on the case refers to "ERISA, Employee Retirement Income Security Act of 1974, Sec. 415(a) as amended, 29 U.S.C.A., Sec. 1144(a)," and states that "the ERISA preemption provision was designed to have sweeping preemptive effect in the employment benefit field, and the various exceptions to preemption are meant to be narrow." This information gives John two leads. First, it settles the question presented in Step 2; his jurisdiction will be federal. Second, it gives him a lead into a primary source of law, a statute (29 U.S.C., Sec. 1144(a)). John

---

7/5/84

John   (Retirement Benefits)   Employees

Issue: Does an employer, with the consent of the union and the pension trustees, have the right to reduce or eliminate from its retirement package relative to workers having over ten years of service, such benefits as payment of premiums for health, medical, and hospital insurance, and early retirement provisions?

Fig. 155. Retirement Benefits Issue Card

takes a quick look at the statute mentioned and discovers that it is a part of the Pension Reform Act, or the Employee Retirement Income Security Act of 1974, Public Law 93-406, and actually begins in 29 U.S.C., Sec. 1101. This is a very comprehensive and complex statute. John decides that for his limited purpose of doing a quick, basic review of the material so that he will be able to intelligently discuss the problem with an attorney, he is probably better off sticking to cases, especially since he now has a key number in West's Digest System, "Master and Servant 78.1."

Continuing with Step 5 (examining case finders), John again looks at *West's General Digest, Sixth Series,* Volume 23. Finding no helpful cases at all under 78.1 et seq., he continues to volume 24, the last one published at the time. Here under 78.1 "Pensions, benefits, and relief funds in general," John locates no pertinent cases, so he moves forward and discovers a case under 78.1(3) stating that it is not unlawful per se to alter a pension plan concerning prospective benefits if the change does not violate the requirements of ERISA. Accrued benefits under ERISA are not intended to include such things as conditional benefits, premiums for medical and life insurance, or the value of the right to receive early retirement benefits, all of which may be amended or deleted without violating the act, *Dhayer v. Weirton Steel Div. of Nat'l. Steel Corp.,* 571 F.Supp. 316 (D.C. W.Va. 1983). John places this information on a card (Fig. 156).

Progressing to Step 6, John looks at the case. To make his record complete, John puts this case on a card (Fig. 157).

The case John has found is a Virginia District Court case that was decided under the jurisdiction of the Fourth Circuit Court. John is in the Second Circuit; and in his jurisdiction, the same case may be decided another way. The Dhayer case cannot be used as a percedent for his case, but it might have fairly strong persuasive value. John passes over Step 7 because he has found no new cases to examine. To find out if there is any further action concerning this important case, he turns to *Shepard's Citations* (Step 8). In the June 1984 supplement of *Shepard's Federal Citations* for the *Federal Supplement,* he locates Fed. Supp., Vol. 571 at the top of the page and follows down the column to page 316, under which he finds two references. The first reference is "a724 F.2d 406," indicating that in Volume 724 of *F.2d* on page 406, the case has been affirmed

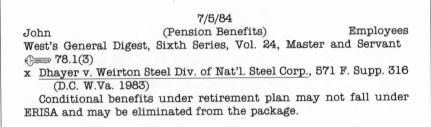

Fig. 156.   West's General Digest, Sixth Series Card

7/5/84

John   (Pension Benefits)   Employees
Dhayer v. Weirton Steel Div. of Nat'l. Steel Corp., 571 F.Supp. 316
(D.C. W.Va. 1983)
    The case involved the purchase of a division of a company by
another company, and an amendment to the retirement plan, reducing retirement benefits. Salaried non-union personnel objected to
the amendment. The case is very similar to the situation under
current investigation. Maxwell, C.J., found among other things, that:
(1) It is not unlawful per se to alter pension plans with respect to
prospective benefits unless they violate ERISA requirements.
(2) ERISA does not require an employer to offer any type of benefit
plan; but if one is offered, it must comply with the minimum
requirements of the act.
(3) Provisions for retirement before the normal age are not required.
(4) Accrued benefits under ERISA are not intended to include such
things as conditional benefits, such as premiums for insurance benefits.
x Shepardized a724 F.2d 406

Fig. 157.   Dhayer v. Weirton Steel Div. of Nat'l. Steel Corp. Card

7/15/84

John   (Pension Benefits)   Employees
Sutton v. Weirton Steel Div. of Nat'l. Steel Corp., 724 F.2d 406 (4th
Cir. 1983)
    Butzner, Sr. J., in a hearing concerning four companion cases,
including the Dhayer case, found no errors and affirmed the lower
court's opinion.
Notation: certiorari denied May 21, 1984. See 104 S.Ct. 2387.
x Shepardized: Appeal to United States Supreme Court

Fig. 158.   Sutton v. Weirton Steel Div. of Nat'l. Steel Corp. Card

by the United States Court of Appeals for the Fourth Circuit. The second
reference, "d723 F.2d [15] 1152," indicates that the facts of Paragraph 15 in
the Dhayer case were distinguished from the facts in the case reported in 723
F.2d 1152.

    According to the Search Process Flow Chart, for new cases found in the
Shepardizing process, John must return to Step 6 for both cases, examine them,
and if necessary, put them on separate cards. So he takes 724 F.2d 406 and 723
F.2d 1152 from the shelves. John looks first at the case affirming the Dahyer
case and enters it on a card (Fig. 158).

    No new cases are referred to that John should investigate (Step 7) so he
continues with Step 8 and Shepardizes the case. He finds a notation in *Shepard's
Citation* that an appeal to the United States Supreme Court is pending. This

fact does not suprise John, because in researching the history of the case before the judge's decision, John had already discovered that the appeal to the United States Supreme Court had been denied. Unless another appeal is taken, the question seems to be settled; and he, along with the other complaining employees, is out of luck.

John returns to Step 6 for the other case found while he was Shepardizing the Dhayer case and finds that it is the case of *Livernois v. Warner-Lambert Co., Inc.*, 723 F.2d 1152. Murnaghan, J., of the Fourth Circuit distinguished the facts in the Livernois case from those in the Dhayer case and found them sufficiently different; therefore, John need not consider the Dhayer case a precedent.

No new cases being discovered, John skips Step 7, bringing him to the final step (Step 9), the writing of a report for the employees, which he does in the form of a Law Library Research Report.

John knows that once the legal issues are resolved, the problems not covered by law must be addressed. These involve the practicality of pursuing and the financial ability to pursue the issue to the desired conclusion. Having the law on one's side, John realizes, does not necessarily mean that one has the power to enforce it.

Law Library Research Report

Title: Pension Benefits

Requested by: John

Submitted by: John

Date Submitted: July 20, 1984

Statement of Facts   The workers in the engineering division of XPD Electronics, which was being sold to ABComputers, had all worked for XPD Electronics for eleven or more years. They were enrolled in the retirement plan, which provided them with a retirement at age sixty-five, the actual vested benefits depending upon the amount contributed by the employer and the employees to their accounts over their years of employment with the company and upon their wages. This amount was not forfeitable. The plan provided that after ten years of employment, the right to retirement benefits was fully and 100 percent vested in the employee. Yearly contributions were made by both the employer and the employee, and the fund was handled by a board of trustees completely independent of the company. The company also provided an early retirement plan if both the employer and employee agreed to it. Also, the package provided for the continuation of the company's payment of premiums on such life insurance, medical insurance, and health insurance as was being covered at the time of retirement.

In the proposed sale of the division to ABComputers, the buyers, seller, union, and trustees for the retirement fund all agreed that the early retirement plan and the insurance premium benefits would be eliminated from the retirement package for those workers staying with the engineering division after the sale.

Question Presented   Does an employer, with the consent of the union and the pension trustees, have the right to reduce or to eliminate from its retirement package relative to workers having over ten years of service, such benefits as payment of premiums for health, medical, and hospital insurance, and early retirement provisions?

Discussion   The Employee Retirement Income Security Act of 1974, 29 U.S.C. 1101 et seq., provides standards for any pension plans that companies involved in interstate commerce may see fit to establish for their employees. The act provides three methods of vesting benefits in employees, and it provides for funding, the supervision of funds by trustees, tax benefits for those qualifying, and insurance coverage for qualifying plans through the Pension Benefit Guaranty Corporation.

A recent case arose under similar circumstances as the present problem, *Dhayer v. Weirton Steel Div. of Nat'l. Steel Corp.*, 571 F. Supp. 316 (D.C. W.Va. 1983), affirmed with companion cases in *Sutton v. Weirton Steel Div. of Nat'l. Steel Corp.*, 724 F.2d 406 (4th Cir. 1983), cert. den. 104 S.Ct. 2387 (1984). In these cases it was decided that:

(1) It is not unlawful per se to alter pension plans with respect to prospective benefits unless they violate ERISA requirements.

(2) ERISA does not require an employer to offer any type of benefit plan; but if one is offered, it must comply with the minimum requirements of the act.

(3) Provisions for retirement before the normal age are not required.

(4) Accrued benefits under ERISA are not intended to include conditional benefits, such as premiums for insurance benefits.

Bibliography

(Note: The looseleaf materials listed below may set forth the best overview and provide the most up-to-date information. They are not completely described here because the services are tremendously expensive for individuals to purchase, the titles identify the topics, their formats are relatively similar, and most of these materials can be found in law libraries.

If a book cannot be found in your library or in the nearest law library, ask your librarian if it can be obtained through interlibrary loan.)

Bildersee, Robert A. *Pension Regulation Manual.* Rev. ed. 3 vols. Boston: Warren, Gorham, & Lamont, 1978. Vol. 1, *Text and Commentary;* Vol. 2, *Specimen Plans and Practice Aids;* Vol. 3, *Bulletins.*

Boren, Gary I. *Qualified Deferred Compensation Plans.* Wilmette, Ill.: Callaghan & Co., 1983– . With index. In looseleaf for updating.

Bureau of National Affairs, Inc. *BNA Pension Reporter.* Washington, D.C.: BNA Bks., 1984. Provides accurate and authoritative information in the area of pensions. Periodic and cumulative indexes. Weekly, two binders yearly.

———. *Employee Benefit Cases.* Washington, D.C.: BNA Bks., 1984. Covers cases involving employee benefits, text of cases, ERISA, TEFRA, MPPAA, EEO laws, securities laws, state laws, and laws affecting public employee benefits. In looseleaf. Weekly.

————. *Pensions and Other Retirement Benefit Plans.* Washington, D.C.: BNA Bks., 1982. A survey of the types of retirement benefit plans, featuring ERISA, trends in retirement, and pension policies. Contains exhibits.

Canan, Michael J., and David R. Baker. *Qualified Retirement Plans.* St. Paul, Minn.: West, 1987.

Coleman, Barbara J. *Primer on Employee Retirement Income Security Act.* Washington, D.C.: BNA Bks., 1985.

Dunkle, David S. *Guide to Pension and Profit Sharing Plans: Taxation, Selection, Design.* Colorado Springs, Colo.: Shepard's/McGraw-Hill, 1984– . Includes forms. Looseleaf for updating.

Kroll, Arthur H. et al. *Legal and Tax Planning Forms.* 3 vols. Boston: Warren, Gorham, & Lamont, 1981. Covers profit sharing plans, defined benefit pension plans, thrift and employee stock ownership plans (ESOPs), and trust agreements. In looseleaf.

Lynn, Robert J. *The Pension Crisis.* Lexington, Mass.: Lexington Bks., 1983. Offers a clear explanation of the pension system. With index, glossary, and notes.

MacDonald, Jeffrey A., and Anne Bingham. *Pension Handbook for Union Negotiators.* Washington, D.C.: BNA Bks., 1986. Includes bibliographical references and index.

Osgood, R. *Law of Pensions and Profit Sharing.* Boston: Little, 1984.

Pension and Profit Sharing Guide. (P-H). Looseleaf.

Pension Plan Guide. (CCH) Looseleaf.

Prentice-Hall, Inc. *Pension Reform Handbook.* Englewood Cliffs, N.J.: Prentice-Hall, 1982. A complete explanation of ERISA as amended, including the Internal Revenue Code as amended and committee reports. With index. Various pagings.

Appendix A

Selective Legal Abbreviations Table

The left-hand column shows common legal abbreviations. They are listed alphabetically by abbreviations, ignoring numerals in front of the first letter of the abbreviation.

Sample Abbreviation	*Stands for*
101 A. 265	Atlantic Reporter
202 A.2d 789	Atlantic Reporter, Second Series
98 A.B.A.J. 293 (1932)	American Bar Association Journal
22 A.L.I. 76 (1943)	American Law Institute
87 A.L.R. 67 (1945)	American Law Reports
67 A.L.R.2d 33 (1967)	American Law Reports, Second Series
21 A.L.R.3d 98 (1979)	American Law Reports, Third Series
88 A.L.R.Fed. 22 (1968)	American Law Reports, Federal
21 Ad.L.Rev. 65 (1954)	Administrative Law Review
88 Advocate 65 (1977)	The Advocate
16 Akron L.Rev. 7 (1965)	Akron Law Review
34 Ala. 345	Alabama Reporter (Only through 1976; for later cases, see Southern Reporter)
Ala.Code Sec. 2.4 (1977)	Alabama Code
97 Ala.L.Rev. 9 (1977)	Alabama Law Review
25 Alaska 789	Alaska Reports (Only through 1959; for later cases, see Pacific Reporter)
Alaska Stat.Sec. 907.6 (1974)	Alaska Statutes
45 Alb.L.Rev. 345 (1975)	Albany Law Review
21 Am.Bankr.L.J. 8 (1978)	American Bankruptcy Law Journal
16 Am.J.Juris. 78 (1934)	American Journal of Jurisprudence
13 Am.Jur. Tort Sec. 8 (1953)	American Jurisprudence
3 Am.Jur.2d Tort Sec. 8 (1978)	American Jurisprudence, Second Series
5 Am.U.L.Rev. 8 (1954)	American University Law Review
268 Arb.J. 671 (1979)	Arbitration Journal
187 Ariz. 546	Arizona Reports
87 Ariz.L.Rev. 55 (1967)	Arizona Law Review
Ariz.Rev.Stat. Ann. Sec. 3 (1967)	Arizona Revised Statutes Annotated
8 Ariz.St.L.J. 456 (1965)	Arizona State Law Journal

Sample Abbreviation	*Stands for*
89 Ark. 555	Arkansas Reporter
96 Ark.L.Rev. 88 (1977)	Arkansas Law Review
Ark.Stat.Ann. Sec. 398.7 (1977)	Arkansas Statutes Annotated
135 Atom.Energy L.J. 785 (1982)	Atomic Energy Law Journal
183 B.C.L.Rev. 24 (1975)	Boston College Law Review
132 B.U.L.Rev. 895 (1976)	Boston University Law Review
89 B.Y.U.L.Rev. 897 (1973)	Brigham Young University Law Review
77 Banking L.J. 498 (1966)	Banking Law Journal
69 Bankr. 482	Bankruptcy Reporter
77 Baylor L.Rev. 88 (1955)	Baylor Law Review
21 Black L.J. 610 (1970)	Black Law Journal
99 Brooklyn L.Rev. 839 (1956)	Brooklyn Law Review
8 Buffalo L.Rev. 895 (1934)	Buffalo Law Review
99 Bus.Law. 647 (1962)	The Business Lawyer
275 Cal. 679	California Reports
382 Cal.2d 721	California Reports, Second Series
38 Cal.3d 555	California Reports, Third Series
86 Cal.App. 27	California Appellate Reports
73 Cal.App.2d 897	California Appellate Reports, Second Series
93 Cal.App.3d 777	California Appellate Reports, Third Series
85 Cal.Rptr. 870	West's California Reporter
79 Cal.(Ins.) Code Sec. 2.076 (West 1981)	West's Annotated California Code
79 Cal.(Ins.) Code Sec. 2.976 (Deering 1981)	Deering's California Code, Annotated
69 Calif.L.Rev. 76 (1965)	California Law Review
29 Cardozo L.Rev. 5 (1954)	Cardozo Law Review
78 Case & Com. 84 (1966)	Case and Comment
95 Case W.Res. 465 (1974)	Case Western Reserve Law Review
95 Cath.Law. 639 (1954)	Catholic Lawyer
18 Cath.U.L.Rev. 7 (1954)	Catholic University Law Review
146 Chi.-Kent L.Rev. 856 (1982)	Chicago-Kent Law Review
16 Civ.Lib.Rev. 87 (1967)	Civil Liberties Review
61 Civ.Lib.Rptr. 9 (1966)	Civil Liberties Reporter
77 Clev.-Mar.L.Rev. 925 (1957)	Cleveland-Marshall Law Review
9 Clev.St.L.Rev. 9 (1937)	Cleveland State Law Review
283 Colo. 796	Colorado Reports (Only through 1980; for later cases, see Pacific Reporter)
29 Colo.Law. 186 (1945)	Colorado Lawyer
Colo.Rev.Stat. Sec. 29.65 (1966)	Colorado Revised Statutes
8 Colum.J.L. & Soc.Probs. 8 (1964)	Columbia Journal of Law & Social Problems
183 Colum.L.Rev. 97 (1983)	Columbia Law Review
7 Comm.Mkt.L.Rev. 9 (1976)	Common Market Law Review
241 Conn. 982	Connecticut Reports
99 Conn.B.J. 674 (1978)	Connecticut Bar Journal
Conn.Gen.Stat.Sec. 765.90 (1968)	General Statutes of Connecticut
Conn.Gen.Stat.Ann.Sec. 765.90 (West 1968)	Connecticut General Statutes Annotated (West)
88 Conn.L.Rev. 63 (1976)	Connecticut Law Review
452 Conn.Supp. 634	Connecticut Supplement
9 Conv.& Prop.Law.(n.s.) 9 (1922)	Conveyancer and Property Lawyer (New Series)
89 Copyright L.Symp. (ASCAP) 905 (1978)	Copyright Law Symposium (American Society of Composers, Authors, and Publishers)

Sample Abbreviation	Stands for
142 Cornell L.Rev. 879 (1978)	Cornell Law Review
74 Creighton L.Rev. 956 (1967)	Creighton Law Review
58 Cum.L.Rev. 745 (1956)	Cumberland Law Review
9 Cum.-Sam.L.Rev. 3 (1954)	Cumberland-Samford Law Review
9 Current Med.for Att'ys 8 (1964)	Current Medicine for Attorneys
D.C.Code Ann. Sec. 85.80 (1973)	District of Columbia Code Annotated (1973) & Supp. VII 1980)
D.C.Code Encycl. Sec. 85.80 (West 1982)	District of Columbia Code Encyclopedia (West) (Current through 1978)
46 De Paul L.Rev. 9 (1976)	De Paul Law Review
42 Del. 792	Delaware Reports (Only through 1966; for later cases, see Atlantic Reporter)
Del.Code Ann. Tit. 291 Sec. 77.3 (1979)	Delaware Code Annotated
123 Den.L.J. 894 (1984)	Denver Law Journal
88 Det.C.L.Rev. 73 (1967)	Detroit College of Law Review
128 Dick.L.Rev. 67 (1983)	Dickinson Law Review
96 Drake L.Rev. 48 (1963)	Drake Law Review
150 Duke L.J. 869 (1979)	Duke Law Journal
63 Duq.L.Rev. 734 (1955)	Duquesne Law Review
79 Ecology L.Q. 1019 (1977)	Ecology Law Quarterly
142 Emory L.J. 985 (1983)	Emory Law Journal
99 Envtl.L. 845 (1966)	Environmental Law
189 F. 268	Federal Reporter
265 F.2d 1061	Federal Reporter, Second Series
234 F.Supp. 106	Federal Supplement
54 Faculty L.Rev. 62 (1968)	Faculty of Law Review
324 F.R.D. 783	Federal Rules Decisions
79 FDA Cons. 783 (1978)	FDA Consumer
74 Fla. 867	Florida Reports (Only through 1948; for later cases, see Southern Reporter)
Fla.Stat.Sec. 96.4 (1977)	Florida Statutes
Fla.Stat.Ann.Sec. 6.4 (West 1983)	Florida Statutes Annotated (West)
274 Fla.St.U.L.Rev. 845 (1984)	Florida State University Law Review
99 Food Drug Cosm.L.J. 638 (1953)	Food Drug Cosmetic Law Journal
92 Fordham L.Rev. 683 (1966)	Fordham Law Review
241 Forum 888 (1984)	The Forum
785 Ga. 898	Georgia Reports
Ga.Code Ann.Sec. 698 (1974)	Georgia Code Annotated
Ga.Code Ann.Sec. 698 (Harrison 1976)	Georgia Code Annotated (Harrison)
58 Ga.L.Rev. 785 (1947)	Georgia Law Review
28 Geo.Wash.L.Rev. 793 (1934)	George Washington Law Review
286 Geo.L.J. 695 (1982)	Georgetown Law Journal
98 Glendale L.Rev. 357 (1956)	Glendale Law Review
113 Gonz.L.Rev. 956 (1982)	Gonzaga Law Review
19 Hamline L.Rev. 77 (1967)	Hamline Law Review
99 Harv.C.R.-C.L.L.Rev. 8 (1977)	Harvard Civil Rights–Civil Liberties Law Review
98 Harv.Int'l L.J. 691 (1967)	Harvard International Law Journal
107 Harv.J.on Legis. (1968)	Harvard Journal on Legislation
264 Harv.L.Rev. 1072 (1982)	Harvard Law Review
241 Harv.Women's L.J. 888 (1981)	Harvard Women's Law Journal

Sample Abbreviation	*Stands for*
575 Hawaii 978	Hawaii Reports
Hawaii Rev.Stat.Sec. 201.6 (1975)	Hawaii Revised Statutes
85 Hofstra L.Rev. 291 (1968)	Hofstra Law Review
159 Hous.L.Rev. 472 (1982)	Houston Law Review
93 How.L.J. 845 (1968)	Howard Law Journal
79 I.C.C.Prac. J. 6 (1966)	I.C.C. Practitioners' Journal
I.R.C. Sec. 1997.98 (1981)	Internal Revenue Code
86 Idaho 1006	Idaho Reports
Idaho Code Sec. 85.62 (1966)	Idaho Code
54 Idaho L.Rev. 659 (1981)	Idaho Law Review
967 Ill. 888	Illinois Reports
453 Ill.2d 143	Illinois Reports, Second Series
Ill.Ann.Stat.Ch. 348 Sec. 109.2 (Smith-Hurd 1976)	Smith-Hurd Illinois Annotated Statutes
201 Ill.B.J. 947 (1978)	Illinois Bar Journal
Ill.Rev.Stat.Ch. 384 Sec. 109.2 (1970)	Illinois Revised Statutes
876 Ind. 119	Indiana Reports
10 Ind.Advocate 978 (1965)	Indiana Advocate
147 Ind.App. 846	Indiana Court of Appeals Reports
86 Ind.Cl.Comm. 836	Indian Claims Commission Decisions
Ind.Code Sec. 593.91 (1968)	Indiana Code
Ind.Code Ann. Sec. 593.91 (Burns 1977)	Burns Indiana Statutes Annotated Code Edition
Ind.Code Ann. Sec. 593.91 (West 1980)	West's Annotated Indiana Code
187 Ind.L.J. 561 (1982)	Indiana Law Journal
89 Ind.L.Q.Rev. 870 (1975)	Indiana Law Quarterly Review
96 Ind.L.Rev. 687 (1975)	Indiana Law Review
96 Ind.Prop. 876 (1977)	Industrial Property
99 Ind.Prop.Q. (1979)	Industrial Property Quarterly
88 Ind.Rel.J.Econ. & Soc. 9 (1978)	Industrial Relations: Journal of Economy & Society
85 Indian Cas. 967	Indian Cases
39 Indian L.J. 984 (1975)	Indian Law Journal
182 Indian Terr. 759 (1967)	Indian Territory Reports
99 Indus. & Lab.Rel.Rev. 91 (1964)	Industrial and Labor Relations Review
291 Indus. L.J. 960 (1982)	Industrial Law Journal
143 Indus.L.Rev. 682 (1977)	Industrial Law Review
856 Ins.Counsel J. 1078 (1979)	Insurance Counsel Journal
47 Ins.L.Rep. 67 (1955)	Insurance Law Reporter (CCH)
97 Inst.Lab.Rel.Bull. 35 (1967)	Institute for Labor Relations Bulletin
87 Inst.Plan. & Zoning 31 (1974)	Institute on Planning and Zoning
89 Inst.Plan., Zoning & E.D. 197 (1982)	Institute on Planning, Zoning and Eminent Domain (Southwestern Legal Foundation)
34 Inst.Sec.Reg.Sec. 97.62 (1978)	Institute on Securities Regulations (PLI)
197 Iowa 856	Iowa Reports (Only through 1968; for later cases, see Northwestern Reporter)
Iowa Code Sec. 194.68 (1978)	Iowa Code
Iowa Code Ann. Sec. 194.68 (West 1982)	Iowa Code Annotated (West)
87 Iowa L.B. 134 (1973)	Iowa Law Bulletin
85 Iowa L.Rev. 98 (1976)	Iowa Law Review
97 J.A.M.A. 56 (1963)	Journal of the American Medical Association

Sample Abbreviation	*Stands for*
89 J.Accountancy 856 (1952)	Journal of Accountancy
96 J.Air L.& Com. 197 (1967)	Journal of Air Law and Commerce
86 J.Am.Jud.Soc'y 957 (1976)	Journal of the American Judiciary Society
123 J.Am.Soc'y C.L.U. 59 (1979)	Journal of the American Society of Chartered Life Underwriters
86 J.Ass'n L.Teachers 79 (1973)	Journal of the Association of Law Teachers
109 J.B.Ass'n D.C. 683 (1981)	Journal Bar Association of the District of Columbia
84 J.B.Ass'n St.Kan. 856 (1964)	Journal of the Bar Association
95 J.Beverly Hills B.Assn. 946 (1936)	Journal of the Beverly Hills Bar Association
153 J.Bus.L. 894 (1979)	Journal of Business Law
84 J.C.N.P.S. 859 (1968)	Journal of Collective Negotiations in the Public Sector
84 J.Coll.& U.L. 684 (1966)	Journal of College and University Law
57 J.Confl.Res. 784 (1977)	Journal of Conflict Resolution
429 J.Cons.Affairs 732 (1979)	Journal of Consumer Affairs
85 J.Contemp.L. 927 (1976)	Journal of Contemporary Law
123 J.Corp.L. 956 (1982)	Journal of Corporation Law
84 J.Corp.Tax. 53 (1972)	Journal of Corporate Taxation
99 J.Crim.Just. 740 (1955)	Journal of Criminal Justice
152 J.Crim.L.(U.S.) 892 (1979)	Journal of Criminal Law and Criminology (U.S.)
6 J.Crim.L.& Criminology 9 (1955)	Journal of Criminal Law and Criminology
84 J.Crim.L.,C.& P.S. 97 (1957)	Journal of Criminal Law, Criminology and Police Science
196 J.Crim.Sci. 968 (1982)	Journal of Criminal Science
J.D.	Juris Doctor
9 J.Energy & Development 9 (1967)	Journal of Energy and Development
85 J.Fam.L. 572 (1966)	Journal of Family Law
48 J.For.Med. 856 (1962)	Journal of Forensic Medicine
65 J.For.Sci. 485 (1962)	Journal of Forensic Science
53 J.For.Sci.Soc'y 845 (1973)	Journal of the Forensic Science Society
38 J.Ind.L.Inst. 969 (1937)	Journal of the Indian Law Institute
95 J.Juris. 684 (1978)	Journal of Jurisprudence
28 J.Kan.B.Ass'n 894 (1963)	Journal of the Kansas Bar Association
237 J.L. 1009 (1983)	Journal of Law
94 J.L. & Ed. 694 (1968)	Journal of Law and Education
59 J.L.& Pol. 63 (1955)	Journal of Law and Politics
85 J.Land & P.U.Econ. 967 (1967)	Journal of Land and Public Utility Economics
84 J.Law & Econ. 907 (1958)	Journal of Law and Economics
49 J.Law & Econ.Dev. 956 (1975)	Journal of Law and Economic Development
73 J.Law Reform 902 (1966)	Journal of Law Reform
75 J.Legal Ed. 910 (1956)	Journal of Legal Education
132 J.Legal Med. 305 (1981)	Journal of Legal Medicine
294 J.Legal Studies 1004 (1984)	Journal of Legal Studies
285 J.Mar.Law & Comm. 853 (1982)	Journal of Maritime Law and Commerce
274 J.Mo.Bar 865 (1983)	Journal of the Missouri Bar
243 J.Pat.Off.Soc'y 947 (1984)	Journal of the Patent Office Society
83 J.Plan. & Env.L. 845 (1963)	Journal of Planning and Environmental Law
95 J.Pol.Sci. & Admin. 945 (1953)	Journal of Political Science and Administration
143 J.Psyc. & L. 978 (1964)	Journal of Psychiatry and Law
85 J.Pub.L. 685 (1946)	Journal of Public Law
154 J. Radio L. 978 (1976)	Journal of Radio Law

Sample Abbreviation	*Stands for*
284 J.Real Est. Tax 949 (1984)	Journal of Real Estate Taxation
38 J.Space L. 856 (1978)	Journal of Space Law
185 John Marsh.L.J. 490 (1979)	John Marshall Law Journal
95 John Marsh.L.Q. 923 (1969)	John Marshall Law Quarterly
86 Judge Advoc.J. 729 (1957)	Judge Advocate Journal
128 Kan. 856	Kansas Reports
174 Kan.App. 935	Kansas Court of Appeals Reports
83 Kan.App.2d 84	Kansas Court of Appeals Reports, Second Series
85 Kan.B.Ass'n J. 957 (1974)	Kansas Bar Association Journal
59 Kan.C.L.Rep. 745 (1954)	Kansas City Law Reporter
96 Kan.L.J. 835 (1968)	Kansas Law Journal
132 Kan.L.Rev. 957 (1979)	University of Kansas Law Review
Kan.Corp.Code Ann.Sec. 895.1 (Vernon 1981)	Vernon's Kansas Corporation Code Annotated
Kan.Crim.Code Ann.Sec. 796.55 (Vernon 1976)	Vernon's Kansas Criminal Code Annotated
122 Kan.St.L.J. 583 (1976)	Kansas State Law Journal
Kan.Stat.Ann.Sec. 795.9 (1977)	Kansas Statutes Annotated
Kan.U.C.C.Ann.Sec. 8476.906 (Vernon 1978)	Vernon's Kansas Statutes Annotated, Uniform Commercial Code
83 Ky. 684	Kentucky Reports (Only through 1951; for later cases, see Southwestern Reporter)
154 Ky.L.J. 895 (1975)	Kentucky Law Journal
96 Ky.L.R. 956 (1978)	Kentucky Law Reporter
56 Ky.St.B.J. 967 (1971)	Kentucky State Bar Journal
Ky.Rev.Stat.Sec. 85.5 (1966)	Kentucky Revised Statutes
Ky.Rev.Stat.Ann.Sec. 85.5 (Baldwin 1975)	Baldwin's Kentucky Revised Statutes Annotated
Ky.Rev.Stat.Ann.Sec. 85.5 (Bobbs-Merrill 1977)	Kentucky Revised Statutes Annotated (Bobbs-Merrill)
19 L.& Computer Tech. 865 (1976)	Law and Computer Technology
297 L. & Just. 856 (1979)	Law and Justice
153 L. & Lib. 867 (1978)	Law and Liberty
487 L. & Order 839 (1983)	Law and Order
9 L. & Psych.Rev. 9 (1932)	Law and Psychology Review
87 L.A.B.J. 867 (1926)	Los Angeles Bar Journal
43 L.D.L.R. 856 (1968)	Land Development Law Reporter
79 L.Am.Soc'y 976 (1956)	Law in American Society
121 La. 785	Louisiana Reports (Only through 1972; for later cases, see Southern Reporter)
La.Rev.Stat.Ann.Sec. 1009.78 (West 1977)	West's Louisiana Revised Statutes Annotated
La.Civ.Code Ann.Art. 111.2 (West 1978)	West's Louisiana Civil Code Annotated
59 Lab.L.J. 777 (1957)	Labor Law Journal
101 Law & Contemp. Probs. 856 (1979)	Law and Contemporary Problems
85 M.C.J. 852 (1973)	Michigan Civil Jurisprudence
74 M.F.P.D. 965 (1967)	Modern Federal Practice Digest
69 Maine L. Rev. 563 (1965)	Maine Law Review
79 Marijuana 845 (1981)	The Marijuana Review
54 Marq. L.Rev. 196 (1957)	Marquette Law Review

Sample Abbreviation	*Stands for*
143 Mass. 946	Massachusetts Reports
85 Mass. App. Ct. 573	Massachusetts Appellate Court Reports
89 Mass. L.Q. 572 (1963)	Massachusetts Law Quarterly
Mass. Gen. Laws Ann. Ch. 249 Sec. 97.9 (West 1982)	Massachusetts General Laws Annotated (West)
Mass. Ann. Laws Ch. 249 Sec. 97.9 (Michie/Law. Coop 1980)	Annotated Laws of Massachusetts (Michie/Law. Coop)
245 Md. 934	Maryland Reports
Md. (Education) Code Ann. Sec. 154.856 (1978)	Annotated Code of Maryland
Md. Ann. Code Art. 297 Sec. 198.3 (1957)	Annotated Code of Maryland (1957)
486 Md. App. 728	Maryland Appellate Reports
85 Md. B.J. 462 (1957)	Maryland Bar Journal
78 Md. L.F. 856 (1945)	Maryland Law Forum
47 Md. L. Rev. 486	Maryland Law Review
65 Me. 498	Maine Reports (Only through 1965; for later cases, see Atlantic Reporter)
Me. Rev. Stat. Ann. Tit. 197 Sec. 67.454 (1978)	Maine Revised Statutes Annotated
75 Med.-Legal Crim. Rev. 9 (1967)	Medico-Legal and Criminological Review
83 Med. Sci. & L. 978 (1957)	Medicine, Science and the Law
93 Mercer L. Rev. 836 (1966)	Mercer Law Review
89 Miami L.Q. 78 (1968)	Miami Law Quarterly
345 Mich. 1096	Michigan Reports
243 Mich. App. 749	Michigan Appeals Report
Mich. Comp. Laws Ann. Sec. 78.9 (West 1983)	Michigan Compiled Laws Annotated (West)
Mich. Comp. Laws Sec. 78.9 (1970)	Michigan Compiled Laws (1970)
57 Mich.L. Rev. 429 (1956)	Michigan Law Review
48 Mich. St. B.J. 9 (1976)	Michigan State Bar Journal
Mich. Stat. Ann. Sec. 78.9 (Callaghan 1981)	Michigan Statutes Annotated (Callaghan)
96 Mil. L. Rev. 550 (1945)	Military Law Review
287 Minn. 1033	Minnesota Reports (Only through 1977; for later cases, see Northwestern Reporter)
79 Minn. L. Rev. 69 (1966)	Minnesota Law Review
Minn. Stat. Sec. 785.31 (1980)	Minnesota Statutes
Minn. Stat. Ann. Sec. 785.31 (West 1983)	Minnesota Statutes Annotated (West)
283 Misc. 896	Miscellaneous (N.Y.)
149 Misc. 2d 664	Miscellaneous, Second Series (N.Y.)
69 Miss. 197	Mississippi Reports (Only through 1966; for later cases, see Southern Reporter)
Miss. Code Ann. Sec. 879.1 (1975)	Mississippi Code Annotated
57 Miss. L.J. 745 (1936)	Mississippi Law Journal
100 Mo. 846	Missouri Reports (Only through 1956; for later cases, see Southwestern Reporter)
Mo. Ann. Stat. Sec. 197.64 (Vernon 1979)	Vernon's Annotated Missouri Statutes
88 Mo. B.J. 453 (1962)	Missouri Bar Journal
103 Mo.L.Rev. 867 (1978)	Missouri Law Review

Sample Abbreviation	*Stands for*
Mo.Rev. Stat. Sec. 197.64 (1973)	Missouri Revised Statutes
89 Mont. 978	Montana Reports
56 Mont. Code Ann.Sec. 837.33 (1978)	Montana Code Annotated
56 Mont. L.Rev. 845 (1966)	Montana Law Review
49 Month.L.Rev. 675 (1954)	Monthly Law Review
389 Monthly Lab.Rev. 786 (1979)	Monthly Labor Review
264 Mun. Att'y 934 (1979)	Municipal Attorney
152 Mun.L.J. 963 (1979)	Municipal Law Journal
145 N.C. 845	North Carolina Reports
181 N.C.App. 867	North Carolina Court of Appeals Reports
N.C. Gen.Stat.Sec.197.56 (1979)	General Statutes of North Carolina
56 N.C.L.Rev. 85	North Carolina Law Review
186 N.D. 858	North Dakota Reports (Only through 1953; for later cases, see Northwestern Reporter)
N.D.Cent.Code Sec. 895.45 (1976)	North Dakota Century Code
89 N.D.L. Rev. 645 (1959)	North Dakota Law Review
287 N.E. 879	Northeastern Reporter
142 N.E.2d 1096	Northeastern Reporter, Second Series
196 N.Eng. J. Prison L. 853 (1981)	New England Journal of Prison Law
86 N.Eng.L.Rev. 785 (1946)	New England Law Review
187 N.H. 956	New Hampshire Reports
58 N.H.B.J. 785 (1964)	New Hampshire Bar Journal
N.H.Rev.Stat.Ann.Sec.20.7 (1977)	New Hampshire Revised Statutes Annotated
143 N.J. 472	New Jersey Reports
83 N.J.L.J. 396 (1956)	New Jersey Law Journal
35 N.J.L.Rev. 895 (1943)	New Jersey Law Review
N.J.Rev.Stat.Sec.384.87 (1937)	New Jersey Revised Statutes (1937)
N.J.Stat.Ann.Sec.384.87 (West 1978)	New Jersey Statutes Annotated (West)
74 N.J.St.B.J. 906 (1968)	New Jersey State Bar Journal
127 N.J.Super. 823	New Jersey Superior Court Reports
546 N.L.R.B. 898 (1979)	National Labor Relations Board Reports
186 N.M. 734	New Mexico Reports
N.M.Stat.Ann.Sec.745.55 (1981)	New Mexico Statutes Annotated
46 N.Mex.L.Rev. 956 (1968)	New Mexico Law Review
269 N.W. 923	Northwestern Reporter
132 N.W.2d 1097	Northwestern Reporter, Second Series
296 N.Y. 396	New York Reports
128 N.Y.2d 783	New York Reports, Second Series
254 N.Y.S. 87	West's New York Supplement
138 N.Y.S.2d 856	West's New York Supplement, Second Series
N.Y. (Business Law) Sec. 1087.75 (Consol. 1980)	Consolidated Law Service
N.Y. (Business Law) Sec. 1087.75 (McKinney 1979)	McKinney's Consolidated Laws of New York Annotated
95 N.Y. County Law.Ass'n. B.Bull 967 (1968)	New York County Lawyers Association Bar Bulletin
17 N.Y. Jur. (Contracts) Sec. 786 (1976)	New York Jurisprudence
57 N.Y.L.J. 351 (1967)	New York Law Journal
186 N.Y.L.Rev. 784 (1976)	New York Law Review
57 N.Y.Month.L.Bull. 869 (1977)	New York Monthly Law Bulletin
94 N.Y.St.B.J. 868 (1965)	New York State Bar Journal
76 N.Y.U.L.Center Bull. 79 (1979)	New York University Law Center Bulletin

Sample Abbreviation	Stands for
86 N.Y.U.L.Q.Rev. 896 (1965)	New York University Law Quarterly Review
50 N.Y.U.L.Rev. 978 (1945)	New York University Law Review
85 N.Y.U.Rev.Law & Soc.C. 685 (1975)	New York University Review of Law and Social Change
184 Narcotics 1089 (1978)	Narcotics Control Digest
148 Narcotics L.Bull. 498 (1979)	Narcotics Law Bulletin
294 Nat.Corp.Rep. 867 (1976)	National Corporation Reporter
100 Nat.L.Rep. 957 (1978)	National Law Reporter
49 Nat.Munic.Rev. 695 (1932)	National Municipal Review
99 Nat'l Civic Rev.947 (1973)	National Civic Review
204 Nat'l L.F. 845 (1978)	Natural Law Forum
89 Nat'l Income Tax Mag. 8 (1977)	National Income Tax Magazine
82 Nat'l J. Crim.Defense 9 (1977)	National Journal of Criminal Defense
85 Nat'l Legal Mag. 869 (1955)	National Legal Magazine
99 Nat'l Mun.Rev. 863 (1963)	National Municipal Review
106 Nat'l Tax J. 845 (1978)	National Tax Journal
54 Natural Resources J. 77 (1965)	Natural Resources Journal
85 Neb. 782	Nebraska Reports
69 Neb. L.Bull. 896 (1966)	Nebraska Law Bulletin
59 Neb.L.Rev. 449 (1959)	Nebraska Law Review
Neb.Rev.Stat.Sec. 969.9 (1967)	Revised Statutes of Nebraska
34 Neb.St.B.J. 832 (1962)	Nebraska State Bar Journal
96 Negl. & Comp.Cas.Ann. 7 (1957)	Negligence & Compensation Cases Annotated
2 Negl. & Comp.Cas.Ann. (N.S.) 846 (1967)	Negligence & Compensation Cases Annotated (New Series)
3 Negl. & Comp.Cas.Ann.3d 574 (1977)	Negligence & Compensation Cases Annotated, Third Series
6 Negl.Cas. (CCH) Auto Sec. 32.6	Negligence Cases (CCH)
3 Negl.Cas.2d (CCH) Auto Sec. 47	Negligence Cases, Second Series (CCH)
274 Nev. 888	Nevada Reports
Nev.Rev.Stat.Sec. 196.33 (1978)	Nevada Revised Statutes
76 Nev.St.Bar J. 845 (1975)	Nevada State Bar Journal
88 Notre Dame Law. 835 (1969)	Notre Dame Lawyer
89 Nuclear Reg.Rep. (CCH) (Melt Down) Sec. 998.67	Nuclear Regulations Reporter (CCH)
55 Nw.U.L.Rev. 967 (1934)	Northwestern University Law Review
75 O.C.S. 835	Office of Contract Settlement Decisions
77 O.G.Pat.Off. 572 (1935)	Official Gazette (U.S.) Patent Office
57 O.S.H.Dec. (CCH) Sec. 4629.49	Occupational, Safety, and Health Decisions
187 Ohio App. 684	Ohio Appellate Reports
78 Ohio App.2d 733	Ohio Appellate Reports, Second Series
38 Ohio Bar 461 (1945)	Ohio State Bar Association Reports
23 Ohio Jur. (Tort) Sec. 967.84	Ohio Jurisprudence
3 Ohio Jur.2d (Tort) Sec. 967.84	Ohio Jurisprudence, Second Edition
93 Ohio L.R. 361 (1945)	Ohio Law Reporter
99 Ohio Law R. 77 (1956)	Ohio Law Review
55 Ohio Misc. 687	Ohio Miscellaneous
78 Ohio North U.L. 999	Ohio Northern University Law Review
67 Ohio Op. 194	Ohio Opinions
56 Ohio Op.2d 823	Ohio Opinions, Second Series
26 Ohio Op.3d 1204	Ohio Opinions, Third Series
Ohio Rev.Code Ann.Sec. 1072.1 (Baldwin 1980)	Ohio Revised Code Annotated (Baldwin)

Sample Abbreviation	*Stands for*
Ohio Rev. Code Ann. Sec. 1072.1 (Page 1976)	Ohio Revised Code Annotated (Page)
281 Ohio St. 1067	Ohio State Reports
43 Ohio St.2d 785	Ohio State Reports, Second Series
78 Oil & Gas Compact Bull. 845 (1966)	Oil and Gas Compact Bulletin
66 Oil & Gas Inst. 684 (1933)	Oil and Gas Institute
57 Oil & Gas J. 986 (1977)	Oil and Gas Journal
198 Oil & Gas L. & Tax. Inst. (S.W. Legal Fdn.) 74 (1957)	Oil & Gas Law & Taxation Institute (Southwestern Legal Foundation)
78 Oil & Gas Rptr. 846 (1945)	Oil and Gas Reporter
173 Oil & Gas Tax Q. 995 (1978)	Oil and Gas Tax Quarterly
187 Okla. 777	Oklahoma Reports (Only through 1953; for later cases, see Pacific Reporter)
Okla.Stat.Tit.374, Sec. 19.86 (1971)	Oklahoma Statutes (1971)
Okla.Stat. Ann.Tit.374, Sec. 19.86 (West 1983)	Oklahoma Statutes Annotated (West)
66 Okla.B.Ass'n J. 684 (1976)	Oklahoma Bar Association Journal
59 Okla.L.Rev. 675 (1965)	Oklahoma Law Review
8 Op.Att'y Gen. 777 (1923)	Opinions of the Attorney General, United States
345 Op.Sol.Dep. 49 (1966)	Opinions of the Solicitor, U.S. Department of Labor
189 Or. 787	Oregon Reports
88 Ore.App. 571	Oregon Reports, Court of Appeals
89 Or.T.R. 289	Oregon Tax Reports
99 Or.L.Rev. 675 (1968)	Oregon Law Review
Or.Rev.Stat.Sec.856 (1978)	Oregon Revised Statutes
145 P. 185	Pacific Reporter
181 P.2d 839	Pacific Reporter, Second Series
68 P.Coast L.J. 786 (1978)	Pacific Coast Law Journal
298 PEAL 893 (1977)	Publishing, Entertainment, Advertising, and Allied Fields Law Quarterly
P-H Am.Lab.Arb. Awards (Strikes) Sec.834.956 (1983)	American Labor Arbitration Awards (P-H)
P-H Am.Lab.Cas. (Strikes) Sec. 666.777 (1979)	American Labor Cases (P-H)
P-H Corp. (Strikes) Sec. 5648.95	Corporations (P-H)
P-H Est.Plan. (Trusts) Sec. 555.1 (1982)	Estate Planning (P-H)
P-H Fed.Taxes (Fraud) Sec. 1000.01 (1984)	Federal Taxes (P-H)
P-H Fed. Wage & Hour (Overtime) Sec. 98.5 (1983)	Federal Wage and Hour (P-H)
P-H Ind.Rel., Lab.Arb. (Wages) Sec. 77.956 (1976)	Industrial Relations, Labor Arbitration (P-H)
P-H Ind.Rel. Union Conts. (Boycotts) Sec. 8888.65 (1981)	Industrial Relations, Union Contracts, and Collective Bargaining (P-H)
P-H Soc.Sec.Taxes (Self-employed) Sec. 10.8 (1982)	Social Security Taxes (P-H)
P-H State & Local Taxes (Appeals) Sec. 856.4009 (1977)	State and Local Taxes (P-H)
P-H Tax Ct. Mem. (Fraud) Sec. 10978.563 (1979)	Tax Court Memorandum Decisions (P-H)

Sample Abbreviation	Stands for
58 P.L.E. (Tort) Sec. 8.1 (1977)	Pennsylvania Law Encyclopedia
79 P.L.Mag. 687 (1957)	Pacific Law Magazine
68 P.L.Rep. 768	Pacific Law Reporter
79 P.R. 674	Puerto Rico Reports (Only through 1972; for later cases, see Decisiones de Puerto Rico)
37 P.R.Dec. 845	Decisiones de Puerto Rico
P.R.Laws Ann.Tit. 78 Sec. 198.1 (1978)	Puerto Rico Laws Annotated
583 P.U.R. 923 (1965)	Public Utilities Reports
477 P.U.R. (N.S.) 986 (1975)	Public Utilities Reports (New Series)
289 P.U.R.3d 895 (1983)	Public Utilities Reports, Third Series
288 Pa. 967	Pennsylvania State Reports
297 Pa.B.Ass'n Q. 994 (1981)	Pennsylvania Bar Association Quarterly
39 Pa.Cons.Stat.Sec. 98.7 (1984)	Pennsylvania Consolidated Statutes
86 Pa.Cons.Stat.Ann. Sec. 76.2 (Purdon 1976)	Pennsylvania Consolidated Statutes Annotated (Purdon)
366 Pa.D. & C. 498	Pennsylvania District & County Reports
297 Pa.D. & C.2d 865	Pennsylvania District & County Reports, Second Series
154 Pa.D.&C.3d 1074	Pennsylvania District & County Reports, Third Series
177 Pa.Fiduc. 1096 (Purdon 1966)	Pennsylvania Fiduciary Reporter Annotated (Purdon)
88 Pa.L.J. 88 (1954)	Pennsylvania Law Journal
P.A.Stat.Ann.Tit. 85 Sec. 298.7 (Purdon 1975)	Purdon's Pennsylvania Statutes Annotated
296 Pa.Super. 822	Pennsylvania Superior Court Reports
484 Pac. 784	Pacific Reporter
201 Pac. 2d. 783	Pacific Reporter, Second Series
198 Pacific L.J. 967 (1953)	Pacific Law Journal
292 Pat. & Tr.Mk.Rev. 38 (1942)	Patent & Trade Mark Review
67 Pat.L.Rev. 759 (1924)	Patent Law Review
526 Pat.T.M.&Copy.Journal 895 (1965)	Patent, Trademark & Copyright Journal
468 Penn.B.A.Q. 679 (1974)	Pennsylvania Bar Association Quarterly
88 Pension Rep. (BNA) 96 (1966)	Pension Reporter (BNA)
85 Pepperdine L. Rev. 864 (1967)	Pepperdine Law Review
159 Pers.Finance L.Q. 97 (1979)	Personal Finance Law Quarterly Report
87 Pers.Inj. Comment'r 6 (1965)	Personal Injury Commentator
85 Plan. & Comp. 687 (1947)	Planning and Compensation Reports
96 Plan.,Zoning & E.D.Inst. 83 (1978)	Planning, Zoning & Eminent Domain Institute
586 Pol.Sci.Q. 786 (1979)	Political Science Quarterly
64 Police J. 674 (1943)	Police Journal
99 Police L.Q. 564 (1965)	Police Law Quarterly
86 Poll.Contr.Guide (Smoke) Sec. 893.33 (1977)	Pollution Control Guide (CCH)
687 Pollution Abs. 666 (1983)	Pollution Abstracts
77 Poor L.& Local Gov't Mag. 687 (1965)	Poor Law and Local Government Magazine
78 Portia L.J. 87 (1946)	Portia Law Journal
98 Portland U.L. Rev. 897 (1968)	Portland Law Review
34 Prob. & Prop. 87 (1925)	Probate and Property
321 Prob.Law. 896 (1978)	Probate Lawyer
48 Prod.Safety & Liab.Rep. (BNA) (Belts) Sec. 19.9 (1976)	Product Safety and Liability Reporter (BNA)

Sample Abbreviation	Stands for
87 Prop. & Comp. 76 (1965)	Property and Compensation Reports
35 Pub.Ad.Rev. 997 (1963)	Public Administration Review
79 Pub.Employee Rel.Rep. 978 (1966)	Public Employee Relations Reporter
86 Pub.Land & Res.L.Dig. 8 (1964)	Public Land and Resources Law Digest
89 Pub.Util.Fort. 786 (1966)	Public Utilities Fortnightly
181 R.I. 888	Rhode Island Reports
R.I.Gen.Laws Sec. 298.46 (1978)	General Laws of Rhode Island
68 R.L.B. 452	U.S. Railroad Labor Board Decisions
398 Race Rel.L.Survey 75 (1978)	Race Relations Law Survey
78 Real Est.L.J. 865 (1965)	Real Estate Law Journal
67 Rev.Contemp.L. 453 (1957)	Review of Contemporary Law
59 Rev.Jud., & Police J. 3 (1965)	Revenue, Judicial, and Police Journal
286 Rev.L. & Soc.Change 97 (1968)	Review of Law and Social Change
461 Rev.Sec.Reg. 79 (1976)	Review of Securities Regulations
37 Rocky Mt.L. Rev. 553 (1967)	Rocky Mountain Law Review
87 Rocky Mt.Min.L.Inst. 8 (1974)	Rocky Mountain Mineral Law Institute
9 Rocky Mt.Miner.L.Rev. 6 (1925)	Rocky Mountain Mineral Law Review
69 Rutgers J.Computers & Law 536 (1979)	Rutgers Journal of Computers and the Law
86 Rutgers L.Rev. 849 (1949)	Rutgers Law Review
285 Rutgers U.L.Rev. 46 (1982)	Rutgers University Law Review
85 Rutgers-Camden L.J. 7 (1966)	Rutgers-Camden Law Journal
247 S. 895	Southern Reporter
157 S. 2d 563	Southern Reporter, Second Series
143 S.C. 832	South Carolina Reports
S.C. Code Ann. Sec. 1987.4 (Law.Coop 1976)	Code of Laws of South Carolina 1976 Annotated (Law.Coop)
89 S.C.L.Q. 987 (1957)	South Carolina Law Quarterly
98 S.C.L. Rev. 783 (1966)	South Carolina Law Review
119 S.Cal.L. Rev. 923 (1977)	Southern California Law Review
284 S.Ct. 888	Supreme Court Reporter (U.S.)
106 S.D. 884	South Dakota Reports (Only through 1976; for later cases, see Northwestern Reporter)
S.D. Codified Laws Ann. Sec. 23.8 (1978)	South Dakota Codified Laws Annotated
S.D. Comp. Laws Ann. Sec. 23.8 (1982)	South Dakota Complied Laws Annotated
83 S.D.L. Rev. 764 (1974)	South Dakota Law Review
99 S.D. St. B.J. 991 (1975)	South Dakota State Bar Journal
378 S.E. 855	Southeastern Reporter
85 S.E.2d 777	Southeastern Reporter, Second Series
269 S.F.L.J. 345 (1978)	San Francisco Law Journal
176 S.W. 1094	Southwestern Reporter
165 S.W.2d 99	Southwestern Reporter, Second Series
89 S.W.L.J. 98 (1975)	Southwestern Law Journal (Nashville)
118 St. John's L.Rev. 987 (1981)	St. John's Law Review
95 St. Louis L. Rev. 78 (1947)	St. Louis Law Review
68 St. Louis U.L.J. 75 (1965)	St. Louis University Law Journal
66 St. Mary's L.J. 796 (1954)	St. Mary's Law Journal
55 San Diego L. Rev. 777 (1968)	San Diego Law Review
48 San Fran. L.J. 785 (1955)	San Francisco Law Journal
186 Santa Clara L. Rev. 67 (1982)	Santa Clara Law Review
149 Search & Seizure 809 (1983)	Search and Seizure Bulletin

Sample Abbreviation	Stands for
276 Sec.L. Rev. 87 (1980)	Securities Law Review
119 Sec. Reg. L.J. 973 (1975)	Securities Regulation Law Journal
97 Seton Hall L. Rev. 967 (1974)	Seton Hall Law Review
187 So. 887	Southern Reporter
98 So.2d 567	Southern Reporter, Second Series
354 So.Calif.L.Rev. 872 (1978)	Southern California Law Review
94 So.L.J. 453 (1968)	Southern Law Journal (Nashville)
138 So.L.Q. 768 (1978)	Southern Law Quarterly
69 So.L.Rev. 59 (1954)	Southern Law Review (Nashville)
58 So. L. Rev. 88 (1942)	Southern Law Review (St. Louis)
12 So. L.Rev. (N.S.) 964	Southern Law Review (New Series) (St. Louis)
87 So.Law T. 55 (1966)	Southern Law Times
84 So. Tex. L.J. 896 (1937)	Southern Texas Law Journal
96 So. U.L. Rev. 784 (1940)	Southern University Law Review
31 Soc. & Lab. Bull. 895 (1924)	Social and Labor Bulletin
96 Soc. Action & L.395 (1945)	Social Action and the Law
85 Soc. Sec.Bull. 873 (1969)	Social Security Bulletin
183 Stan. L. Rev. 967 (1982)	Stanford Law Review
173 Stud. L. & Econ. Dev. 54 (1978)	Studies in Law and Economic Development
123 Suffolk U.L. Rev. 675 (1982)	Suffolk University Law Review
89 Sup. Ct. Hist. Soc't Y.B. 666 (1964)	Supreme Court Historical Society Yearbook
267 Sw. L.J. 785 (1979)	Southwestern Law Journal
129 Sw. U.L. Rev. 975 (1976)	Southwestern University Law Review
154 Syracuse L. Rev. 944 (1965)	Syracuse Law Review
56 T.C. 198	Tax Court of the United States Reports
55 T.M. Bull. 547 (1953)	Trade Mark Bulletin (U.S.)
36 T.M.Bull.(N.S.) 87 (1967)	Trade Mark Bulletin (U.S.) (New Series)
79 T.M.M. (BNA) Sec. 96.9 (1978)	Tax Management Memorandum (BNA)
77 Tax Adm'rs News 967 (1945)	Tax Administrators News
197 Tax Advisor 85 (1978)	The Tax Advisor
523 Tax L. Rev. 253 (1984)	Tax Law Review
68 Temp. L.Q. 593 (1956)	Temple Law Quarterly
220 Tenn. 895	Tennessee Reports (Only through 1971; for later cases, see Southwestern Reporter)
179 Tenn.L.Rev. 98 (1981)	Tennessee Law Review
Tenn. Code Ann. Sec.203.7 (1975)	Tennessee Code Annotated
87 Tenn. B.J. 598 (1943)	Tennessee Bar Journal
186 Tex. 978	Texas Reports (Only through 1962; for later cases, see Southwestern Reporter)
296 Tex. B.J. 486 (1976)	Texas Bar Journal
Tex.(Fam.) Code Ann. Sec. 198.4 (Vernon 1975)	Texas Code Annotated (Vernon)
8 Tex.Jur.(Tort) Sec. 87.2 (1968)	Texas Jurisprudence
9 Tex.Jur.2d (Tort) Sec. 87.2 (1982)	Texas Jurisprudence, Second Series
78 Tex.L.J. 245 (1945)	Texas Law Journal
35 Tex.L.Rev. 231 (1941)	Texas Law Review
678 Tex.So.U.L.Rev. 86 (1982)	Texas Southern University Law
7 Tex.Tech L.Rev. 987 (1964)	Texas Tech Law Review
98 Trademark Bull. 864 (1957)	Trademark Bulletin
43 Trademark Bull.(N.S.) 4 (1977)	Trademark Bulletin (New Series)
154 Transp.L.J. 785 (1978)	Transportation Law Journal
8 Trial Law.Forum 483 (1924)	Trial Lawyers' Forum

Sample Abbreviation	*Stands for*
95 Trial Law.Q. 846 (1976)	Trial Lawyers' Quarterly
182 Trust Bull. 76 (1975)	Trust Bulletin
45 Tul.L.Rev. 756 (1953)	Tulane Law Review
55 Tul.Tax Inst. 967 (1966)	Tulane Tax Institute
94 Tulane L.Rev. 346 (1977)	Tulane Law Review
78 Tulsa L.J. 459 (1978)	Tulsa Law Journal
87 U.Balt.L.Rev. 8 (1968)	University of Baltimore Law Review
386 U.C.C.Rep.Serv. 467 (1976)	Uniform Commercial Code Reporting Service
45 U.C.C.A.L.Rev. 876 (1955)	U.C.C.L.A. Law Review
86 U.C.L.A.-Alaska L.Rev. 756 (1978)	U.C.L.A.-Alaska Law Review
89 U.Chi.L.Rec. 945 (1966)	University of Chicago Law School Record
97 U.Chi.L.Rev. 1001 (1953)	University of Chicago Law Review
296 U.Cin.L.Rev. 957 (1978)	University of Cincinnati Law Review
85 U.Col.L.Rev. 84 (1965)	University of Colorado Law Review
175 U.Det.L.J. 834 (1982)	University of Detroit Law Journal
98 U.Fla.L.Rev. 745 (1975)	University of Florida Law Review
91 U.Ill.L.F. 976 (1982)	University of Illinois Law Forum
168 U.Kan.City L.Rev. 962 (1978)	University of Kansas City Law Review
99 U.Miami L.Rev. 494 (1954)	University of Miami Law Review
85 U.Mich.J.Law Reform 87 (1974)	University of Michigan Journal of Law Reform
179 U.Mo.Bull.L.Ser. 864 (1981)	University of Missouri Bulletin Law Series
98 U.Mo.K.C.L.Rev. 864 (1974)	University of Missouri at Kansas City Law Review
352 U.N.B.L.J. 856 (1983)	University of New Brunswick Law Journal
88 Unempl.Ins.Rep.(CCH)	Unemployment Insurance Reporter (CCH)
88 U.Newark L. Rev. 463 (1974)	University of Newark Law Review
78 Un.Prac.News 785 (1963)	Unauthorized Practice News
89 Uniform L.Rev. 856 (1952)	Uniform Law Review
397 U.Pa.L.Rev. 548 (1983)	University of Pennsylvania Law Review
79 U.Pitt.L.Rev. 856 (1953)	University of Pittsburgh Law Review
58 U.Rich.L.Rev. 392 (1942)	University of Richmond Law Review
351 U.S. 1002	United States Reports
98 U.S.C. Sec. 100.1090 (1977)	United States Code
98 U.S.C.S. Sec. 100.1090 (1978)	United States Code Service
1982 U.S.Code Cong. & Ad.News 9870, 9881	United States Code Congressional & Administrative News
354 U.S.L.Ed. 986	United States Supreme Court Reports, Lawyer's Edition
756 U.S.L.J. 888 (1976)	United States Law Journal
86 U.S.L.Mag. 785 (1956)	United States Law Magazine
466 U.S.L.Rev. 777 (1978)	United States Law Review
384 U.S.C.S. Sec. 203.3 (Law. Coop. 1981)	United States Code Service
59 U.S.L.W. 684 (1945)	United States Law Week
46 U.S.P.Q. 674 (1945)	United States Patent Quarterly
57 U.S.Sup.Ct.Rep. 867	United States Supreme Court Reporter (West)
44 U.S.V.A.A.D. 687	U.S. Veterans Administrator's Decisions
163 U.San.Fran.L.Rev. 896 (1968)	University of San Francisco Law Review
55 U.Toledo L.Rev. 295 (1950)	University of Toledo Law Review
87 U.W.L.A.L. Rev. 785 (1967)	University of West Los Angeles Law Review
49 U.Wash.L.Rev. 673 (1952)	University of Washington Law Review

Sample Abbreviation	*Stands for*
65 Urban Law Ann. 784 (1956)	Urban Law Annual
89 Uniform L.Rev. 856 (1952)	Uniform Law Review
78 Urban Law Rev. 435 (1958)	Urban Law Review
143 Utah 840	Utah Reports
167 Utah 2d 835	Utah Reports, Second Series (Only through 1974; for later cases, see Pacific Reporter)
Utah Code Ann.Sec. 29.55 (1974)	Utah Code Annotated
69 Utah L.Rev. 756 (1943)	Utah Law Review
84 Util.L.Rep. (CCH) Sec. 4975.2545 (1981)	Utilities Law Reporter (CCH)
14 Util.Sect.Newsl. 785 (1934)	Utility Section Newsletter
85 V.I. 678	Virgin Islands Reports
68 V.I.B.J. 78 (1967)	Virgin Islands Bar Journal
V.I.Code Ann.Tit.24 Sec. 106 (1967)	Virgin Islands Code Annotated
288 Va. 985	Virginia Reports
85 Va.Bar News 823 (1965)	Virginia Bar News
Va.Code Sec. 88.432 (1979)	Code of Virginia
78 Va.L.J. 749 (1933)	Virginia Law Journal
64 Va.L.Reg. 875 (1931)	Virginia Law Register
121 Va.L.Reg. (N.S.) 85 (1965)	Virginia Law Register (New Series)
189 Va.L.Rev. 845 (1968)	Virginia Law Review
78 Val.U.L.Rev. 894 (1977)	Valparaiso University Law Review
164 Vand.L.Rev. 241 (1978)	Vanderbilt Law Review
187 Vt. 844	Vermont Reports
Vt.Stat.Ann.Tit. 791 Sec. 897.32 (1976)	Vermont Statutes Annotated
687 W.C.Rep. 197	Workmen's Compensation Reports
78 W.F.P.D.2d 785	West's Federal Practice Digest, Second Series
66 W.H.Man. 784 (1966)	Wage & Hours Manual
85 W.L.J. (1955)	Western Law Journal
86 W.Res.L.Rev.	Western Reserve Law Review
142 W.Va. 962	West Virginia Reports (Only through 1973; for later cases, see Southeastern Reporter)
W.Va.Code Sec.1089.9 (1978)	West Virginia Code
86 W.Va.L.Q. 482 (1945)	West Virginia Law Quarterly
188 W.Va.L.Rev. 591 (1976)	West Virginia Law Review
47 Wage & Hour Cas. (BNA) Sec. 784.29 (1979)	Wage and Hour Cases (BNA)
98 Wake For.L.Rev. 857 (1954)	Wake Forest Law Review
197 Wash. 977	Washington Reports
142 Wash.2d 795	Washington Reports, Second Series
187 Wash.App. 888	Washington Appellate Reports
Wash.Rev.Code Ann.Sec. 1984.86 (1983)	Revised Code of Washington Annotated
Wash.Rev.Code Sec. 1984.86 (1974)	Revised Code of Washington (1974)
176 Wash.L.Rev. 483 (1978)	Washington Law Review
422 Wash.U.L.Q. 894 (1984)	Washington University Law Quarterly
75 Welfare L.News 685 (1968)	Welfare Law News
66 West.L.J. 967 (1967)	Western Law Journal
85 West.School L. Rev. 96 (1968)	Western School Law Review

Sample Abbreviation	Stands for
352 West.St.U.L.Rev. 763 (1981)	Western State University Law Review
154 Western Res.L.Rev. 82 (1978)	Western Reserve Law Review
284 Wis. 968	Wisconsin Reports
85 Wis.2d 529	Wisconsin Reports, Second Series
86 Wis.B.Bull. 885 (1945)	Wisconsin Bar Bulletin
169 Wis.L.Rev. 735 (1969)	Wisconsin Law Review
Wis.Stat.Ann.Sec.1061.98 (West 1980)	West's Wisconsin Statutes Annotated
Wis.Stat.Sec.1061.89 (1975)	Wisconsin Statutes
246 Wm. & Mary L.Rev. 998 (1982)	William & Mary Law Review
78 Women Law.J. 967 (1977)	Women Lawyer's Journal
68 Women Lawyer's J. 856 (1976)	Women Lawyer's Journal
9 Women's Rights L. Rptr. 9 (1967)	Women's Rights Law Reporter
56 Workmen's Comp.L.Rev. 9 (1965)	Workmen's Compensation Law Review
143 Wyo. 870	Wyoming Reports (Only through 1959; for later cases, see Pacific Reporter)
Wyo.Stat.Sec.1001.9 (1971)	Wyoming Statutes
58 Yale L.J. 784 (1904)	Yale Law Journal
158 Y.B. Human Rights 909 (1984)	Yearbook of Human Rights
88 Yale Rev.Law & Soc.Act'n 83 (1965)	Yale Review of Law and Social Action

Appendix B

State Uniform Commercial Code References

Some states have more than one printing of their code. All states have one official code, and some have one or more unofficial printings by the commercial press. Although only one version is entered here for each state—not necessarily the official version—in most states having both official and unofficial versions, the numbering system is consistent in all versions.

State	*Uniform Commercial Code Reference*
Alabama	Ala. Code Sec. 7-1-101 et seq. (1977)
Alaska	Alaska Stat. Sec. 45.01.101 et seq. (1980)
Arizona	Ariz. Rev. Stat. Ann. Sec. 44-2301 et seq. (1967)
Arkansas	Ark. Stat. Ann. Sec. 85-1-101 et seq. (1961)
California	Cal. Com. Code Sec. 1101 et seq. (West 1964)
Colorado	Colo. Rev. Stat. Sec. 4-1-101 et seq. (1974)
Connecticut	Conn. Gen. Stat. Ann. Sec. 42a-1-101 et seq. (West 1960)
Delaware	Del. Code Ann. Tit. 6 Sec. 1-101 et seq. (1975)
District of Columbia	D.C. Code Ann. Sec. 28-1-101 et seq. (1973)
Florida	Fla. Stat. Ann. Sec. 671.1-101 et seq. (1966)
Georgia	Ga. Code Ann. Sec. 109A-101 et seq. (Harrison 1979)
Hawaii	Hawaii Rev. Stat. Sec. 490-1-101 et seq. (1968)
Idaho	Idaho Code Sec. 28-1-101 et seq. (1980)
Illinois	Ill. Ann. Stat. Ch. 26 Sec. 1-101 et seq. (1963)
Indiana	Ind. Code Ann. Sec. 26-1-101 et seq. (Burns 1974)
Iowa	Iowa Code Ann. Sec. 554.1101 et seq. (West 1967)
Kansas	Kan. Stat. Ann. Sec. 84-1-101 et seq. (1983)
Kentucky	Ky. Rev. Stat. Sec. 355.1-101 et seq. (1972)
Louisiana	La. Rev. Stat. Ann. Sec. 10:1-101 et seq. (West 1983)
Maine	Me. Rev. Stat. Ann. Tit. 11 Sec. 1-101 et seq. (1964)
Maryland	Md. Com. Law Code Ann. Sec. 101-1 et seq. (1983)
Massachusetts	Mass. Gen. Laws Ann. Ch. 106 Sec. 1-101 et seq. (West 1958)
Michigan	Mich. Comp. Laws Ann. Sec. 440.1101 et seq. (West 1967)
Minnesota	Minn. Stat. Ann. Sec. 336.1-101 et seq. (West 1966)
Mississippi	Miss. Code Ann. Sec. 75-1-101 et seq. (1981)

State	Uniform Commercial Code Reference
Missouri	Mo. Ann. Stat. Sec. 400.1-101 et seq. (Vernon 1965)
Nebraska	Neb. Rev. Stat. U.C.C. Sec. 1-101 et seq. (1980)
Nevada	Nev. Rev. Stat. Sec. 104.1101 et seq. (1965)
New Hampshire	N.H. Rev. Stat. Ann. Sec. 382-A:1-101 et seq. (1961)
New Jersey	N.J. Stat. Ann. Sec. 12A:1-101 et seq. (West 1962)
New Mexico	N.M. Stat. Ann. Sec. 55-1-101 et seq. (1978)
New York	N.Y. U.C.C. Law Sec. 1-101 et seq. (McKinney 1964)
North Carolina	N.C. Gen. Stat. Sec. 25-1-101 et seq. (1965)
North Dakota	N.D. Cent. Code Sec. 41-01-01 et seq. (1983)
Ohio	Ohio Rev. Code Ann. Sec. 1301.01 et seq. (Page 1979)
Oklahoma	Okla. Stat. Ann. Tit. 12A Sec. 1-101 et seq. (West 1963)
Oregon	Or. Rev. Stat. Sec. 71.1010 et seq. (1983)
Pennsylvania	Pa. Stat. Ann. Tit. 12A Sec. 1-101 et seq. (Purdon 1970)
Puerto Rico	P.R. Laws Ann. Tit. 10 Appendix Sec. 1001 et seq. (1978)
Rhode Island	R.I. Gen. Laws Sec. 6A-1-101 et seq. (1970)
South Carolina	S.C. Code Ann. Sec. 36-1-101 et seq. (Law. Coop 1976)
South Dakota	S.D. Codified Laws Ann. Sec. 57A-1-101 et seq. (1980)
Tennessee	Tenn. Code Ann. Sec. 47-1-101 (1979)
Texas	Tex. (Bus. & Comm.) Code Ann. Sec. 1.101 et seq. (Vernon 1968)
Utah	Utah Code Ann. Sec. 70A-1-101 et seq. (1981)
Vermont	Vt. Stat. Ann. Tit. 9A Sec. 1-101 et seq. (1966)
Virgin Islands	V.I. Code Ann. Tit. 11A Sec. 1-101 et seq. (1965)
Virginia	Va. Code Sec. 8.1-101 et seq. (1965)
Washington	Wash. Rev. Code Ann. Sec. 62A.1-101 et seq. (1966)
West Virginia	W. Va. Code Sec. 46-1-101 et seq. (1966)
Wisconsin	Wis. Stat. Ann. Sec. 401.101 et seq. (West 1964)
Wyoming	Wyo. Stat. Ann. Sec. 34-21-101 et seq. (1977)

Glossary

ABSENTEE: One who is not present, usually a husband, wife, or child who has departed for parts unknown.

ACCIDENT INSURANCE: *See* under INSURANCE.

ACTUARIALLY FUNDED PENSION PLAN: A pension plan funded according to life expectancy tables, similar to those used by insurance companies, to estimate the reserves needed to meet obligations.

ADOPTION: The process of taking a person into one's own family by a legal process.

ADMINISTRATION (of Estates): The management and settlement of an estate.

ADMINISTRATIVE AGENCY: An agency established by the executive branch of the government under constitutional or legislative authority to conduct specific functions of the executive branch.

ADMINISTRATIVE LAW: A body of law that has grown up around the operations of the administrative and executive agencies.

ADMINISTRATOR (of Estates): A person appointed by the court to settle an estate of a deceased person who left no will.

AGENCY: A situation where one person acts for and upon the direction of another. The principal is responsible for the acts of the agent as long as the agent is acting within the scope of his or her authority. Agency is a consentual contract that may be created in writing, orally, or through the actions of the parties. The principal must compensate the agent, warn him or her of anything that might cause loss to the agent, reimburse him or her for losses while acting as agent, and be responsible for damages caused by acts of the agent. The agent must be loyal and act in good faith, notify the principal of any circumstances creating a conflict of interest, not benefit from a transaction made for the principal without permission, not violate confidences, follow instructions, and account to the principal.

AGENCY SHOP: A union security device whereby in order to continue employment, any non-union employee is required to pay the union sums equivalent to those paid by union members.

ALIMONY: Financial support, usually of the wife by her divorced husband. May be for various periods, such as pendente lite (during the pendency of the suit for divorce), for a limited time, or permanently.

ANNOTATED REPORTS: Reports of the proceedings of stated courts, to which have been added statements analyzing other cases that deal with the various points of law set forth in the reported case.

ANNOTATION: A statement, usually a footnote to a point of law decided in a case, in which a particular point of law is discussed in conjunction with other cases covering the same point of law.

ANNUITY: An investment yielding a fixed payment during the holder's lifetime or for a stated number of years.

ANNULMENT OF MARRIAGE: The invalidation of a marriage, or its being declared void by a court of proper jurisdiction, stating in effect that the marriage never took place.

APPRECIATION PARTICIPATION MORTGAGES (APMS), Shared Appreciation Mortgages (SAMS), and Tenant in Common Keeping Equity (TICKET): All approximately the same. Such a loan has a low interest rate, payable in fixed monthly installments of principal and interest for a set term. At the end of the term or upon sale, the lender shares in the increase in value of the property according to an agreed-upon ratio.

ARBITRATION: The settlement of a dispute by a person or persons chosen to hear both sides and to come to a conclusion.

AS IS: A statement that the goods are to be taken just as they stand without any obligation to make any changes or repairs on the part of the party delivering them.

ASSAULT: A threat to physically harm another person.

ASSAULT AND BATTERY: Physically injuring or beating a person.

ADVALORUM TAX: *See* DIRECT TAX.

ASSESSMENT: An official estimate of the value of property within a given jurisdiction.

ASSESSMENT LIFE INSURANCE: *See* under INSURANCE.

ASSESSMENT ROLL: A listing of persons and their taxable property.

ASSESSORS: Appointed or elected officials charged with making assessments of property.

ASSOCIATIONS: If organized for a profit, the members are in effect legal partners and individuals, making them jointly and severally liable. An association has no existence outside of its members and no powers outside of its contract of association. It does not exist as an entity; therefore, in common law, all members must act in unison and all must be sued together. However, now most states have passed statutes simplifying this process by allowing associations to sue and be sued in their own name. Associations may draw their own bylaws. The law generally will not interfere in the internal operations of associations.

ASSURANCE: *See* INSURANCE.

ATTORNEY GENERAL OPINIONS: Non-binding opinions that interpret the law and that are issued by the chief counsel of the government upon the request of some government body.

ATTRACTIVE NUISANCE: An attractive nuisance is created by maintaining on a premises a condition dangerous to children of tender age by reason of their inability to appreciate the danger. In some jurisdictions, under these conditions, individuals are required to use reasonable care to protect children against the danger.

BAILEE: A person who receives property from another under a contract of bailment requiring that person to return the property upon the request of the bailor or upon the happening of some event.

BAILMENT: Delivery of personal property to a person for a specific purpose, following which the property is to be returned to its owner or disposed of upon the instructions of the owner.

BAILOR: A person who delivers property to another under a contract of bailment and to whom the property is to be returned as agreed.

BATTERY: An illegal touching or beating of another person.

BENEFICIARY: Under a trust, the person receiving the proceeds or benefits thereof. *See also* under INSURANCE.

BILATERAL CONTRACT: A contract in which both parties have bound themselves to an obligation to the other party.

BILL OF RIGHTS: The first ten amendments to the Constitution of the United States guaranteeing certain rights to the people.

BINDER: *See* under INSURANCE.

BOND: A certificate evidencing a debt of a corporation or of a governmental body, agreeing to pay the holder a set rate of interest for a specific period of time, and then to repay the principal sum loaned.

BUILDING CODES: Laws passed by state or local governments regulating standards for construction, maintenance, operation, occupancy, use, appearance, or fitness of buildings for habitation.

BULK TRANSFER: In commercial law, any transfer in bulk not in the ordinary course of the transferor's business, of a majority part of the materials, supplies, merchandise, or other inventory of an enterprise.

BURDEN OF PROOF: The responsibility of producing specified evidence for the court.

C CORPORATIONS: *See* CORPORATIONS.

CAPITATION TAX: *See* POLL TAX.

CASE FINDERS: Useful tools in locating a case covering a specific subject. Digests, encyclopedias, and indexes are popular tools.

CASE NOTES: Notes found in Digests, encyclopedias, annotated statutes, and annotated reporters, in which cases discussing a particular point of law are cited.

CASE REPORT: A report of a legal action in volumes kept for that purpose.

CASUALTY INSURANCE: *See* ACCIDENT INSURANCE under INSURANCE.

CAUSE OF ACTION: The grounds for an action; a claim factually and legally sufficient to bring a case to court.

CERTIORARI: A request that the records be produced. A process used by the Supreme Court to select cases it will consider.

CHANCERY COURT: A court of equity.

CHARTER, CITY: A document given by the state legislatures to corporate cities that validates their existence.

CHARTER, CORPORATE: A written grant of rights made by a government to a corporation, allowing it to conduct specified businesses.

CHATTEL: An article of personal property.

CHATTEL MORTGAGE: Security interest in personal property, generally superseded by security agreements under Article IX of the Uniform Commercial Code.

CHECKS AND BALANCES: A balance of power between the executive department, the legislative department, and the judicial department of government, maintained by the power of any one branch to exert control over the others and keeping each from obtaining complete control of governmental operations.

CHILD: *See* INFANT.

CHILD SUPPORT: Money paid by one parent to the other for the expenses of their children, including education.

CHOSE IN ACTION: A right to sue to recover a chattel or debt, or for damages to property not in the possession of the party suing.

CIRCUIT COURT OF APPEALS: *See* UNITED STATES COURT OF APPEALS.

CITATION: A reference to an authority, usually a statute or case, that backs up a legal position.

CIVIL ACTION: A legal action involving non-criminal matters.

CIVIL COMMOTION INSURANCE: *See* RIOT INSURANCE under INSURANCE.

CIVIL CONSPIRACY: A secret planning and acting together that does not constitute an illegal act.

CIVIL LAW: That part of the law concerning itself with non-criminal matters.

CLEAN-HANDS DOCTRINE: A doctrine in equity stating that someone who wishes the court to give him or her relief must him- or herself approach the court with clean hands. In other words, if an individual is guilty, he or she may have no relief.

CLOSED SHOP: A requirement by contract that an employer hire only union members and discharge non-union employees, and requiring employees to remain union members as a condition of their employment.

CODE: A body of laws and rules of a government or of a government agency, collected together and organized in a systematic way for easy reference.

CODE OF FEDERAL REGULATIONS: A codification of the rules and regulations of the administrative and regulatory agencies of the United States, arranged by subjects in fifty titles.

CODICIL: An addition to a will that changes or explains some provisions, or adds new provisions.

CODIFICATION: The collecting together of laws systematically by subjects.

COHABITATION: Living together as husband and wife, usually applied to those who have not acquired a license to marry and who have had neither a civil nor a religious marriage ceremony.

CO-INSURANCE *See* under INSURANCE.

COLLECTIVE BARGAINING: Negotiations between organized workers, usually represented by a union, and their employer for reaching an agreement concerning wages, hours, and other terms of employment.

COLLISION INSURANCE: *See* under INSURANCE.

COLOR OF LAW: Having the outward appearance, or semblance, of the backing of the law.

COMMERCIAL INSURANCE: *See* under INSURANCE.

COMMERCIAL PAPER: Checks, promissory notes, bills of exchange, and other negotiable paper used in business.

COMMON CARRIER: Someone in the business of transporting people or goods and who offers this service to the general public.

COMMON LAW: A body of law built up from decided cases, in contrast with laws set forth in statutes.

COMMON-LAW MARRIAGE: A marriage not solemnized by religious or civil ceremony and not licensed by the state, but effected by agreement to live together as husband and wife. Authorized by statute in some states.

COMMON-LAW SYSTEM: Concerning marriage, a system of laws that considers that each spouse owns whatever he or she earns during the existence of the marriage, in contrast with the Community Property System.

COMMON STOCK: Represents ownership of a corporation, the owners of which receive dividends after the creditors and the preferred stockholders have been paid. Such owners may have voting rights and are the last to share in the distribution of assets upon the dissolution of the corporation.

COMMUNITY PROPERTY SYSTEM: A system of laws that considers that one-half of the earnings of either spouse during marriage is owned by the other spouse, in contrast with the Common-Law System.

COMPARABLE WAGES: Wages that are paid equally, regardless of sex, for jobs that require equal skills, effort, and responsibility, and that are performed under similar working conditions.

COMPREHENSIVE INSURANCE: *See* under INSURANCE.

CONCILIATION: The attempt to bring together, or to reconcile, the differences between labor and management in any disputed situation.

CONCURRENT RESOLUTION: A formal non-binding opinion issued by both houses of a legislature.

CONDITIONAL SALE: A sales contract in which the seller retains title until the goods are paid for. (Now comes under U.C.C. Sec. 9–105(h).)

CONFISCATION INSURANCE: *See* under INSURANCE.

CONSIDERATION: Something of value done or given by a person in exchange for the other person's doing or giving something in order to make a contract.

CONSPIRACY: A planning and acting together secretly.

CONSTRUCTIVE DIVIDEND: Dividends imputed to a shareholder of a corporation by the Internal Revenue Service from a reconstruction or interpretation of the taxpayer's conduct, as distinguished from an actually declared dividend.

CONSTRUCTIVE EVICTION: An eviction in which the landlord does not actually deprive the tenant of possession, but has done, or has permitted to be done, some act that makes the premises uninhabitable.

CONTRACT: An agreement, either oral or written, between two or more people to do or to refrain from doing something legal, which is enforceable by law.

CONTRIBUTORY NEGLIGENCE: A theory of law in which parties to an accident are held responsible according to the proportion in which their own negligent actions contributed to the cause of the accident.

CONVERSION: The unlawful appropriation and use of the property of another.

COPYRIGHT: The exclusive right to publish, produce, or sell the rights to a literary, dramatic, musical, or artistic work, granted by law for a definite period of years.

CORPORATIONS: Have no existence outside of the legislative enactments allowing their creation. Corporations are formed by enacting a charter, which is filed where the legislature directs. Corporations are governed by the statutes of the state of incorporation, the charter, and their own bylaws. Corporations are owned by stockholders who elect boards of directors, who in turn hire the operating officers. Corporations come in all sizes ranging from a corner store to General Motors.

COVERAGE: *See* under INSURANCE.

CREDIT INSURANCE: *See* under INSURANCE.

CRIME: An act committed in violation of a law prohibiting the act, or omitting an act in violation of a law requiring the act.

CRIMINAL CONSPIRACY: A secret planning and acting together that constitutes an illegal act.

CRIMINAL LAW: That part of the law dealing with illegal actions.

CURTESY: The rights of a husband in the lands of his deceased wife when there has been born to the couple a child capable of inheriting.

CUSTODY, OF CHILDREN: The safekeeping of children, by a guardian, a parent, a grandparent, or another person appointed by a court, who is put in charge of the upbringing of the children.

DANGEROUS AGENCY: *See* ATTRACTIVE NUISANCE.

DANGEROUS INSTRUMENTALITY: *See* ATTRACTIVE NUISANCE.

DEBENTURE: An interest-bearing bond, often issued by a corporation without security.

DEED: A document, signed and sealed, that transfers real estate from one party to another.

DEFERRED DIVIDEND INSURANCE. *See* under INSURANCE.

DEPOSITORY FOR GOVERNMENT DOCUMENTS: A library that, in exchange for the privilege of receiving published depository government documents, has agreed to keep its government document section open to the public.

DEPOSITORY GOVERNMENT DOCUMENTS: Those documents selected by the Superintendant of Government Documents for shipment to libraries designated as depositories for government documents.

DESCENT: The transfer of real estate to heirs by inheritance according to statute.

DIGEST: An index of reported cases arranged by subject matter, subdivided by jurisdiction and courts, containing a brief statement of the holdings or facts of the cases.

DIRECT TAX: A tax imposed directly upon the property according to its value.

DIRECTORS: Members of a board chosen to form the policies and direct the affairs of a corporation or institution.

DISCRIMINATION: The showing of a difference or favoritism in treatment, usually concerning race, color, creed, sex, age, or national origin.

DISQUALIFIED PERSONS: In a pension plan, certain individuals who might have a conflict of interest in dealing with a pension plan, all as set forth in 29 U.S.C. 1101 et seq.

DISSOLUTION OF MARRIAGE: *See* DIVORCE.

DISTRIBUTION: The transfer of personal property to the next of kin according to statute.

DISTRICT COURTS: The general trial courts of the federal judiciary system.

DIVIDEND: Money or property derived from the income of the corporation and divided among the stockholders of a corporation, as declared by the board of directors of the corporation.

DIVIDEND ADDITION: *See* under INSURANCE.

DIVORCE: The legal separation of a husband and wife by decree of the court.

DOMICILE: The legal and official residence of a person or thing.

DOMICILE OF A MARRIAGE: Chronologically, the last place a husband and wife lived together as husband and wife.

DOWER: Originally, a life estate given to a widow in her deceased husband's estate. By statutes, dower now varies from state to state.

EJECTMENT: An action to regain possession of real estate.

ENDOWMENT INSURANCE: *See* under INSURANCE.

ENVIRONMENT: All of the conditions, circumstances, and influences surrounding and affecting the growth and development of organisms on earth.

EQUITY: (1) A system of doctrines and rules supplementing and superseding common and statutory law when such law is inadequate for a just settlement. (2) The administration of justice according to fairness instead of the strict rules of law. Such proceedings cover situations in which the application of law creates an unjust situation, and are handled in a Court of Equity in contrast with a Court of Law.

ESTATE (in property): The interest one has in property, either real or personal.

ESTATE (of a deceased person): The assets and liabilities of a deceased person, settled by an administration if no will is left, and settled by the probate of the will if one is found. Both proceedings are handled in the same court, frequently called Probate Court or Surrogate Court.

ESTATE FOR YEARS: Estate less than a freehold where a person has an interest in land for some fixed period of time.

ESTATE TAX: Tax upon the right to transfer property from the deceased to the living through an estate or by a will.

EVICTION: The removal from a premises by the person having the legal right to occupy the premises, of people not having the legal right of occupancy.

EXECUTED CONTRACT: One in which one of the parties has completed his or her part of the bargain.

EXECUTIVE ORDERS: Orders issued by the president, under authority of Congress, relating to the organization of the executive department, or to government business. To have legal effect, they are published in the *Federal Register*.

EXECUTOR: A person named in a will and appointed by the court to carry out the terms of the will.

EXECUTORY CONTRACT: A contract in which one of the parties is bound to perform some action.

FACE: *See* under INSURANCE.

FAMILY INSURANCE: *See* INDUSTRIAL INSURANCE under INSURANCE.

FAULT DIVORCE: Before the institution of no-fault divorce, it was necessary (and still is in some jurisdictions) that the party from whom the divorce was requested committed a fault against the other spouse and the marriage. It connotes an act to which blame is attached.

FELONY: A crime that can be punished by death or imprisonment in a penitentiary.

FEOFFMENT: An Old English expression for the granting or selling of land.

FEOFFMENT TO USE: The granting or selling of real estate to a person who will hold the title, but who will hold the land for the use of another person.

FEUDAL SYSTEM: A system of land holdings developed in England in which all lands were owned by the king, who granted the use of the land to his subjects upon the consideration that they perform certain duties. The occupant was said to have tenure and could, in turn, create a subtenure if desired.

FIDELITY INSURANCE: *See* GUARANTY INSURANCE under INSURANCE.

FIDUCIARY (Pension Plan): An individual or individuals charged with the management and operation of a trust or pension plan.

FINANCING STATEMENT: A statement signed by the debtor and creditor, giving the creditor a claim on personal property of the debtor, which vests when properly filed in the correct recording office.

FIRST IMPRESSION: When a particular point of law has never previously been presented to a court, the case first presenting the question for decision is called "a case of first impression."

FLOATING POLICY: *See* under INSURANCE.

FLOOR TAX: A tax on all distilled spirits "on the floor" in a warehouse.

FRANCHISE TAX: A tax on the privilege of carrying on a business and figured in a variety of ways.

FRAUD: A deception depriving a person of his or her property or a legal right.

FREEHOLD ESTATE: The holding of land for life with the right to sell it or pass it on by inheritance.

FUNDED PENSION PLAN: A pension plan in which funds are set aside yearly to cover the costs of the plan.

GENERAL TAX: A tax imposed throughout a state for the general support of the government.

GUARDIAN: A person appointed by a court to take charge of the affairs of another, usually an infant or someone incapable of managing for him- or herself.

GUARDIAN AD LITEM: A guardian appointed by a court to represent a person for the duration of a specific trial.

HAZARD: *See* under INSURANCE.

HEADNOTES: Paragraphs below the title of a case that summarize each point of law decided by the court.

HOLDOVER TENANT: A tenant who retains possession after the expiration of a lease or after a tenancy at will has been terminated.

HOLOGRAPHIC WILL: A will written entirely in the handwriting of the person signing it.

HOUSING CODE: *See* BUILDING CODES.

IMPLIED CONTRACT: If the recipient of benefits knows of acts being performed for his or her benefit and does not object, a contract to pay for the reasonable cost of such services may arise by implication.

IMPLIED INVITATION: *See* ATTRACTIVE NUISANCE.

INCOME TAX: A tax upon the income or profit of a person or of any form of business.

INDEMNITY INSURANCE: *See* under INSURANCE.

INDIRECT TAX: A tax on the privilege of doing something, such as on a franchise or right.

INFANT: A person under the legal age, at which time that person has full control of and responsibility for his or her own actions. Generally, the legal age is 21, however, states vary in making exceptions for many situations, for example, for hunting, driving, marrying, holding public office, or attending school.

INFANT TRESPASSER: *See* ATTRACTIVE NUISANCE.

INFERRED CONTRACT: A contract that is made by the action of the parties. If the parties act as if a contract has been made between them, an enforceable contract may be inferred.

INFRINGEMENT (of a Copyright, Patent, Trademark or Tradename): An encroachment or trespass on the rights of the legal holders thereof by copying or otherwise using their work without permission.

INHERITANCE TAX: A tax upon the transfer of property through an estate or by will. Not a tax on the property, but upon the right to acquire the property by such means.

INJUNCTION: An order by a judge that a person should do or refrain from doing a certain act.

INSURANCE: A contract whereby for a fee, one party agrees to pay a fixed sum to another party for a specified loss by specific perils on a stated subject.

> ACCIDENT INSURANCE: Insurance indemnifying against expenses, loss of time, and suffering resulting from accidents.

> ANNUITY: An investment yielding a fixed payment during the holder's lifetime or for a stated number of years.

> ASSESSMENT LIFE INSURANCE: Insurance whose benefits paid depend upon the collection of the assessments that are needed to pay the amount involved.

> ASSURANCE: A term used in reference to life insurance only.

> BENEFICIARY: The person to whom the proceeds of the policy are payable.

> BINDER: A written memorandum of the important insurance terms, given for temporary protection pending the issuance of a policy.

> CASUALTY INSURANCE: See ACCIDENT INSURANCE.

> CIVIL COMMOTION INSURANCE: See RIOT INSURANCE.

> CO-INSURANCE: A policy in which property is insured for less than its full value and the insured absorbs the loss above the policy limit.

> COLLISION INSURANCE: In automobile insurance, coverage against loss from collision with another vehicle.

> COMMERCIAL INSURANCE: Insurance against breach of contract in a commercial contract.

> COMPREHENSIVE INSURANCE: A policy of insurance combining both fire and casualty insurance, or in the case of an automobile, covering fire, theft, wind, water, and malicious mischief and generally protecting against all damages except collision and upset.

> CONFISCATION INSURANCE: Insurance issued to mortgages of automobiles, insuring against confiscation of the vehicle.

> COVERAGE: The object or person insured.

> CREDIT INSURANCE: Insurance coverage for monetary loss on loans.

> DEFERRED DIVIDEND INSURANCE: See TONTINE INSURANCE.

> DISABILITY INSURANCE: Insurance covering loss of wages caused by an injury.

> DIVIDEND ADDITION: Paid-up insurance in addition to the face value of a life insurance policy, purchased by dividends generated by excessive premiums.

> ENDOWMENT INSURANCE: Insurance for which the premium is fixed or is paid in advance, and if the insured survives a specified time, he or she is paid according to a schedule; or if the insured does not survive, the policy is paid to a designated party.

> FACE: The entire insurance contract.

> FAMILY INSURANCE: See INDUSTRIAL INSURANCE.

> FIDELITY INSURANCE: See GUARANTY INSURANCE.

> FLOATING POLICY: The details of losses under an insurance policy to be determined later as stipulated in the policy.

> GUARANTY INSURANCE: Indemnity for loss arising from want of integrity or fidelity of employees or persons holding a position of trust.

HAZARD: The risk, danger, or probability involved in an insurance contract.

INDEMNITY INSURANCE: An insurance policy insuring against loss or damage due to one's own negligence.

INDUSTRIAL INSURANCE: Life insurance in which agents collect premiums periodically, i.e, weekly or monthly.

INSURED: The person whose life or property is insured.

INSURER: The insurance company issuing an insurance policy.

LIABILITY INSURANCE: An insurance policy insuring the policyholder against liability for loss or damage to the person or property of another.

MIXED INSURANCE: An insurance policy with elements of several types of policies.

MUTUAL LIFE INSURANCE: Insurance coverage in which the owners of the insurance company are the policyholders and dividends are declared yearly to the policyholders. A large percentage of life insurance companies are mutual companies.

NO-FAULT INSURANCE: Automobile insurance in which the owner of a vehicle looks to his or her own insurance company for the payment of accident claims.

OPEN INSURANCE: An insurance policy in which the value of the thing insured is proved at the time of loss.

OWNER: The person who owns the policy and pays the premiums.

PEOPLE'S INSURANCE: See INDUSTRIAL INSURANCE.

POLICY: The contract between the insurer and the insured.

PREMIUM: The money paid for insurance coverage.

RE-INSURANCE: Insurance issued by a second insurance company to the initial insurer against loss due from the original insurance.

RIOT INSURANCE: Insurance against the disruption of a business or distruction of property as a result of a riot.

RUNNING INSURANCE: A policy issued in which the details are determined later as stipulated in the policy.

SINGLE-PREMIUM LIFE INSURANCE: Insurance for which the premium is paid in advance as a lump sum.

STATE INSURANCE: Insurance provided by the state, such as old age insurance, unemployment insurance, and sickness and health insurance.

STRAIGHT LIFE INSURANCE: Ordinary life insurance in which the premium is paid during the life of the insured or until a stated age.

SURRENDER VALUE: The value of a life insurance policy based on the reserve value, considerably below the actual reserve, that will be paid to the policyholder if he or she cancels the policy.

TERM INSURANCE: Life insurance for only a set term of years.

TIME INSURANCE: Insurance issued for a specific period of time.

TITLE INSURANCE: Insurance covering losses due to defects in titles to real estate.

TONTINE INSURANCE: Insurance in which the dividend payments are postponed and the surpluses are accumulated until a specific time, and then are distributed to only those surviving with policies still in force.

UNIVERSAL LIFE INSURANCE: A life insurance policy under which the policyholder may change the premium and the death benefits, while the interest on cash value changes with market rates.

UNIVERSAL VARIABLE LIFE INSURANCE: A life insurance policy under which the policyholder may change the premium and the death benefits, and the cash value and additional death benefits vary with the performance of the investment programs chosen by the policyholder.

UNVALUED INSURANCE: See OPEN INSURANCE.

VALUED INSURANCE: Insurance in which the parties have agreed in advance to the value of the thing insured.

VARIABLE ANNUITY CONTRACT: A contract guaranteeing that the annuitant, upon reaching a certain age, will receive payments, the amount of which is not fixed and has no minimum, but varies according to the return on investments.

VARIABLE LIFE INSURANCE: A life insurance policy in which the premium remains constant, but the cash value and the additional death benefits may vary according to the performance of the investment portfolio the policyholder has selected.

WAGER INSURANCE: An insurance policy issued to a person who has no interest in the thing being insured and thus would sustain no loss by its damage or loss.

WHOLE LIFE INSURANCE: A policy in which the premiums and death benefits remain constant, while the cash value increases by at least a minimum stated amount.

INTANGIBLE PROPERTY: Property that cannot be touched, easily defined, or grasped, such as the goodwill of a business.

INTENT: Having the mind directed or fixed on some purpose or plan.

INTER VIVOS TRUST: A trust drawn up and activated while the settlor is living.

IRREVOCABLE TRUST: A trust that may not be recalled or revoked.

JUDICIAL OPINIONS: Decisions by the justice presiding over a case concerning the points in contention, together with the justice's reasons for his or her position.

JURISDICTION: The power given by a constitution or a legislature to make legally binding decisions over people or property.

JUVENILE: *See* INFANT.

KEY NUMBER: A fixed, permanent number assigned by West Publishing Co. to a specific legal point under which all cases discussing this point of law are collected.

KEY NUMBER SYSTEM: A method devised by West Publishing Co. and used throughout the publisher's reporters and digests, by which areas of the law are identified by subject and are further subdivided by a system of key numbers. The consistent use of the key numbers allows a point of law found in a West reporter to be examined also in West's digest system for additional cases covering the same point of law.

KIN: A family relationship connected by birth.

LAND TAX: A tax levied on the owner of, or on the person receiving the benefits from, real estate, and based upon the assessed value of the land.

LANDLORD: The owner, or party having the right of occupancy, of certain real estate, who allows another person to use that property for a specified or unspecified time, usually for a set rent payment.

LANDLORD AND TENANT: A contractual relationship between two people for the right to occupy real estate.

LAW: The rules of conduct established by legislation and enforced by the authority of the community.

LAW LIBRARY RESEARCH REPORT: A written outline examining the points of law covering a given factual situation, which are found by an examination of the research material in a law library.

LEACHATE: Liquid material that leaches, or drains, from an area, usually a trash disposal site.

LEASE: A grant by a landlord to a tenant of an interest in real estate for a specific period of time, or at will, usually for consideration, and upon certain conditions. At the temination of the lease period, the right of possession reverts to the landlord.

LESSEE: A person to whom a lease is given; a tenant.

LESSOR: A person who gives a lease; a landlord.

LEGAL CONCEPT: The formation of an idea into a point of law.

LEGAL DUTY: A situation in which one is by law required to do or to refrain from doing some act.

LEGAL ENCYCLOPEDIA: A set of books giving information on legal topics, in articles alphabetically arranged. (Examples, include *Corpus Juris Secundum (C.J.S.)*, published by West, and *American Jurisprudence 2d (Am. Jur.2d)*, published by Lawyers Cooperative/Bancroft-Whitney.)

LEGAL ISSUE: The legal question or point of law that is disputed, or to be decided.

LEGAL SEPARATION: A situation in which a person lives apart from his or her spouse under a decree of court.

LETTER OF CREDIT: A letter from a bank asking that the holder of the letter be allowed to draw specified sums of money from other banks or agencies, to be charged to the account of the writer of the letter.

LEVY: An official action by a legislature whereby the legislature determines and declares that a tax of a certain amount or percentage value shall be imposed upon some object or act.

LIABILITY: Responsibility for damages resulting from an injurious act, or for the discharge of a debt or obligation.

LIABILITY INSURANCE: *See* under INSURANCE.

LIEN: A claim against property; or if the property is in the hands of creditors, the right to retain the property for the payment of a debt.

LIVES IN BEING: A term used in measuring the maximum time into the future that property may be tied up. Property must vest during the lifetime of a person who is living at the time a trust takes effect, with the additional allowance of twenty-one years and another additional period for gestation.

LIVING APART FOR JUSTIFIABLE CAUSE: *See* LEGAL SEPARATION.

LIVING TRUST: See INTER VIVOS TRUST.

LOCAL TAX: A tax assessed, collected, and used by political subdivisions of a state, such as a county, city, village, or town.

LOCKOUT: The keeping of workers from their place of employment in an attempt to make them accept the terms of employment set forth by management.

LOOSELEAF SERVICE: A collection of state and federal regulations, court decisions, and editorial material on a legal topic, in special binders that allow the insertion of leaves containing new material and the removal of leaves containing out-dated material.

MARRIAGE: The civil status of one man and one woman united by contract and mutual consent for the discharge to each other and to the community of the duties imposed upon the association, founded on the distinction of sex.

MECHANISTIC THEORY OF STATE: A theory that holds that state is established by the citizens as a mechanism for governing the center of interest being the individual citizen.

MEDIATION: An intervention by a third party, either by consent or by request, attempting thereby to settle the differences between labor and management in a dispute.

MEMORANDUM OF LAW: A written discussion of the merits of a legal situation, usually prepared by an attorney or a law clerk.

MINOR: *See* INFANT.

MISDEMEANOR: A minor crime for which the punishment is less than that of a felony (death or imprisonment in a penitentiary).

MIXED INSURANCE: *See* under INSURANCE.

MORTGAGE: An instrument pledging property to a creditor to secure the performance of an obligation.

MUTUAL LIFE INSURANCE: *See* under INSURANCE.

NATURAL RIGHTS: Those rights inherently existing in the relations among human beings and not based upon constitutions or statutes, but which may be limited by constitutions and statutes.

NEGLIGENCE: The failure to exercise due care when required.

NO-FAULT DIVORCE: A divorce obtained in some states upon the allegation that the marriage has "irretrievably" broken down because of "irreconcilable" differences.

NO-FAULT INSURANCE: *See* under INSURANCE.

OCCUPATION TAX: A tax on an occupation, or business, trade, or profession. It is not a tax on the property of the business, but is instead for the privilege of carrying on the business.

OFFICIAL REPORTS: Books in which are recorded the decisions of courts, directed to be published by the state.

OLOGRAPHIC WILL: *See* HOLOGRAPHIC WILL.

OPEN INSURANCE: *See* under INSURANCE.

OPINION, COURT: The final judgement made by a court in settling a case within its jurisdiction.

OPTION: An agreement by a person, for a consideration, to perform an act for a set price within a limited time, leaving the right to exercise the option to the other party.

ORDERS, AGENCY: Directions given to a person by an executive or a regulatory agency to comply with the agency's rules and decisions.

ORGANIC THEORY OF STATE: A theory that holds that the interests of the state are supreme and that individuals must be cared for by the state and are to be used by the state in its own best interests. The function of a good citizen is to perform for the benefit of the state, according to this theory.

OWNER: *See* under INSURANCE.

PARENTAL RIGHTS: Those legal rights given to parents by common law or by statutes and that may involve, among others, the right to select the child's associates and education.

PAROLE EVIDENCE: Oral, or verbal, evidence.

PAROLE EVIDENCE RULE: A rule stating that when parties put their agreement in writing, all previous oral agreements merge in the writing, and the contract as written cannot be changed by parole evidence.

PARTNERSHIP: The joining of two or more legal persons together under a partnership agreement for the purpose of jointly carrying on a business. The partners are jointly and severally liable for the partnership's obligations. The partnership may own and dispose of the business property, the signature of any partner in the name of the partnership being sufficient.

PATENT: An exclusive right to produce, use, and sell an invention or process.

PENSION: Regular payments, not wages, to former employees who have fulfilled certain conditions of employment and reached an established age.

PEOPLE'S INSURANCE: *See* under INSURANCE.

PERIODIC TENANCY: The lease of property which endures for a certain length of time and then automatically renews for successive like periods of time unless the lease is terminated by due notice.

PERIODICALS: Newspapers or magazines that are published frequently and that often contain the most up-to-date discussions of points of law.

PERSONAL PROPERTY: All property other than real estate, including goods, chattels, money, notes, bonds, stocks, intangibles and chose in actions.

PLAYGROUND RULE: *See* ATTRACTIVE NUISANCE.

PLEADINGS: The technical proceedings by which parties bring their complaints before the court.

PLEDGE: The bailment of goods of a creditor in order to secure a debt or agreement. Replaced now by U.C.C. Article IX.

POCKET PART: A paper supplement to a book which is inserted into a pocket built into the back cover of the book. The supplemental material is usually cumulative.

POLL TAX: A tax of a specific sum, levied upon each person within the jurisdiction and within a certain class.

POLICY: *See* under INSURANCE.

POLITICAL RIGHTS: The rights of citizens to participate in the establishment and management of their government.

PORTABLE PENSION: A pension that has vested in an employee after a certain term of employment and that is payable to him or her at retirement age even though the employee leaves the company before retirement age.

POUR-OVER TRUST: A trust established during the lifetime of a testator, which provides for the acceptance of assets under the will of the testator.

POUR-OVER WILL: A will that provides that some or all of the assets of an estate will be "poured over" into an existing trust that is established to receive the assets.

PRECEDENT: A legal decision that is used as an example or justification for a legal position taken.

PREFERRED STOCK: Stock with a preferential claim on set dividends of a corporation, usually having a fixed rate of return, and with a claim on assets of the corporation upon the corporation's dissolution which takes priority over the claim of the common stockholder.

PREMIUM : *See* under INSURANCE.

PRESIDENTIAL DOCUMENTS: Executive orders, proclamations, speeches, press conferences, and other documents of legal effect and significance. Most are compiled in the *Weekly Compilation of Presidential Documents* issued by the U.S. Government Printing Office.

PRESIDENTIAL PROCLAMATION: A formal announcement of a policy or public notice of an event, published in the Federal Register.

PRIMARY SOURCE: The original source of the law, i.e., statutes and cases.

PRIVATE LAW: A law passed that has no general effect and that deals only with individuals.

PROBATE: The official establishment of the genuineness of a will by a court of competent jurisdiction.

PROBATE COURT: A court established for the purpose of settling the estates of deceased persons leaving no wills and of probating the wills of those persons leaving wills. The jurisdiction of the court frequently includes divorces, annulments, and children.

PROCEDURAL LAW: Laws concerning the internal mechanical operations of the courts and agencies.

PROCEDURAL UNCONSCIONABILITY: Concerning contracts, the results of the contract-forming process itself, focusing on high-pressure tactics of a party to the contract, fine print in contracts, misrepresentation, or unequal bargaining positions.

PROFESSIONAL CORPORATIONS: Corporations formed for doctors, attorneys, and other professional people. Such corporations were formerly prohibited but now may exist under special statutes.

PROPORTIONAL TAX: A tax wherein the proportion paid by each taxpayer is in relation to the amount raised as the value of the property bears to the total taxable value.

PSEUDONYM: A pen name, or fictitious name, assumed by and author.

PUBLIC DOMAIN: The condition of being free from a copyright or patent.

QUALIFYING PENSION PLAN: A pension plan that meets the requirements of 29 U.S.C. 1101 et seq., thereby qualifying the corporation having such a plan for certain tax benefits.

REAL PROPERTY: Land and things permanently attached thereto.

RECORDING (Deeds, Mortgages, etc.): The placing of instruments with a public office established for that purpose, so that public notice may be given of the transfers and transactions.

REGIONAL REPORTERS: The National Reporter System, published by West, in which cases are reported for all states in seven geographic regional reporters.

REGULATORY AGENCIES: Agencies established by Congress to govern certain aspects of government and frequently authorized to make rules having the power of law, to provide penalties for non-compliance, and to enforce the rules through the court system (example: the Federal Trade Commission).

RE-INSURANCE: *See* under INSURANCE.

REMAND: The return of a case to a lower court with directions for further proceedings.

REORGANIZATION PLANS: Presidential proposals for changes in the form of the agencies of the executive branch which are sent to Congress as executive orders. Unless Congress disapproves within a specific period of time, such proposals become law.

REPORT: The decision of a court.

REPORTER: Volumes in which the decisions of court cases are recorded.

RESIDENCE: A place where a person lives for a long time or where a person lives while working.

RESIDENT: A person who lives in a place as distinguished from a visitor or transient.

RESOLUTION: A formal expression of opinion by a legislative body, having no legal effect.

RETALIATORY EVICTION: An eviction of a tenant by a landlord to avenge some act of the tenant against the landlord.

RETIREMENT BENEFITS (Pension Plan): Those benefits that are received by employees upon retirement, including pensions, insurance premium payments, club memberships, early retirement benefits, and the like.

REVOCABLE TRUST: A trust in which the settlor reserves the right to revoke and cancel the trust.

RIGHT-TO-WORK STATUTES: Laws providing that employees are not required to join a union as a condition of obtaining or retaining employment.

RULE AGAINST PERPETUITIES: A rule prohibiting property to be held in trust indefinitely, accomplished by limiting the existence of trusts to "lives in being" at the time the trust is established, plus twenty-one years and a period of gestation.

RULES OF PROCEDURE: Regulations issued by a court governing how practice in that court shall be conducted.

RUNNING INSURANCE: *See* under INSURANCE.

S CORPORATION: *See* SUBCHAPTER S CORPORATION.

SECURITY AGREEMENT: An agreement giving a creditor a claim on personal property, usually indicated by the filing of a financing agreement in a specified office in a town, city, county, or state.

SETOFF: A balancing of equities. (Example: When "A" owes "B" one hundred dollars, and "A" sues "B" for three hundred dollars concerning some unrelated claim, "B" can claim a setoff in the action of the one hundred dollars owed him by "A," instead of having to start another suit.)

SETTLOR: A person who establishes a trust to manage his or her property, either while that person is living or upon his or her death.

SHEPARDIZE: The process of tracing the history of a case since the time of its decision in order to determine any changes in its legal effect, by the use of *Shepard's Citations*.

SINGLE-PREMIUM LIFE INSURANCE: *See* under INSURANCE.

SOLE PROPRIETORSHIP: A business that is owned entirely by one individual who is responsible for everything (e.g., he or she must make all decisions, see that all work is done, and pay all obligations) and who receive all of the profit.

SPECIAL RULE: *See* ATTRACTIVE NUISANCE.

SPECIAL TAX: A tax levied for specific local purpose and that benefits only a portion of the general public.

SPECIFIC TAX: A fixed sum imposed on each article or item of property of a given class without consideration of the item's value.

SPENDTHRIFT TRUST: A trust written in such a way as to prevent creditors of a beneficiary from obtaining access to the trust property or income before its being delivered to the beneficiary.

STARE DECISIS: An English doctrine of law carried over to the United States, in which a court will decide a case in the same way another court has decided it, if the facts and law appear the same.

STATE INSURANCE: *See* under INSURANCE.

STATUS: A position or condition with regard to the law. (Example: Marriage is considered a status.)

STATUTE: An act passed by a legislative body setting forth the law on a particular subject.

STATUTE FINDERS: Indexes, lists, and other volumes used in locating specific statutes.

STATUTE OF FRAUDS: A statute stating that no suit or action shall be maintained on certain classes of contracts unless there is a note or memorandum in writing, signed by the party to be charged.

STATUTORY PARENT: A person legally appointed by the court to act as a parent to an infant.

STOCK: In a corporation, represents an ownership interest in the corporation.

STRAIGHT LIFE INSURANCE: *See* under INSURANCE.

STRICT LIABILITY: A condition in which persons engaged in inherently dangerous activities, or using inherently dangerous materials, are held strictly responsible for seeing that the material does not injure other persons or property.

SUBCHAPTER S CORPORATION: A corporation formed under special rules that give the shareholders the same federal tax benefits as does a partnership and under which any income or loss is passed directly to the stockholders, thereby eliminating a corporate tax.

SUBSTANTIVE LAW: The law of the land as passed by Congress and which has general application.

SUBSTANTIVE UNCONSCIONABILITY: Concerning contracts, the results of an undue harshness in the contract terms themselves.

SUCCESSION TAX: *See* INHERITANCE TAX.

SUMMARY PROCEEDING: A relatively quick court proceeding for handling matters in which time is of the essence.

SUPPLEMENTAL PAMPHLET: A paperback pamphlet issued to update statute books, digests, or other books.

SUPREME COURT: The highest court of the United States court system, whose decisions are binding on all other courts concerning matters involving federal law. Generally, cases reach this court from one of the United States Courts of Appeals.

SURRENDER VALUE: *See* under INSURANCE.

SURROGATE COURT: *See* PROBATE COURT.

SURTAX: An additional tax upon certain types of income, frequently imposed if the income exceeds a certain amount.

TANGIBLE PROPERTY: Property that can be touched, or that can be felt by touching, having actual form and substance, and that can be appraised for value.

TAX EXEMPTION: The exempting, or releasing, from a portion of a person's taxable income a specified sum for that individual and each of his or her dependents.

TAX LIEN: A statutory lien in favor of the government on the lands of a delinquent taxpayer.

TENANCY AT SUFFERANCE: A tenancy arising out of the neglect of the landlord to do anything to create another type of tenancy, giving the tenant only possession—wrongfully, and without right—no term, and no title.

TENANCY AT WILL: One who has possession of premises by permission of the owner, but without a fixed term.

TENANT: A person who pays rent for the privilege of occupying real estate.

TENURE: The right to hold or possess real estate.

TERM INSURANCE: *See* under INSURANCE.

TESTAMENTARY TRUST: A trust that has its provisions incorporated in the will of a testator and that takes effect upon the death of the testator.

TESTATOR: A person who has made a will.

TIME INSURANCE: *See* under INSURANCE.

TITLE INSURANCE: *See* under INSURANCE.

TONTINE INSURANCE: *See* under INSURANCE.

TORT: A civil wrong, in contrast to a criminal wrong, not involving a contract. Brought about by a person doing something that he or she legally should not have done, or not doing something that he or she should legally have done.

TRADEMARK: A symbol, word, design, or letter used by a manufacturer or dealer to distinguish his or her products from those of a competitor.

TRADE NAME: A name used as a trademark.

TRUST: An instrument providing for one person or persons (trustees) to own the legal title to property, but to manage that property solely for the benefit of another person or persons (beneficiaries).

TRUST (BUSINESS): Frequently called a "Massachusetts Business Trust," a trust established under an agreement between the parties involved. The trustees own all property, conduct all business, and decide how much of the profits goes to the beneficiaries, all according to the trust agreement. Generally, the agreement must be recorded with the state, and the trust is taxed as a corporation. Such a trust was more popular before statutes allowed certain professions to incorporate.

TRUSTEE: A person—either individual, corporate, or both—charged with the duty of carrying out the terms of a trust.

UNCONSCIONABLE CONTRACT: A contract whose clauses, in the light of the general commercial background and the commercial needs of the particular trade or case, are so one-sided as to be unconscionable under the circumstances existing at the time the contract was made.

UNFAIR LABOR PRACTICE: Under the National Labor Relations Act, it is an unfair labor practice for an employer to (1) interfere with, restrain, or coerce employees in their right to unionize; (2) interfere with the formation or administration of a labor organization, or to support it in any way; (3) discriminate concerning hiring or tenure; (4) discharge or discriminate against an employee because he or she has filed charges or given testimony under the act; or (5) refuse to bargain collectively with a union in good faith.

UNFUNDED PENSION PLAN: A pension plan that has no funds set aside from which to pay benefits and that instead relies on company earnings or some other source to create the funds when needed.

UNIFORM COMMERCIAL CODE: A code covering commercial transactions which, with local variations, has been enacted into law by most states.

UNIFORM LAWS: An attempt to make uniform throughout the United States various areas of the law, the Uniform Commercial Code being the most successful.

UNILATERAL CONTRACT: Resides in the nature of an agreement to make a contract. One party to the unilateral contract states that he or she will perform a certain act provided that the other party does a specified thing. Once the "thing" is done, the contract is made and the person doing the thing is entitled to enforce the contract.

UNION SECURITY PROVISIONS: Provisions in a union contract establishing the status of the union, providing for the relationship of the union to the workers and their positions.

UNION SHOP: *See* CLOSED SHOP.

UNITED STATES CODE: The laws of the United States collected into fifty logical subject classifications called titles.

UNITED STATES COURT OF APPEALS: (Formerly the United States Circuit Court of Appeals). A system of courts to whom appeals may be taken from the trial courts of the United States, consisting of thirteen circuits. The decisions of these courts may be further appealed to the United States Supreme Court.

UNIVERSAL LIFE INSURANCE: *See* under INSURANCE.

UNIVERSAL VARIABLE LIFE INSURANCE: *See* under INSURANCE.

UNVALUED INSURANCE: *See* OPEN INSURANCE under INSURANCE.

USE: In law, the right to a beneficial interest in property that is legally owned by another person (trustee).

VALUED INSURANCE: *See* under INSURANCE.

VARIABLE ANNUITY CONTRACT: *See* under INSURANCE.

VARIABLE LIFE INSURANCE: *See* under INSURANCE.

VESTED PENSION: A pension that an employee has earned and is entitled to and that may not be taken away from that individual if he or she leaves the employment of the company before reaching the retirement age.

VESTING: In trust law and property law, the passing to a person the possession, power of control over, and absolute use of property.

VETO: The Constitutional power of the president to refuse to sign into law enactments of the legislative department of the government.

WAGER INSURANCE: *See* under INSURANCE.

WARD OF THE STATE: A person under the guardianship of the state, such as certain children placed in foster homes or in institutions.

WAREHOUSE RECEIPT: A receipt issued by a warehouse for goods stored there; usually a negotiable instrument.

WHOLE LIFE INSURANCE: *See* under INSURANCE.

WILL: A document stating how a person wishes his or her estate to be disposed of upon his or her death.

John Corbin is associate professor of law and library director at the Reynaldo G. Garza School of Law in Edinburgh, Texas. For 25 years, Corbin served as senior partner of Corbin, Sarapas, and Madaus of Worcester, Massachusetts.